Story and Art by
Rumiko Takahashi

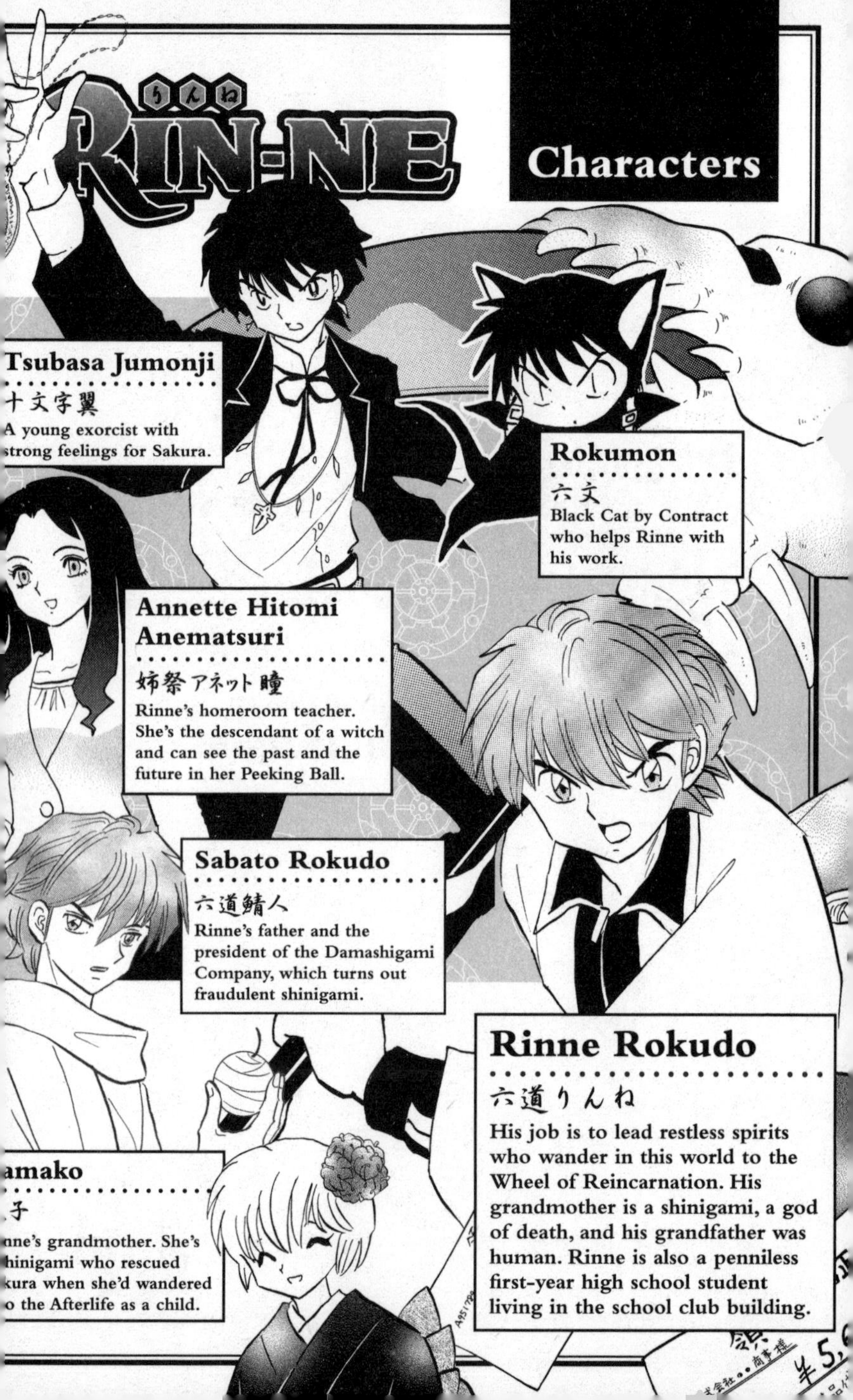
RIN-NE
りんね

Characters

Tsubasa Jumonji

十文字翼

A young exorcist with strong feelings for Sakura.

Rokumon

六文

Black Cat by Contract who helps Rinne with his work.

Annette Hitomi Anematsuri

姉祭アネット瞳

Rinne's homeroom teacher. She's the descendant of a witch and can see the past and the future in her Peeking Ball.

Sabato Rokudo

六道鯖人

Rinne's father and the president of the Damashigami Company, which turns out fraudulent shinigami.

Rinne Rokudo

六道りんね

His job is to lead restless spirits who wander in this world to the Wheel of Reincarnation. His grandmother is a shinigami, a god of death, and his grandfather was human. Rinne is also a penniless first-year high school student living in the school club building.

amako

子

nne's grandmother. She's hinigami who rescued kura when she'd wandered o the Afterlife as a child.

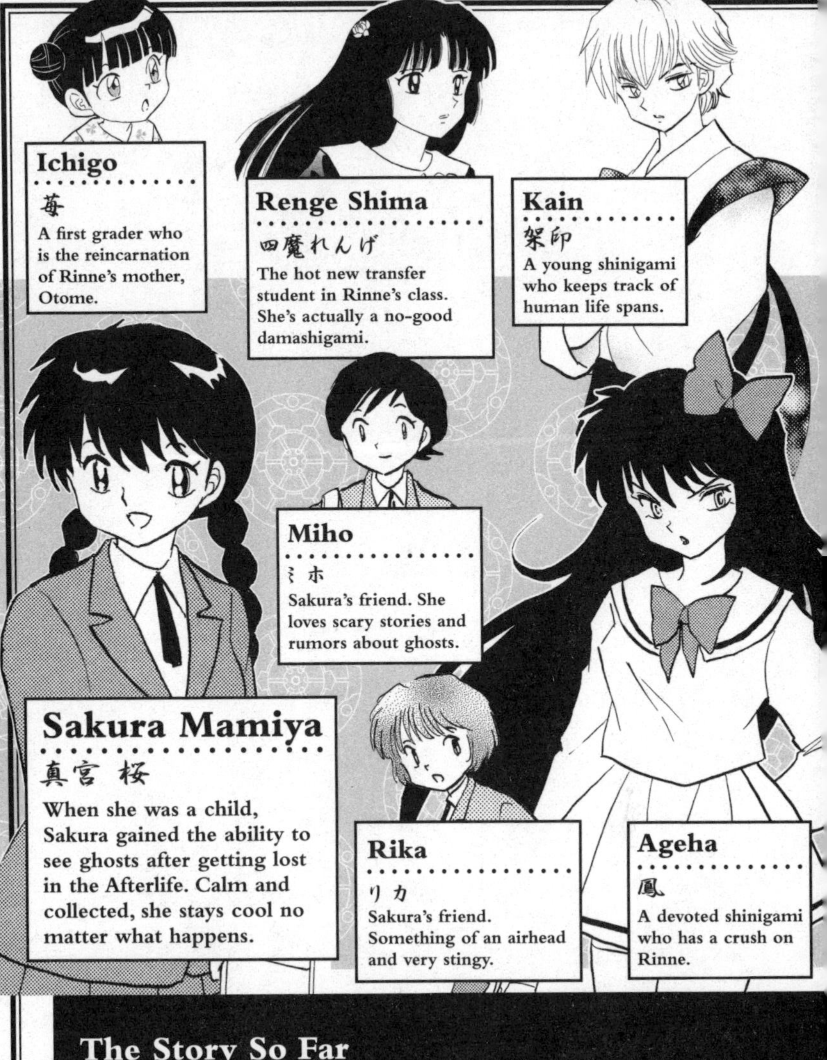

Ichigo

苺

A first grader who is the reincarnation of Rinne's mother, Otome.

Renge Shima

四魔れんげ

The hot new transfer student in Rinne's class. She's actually a no-good damashigami.

Kain

架印

A young shinigami who keeps track of human life spans.

Miho

ミホ

Sakura's friend. She loves scary stories and rumors about ghosts.

Sakura Mamiya

真宮 桜

When she was a child, Sakura gained the ability to see ghosts after getting lost in the Afterlife. Calm and collected, she stays cool no matter what happens.

Rika

リカ

Sakura's friend. Something of an airhead and very stingy.

Ageha

鳳

A devoted shinigami who has a crush on Rinne.

The Story So Far

Sakura, the girl who can see ghosts, and Rinne, the shinigami (sort of), spend their days together helping spirits that can't pass on reach the Afterlife and dealing with all kinds of strange phenomena at their school.

Renge's working in a beach hut when Kain surprises her with a visit, asking her to meet him later that night. However, just before they can rendezvous, she's devastated to learn that Kain's been approached about an arranged marriage! Then a spirit starts impersonating Sakura and Ageha takes all his exorcism work. This volume is the last we'll see of the poverty-stricken Rinne's exploits and deeds. What is the final misadventure that will befall our young hero…?

Contents

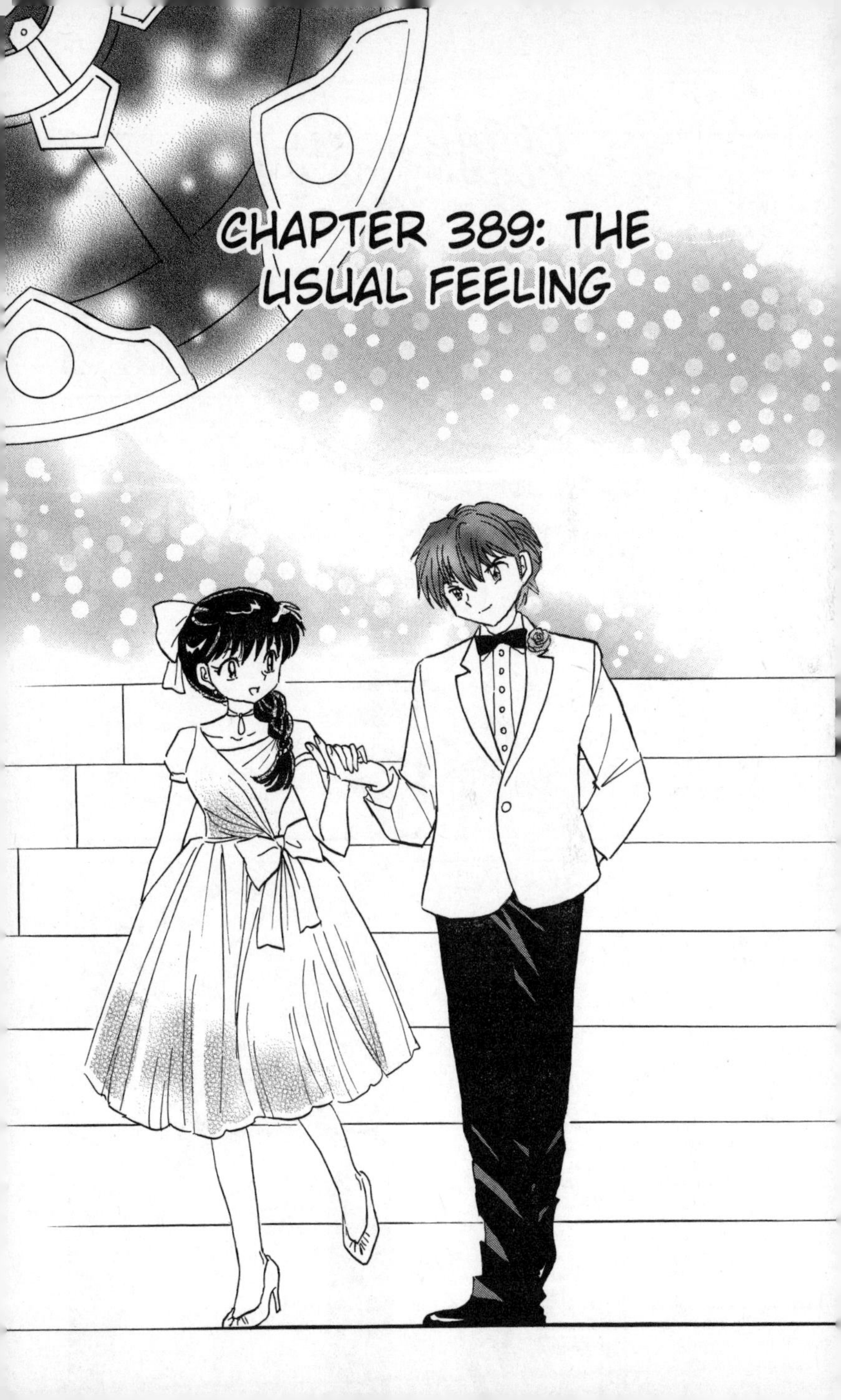
CHAPTER 389: THE USUAL FEELING

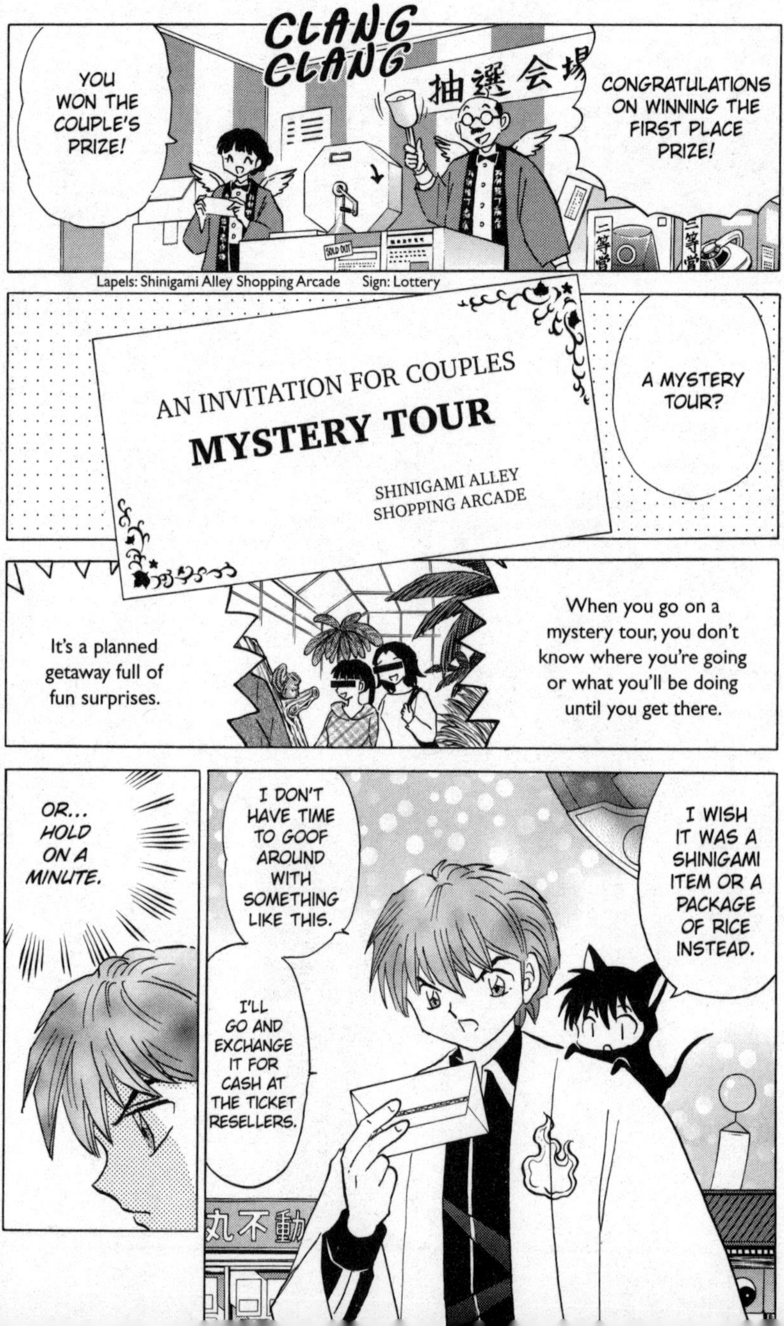
CONGRATULATIONS ON WINNING THE FIRST PLACE PRIZE!
CLANG CLANG
抽選会場
YOU WON THE COUPLE'S PRIZE!
A MYSTERY TOUR?
AN INVITATION FOR COUPLES
MYSTERY TOUR
SHINIGAMI ALLEY SHOPPING ARCADE
When you go on a mystery tour, you don't know where you're going or what you'll be doing until you get there.
It's a planned getaway full of fun surprises.
I WISH IT WAS A SHINIGAMI ITEM OR A PACKAGE OF RICE INSTEAD.
I DON'T HAVE TIME TO GOOF AROUND WITH SOMETHING LIKE THIS.
I'LL GO AND EXCHANGE IT FOR CASH AT THE TICKET RESELLERS.
OR... HOLD ON A MINUTE.

Lapels: Shinigami Alley Shopping Arcade Sign: Lottery

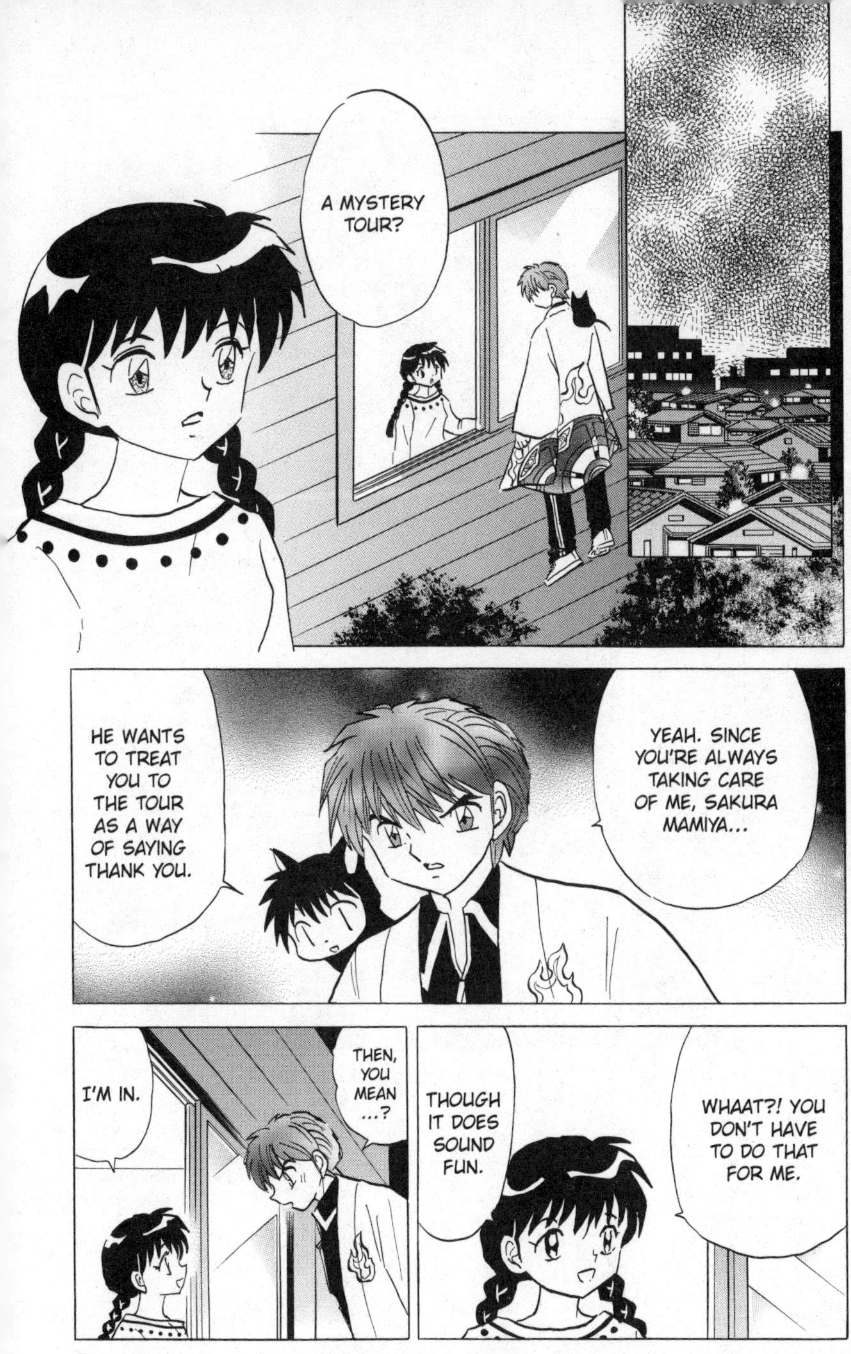
A MYSTERY TOUR?
YEAH. SINCE YOU'RE ALWAYS TAKING CARE OF ME, SAKURA MAMIYA...
HE WANTS TO TREAT YOU TO THE TOUR AS A WAY OF SAYING THANK YOU.
WHAAT?! YOU DON'T HAVE TO DO THAT FOR ME.
THOUGH IT DOES SOUND FUN.
THEN, YOU MEAN ...?
I'M IN.

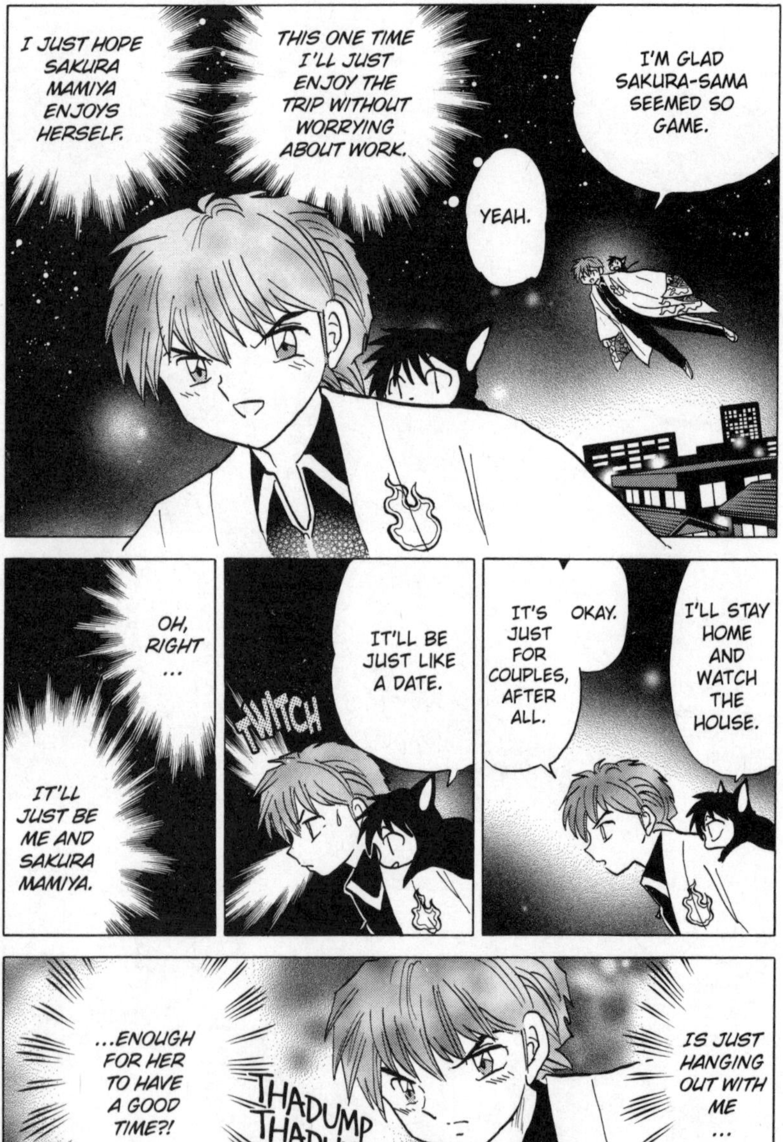
I'M GLAD SAKURA-SAMA SEEMED SO GAME.
YEAH.
THIS ONE TIME I'LL JUST ENJOY THE TRIP WITHOUT WORRYING ABOUT WORK.
I JUST HOPE SAKURA MAMIYA ENJOYS HERSELF.
I'LL STAY HOME AND WATCH THE HOUSE.
OKAY.
IT'S JUST FOR COUPLES, AFTER ALL.
IT'LL BE JUST LIKE A DATE.
TWITCH
OH, RIGHT ...
IT'LL JUST BE ME AND SAKURA MAMIYA.
IS JUST HANGING OUT WITH ME ...
THADUMP THADUMP THADUMP
...ENOUGH FOR HER TO HAVE A GOOD TIME?!

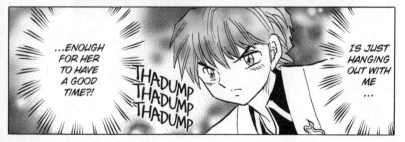

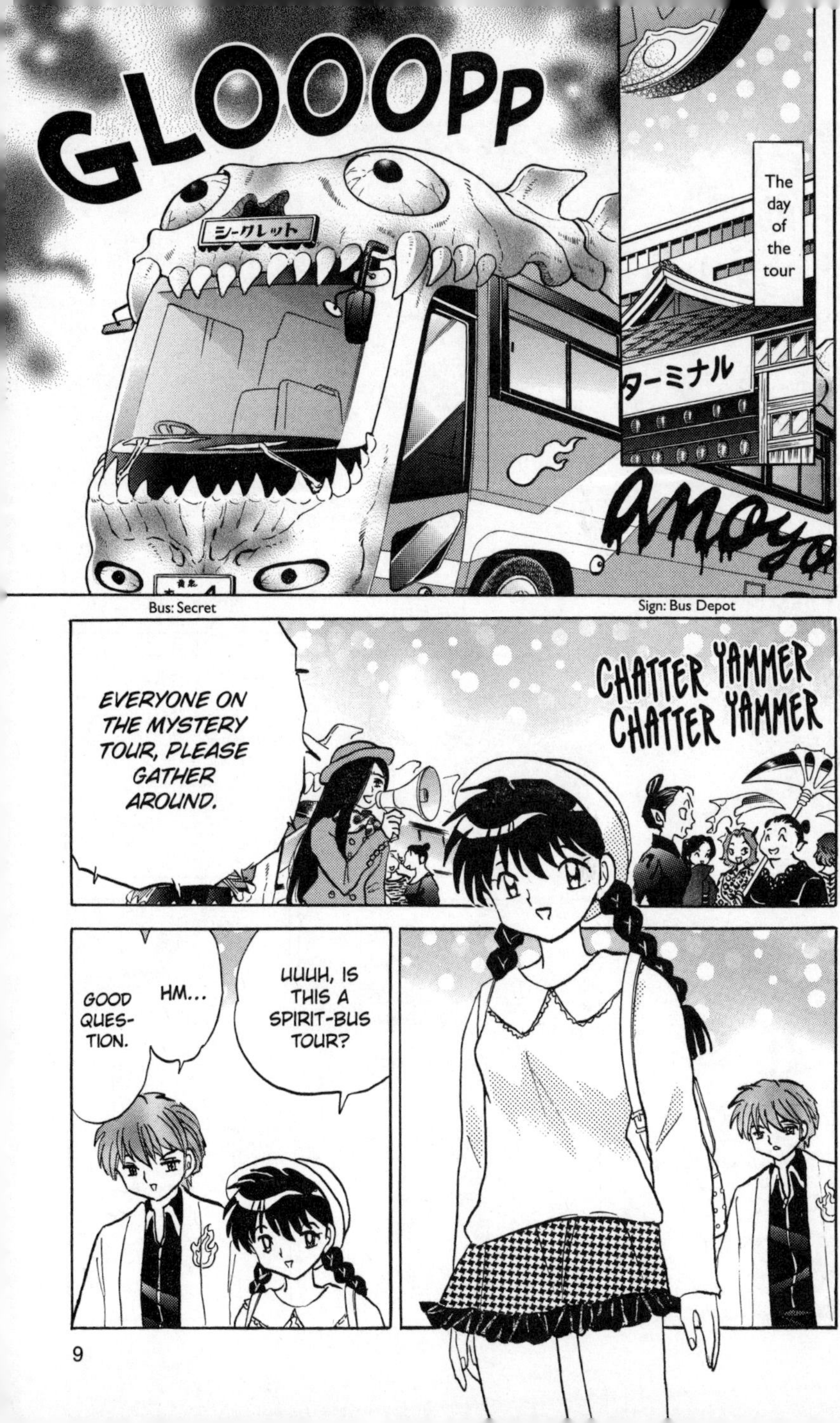
The day of the tour
GLOOOPP
シークレット
ターミナル
amoyo
Bus: Secret
Sign: Bus Depot
CHATTER YAMMER
CHATTER YAMMER
EVERYONE ON THE MYSTERY TOUR, PLEASE GATHER AROUND.
UUUH, IS THIS A SPIRIT-BUS TOUR?
HM...
GOOD QUES-TION.

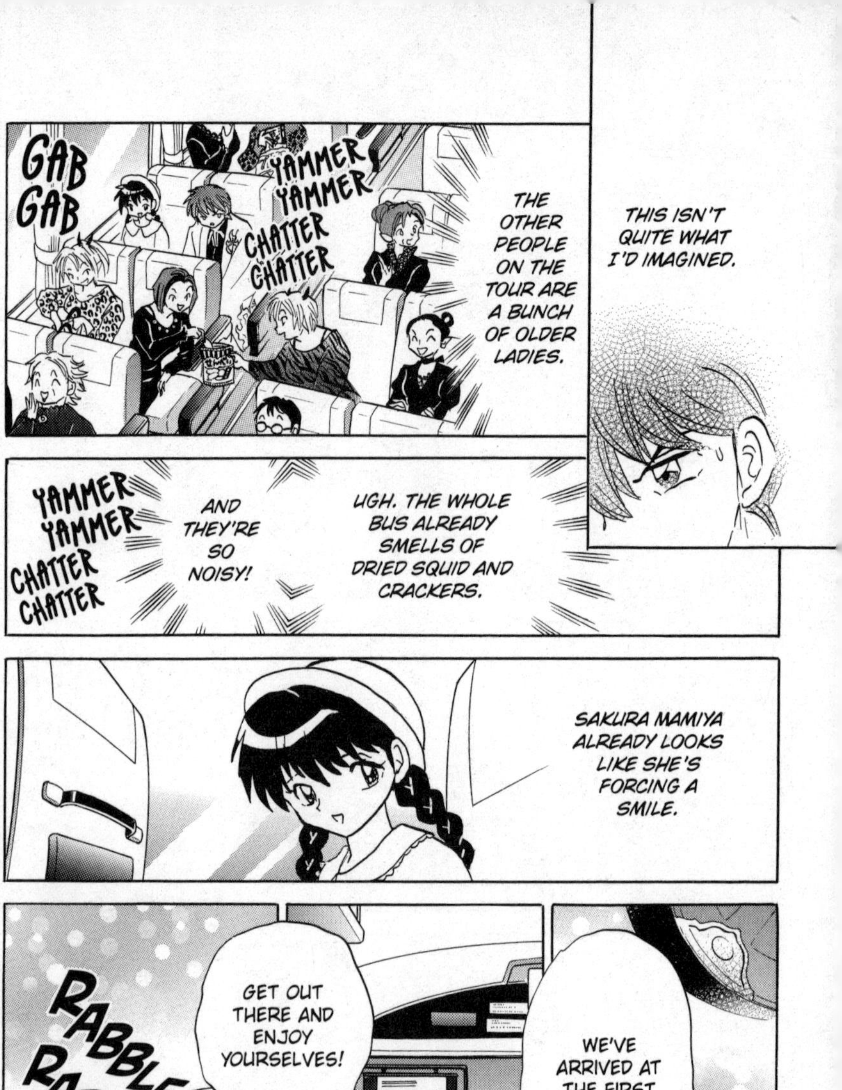
THIS ISN'T QUITE WHAT I'D IMAGINED.
THE OTHER PEOPLE ON THE TOUR ARE A BUNCH OF OLDER LADIES.
YAMMER YAMMER
CHATTER CHATTER
GAB GAB
UGH. THE WHOLE BUS ALREADY SMELLS OF DRIED SQUID AND CRACKERS.
AND THEY'RE SO NOISY!
YAMMER YAMMER
CHATTER CHATTER
SAKURA MAMIYA ALREADY LOOKS LIKE SHE'S FORCING A SMILE.
WE'VE ARRIVED AT THE FIRST STOP ON OUR SECRET TOUR.
PSSSHH
GET OUT THERE AND ENJOY YOURSELVES!
RABBLE RABBLE RABBLE

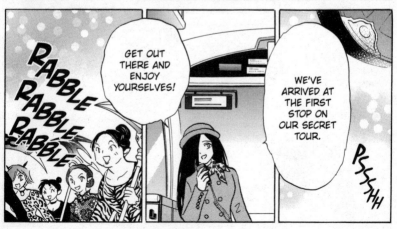

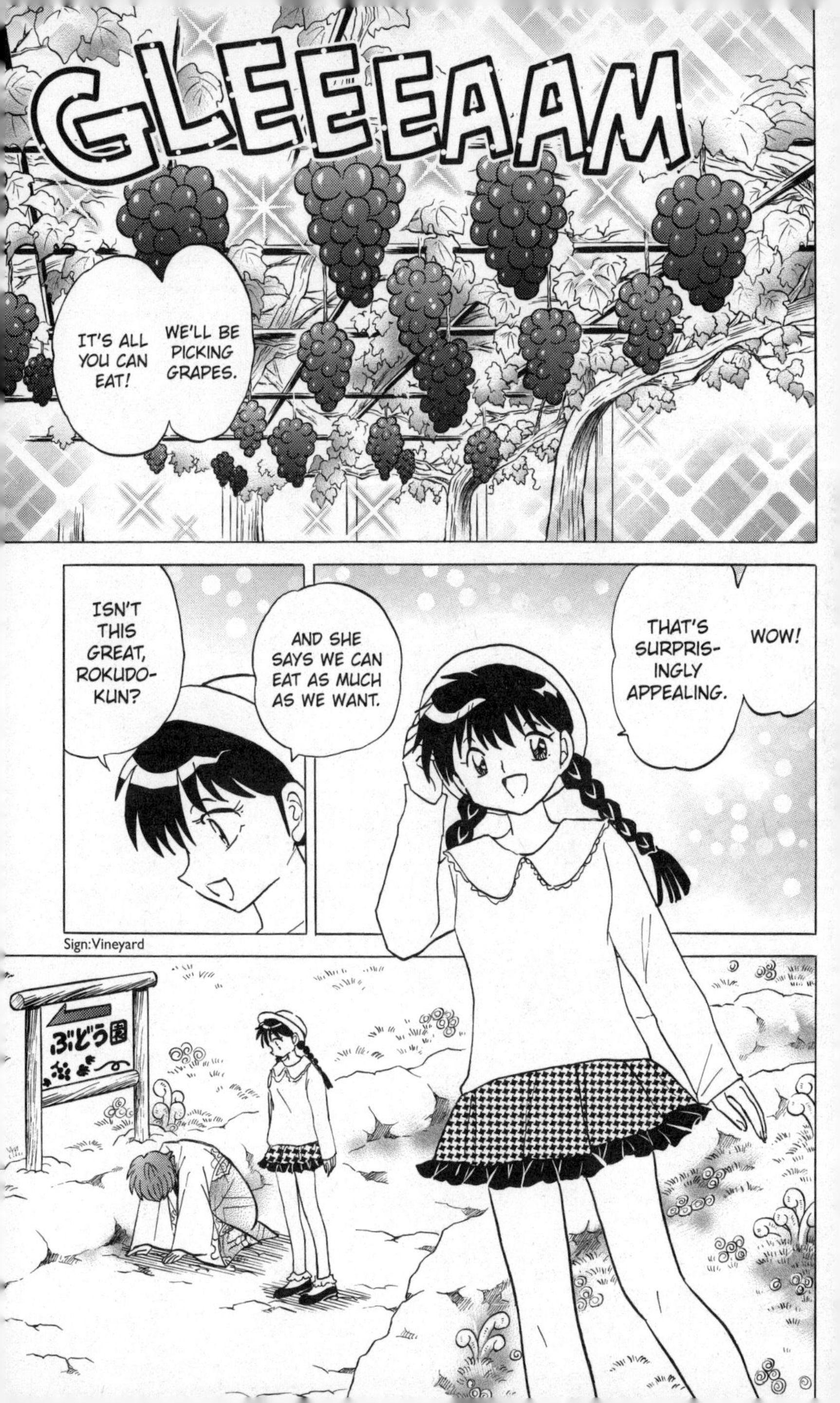
GLEEEAAM
WE'LL BE PICKING GRAPES.
IT'S ALL YOU CAN EAT!
WOW!
THAT'S SURPRISINGLY APPEALING.
ISN'T THIS GREAT, ROKUDO-KUN?
AND SHE SAYS WE CAN EAT AS MUCH AS WE WANT.
Sign: Vineyard
ぶどう園

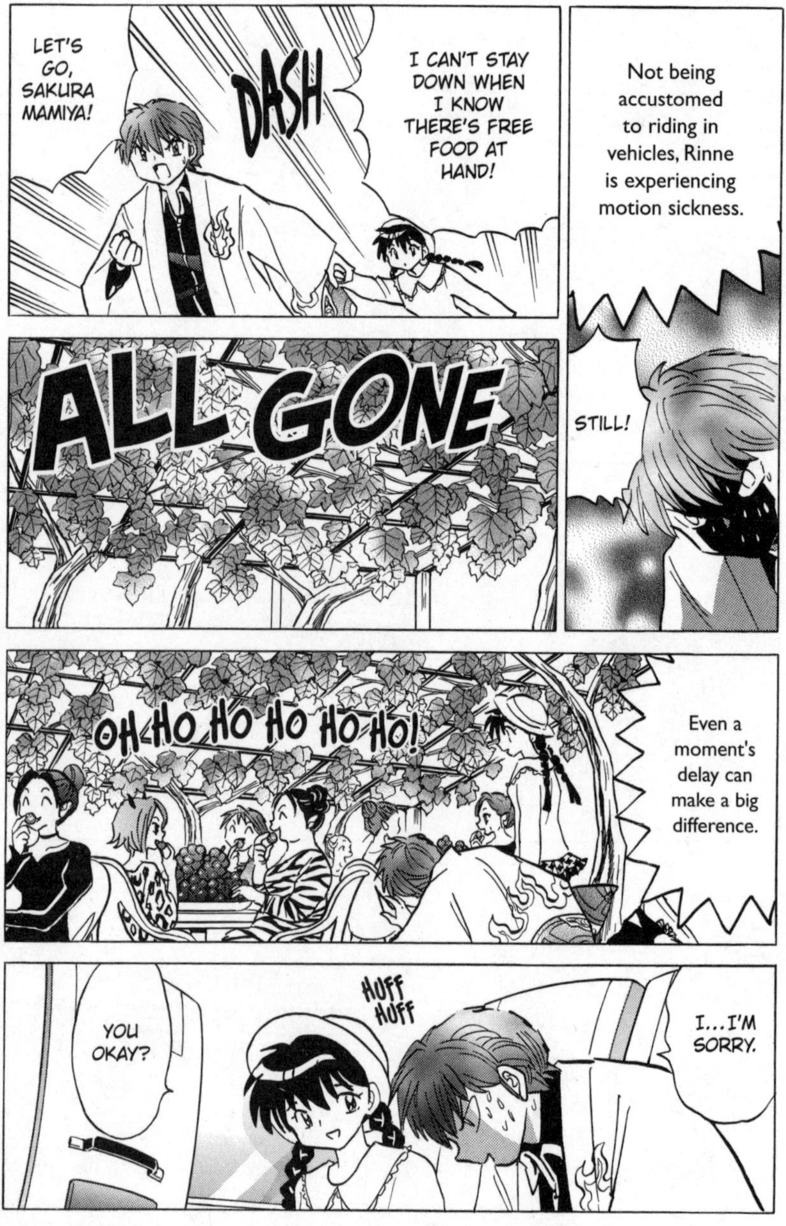
Not being accustomed to riding in vehicles, Rinne is experiencing motion sickness.
STILL!
I CAN'T STAY DOWN WHEN I KNOW THERE'S FREE FOOD AT HAND!
DASH
LET'S GO, SAKURA MAMIYA!
ALL GONE
Even a moment's delay can make a big difference.
OH HO HO HO HO HO!
I...I'M SORRY.
HUFF HUFF
YOU OKAY?

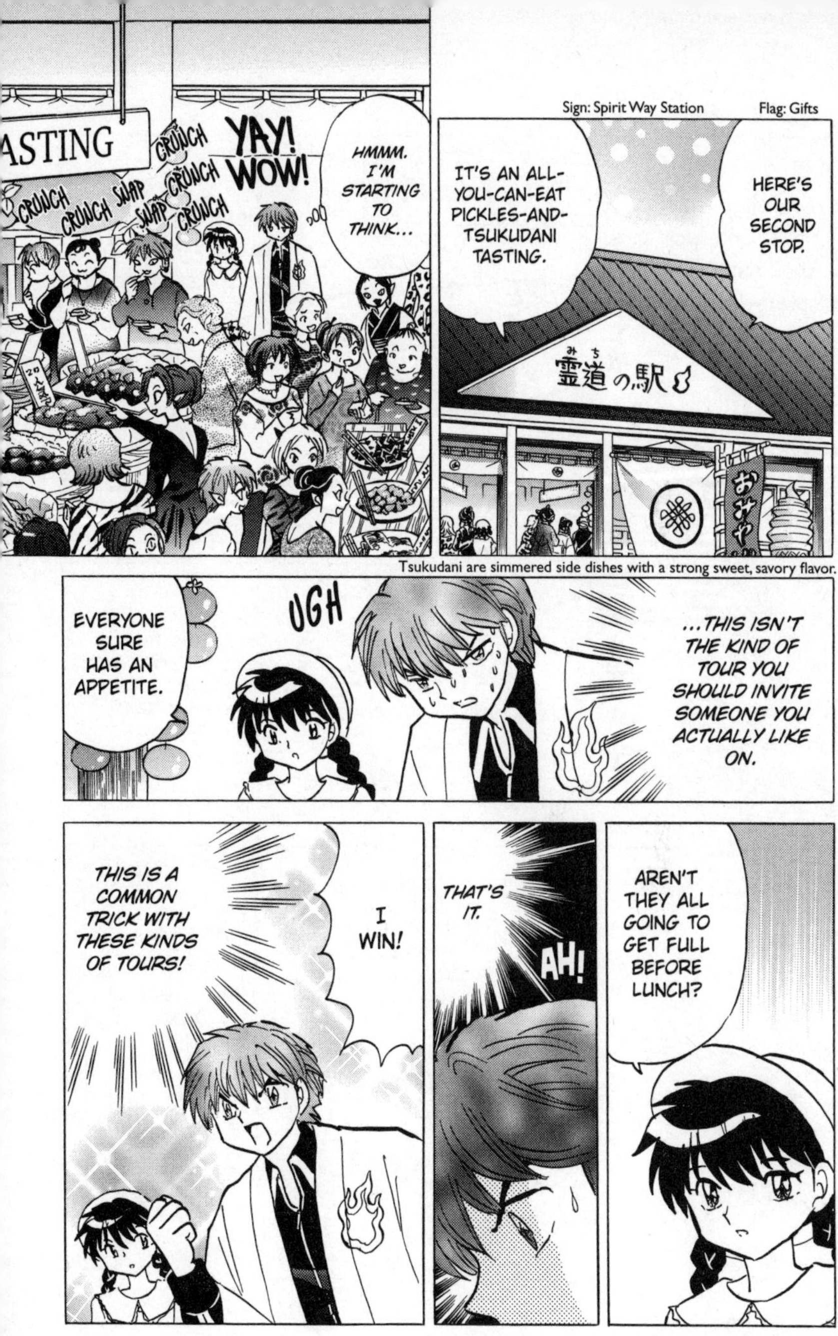

Sign: Spirit Way Station
Flag: Gifts
HERE'S OUR SECOND STOP.
IT'S AN ALL-YOU-CAN-EAT PICKLES-AND-TSUKUDANI TASTING.
霊道の駅
HMMM. I'M STARTING TO THINK...
YAY! WOW!
CRUNCH
CRUNCH
CRUNCH
SNAP
SNAP
CRUNCH
CRUNCH
ASTING
...THIS ISN'T THE KIND OF TOUR YOU SHOULD INVITE SOMEONE YOU ACTUALLY LIKE ON.
UGH
EVERYONE SURE HAS AN APPETITE.
AREN'T THEY ALL GOING TO GET FULL BEFORE LUNCH?
THAT'S IT.
AH!
I WIN!
THIS IS A COMMON TRICK WITH THESE KINDS OF TOURS!

Tsukudani are simmered side dishes with a strong sweet, savory flavor.

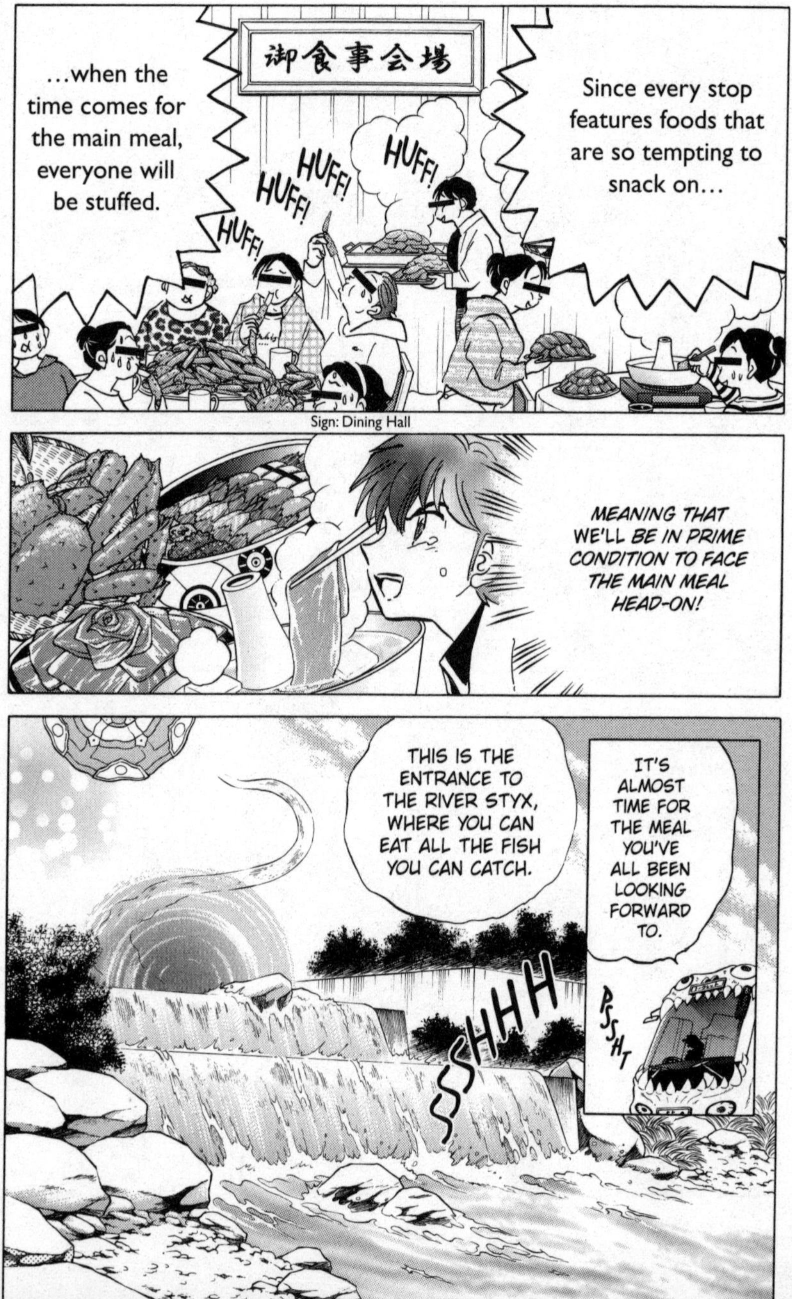

御食事会場
Since every stop features foods that are so tempting to snack on…
HUFF!
HUFF!
HUFF!
HUFF!
…when the time comes for the main meal, everyone will be stuffed.
MEANING THAT WE'LL BE IN PRIME CONDITION TO FACE THE MAIN MEAL HEAD-ON!
IT'S ALMOST TIME FOR THE MEAL YOU'VE ALL BEEN LOOKING FORWARD TO.
THIS IS THE ENTRANCE TO THE RIVER STYX, WHERE YOU CAN EAT ALL THE FISH YOU CAN CATCH.
PSSHT
SSHHH

Sign: Dining Hall

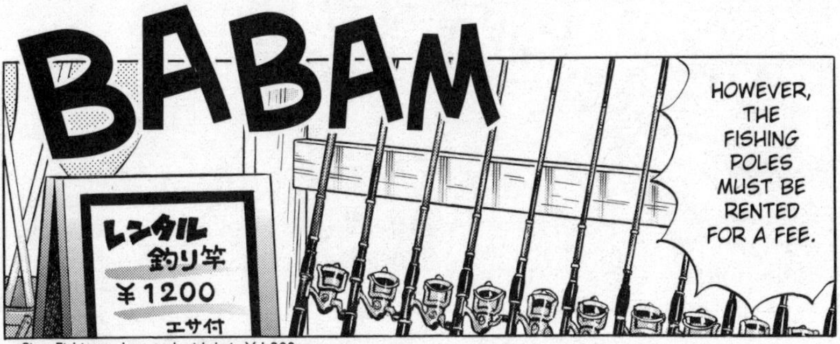
HOWEVER, THE FISHING POLES MUST BE RENTED FOR A FEE.
BABAM
レンタル
釣り竿
¥1200
エサ付
Sign: Fishing pole rental with bait, ¥1,200

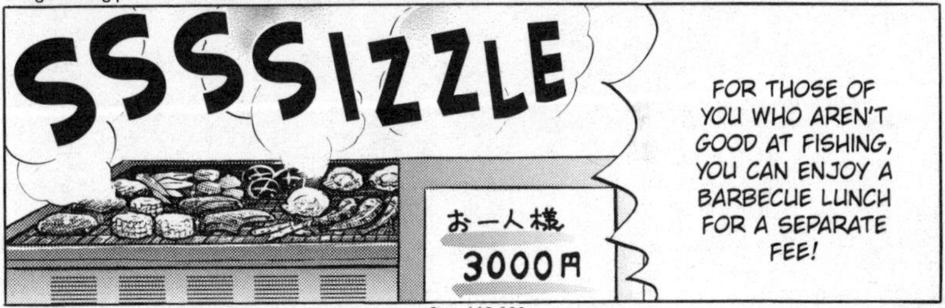
FOR THOSE OF YOU WHO AREN'T GOOD AT FISHING, YOU CAN ENJOY A BARBECUE LUNCH FOR A SEPARATE FEE!
SSSSIZZLE
お一人様
3000円
Sign: ¥3,000 per person

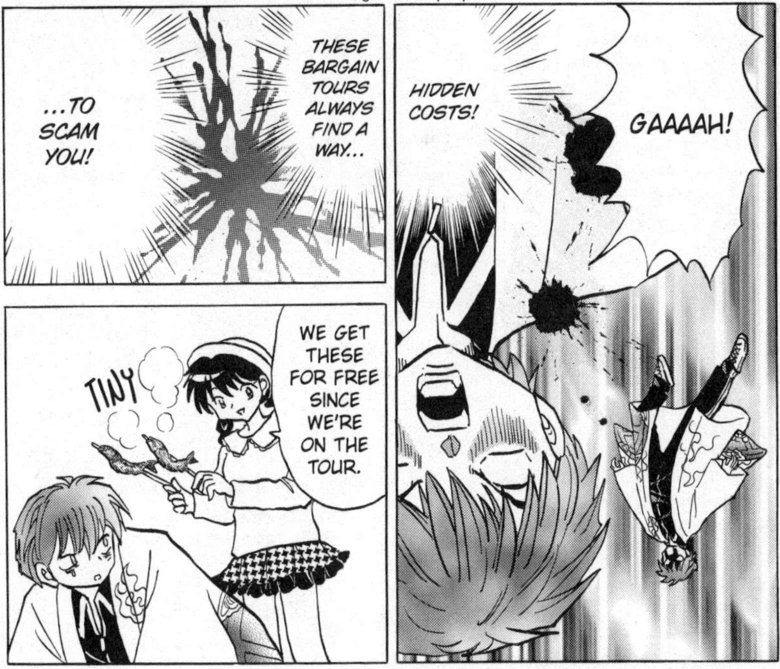
GAAAAH!
HIDDEN COSTS!
THESE BARGAIN TOURS ALWAYS FIND A WAY...
...TO SCAM YOU!
WE GET THESE FOR FREE SINCE WE'RE ON THE TOUR.
TINY

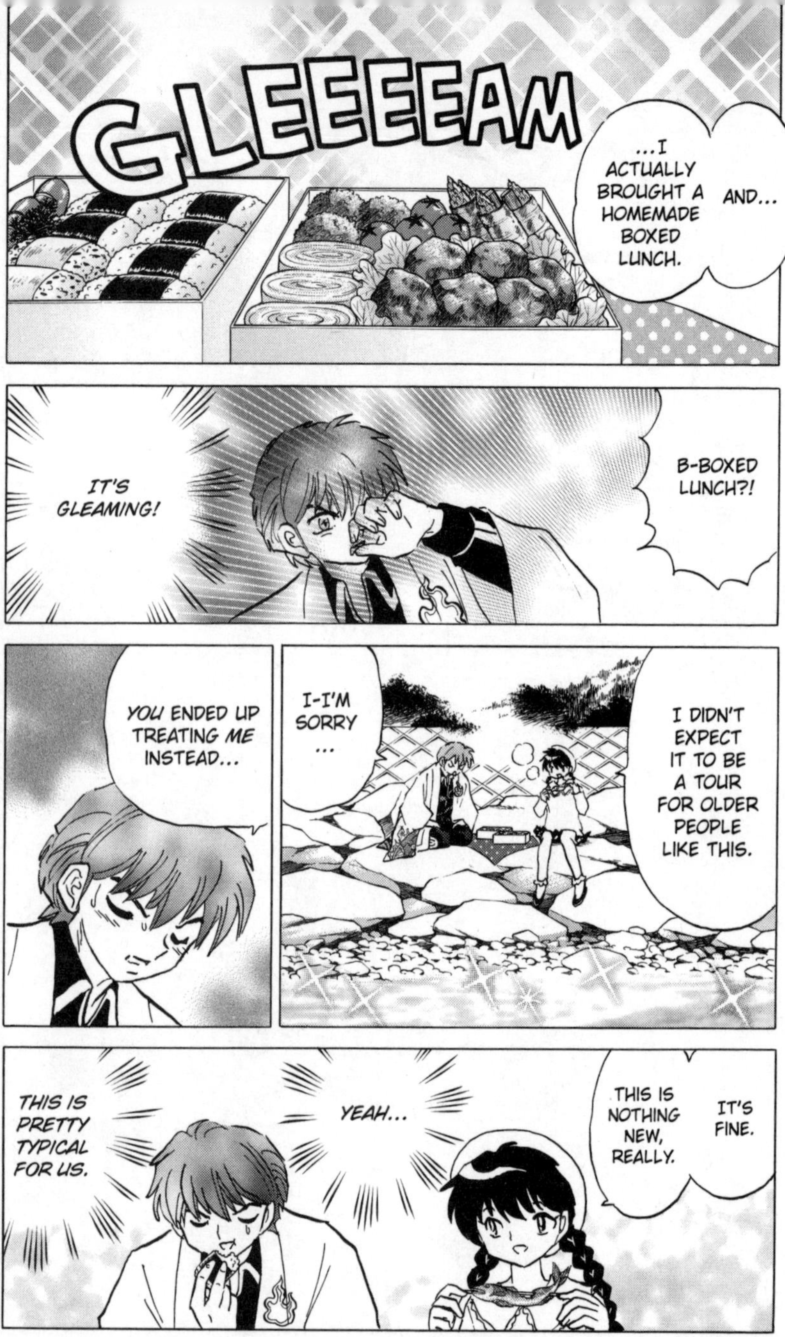
AND...
...I ACTUALLY BROUGHT A HOMEMADE BOXED LUNCH.
GLEEEEAM
B-BOXED LUNCH?!
IT'S GLEAMING!
I DIDN'T EXPECT IT TO BE A TOUR FOR OLDER PEOPLE LIKE THIS.
I-I'M SORRY...
YOU ENDED UP TREATING ME INSTEAD...
IT'S FINE.
THIS IS NOTHING NEW, REALLY.
YEAH...
THIS IS PRETTY TYPICAL FOR US.

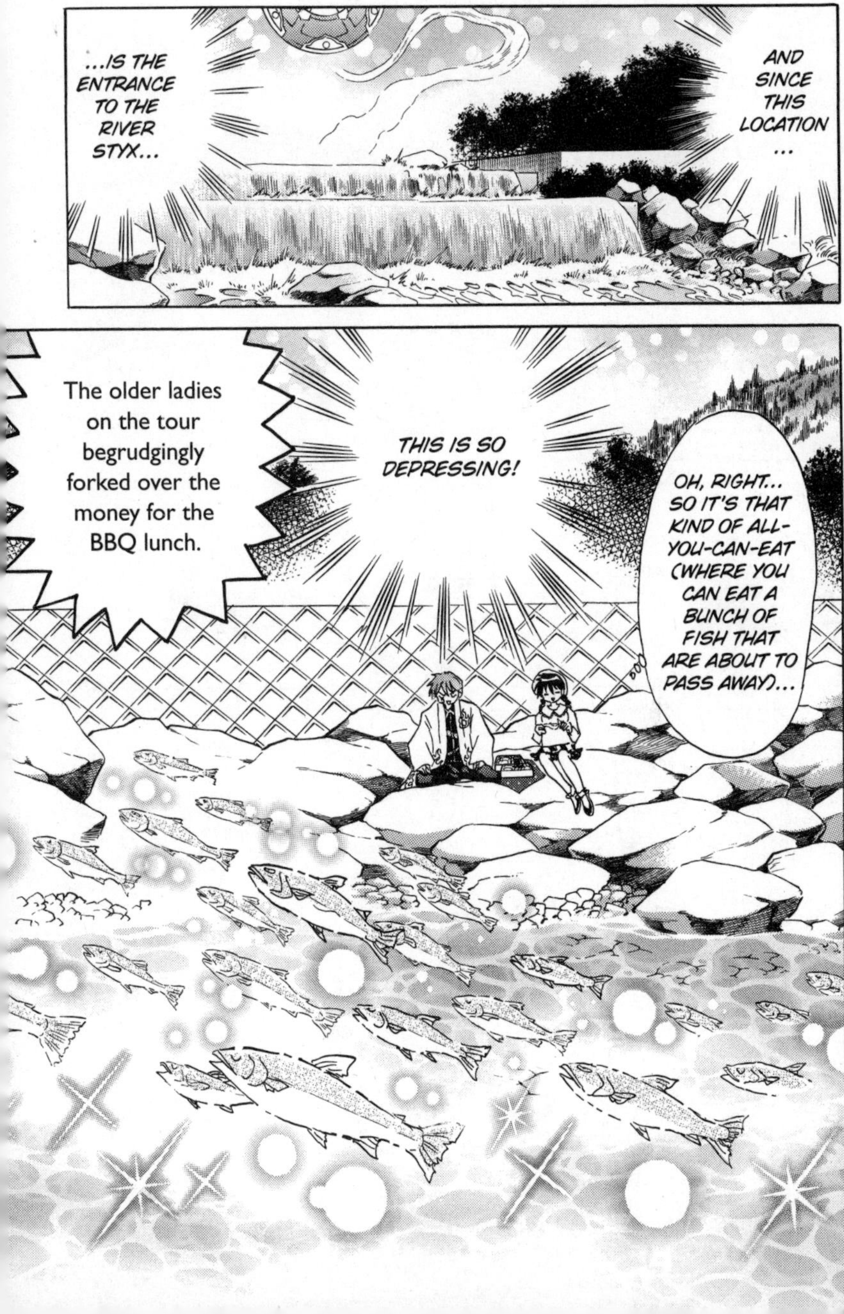
AND SINCE THIS LOCATION...
...IS THE ENTRANCE TO THE RIVER STYX...
OH, RIGHT... SO IT'S THAT KIND OF ALL-YOU-CAN-EAT (WHERE YOU CAN EAT A BUNCH OF FISH THAT ARE ABOUT TO PASS AWAY)...
THIS IS SO DEPRESSING!
The older ladies on the tour begrudgingly forked over the money for the BBQ lunch.

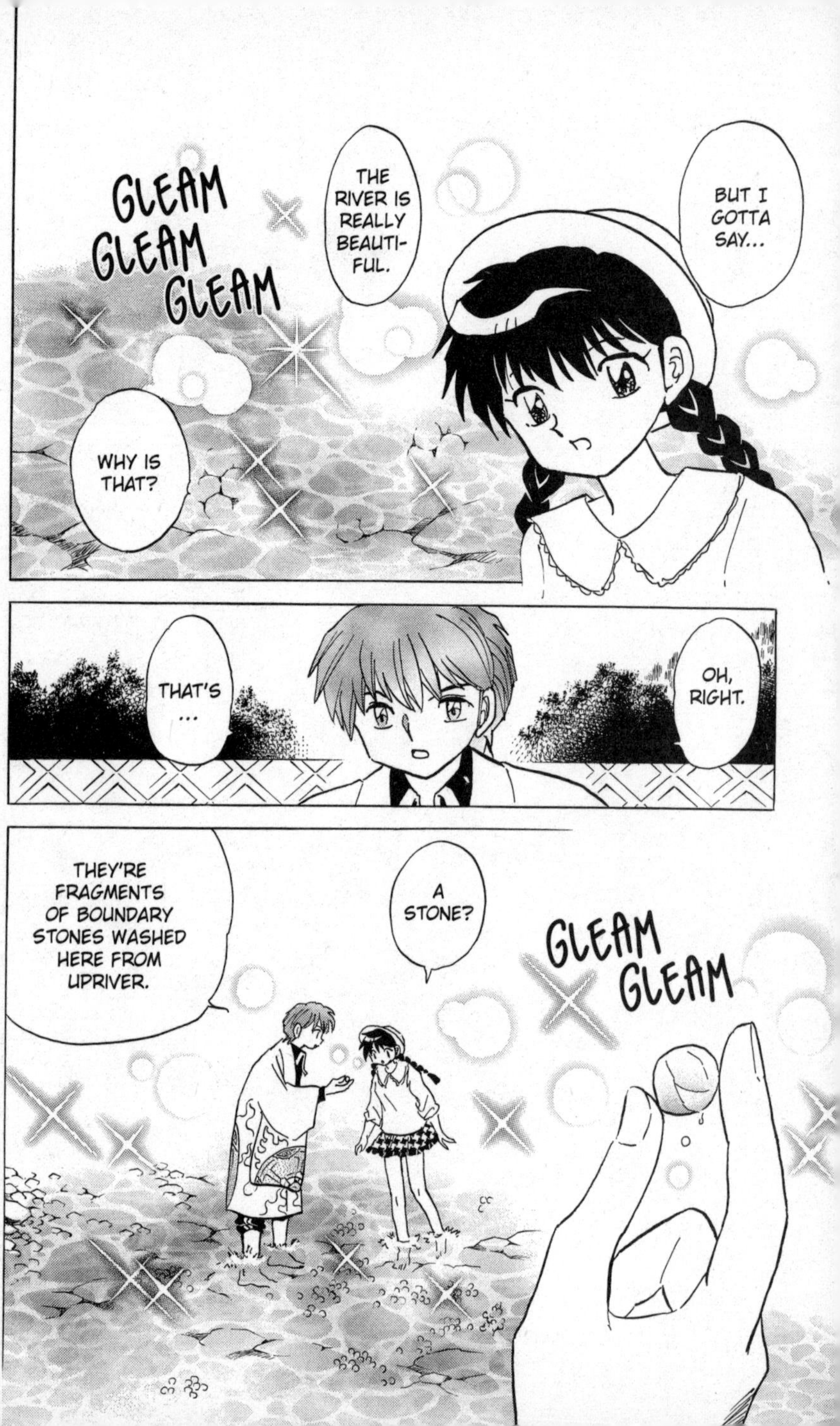
BUT I GOTTA SAY...
THE RIVER IS REALLY BEAUTIFUL.
GLEAM GLEAM GLEAM
WHY IS THAT?
OH, RIGHT.
THAT'S ...
GLEAM GLEAM
A STONE?
THEY'RE FRAGMENTS OF BOUNDARY STONES WASHED HERE FROM UPRIVER.

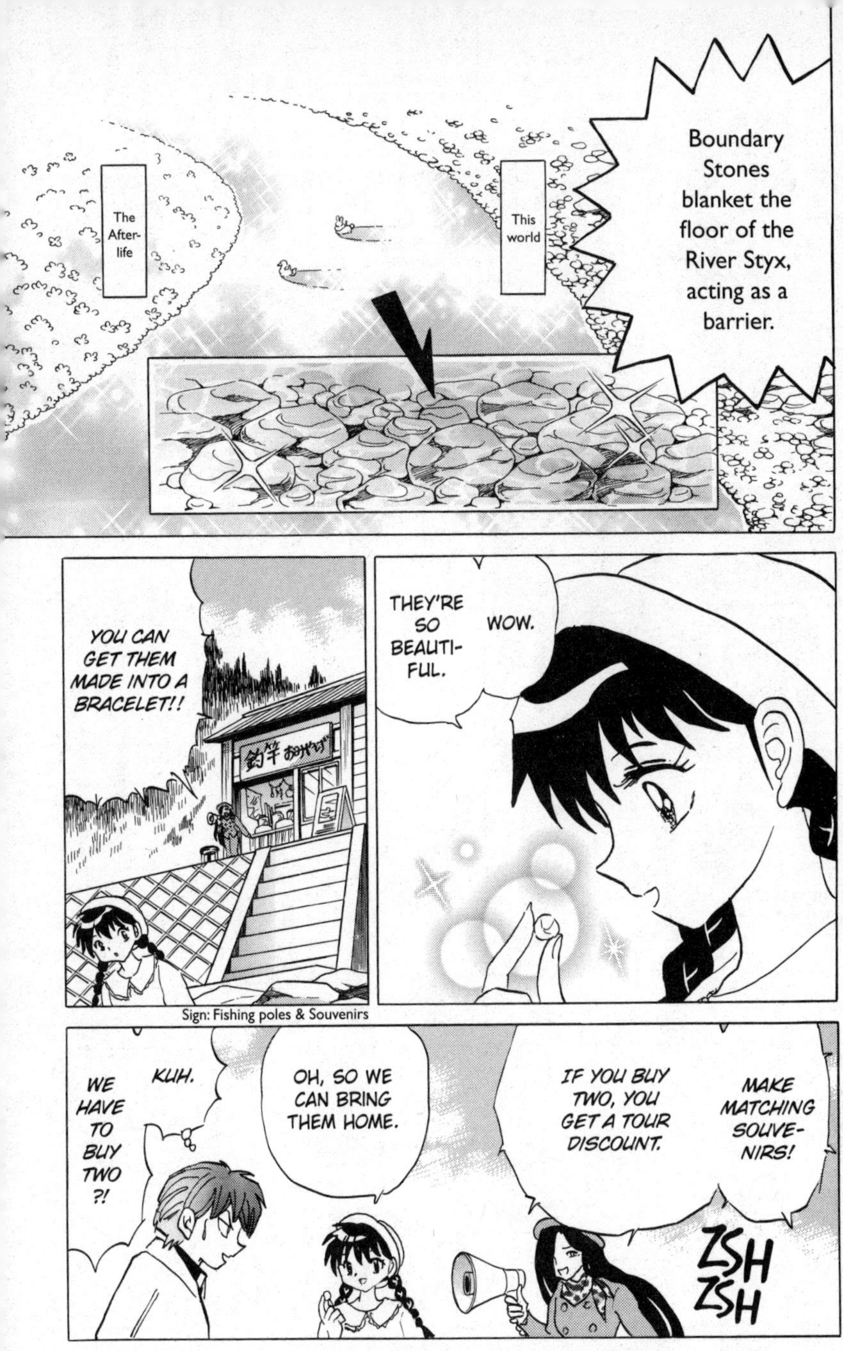
Boundary Stones blanket the floor of the River Styx, acting as a barrier.
This world
The After-life
WOW.
THEY'RE SO BEAUTIFUL.
YOU CAN GET THEM MADE INTO A BRACELET!!
Sign: Fishing poles & Souvenirs
MAKE MATCHING SOUVENIRS!
IF YOU BUY TWO, YOU GET A TOUR DISCOUNT.
ZSH ZSH
OH, SO WE CAN BRING THEM HOME.
KUH.
WE HAVE TO BUY TWO?!

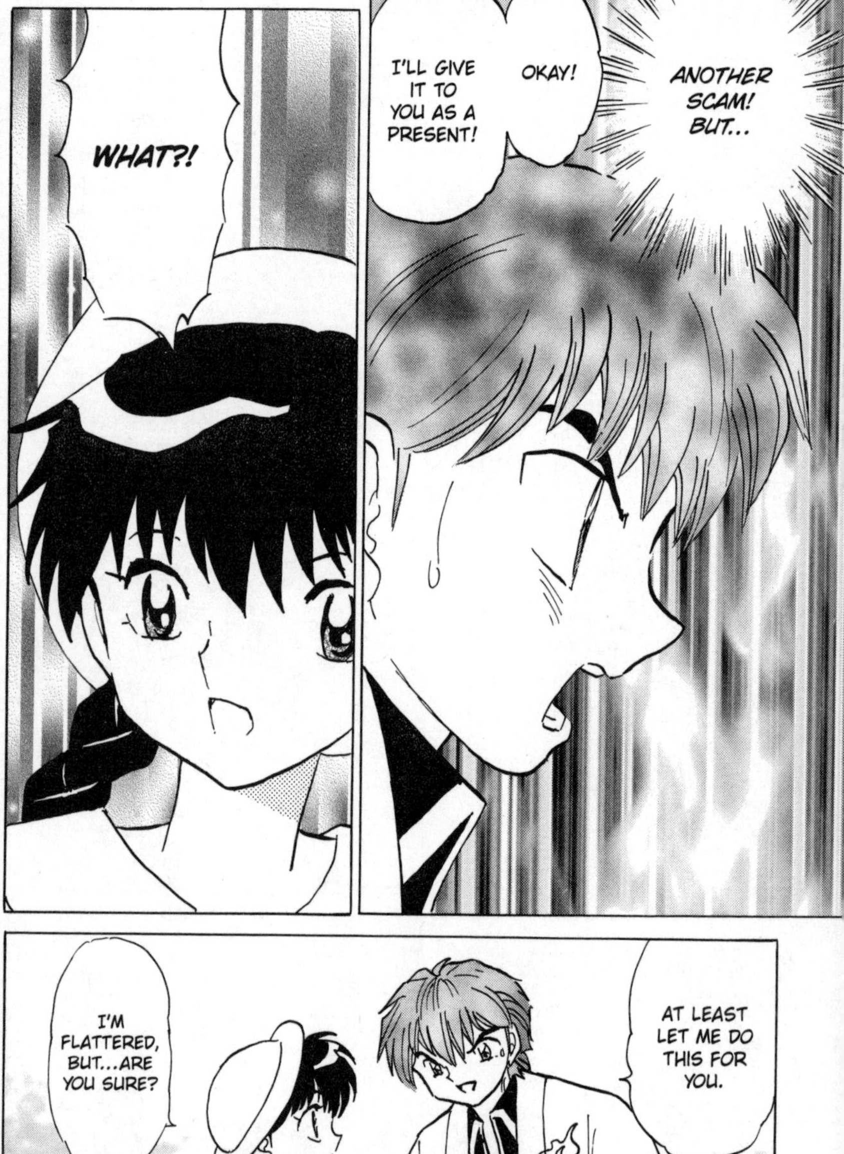
ANOTHER SCAM! BUT...
OKAY!
I'LL GIVE IT TO YOU AS A PRESENT!
WHAT?!
AT LEAST LET ME DO THIS FOR YOU.
I'M FLATTERED, BUT...ARE YOU SURE?

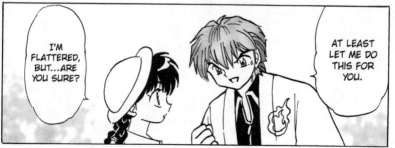

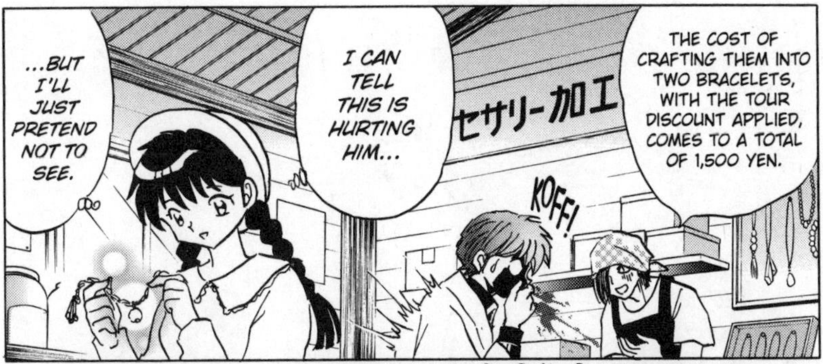
THE COST OF CRAFTING THEM INTO TWO BRACELETS, WITH THE TOUR DISCOUNT APPLIED, COMES TO A TOTAL OF 1,500 YEN.
セサリー加工
KOFF!
I CAN TELL THIS IS HURTING HIM...
...BUT I'LL JUST PRETEND NOT TO SEE.

Sign: Crafting Corner

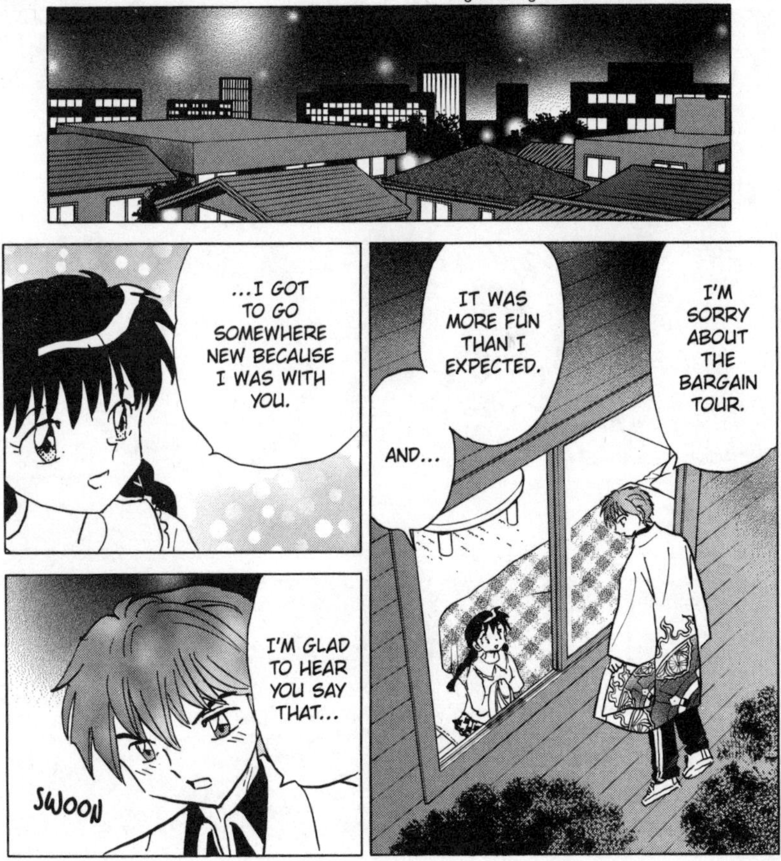
I'M SORRY ABOUT THE BARGAIN TOUR.
IT WAS MORE FUN THAN I EXPECTED.
AND...
...I GOT TO GO SOMEWHERE NEW BECAUSE I WAS WITH YOU.
I'M GLAD TO HEAR YOU SAY THAT...
SWOON

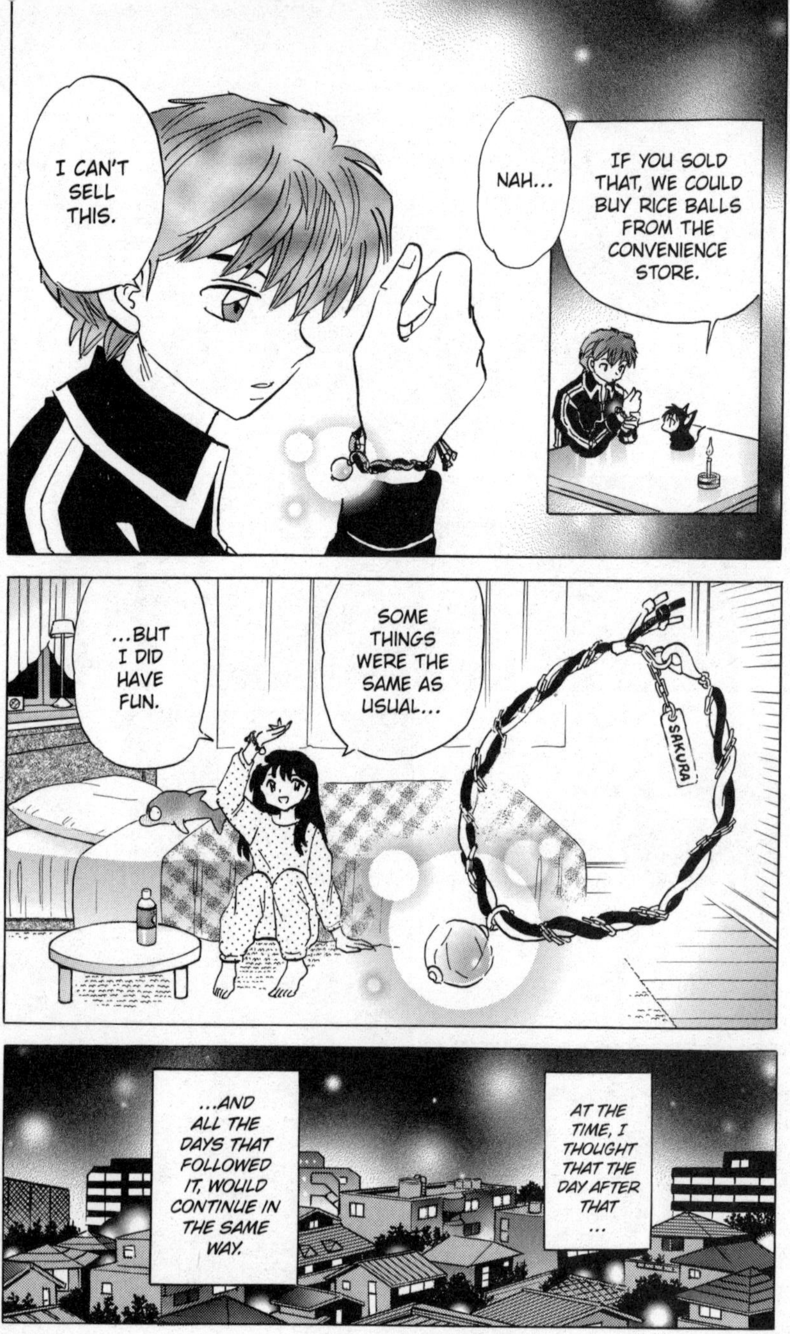
IF YOU SOLD THAT, WE COULD BUY RICE BALLS FROM THE CONVENIENCE STORE.
NAH...
I CAN'T SELL THIS.
SOME THINGS WERE THE SAME AS USUAL...
...BUT I DID HAVE FUN.
SAKURA
AT THE TIME, I THOUGHT THAT THE DAY AFTER THAT ...
...AND ALL THE DAYS THAT FOLLOWED IT, WOULD CONTINUE IN THE SAME WAY.

CHAPTER 390: EXORCISM EXAM

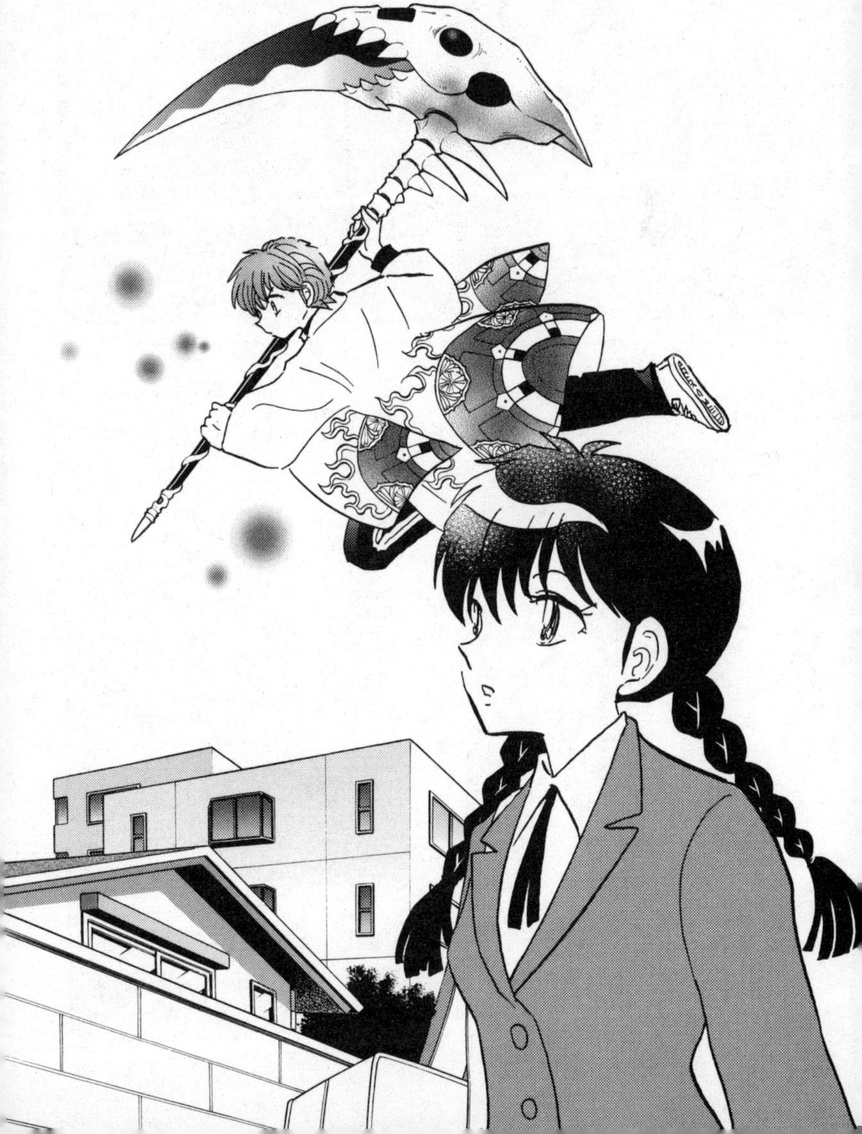

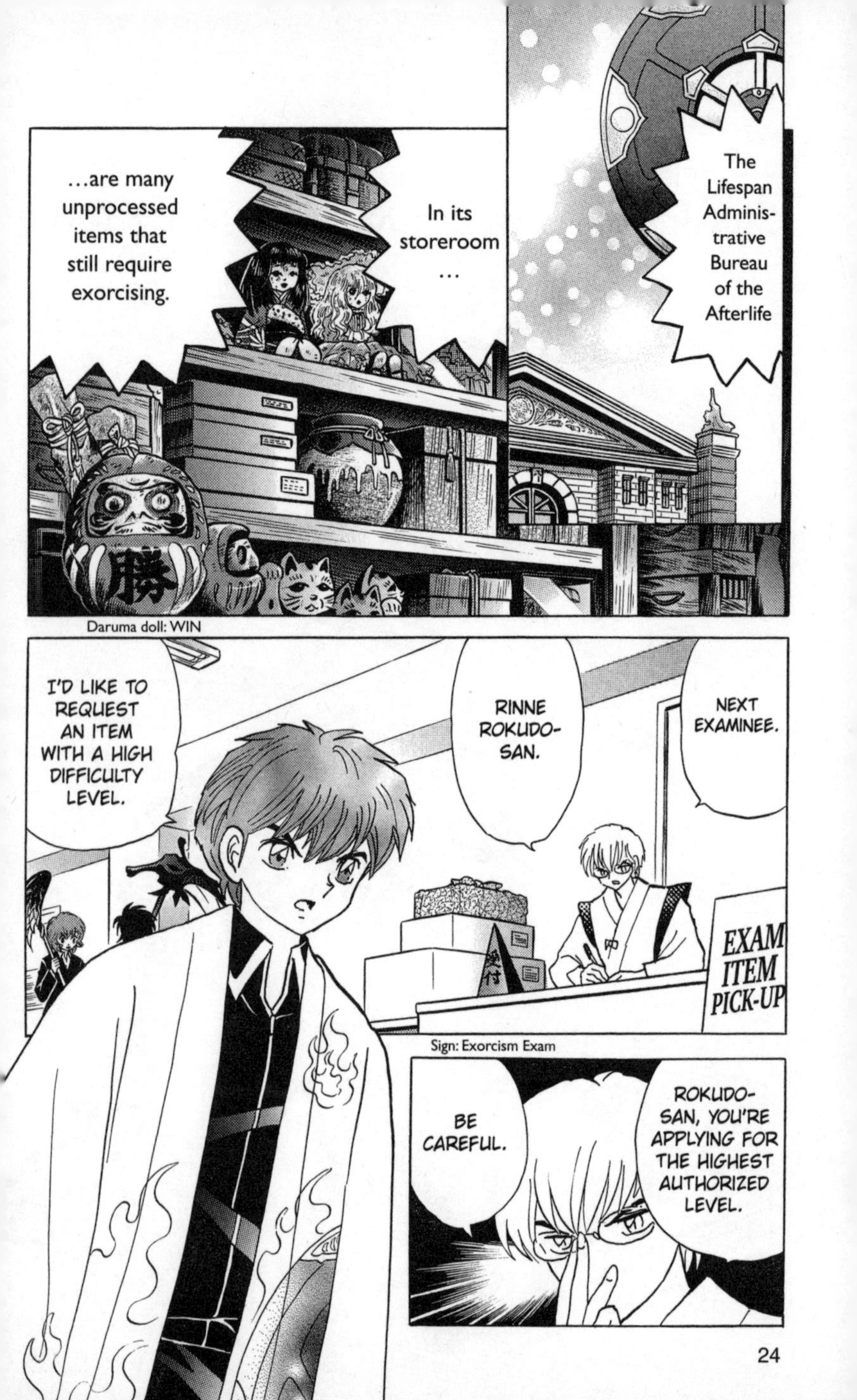
The Lifespan Administrative Bureau of the Afterlife
In its storeroom…
…are many unprocessed items that still require exorcising.
Daruma doll: WIN
NEXT EXAMINEE.
RINNE ROKUDO-SAN.
I'D LIKE TO REQUEST AN ITEM WITH A HIGH DIFFICULTY LEVEL.
EXAM ITEM PICK-UP
Sign: Exorcism Exam
ROKUDO-SAN, YOU'RE APPLYING FOR THE HIGHEST AUTHORIZED LEVEL.
BE CAREFUL.

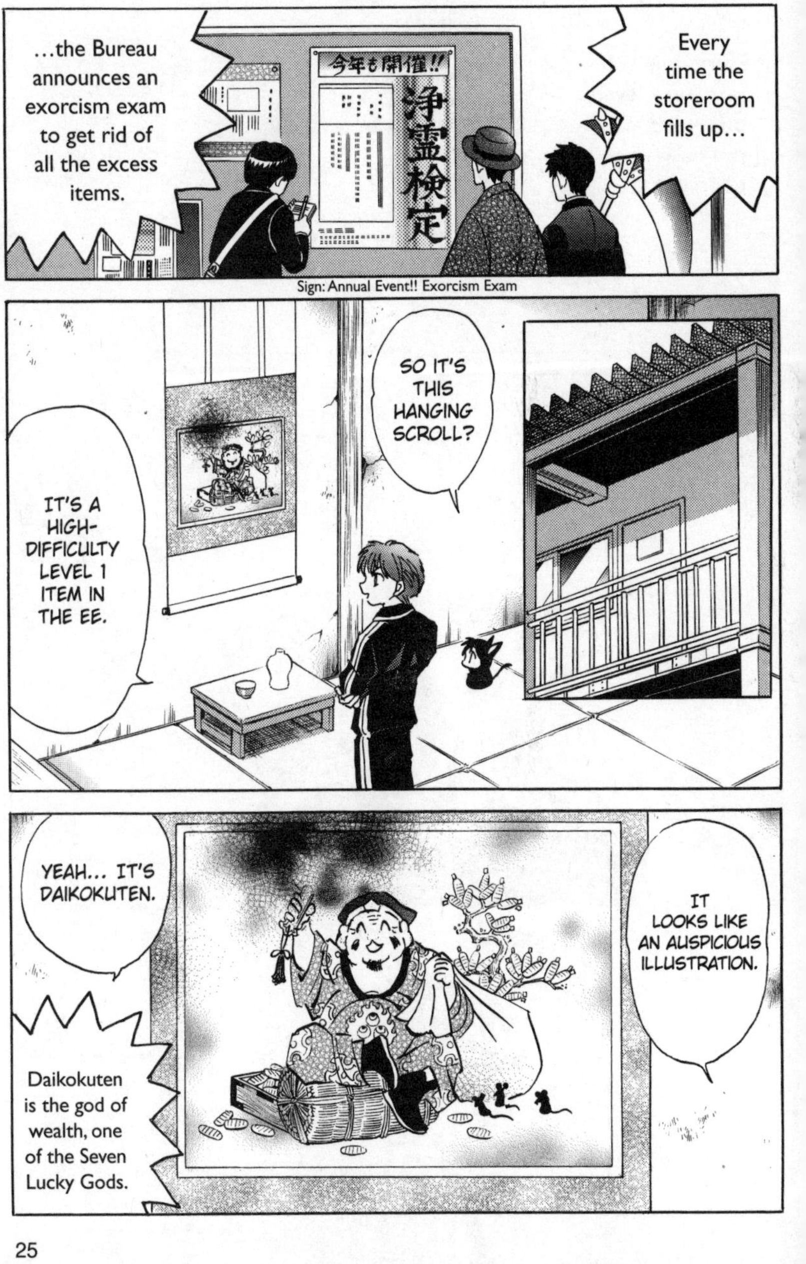
Every time the storeroom fills up…
…the Bureau announces an exorcism exam to get rid of all the excess items.
今年も開催!!
浄霊検定
Sign: Annual Event!! Exorcism Exam
SO IT'S THIS HANGING SCROLL?
IT'S A HIGH-DIFFICULTY LEVEL 1 ITEM IN THE EE.
IT LOOKS LIKE AN AUSPICIOUS ILLUSTRATION.
YEAH… IT'S DAIKOKUTEN.
Daikokuten is the god of wealth, one of the Seven Lucky Gods.

Every time you move up a level on the EE, you can raise your exorcism fees.

Level 1	▶ ¥100 UP
Level 2	▶ ¥70 UP
Level 3	▶ ¥50 UP
Level 4	▶ ¥30 UP
Level 5	▶ ¥10 UP

APPARENTLY, IT USED TO BELONG TO AN OLD MAN WHO LIVED ALONE. HIS DEEP RESENTMENT IS STILL CLINGING TO IT.

YEP! IT'S A HIGH-PAYOUT LEVEL 1 ITEM!

IF YOU EXORCISE THIS, YOU'LL SEE A 100-YEN INCREASE, RIGHT?

ROKUDO-KUUN.

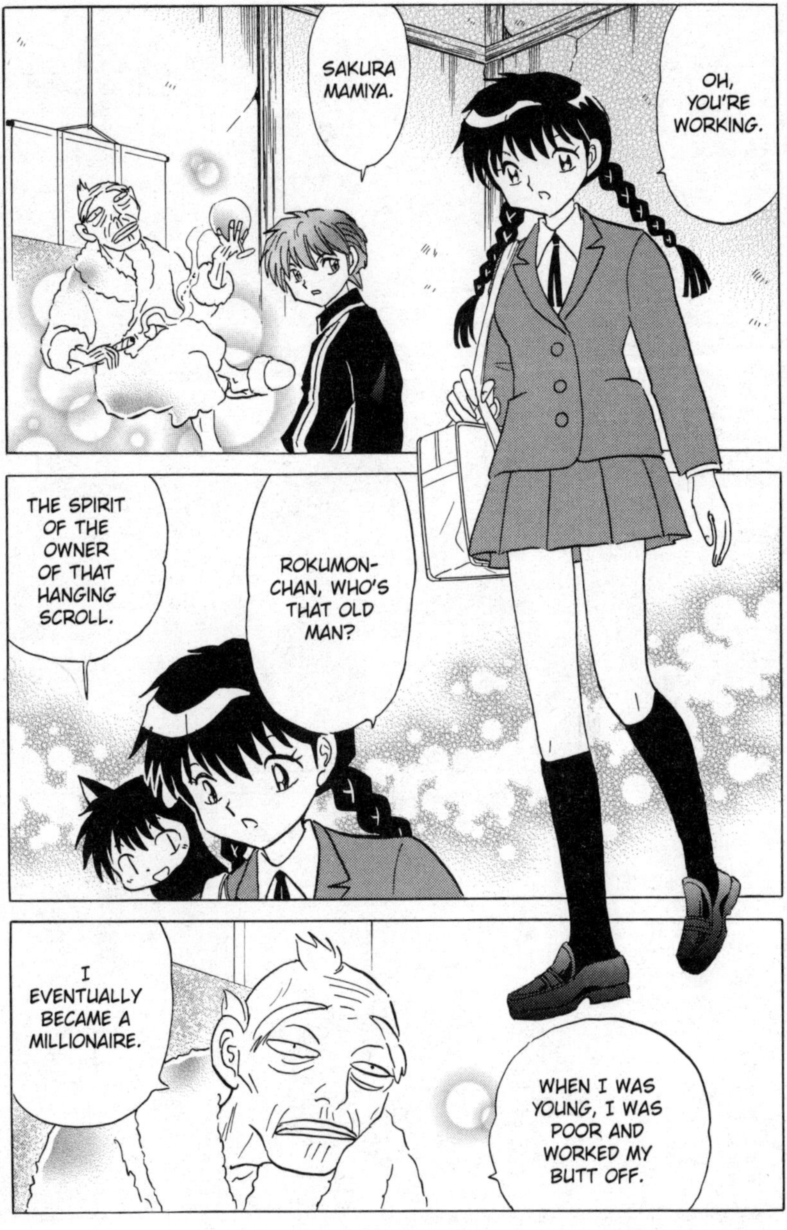
OH, YOU'RE WORKING.
SAKURA MAMIYA.
ROKUMON-CHAN, WHO'S THAT OLD MAN?
THE SPIRIT OF THE OWNER OF THAT HANGING SCROLL.
WHEN I WAS YOUNG, I WAS POOR AND WORKED MY BUTT OFF.
I EVENTUALLY BECAME A MILLIONAIRE.

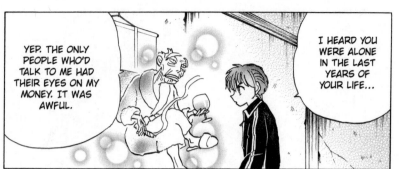

I HEARD YOU WERE ALONE IN THE LAST YEARS OF YOUR LIFE...
YEP. THE ONLY PEOPLE WHO'D TALK TO ME HAD THEIR EYES ON MY MONEY. IT WAS AWFUL.
I BECAME UNABLE TO TRUST ANYBODY...
...AND IN THE END, I WAS ALL ALONE.
OH MY...
SO...
WHAT'S YOUR LINGERING ATTACHMENT?
THE DAY BEFORE I DIED ...
...A HANGING SCROLL ARRIVED.
I HAD COMMISSIONED A TOP ARTIST TO CREATE IT FOR ME AS A WAY TO REWARD MYSELF FOR ALL MY HARD WORK.

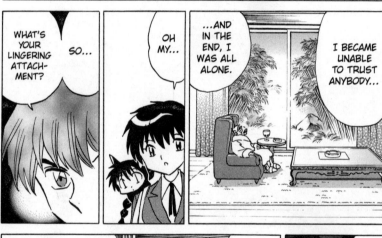

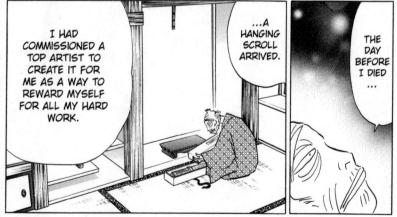

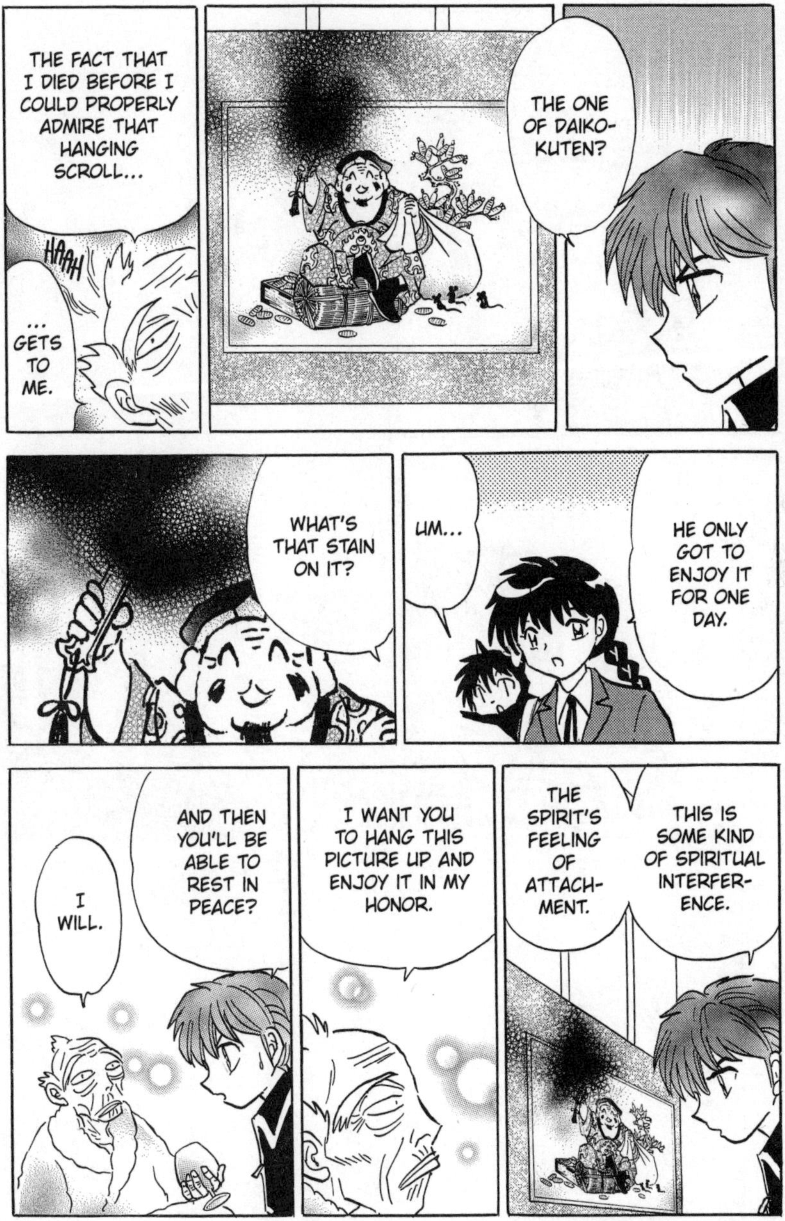
THE ONE OF DAIKO-KUTEN?
THE FACT THAT I DIED BEFORE I COULD PROPERLY ADMIRE THAT HANGING SCROLL...
HAAH
...GETS TO ME.
HE ONLY GOT TO ENJOY IT FOR ONE DAY.
UM...
WHAT'S THAT STAIN ON IT?
THIS IS SOME KIND OF SPIRITUAL INTERFERENCE.
THE SPIRIT'S FEELING OF ATTACHMENT.
I WANT YOU TO HANG THIS PICTURE UP AND ENJOY IT IN MY HONOR.
AND THEN YOU'LL BE ABLE TO REST IN PEACE?
I WILL.

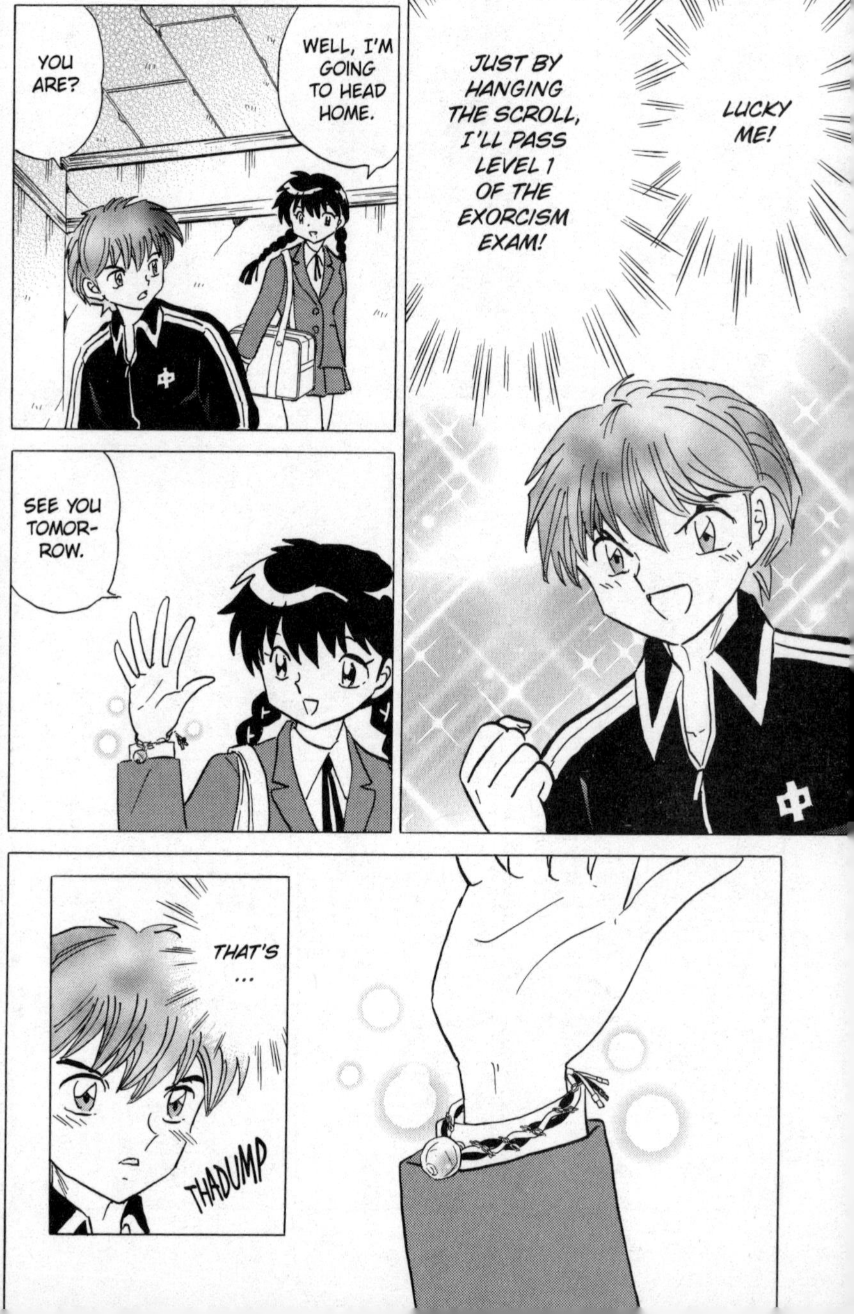
LUCKY ME!
JUST BY HANGING THE SCROLL, I'LL PASS LEVEL 1 OF THE EXORCISM EXAM!
WELL, I'M GOING TO HEAD HOME.
YOU ARE?
SEE YOU TOMOR-ROW.
THAT'S...
THADUMP

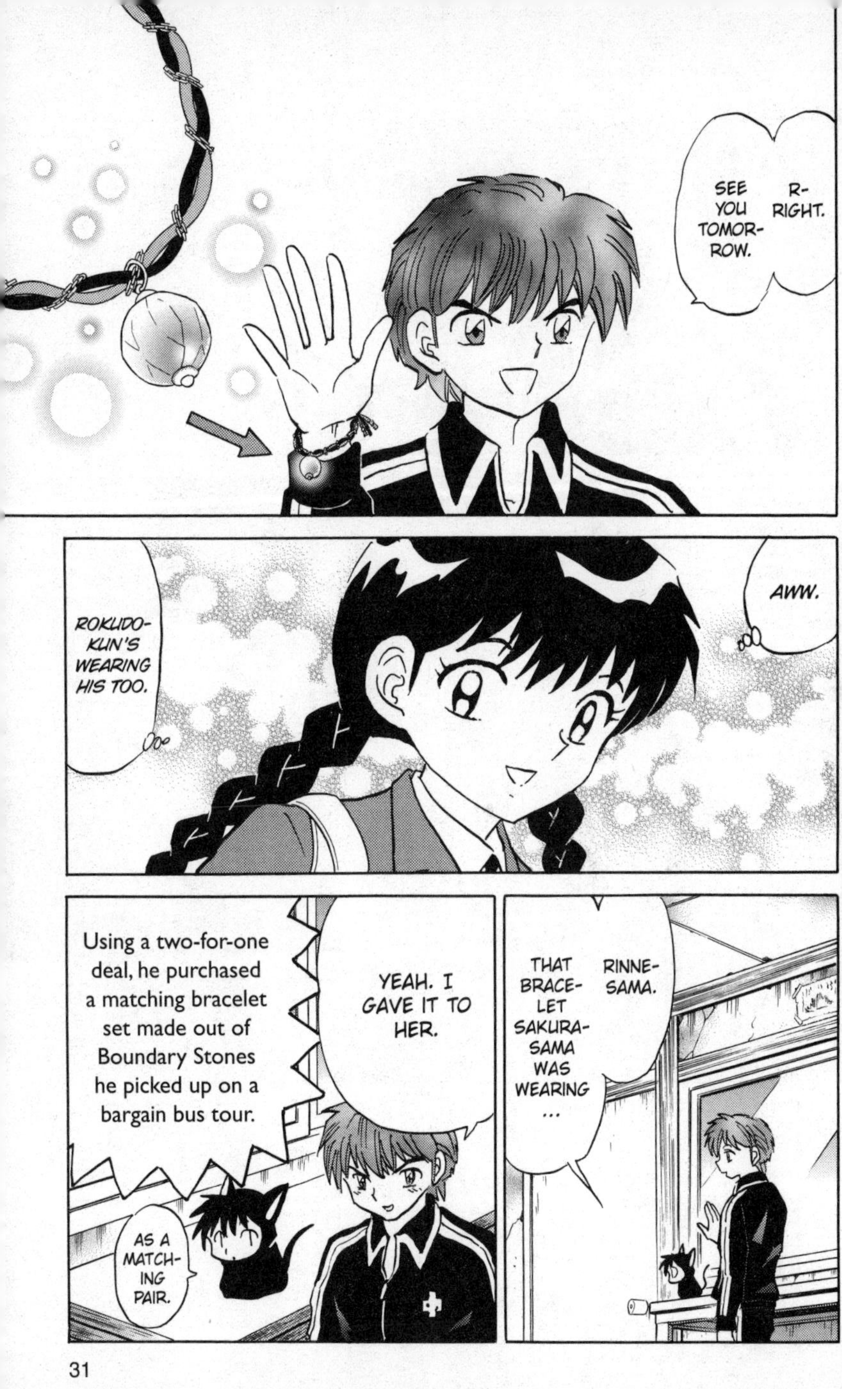
R-RIGHT.
SEE YOU TOMORROW.
AWW.
ROKUDO-KUN'S WEARING HIS TOO.
RINNE-SAMA.
THAT BRACELET SAKURA-SAMA WAS WEARING...
YEAH. I GAVE IT TO HER.
Using a two-for-one deal, he purchased a matching bracelet set made out of Boundary Stones he picked up on a bargain bus tour.
AS A MATCHING PAIR.

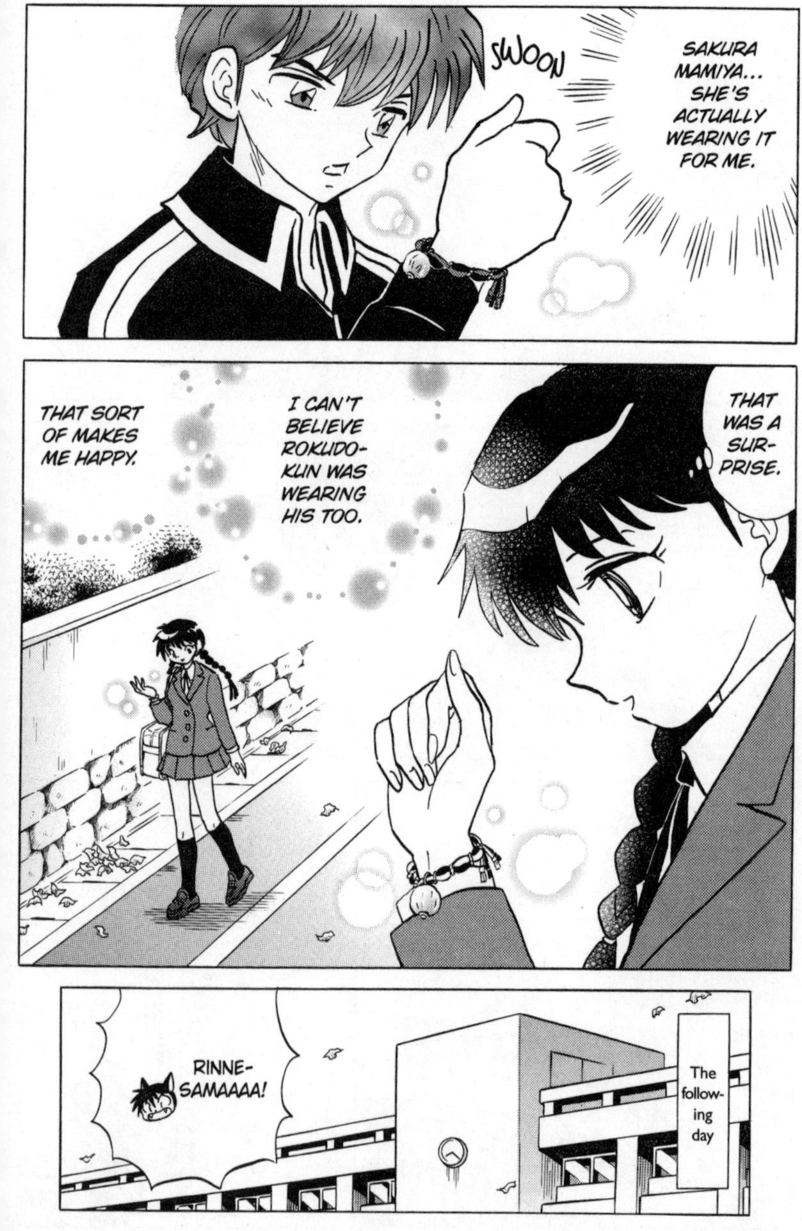
SWOON
SAKURA MAMIYA... SHE'S ACTUALLY WEARING IT FOR ME.
THAT WAS A SUR-PRISE.
I CAN'T BELIEVE ROKUDO-KUN WAS WEARING HIS TOO.
THAT SORT OF MAKES ME HAPPY.
The follow-ing day
RINNE-SAMAAAA!

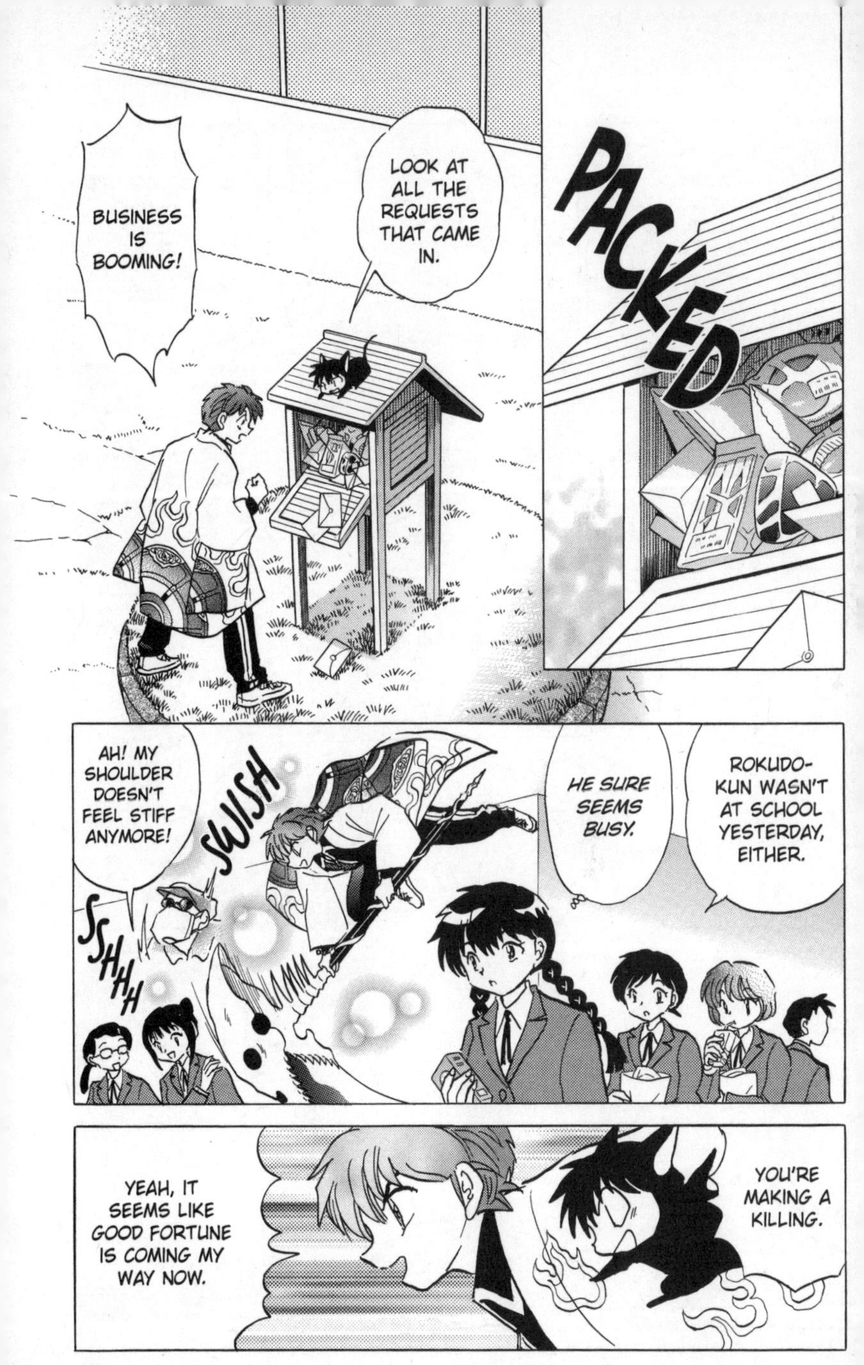
PACKED
LOOK AT ALL THE REQUESTS THAT CAME IN.
BUSINESS IS BOOMING!
ROKUDO-KUN WASN'T AT SCHOOL YESTERDAY, EITHER.
HE SURE SEEMS BUSY.
SWISH
AH! MY SHOULDER DOESN'T FEEL STIFF ANYMORE!
SSHHH
YOU'RE MAKING A KILLING.
YEAH, IT SEEMS LIKE GOOD FORTUNE IS COMING MY WAY NOW.

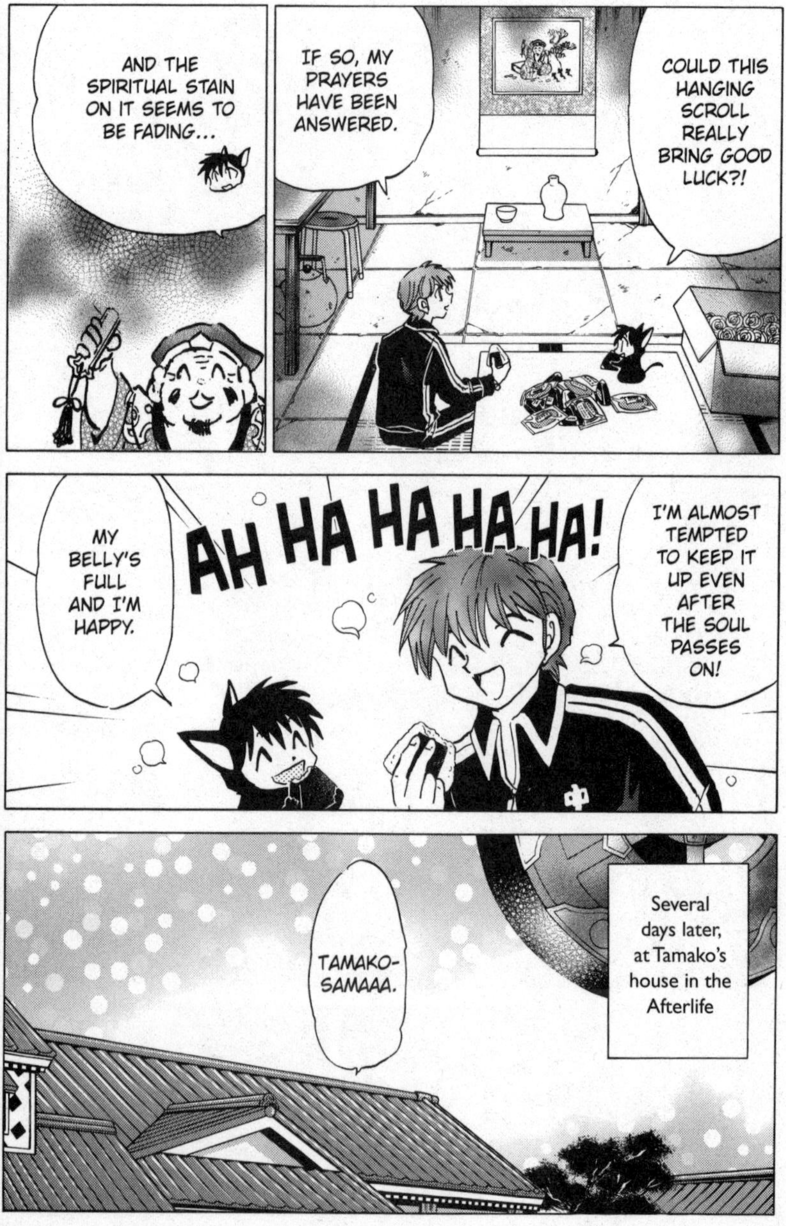
COULD THIS HANGING SCROLL REALLY BRING GOOD LUCK?!
IF SO, MY PRAYERS HAVE BEEN ANSWERED.
AND THE SPIRITUAL STAIN ON IT SEEMS TO BE FADING...
I'M ALMOST TEMPTED TO KEEP IT UP EVEN AFTER THE SOUL PASSES ON!
AH HA HA HA HA!
MY BELLY'S FULL AND I'M HAPPY.
Several days later, at Tamako's house in the Afterlife
TAMAKO-SAMAAA.

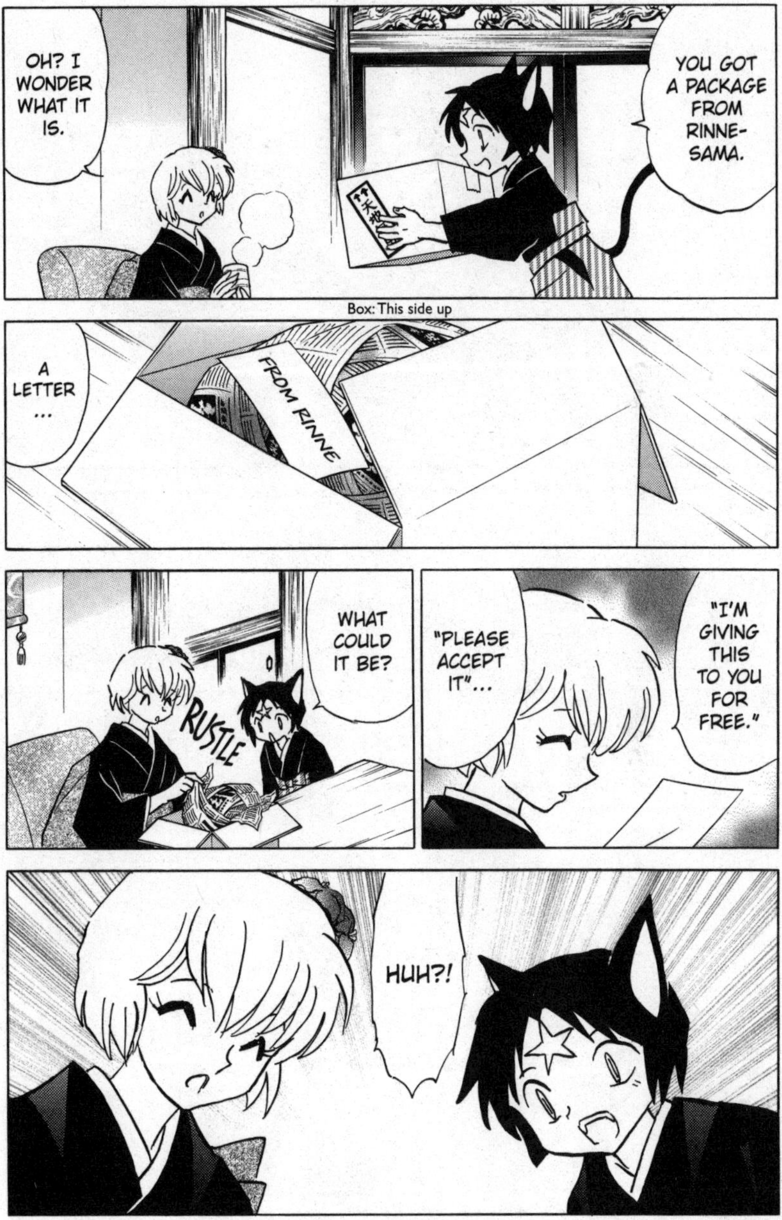
YOU GOT A PACKAGE FROM RINNE-SAMA.
OH? I WONDER WHAT IT IS.
A LETTER ...
FROM RINNE
"I'M GIVING THIS TO YOU FOR FREE."
"PLEASE ACCEPT IT"...
WHAT COULD IT BE?
RUSTLE
HUH?!
Box: This side up

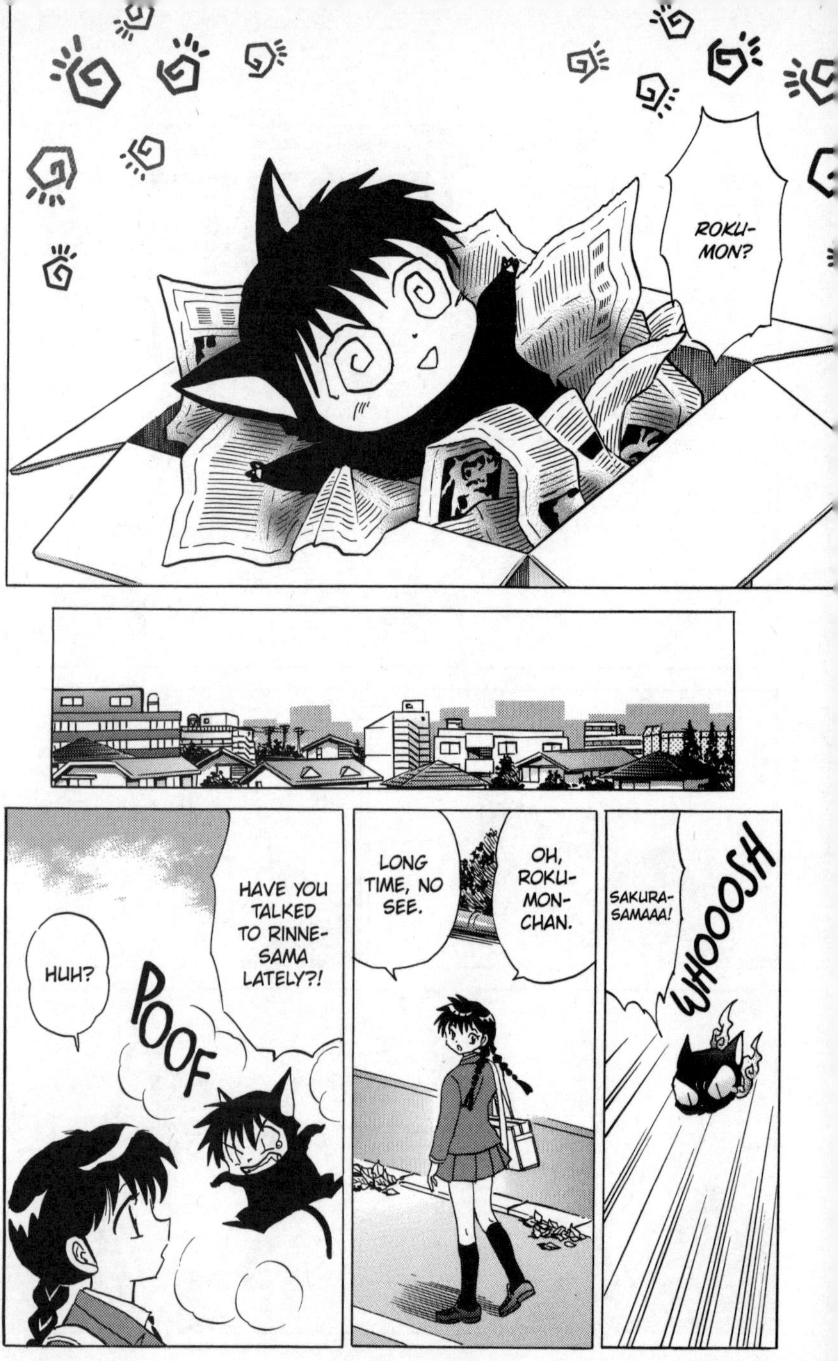
ROKU-MON?
SAKURA-SAMAAA!
WHOOOSH
OH, ROKU-MON-CHAN.
LONG TIME, NO SEE.
HAVE YOU TALKED TO RINNE-SAMA LATELY?!
POOF
HUH?

I'VE BEEN...

...FIRED!

BAM

Contract of Employment

This contract, dated on the 3rd day of June in the year 200_, is made between Rinne Rokudo document constitutes an employment these two parties and is gove... the la... life. The Employer desires to ret... and the Employee desires... register such services... terms and conditions as set for...

Employer:
RINNE ROKUDO

Employee:
ROKUMON 🐾

Stamp: VOID

A "VOID" STAMP? THAT MEANS YOUR CONTRACT IS CANCELED?

HE THREW ME IN THE MAIL ALONG WITH THAT CONTRACT...

THEN, THE OTHER NIGHT...

WE'VE BEEN GETTING A LOT OF JOBS LATELY AND THINGS WERE GOING GREAT.

DID YOU TWO HAVE A FIGHT?

WHAT'S GOING ON?

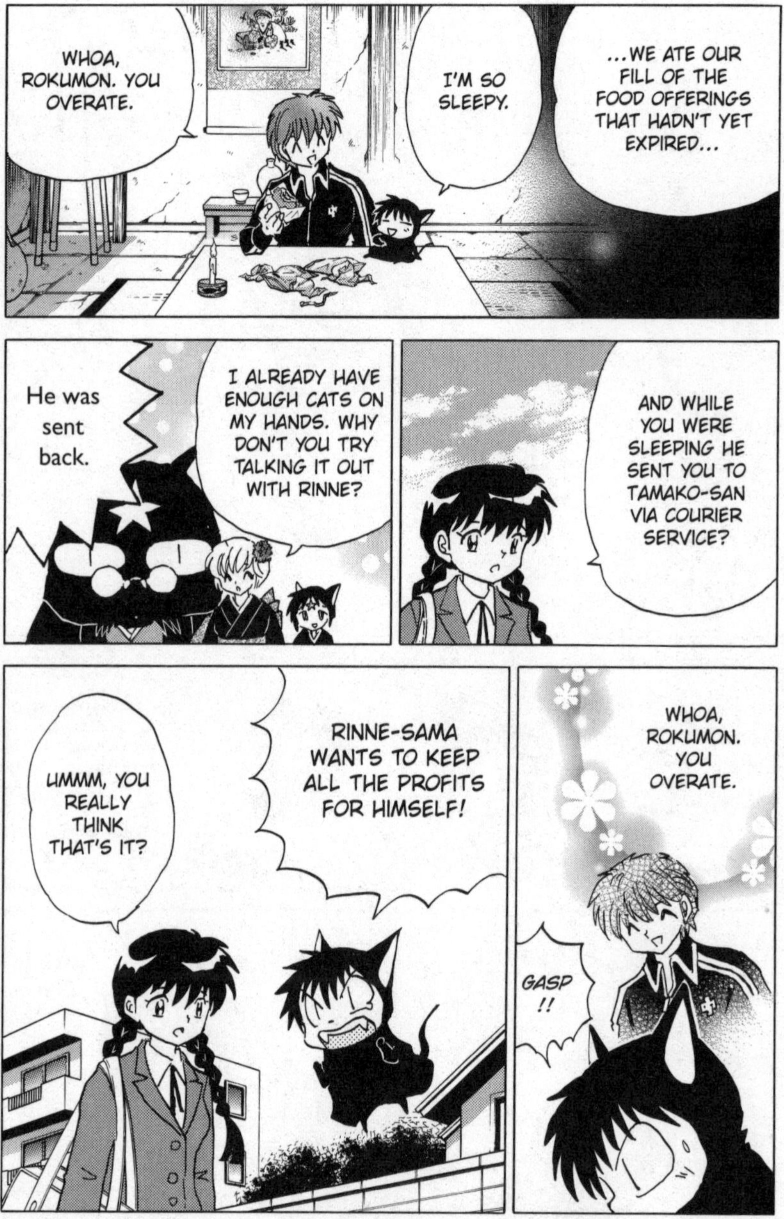
...WE ATE OUR FILL OF THE FOOD OFFERINGS THAT HADN'T YET EXPIRED...
I'M SO SLEEPY.
WHOA, ROKUMON. YOU OVERATE.
AND WHILE YOU WERE SLEEPING HE SENT YOU TO TAMAKO-SAN VIA COURIER SERVICE?
I ALREADY HAVE ENOUGH CATS ON MY HANDS. WHY DON'T YOU TRY TALKING IT OUT WITH RINNE?
He was sent back.
WHOA, ROKUMON. YOU OVERATE.
GASP !!
RINNE-SAMA WANTS TO KEEP ALL THE PROFITS FOR HIMSELF!
UMMM, YOU REALLY THINK THAT'S IT?

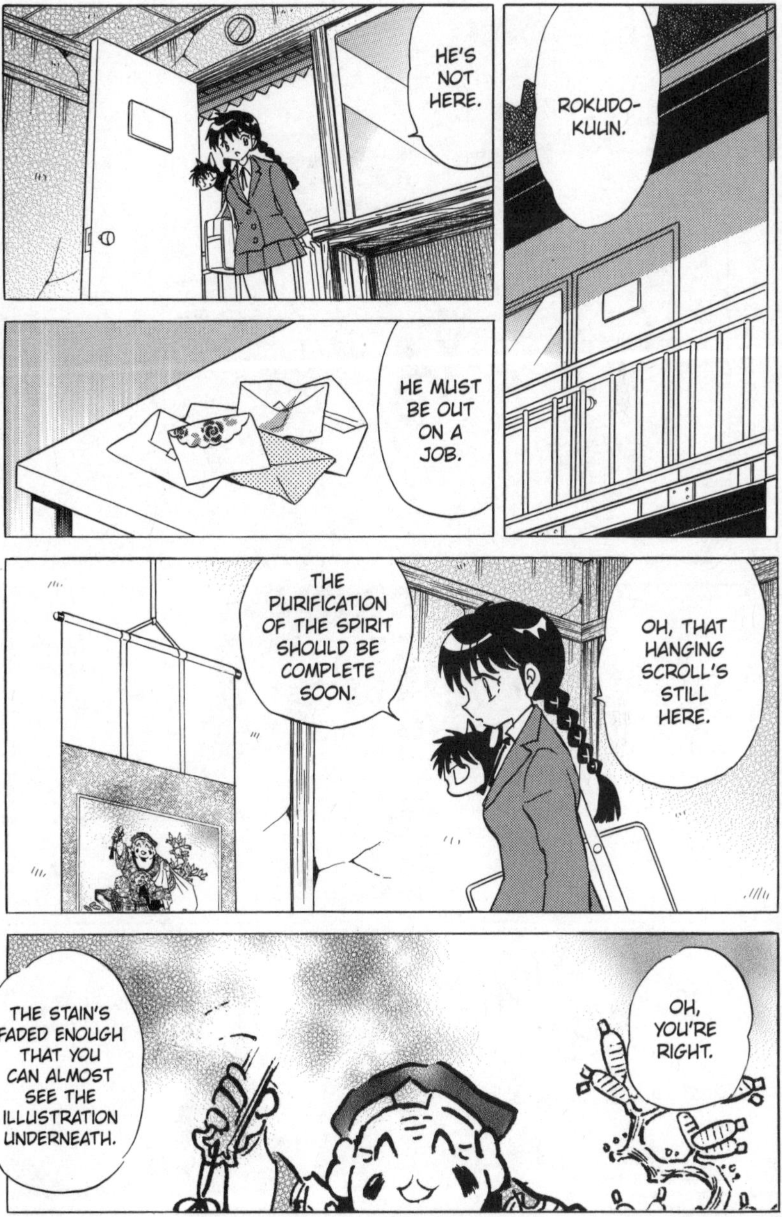
ROKUDO-KUUN.
HE'S NOT HERE.
HE MUST BE OUT ON A JOB.
OH, THAT HANGING SCROLL'S STILL HERE.
THE PURIFICATION OF THE SPIRIT SHOULD BE COMPLETE SOON.
OH, YOU'RE RIGHT.
THE STAIN'S FADED ENOUGH THAT YOU CAN ALMOST SEE THE ILLUSTRATION UNDERNEATH.

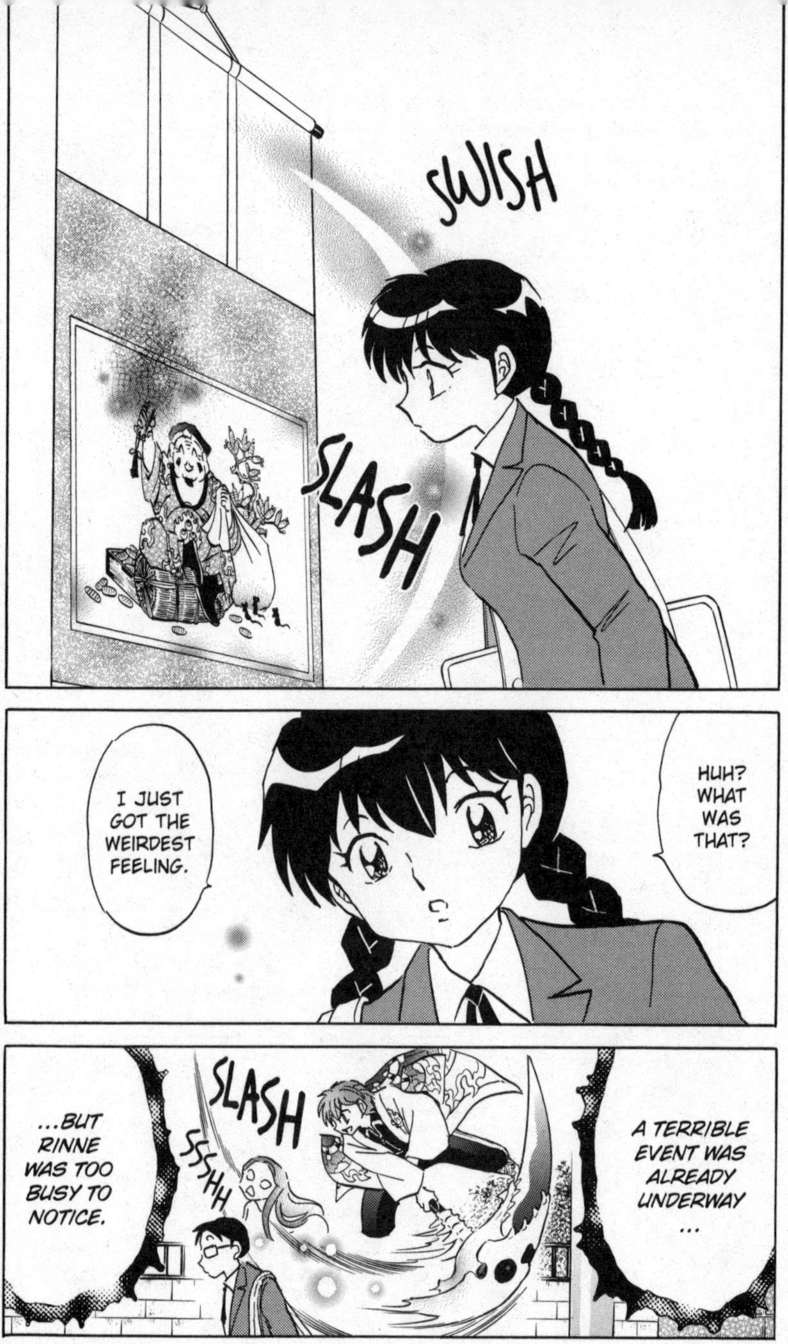
SWISH
SLASH
HUH? WHAT WAS THAT?
I JUST GOT THE WEIRDEST FEELING.
A TERRIBLE EVENT WAS ALREADY UNDERWAY...
SLASH
SSSHH
...BUT RINNE WAS TOO BUSY TO NOTICE.

CHAPTER 391: THE HANGING SCROLL'S TRAP

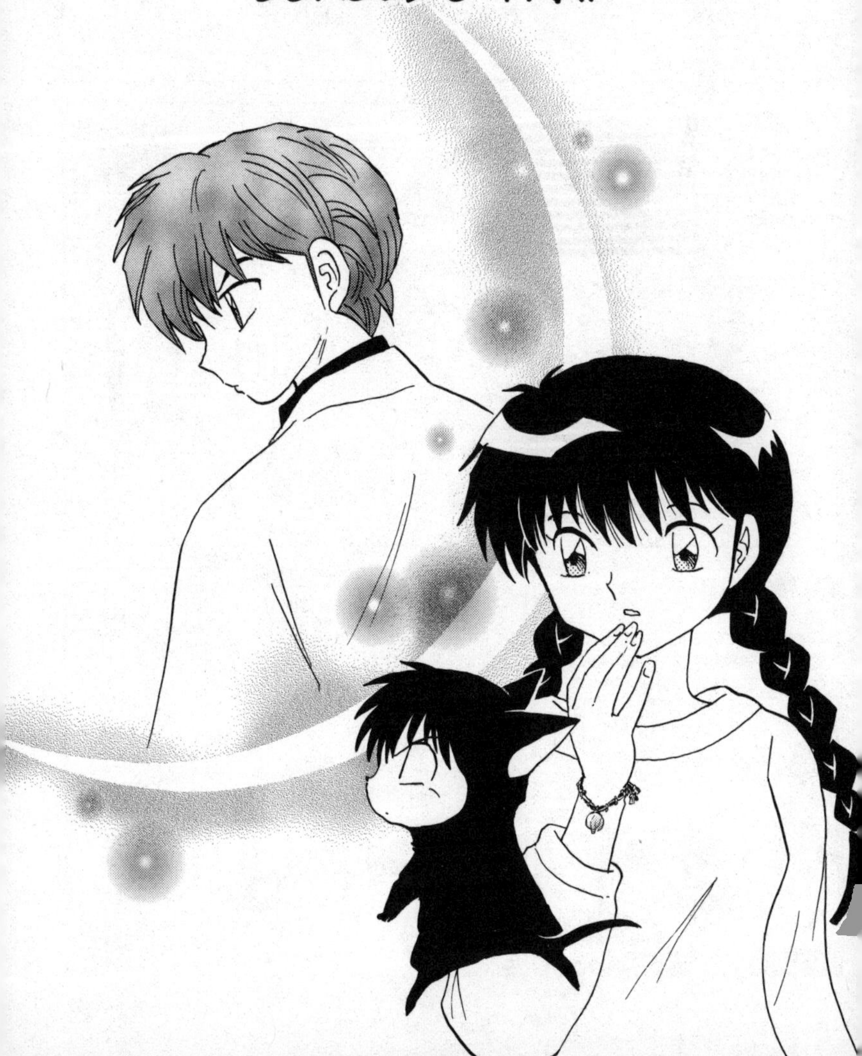

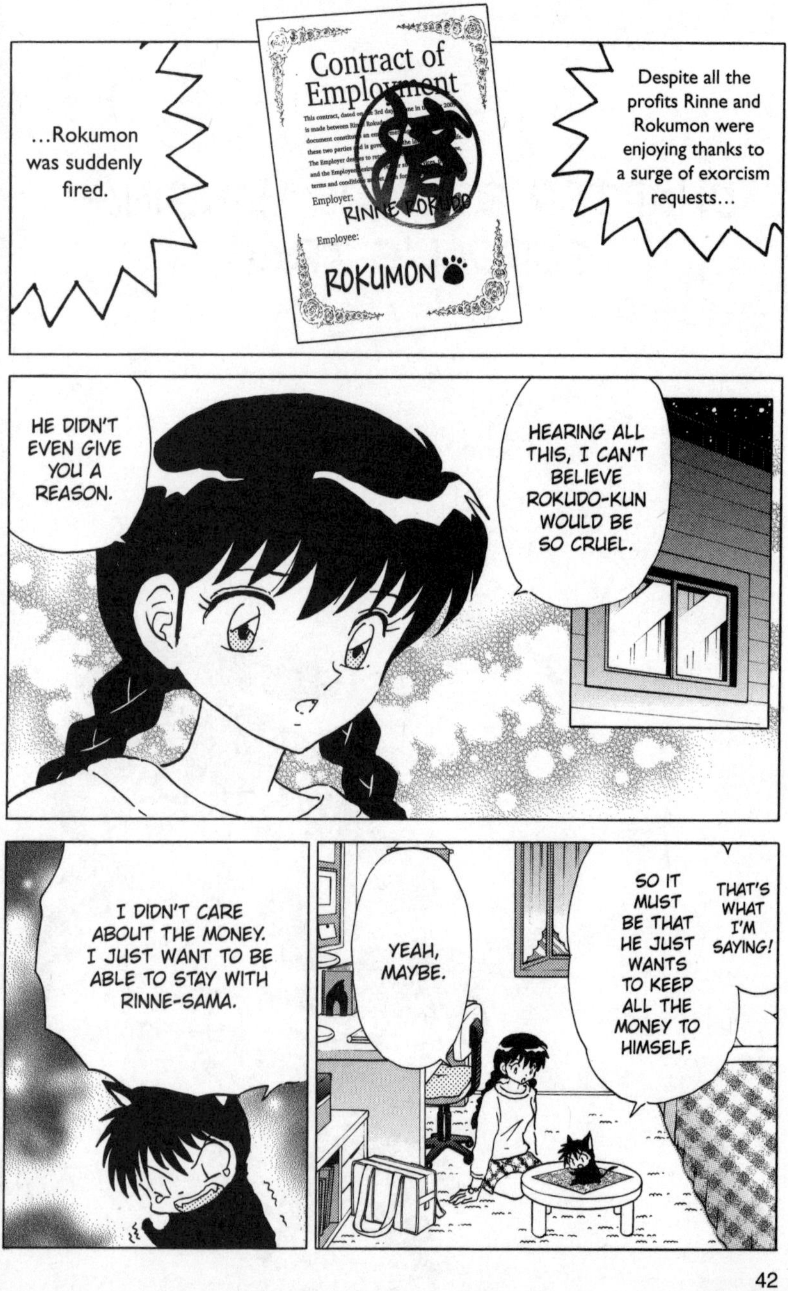
Despite all the profits Rinne and Rokumon were enjoying thanks to a surge of exorcism requests…
Contract of Employment
Employer:
RINNE ROKUDO
Employee:
ROKUMON
…Rokumon was suddenly fired.
HEARING ALL THIS, I CAN'T BELIEVE ROKUDO-KUN WOULD BE SO CRUEL.
HE DIDN'T EVEN GIVE YOU A REASON.
SO IT MUST BE THAT HE JUST WANTS TO KEEP ALL THE MONEY TO HIMSELF.
THAT'S WHAT I'M SAYING!
YEAH, MAYBE.
I DIDN'T CARE ABOUT THE MONEY. I JUST WANT TO BE ABLE TO STAY WITH RINNE-SAMA.

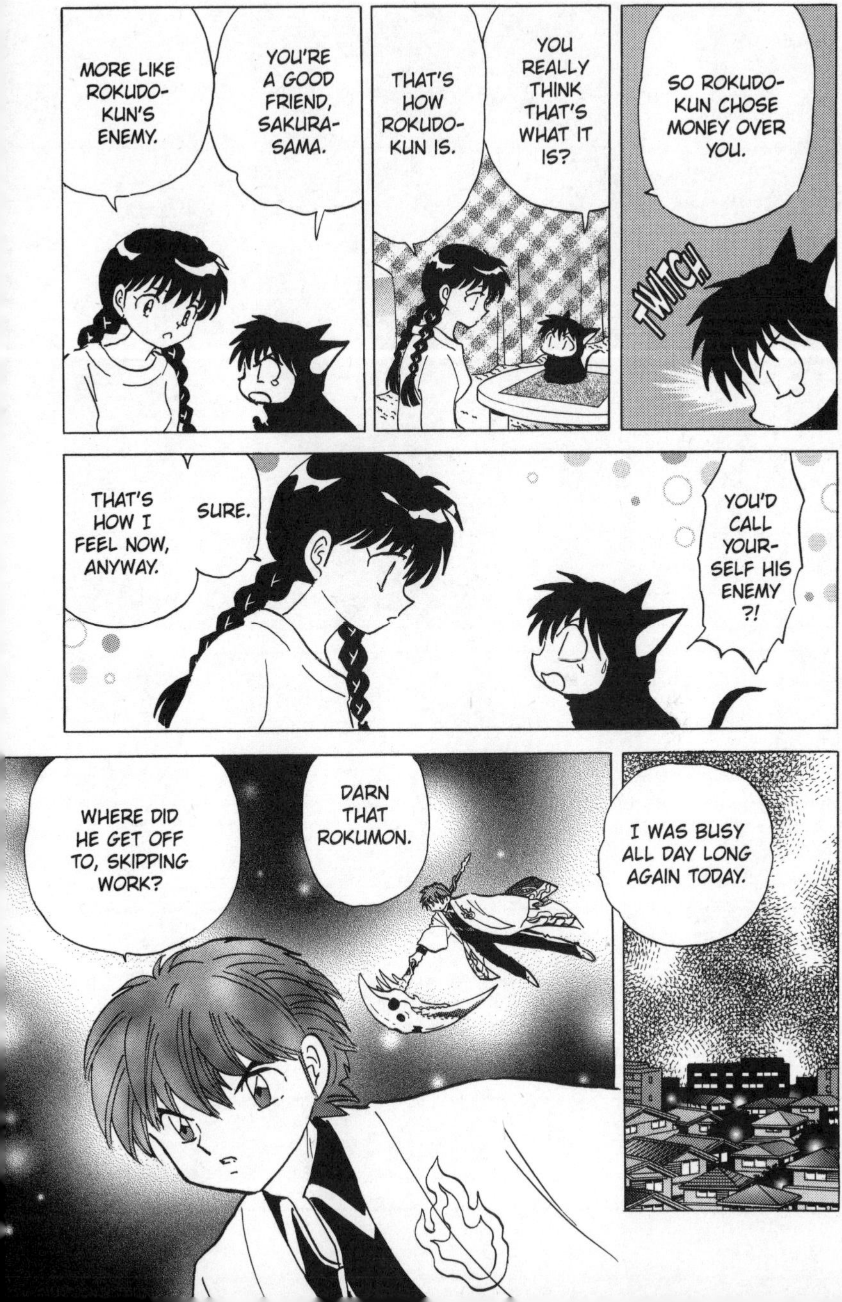
SO ROKUDO-KUN CHOSE MONEY OVER YOU.
TWITCH!
YOU REALLY THINK THAT'S WHAT IT IS?
THAT'S HOW ROKUDO-KUN IS.
YOU'RE A GOOD FRIEND, SAKURA-SAMA.
MORE LIKE ROKUDO-KUN'S ENEMY.
YOU'D CALL YOUR-SELF HIS ENEMY ?!
SURE.
THAT'S HOW I FEEL NOW, ANYWAY.
I WAS BUSY ALL DAY LONG AGAIN TODAY.
DARN THAT ROKUMON.
WHERE DID HE GET OFF TO, SKIPPING WORK?

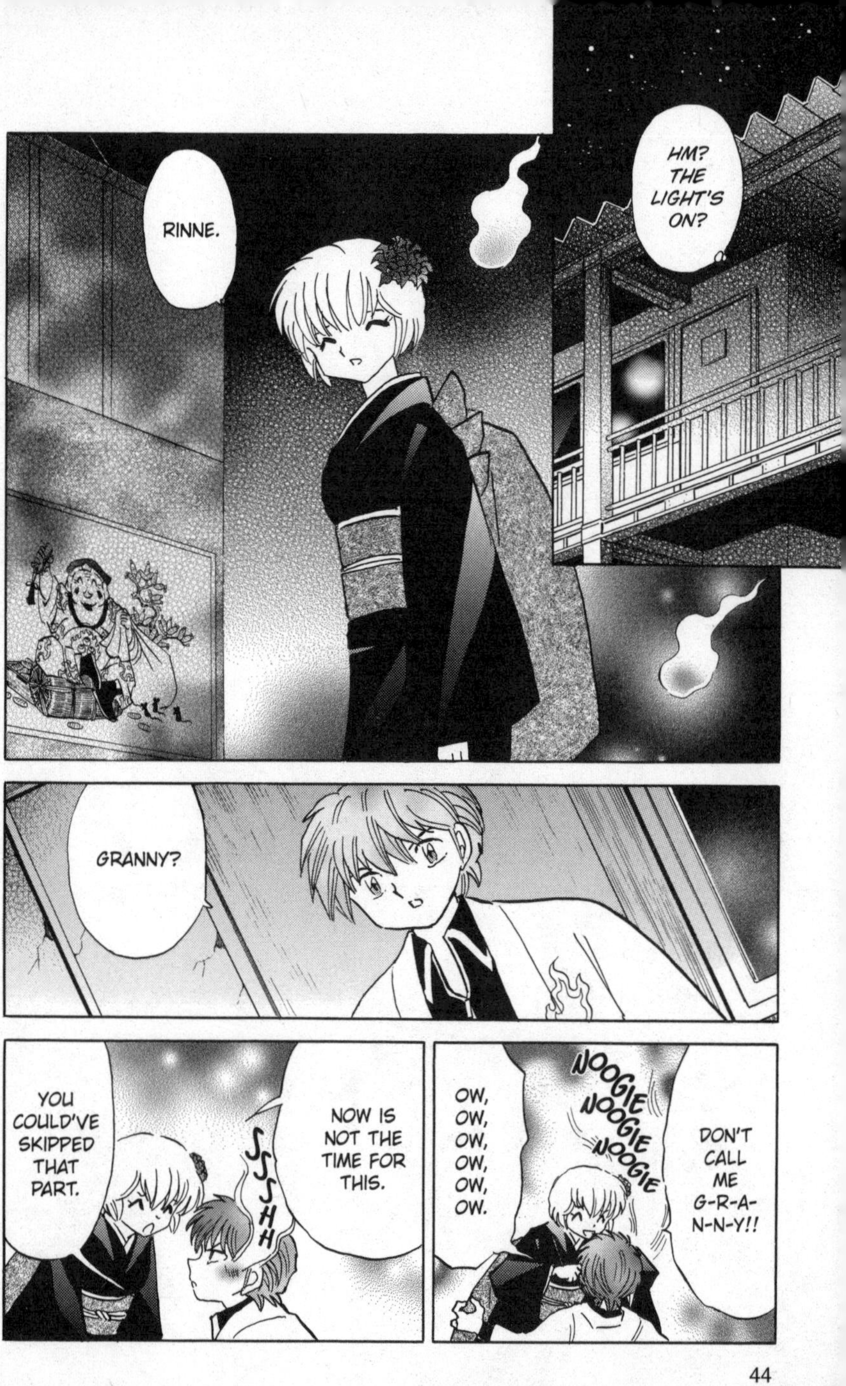
HM? THE LIGHT'S ON?
RINNE.
GRANNY?
DON'T CALL ME G-R-A-N-N-Y!!
NOOGIE NOOGIE NOOGIE
OW, OW, OW, OW, OW, OW.
NOW IS NOT THE TIME FOR THIS.
SSSHH
YOU COULD'VE SKIPPED THAT PART.

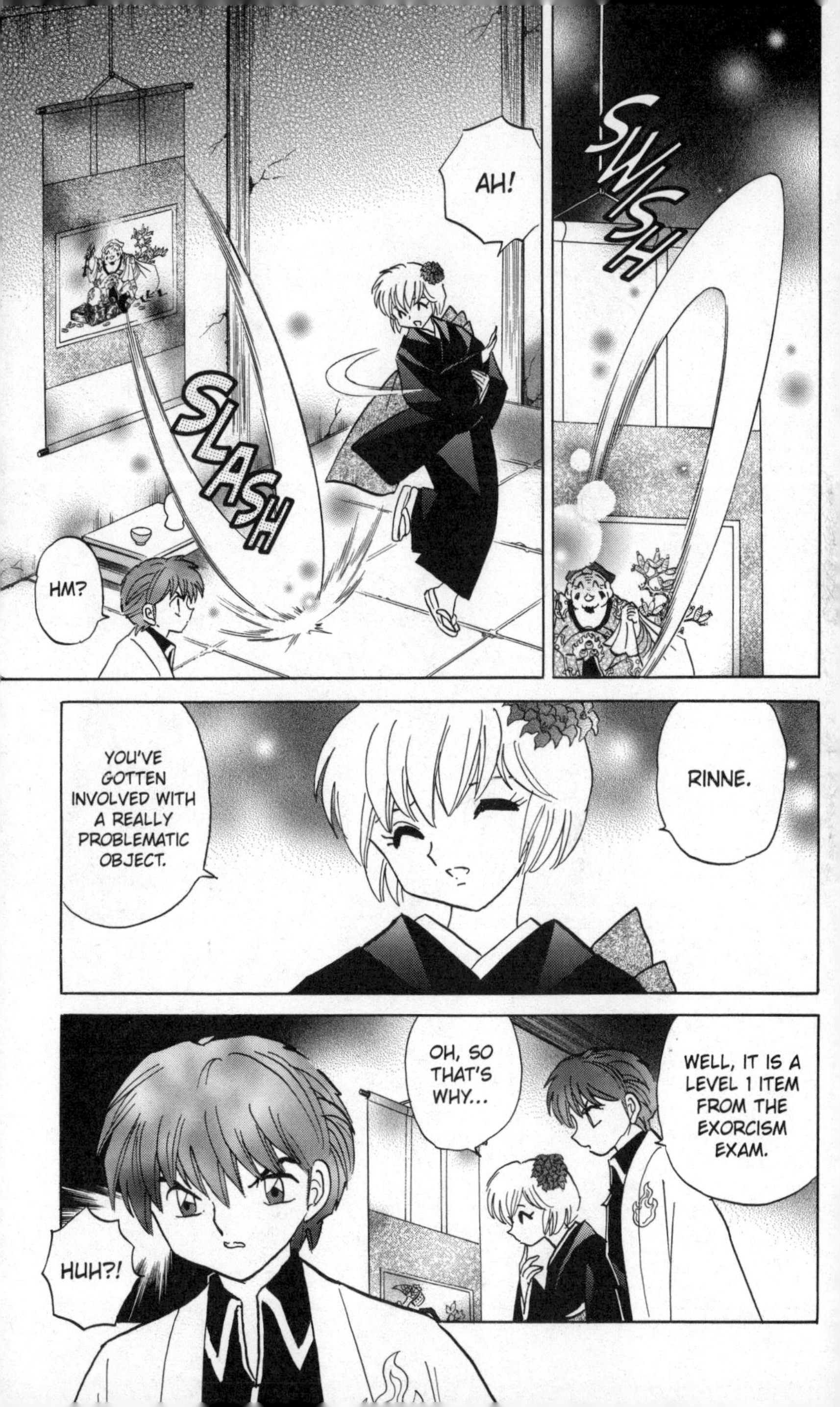
SWISH
AH!
SLASH
HM?
RINNE.
YOU'VE GOTTEN INVOLVED WITH A REALLY PROBLEMATIC OBJECT.
WELL, IT IS A LEVEL 1 ITEM FROM THE EXORCISM EXAM.
OH, SO THAT'S WHY...
HUH?!

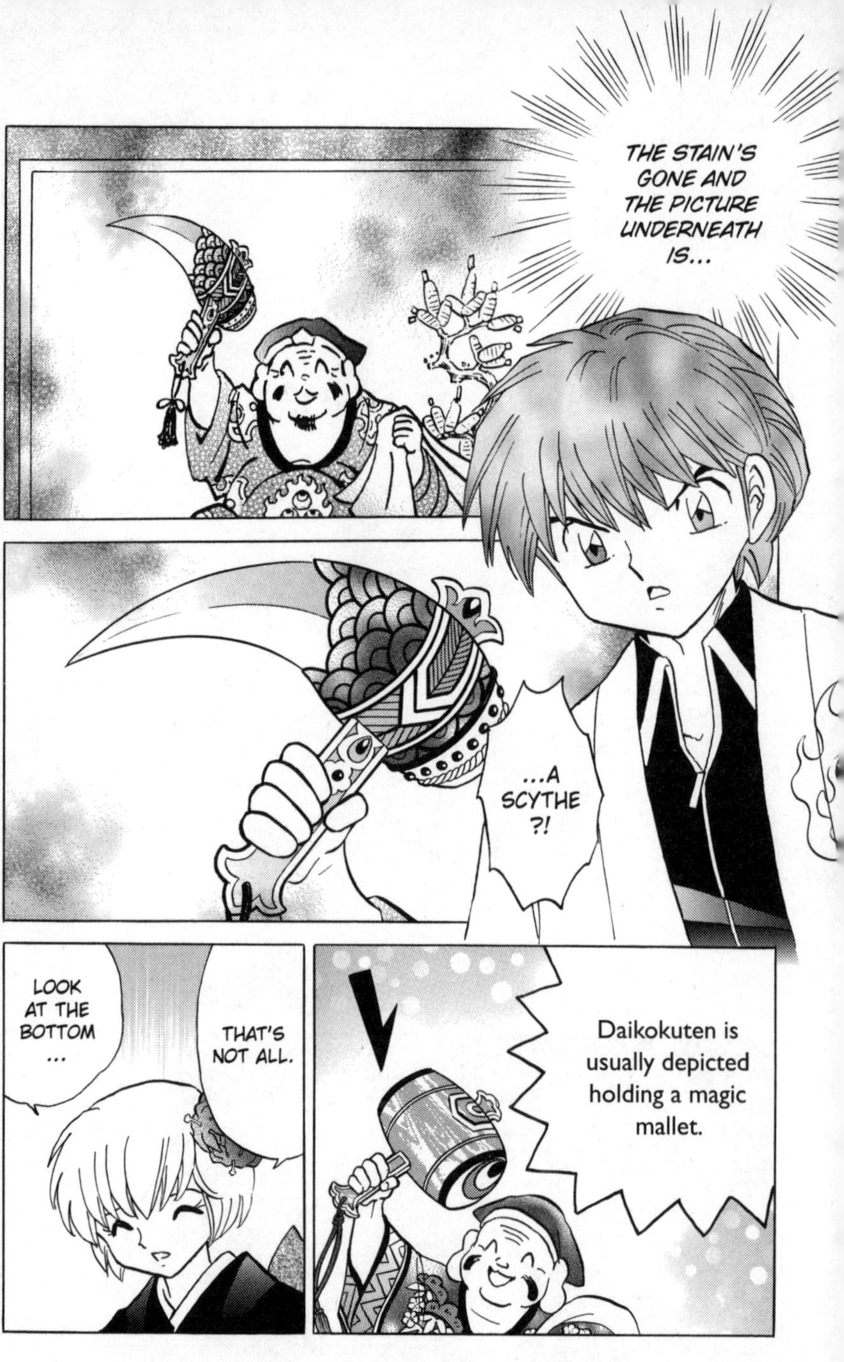
THE STAIN'S GONE AND THE PICTURE UNDERNEATH IS...
...A SCYTHE?!
Daikokuten is usually depicted holding a magic mallet.
THAT'S NOT ALL.
LOOK AT THE BOTTOM...

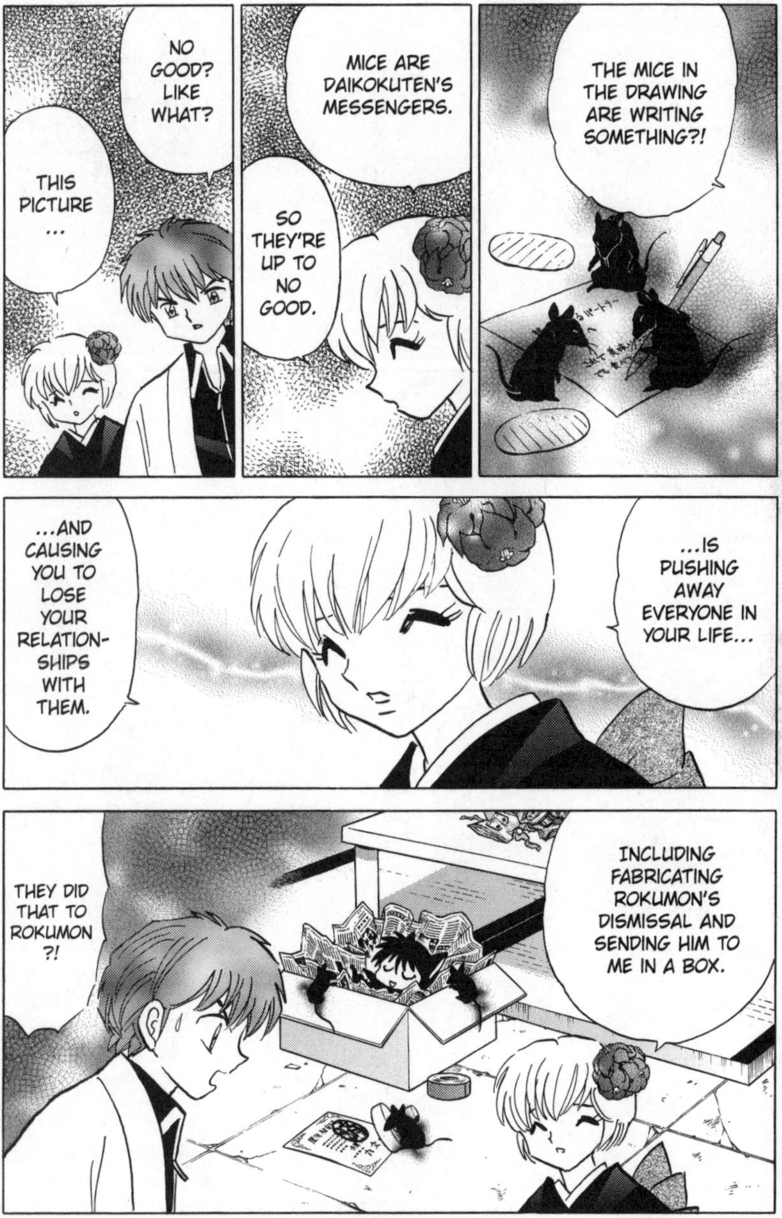
THE MICE IN THE DRAWING ARE WRITING SOMETHING?!
MICE ARE DAIKOKUTEN'S MESSENGERS.
SO THEY'RE UP TO NO GOOD.
NO GOOD? LIKE WHAT?
THIS PICTURE ...
...IS PUSHING AWAY EVERYONE IN YOUR LIFE...
...AND CAUSING YOU TO LOSE YOUR RELATION-SHIPS WITH THEM.
INCLUDING FABRICATING ROKUMON'S DISMISSAL AND SENDING HIM TO ME IN A BOX.
THEY DID THAT TO ROKUMON ?!

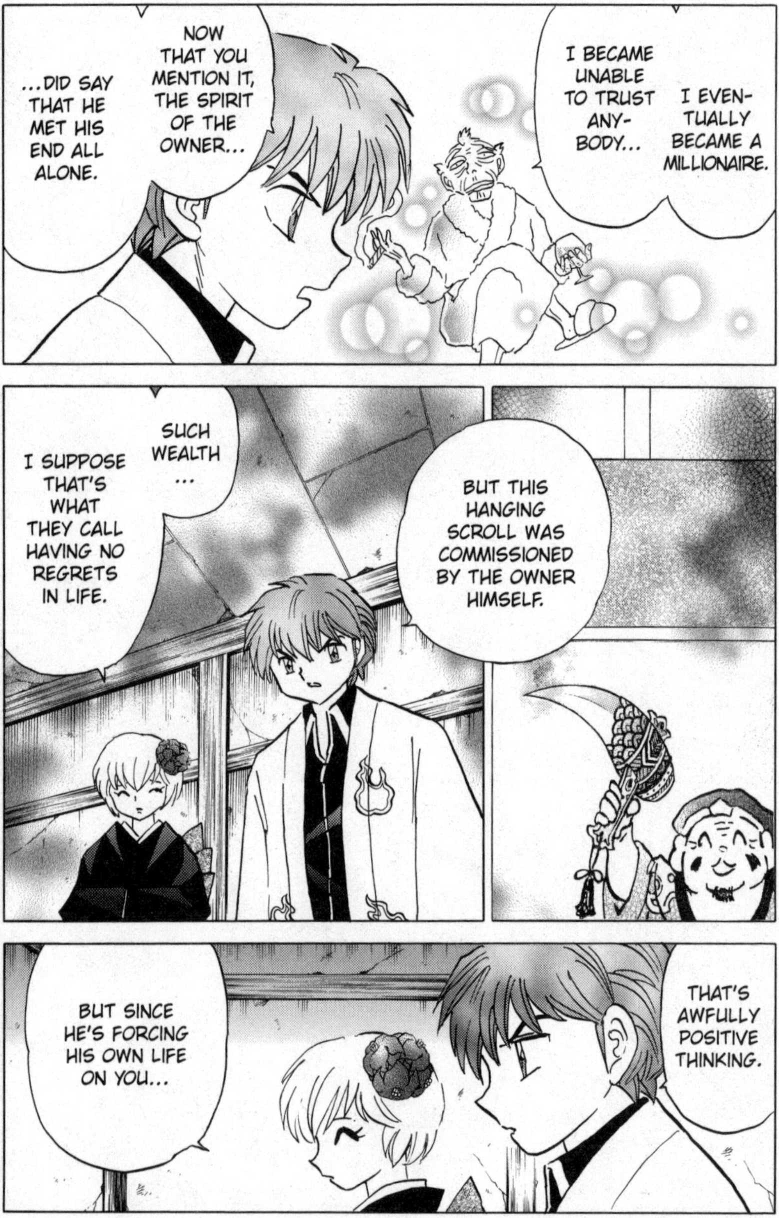
I BECAME UNABLE TO TRUST ANYBODY... I EVENTUALLY BECAME A MILLIONAIRE.
NOW THAT YOU MENTION IT, THE SPIRIT OF THE OWNER...
...DID SAY THAT HE MET HIS END ALL ALONE.
BUT THIS HANGING SCROLL WAS COMMISSIONED BY THE OWNER HIMSELF.
SUCH WEALTH...
I SUPPOSE THAT'S WHAT THEY CALL HAVING NO REGRETS IN LIFE.
THAT'S AWFULLY POSITIVE THINKING.
BUT SINCE HE'S FORCING HIS OWN LIFE ON YOU...

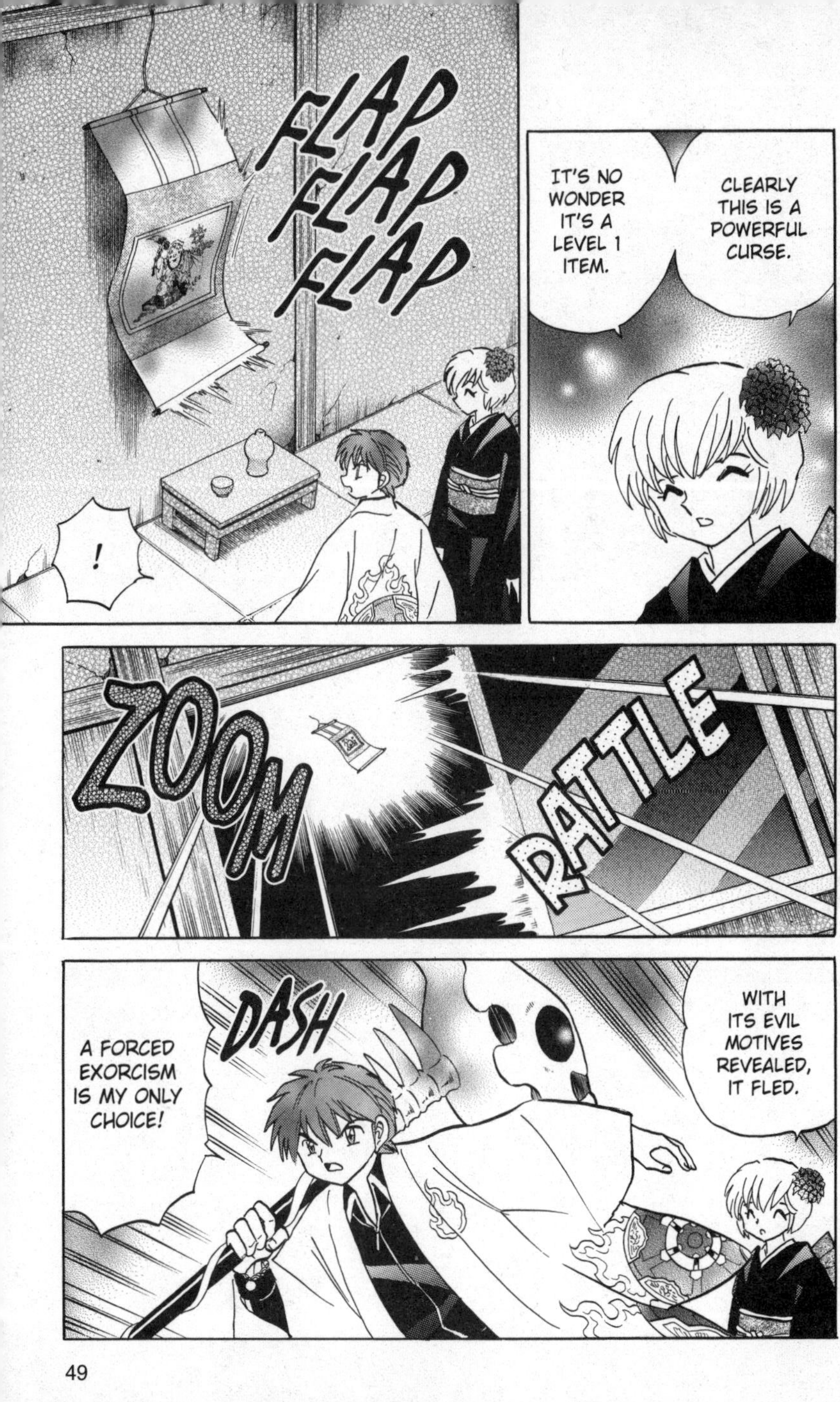
CLEARLY THIS IS A POWERFUL CURSE.
IT'S NO WONDER IT'S A LEVEL 1 ITEM.
FLAP FLAP FLAP
!
RATTLE
ZOOM
WITH ITS EVIL MOTIVES REVEALED, IT FLED.
DASH
A FORCED EXORCISM IS MY ONLY CHOICE!

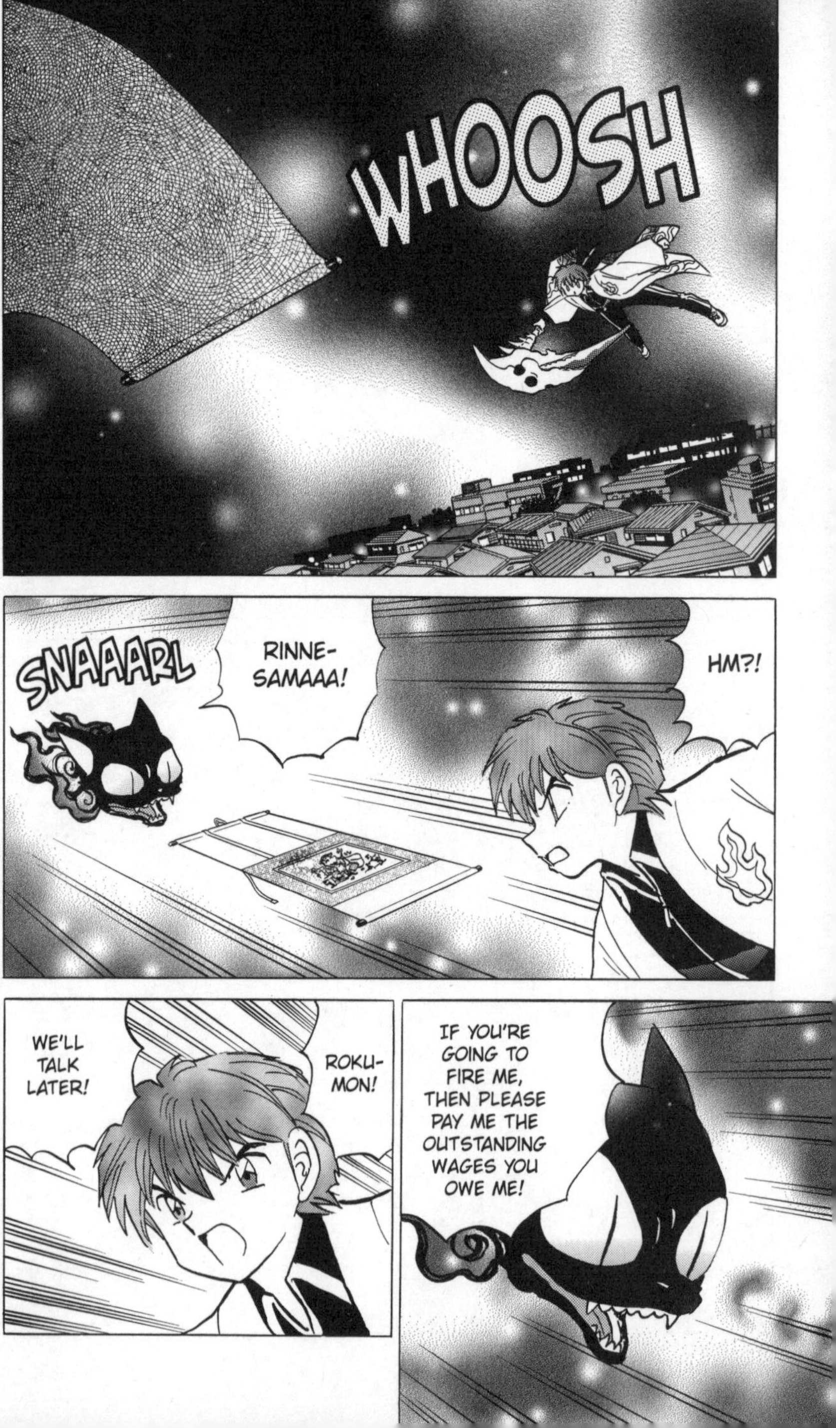
WHOOSH
HM?!
RINNE-SAMAAA!
SNAAARL
IF YOU'RE GOING TO FIRE ME, THEN PLEASE PAY ME THE OUTSTANDING WAGES YOU OWE ME!
ROKU-MON!
WE'LL TALK LATER!

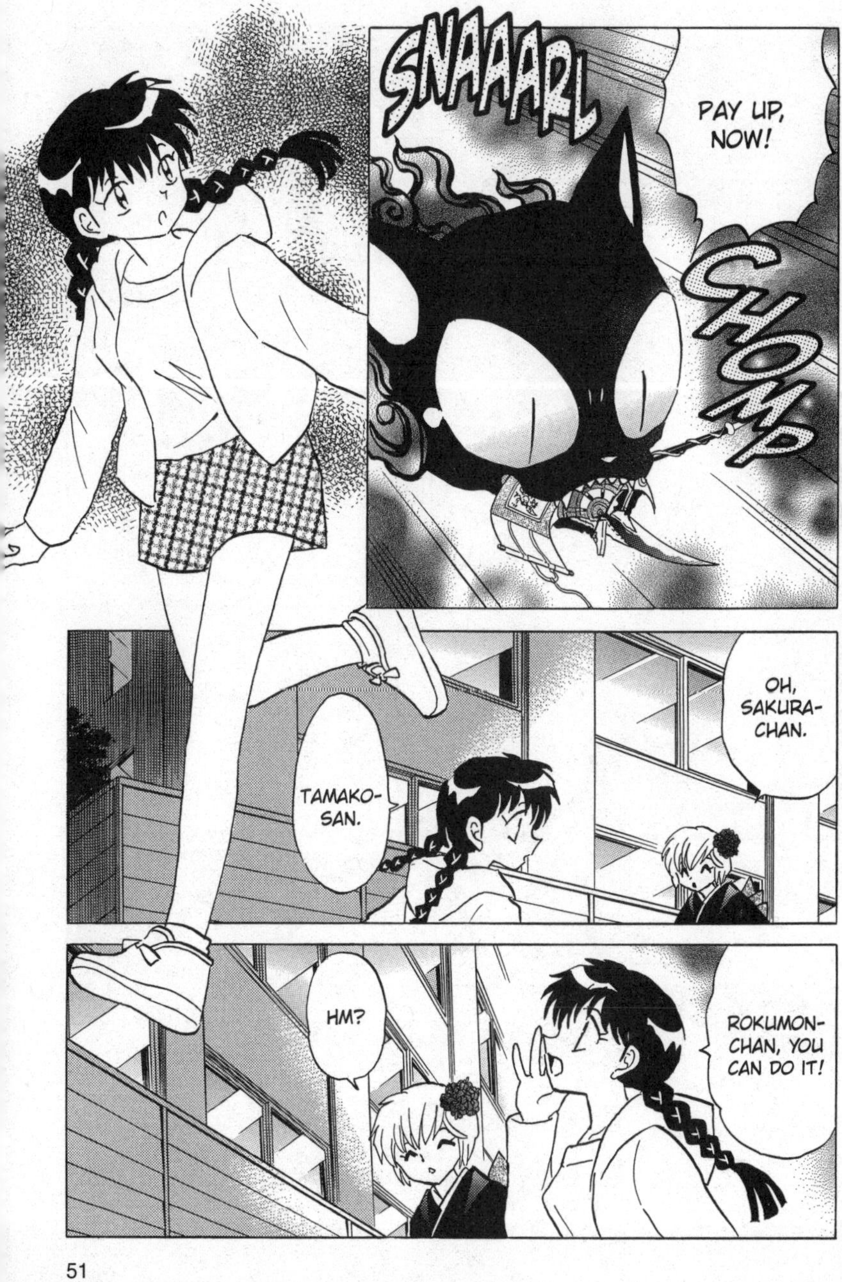
SNAAARL
PAY UP, NOW!
CHOMP
OH, SAKURA-CHAN.
TAMAKO-SAN.
ROKUMON-CHAN, YOU CAN DO IT!
HM?

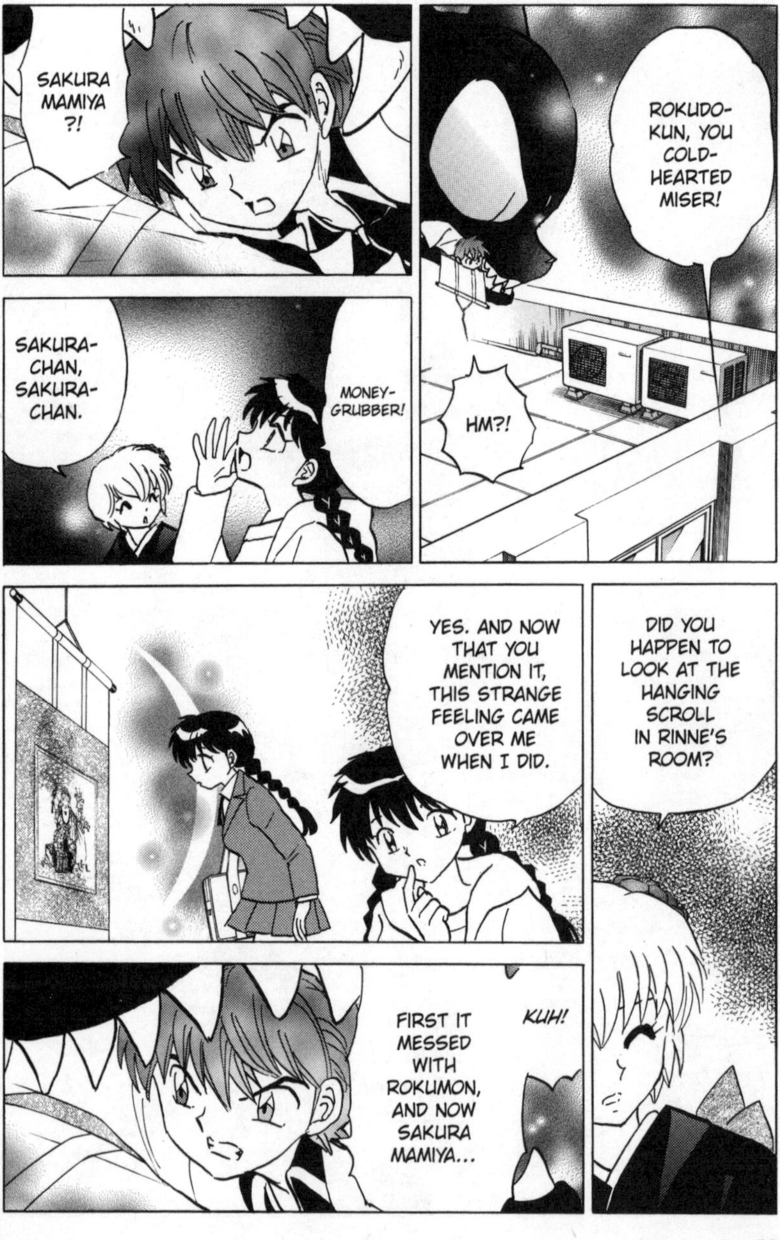
ROKUDO-KUN, YOU COLD-HEARTED MISER!
HM?!
SAKURA MAMIYA ?!
MONEY-GRUBBER!
SAKURA-CHAN, SAKURA-CHAN.
DID YOU HAPPEN TO LOOK AT THE HANGING SCROLL IN RINNE'S ROOM?
YES. AND NOW THAT YOU MENTION IT, THIS STRANGE FEELING CAME OVER ME WHEN I DID.
KUH!
FIRST IT MESSED WITH ROKUMON, AND NOW SAKURA MAMIYA...

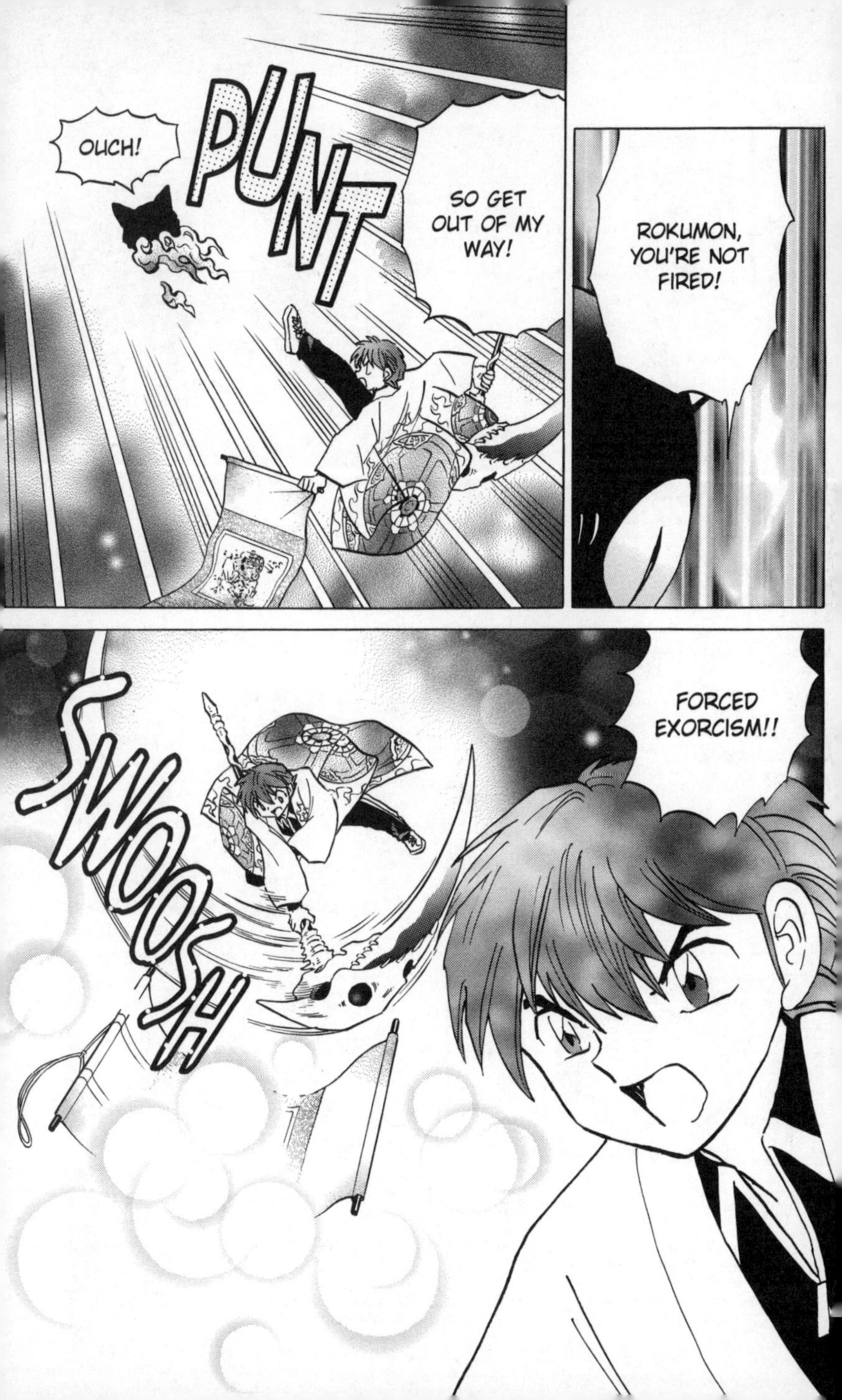
ROKUMON, YOU'RE NOT FIRED!
SO GET OUT OF MY WAY!
PUNT
OUCH!
FORCED EXORCISM!!
SWOOSH

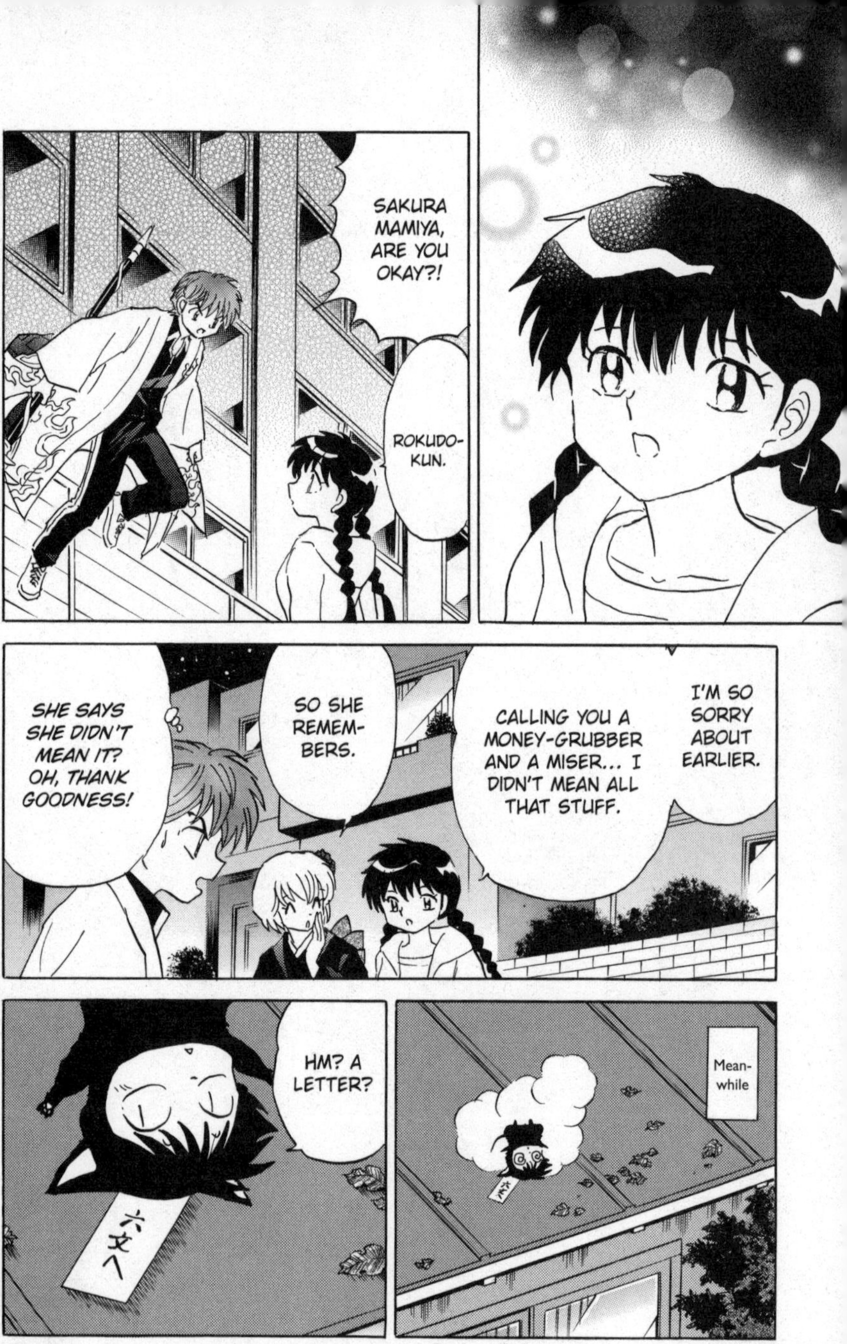
SAKURA MAMIYA, ARE YOU OKAY?!
ROKUDO-KUN.
I'M SO SORRY ABOUT EARLIER.
CALLING YOU A MONEY-GRUBBER AND A MISER... I DIDN'T MEAN ALL THAT STUFF.
SO SHE REMEMBERS.
SHE SAYS SHE DIDN'T MEAN IT? OH, THANK GOODNESS!
Mean-while
HM? A LETTER?
六文へ

Envelope: To Rokumon

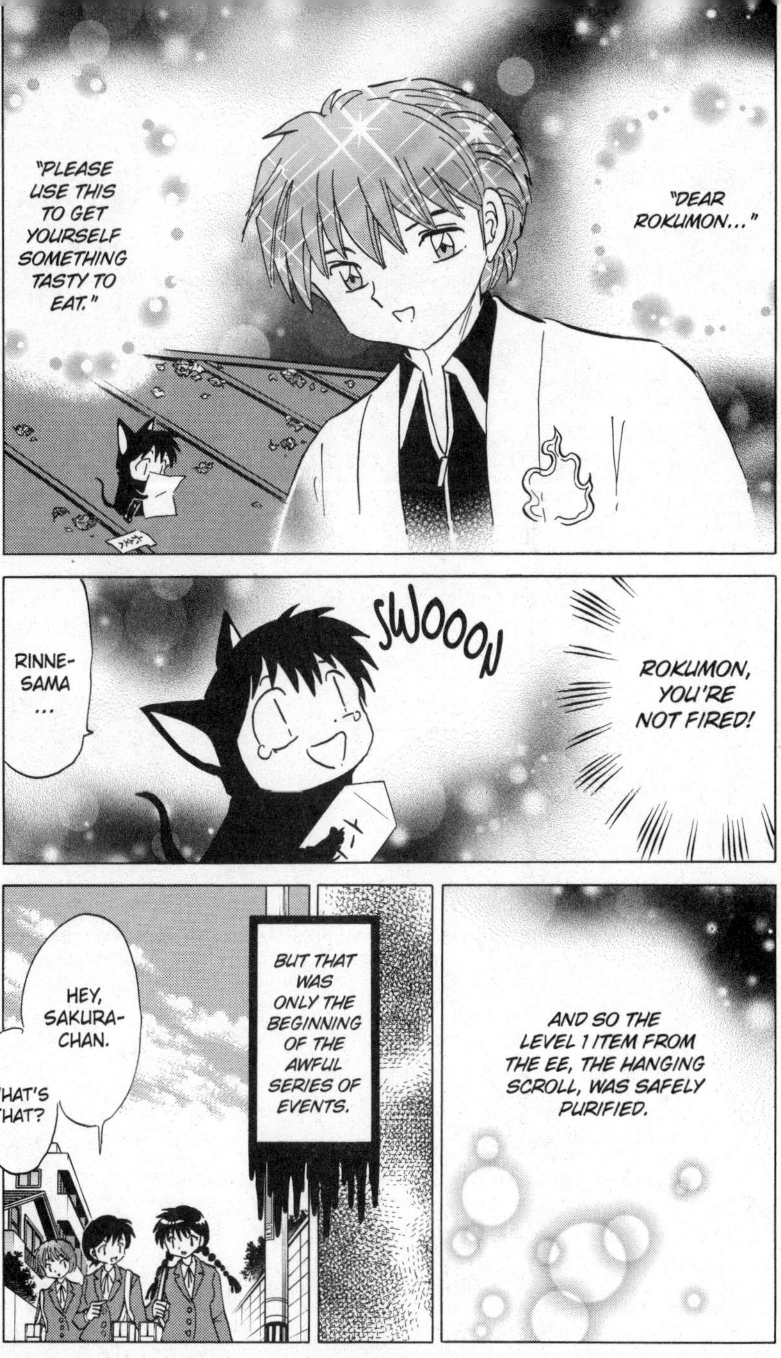
"DEAR ROKUMON..."
"PLEASE USE THIS TO GET YOURSELF SOMETHING TASTY TO EAT."
ROKUMON, YOU'RE NOT FIRED!
SWOOON
RINNE-SAMA ...
AND SO THE LEVEL 1 ITEM FROM THE EE, THE HANGING SCROLL, WAS SAFELY PURIFIED.
BUT THAT WAS ONLY THE BEGINNING OF THE AWFUL SERIES OF EVENTS.
HEY, SAKURA-CHAN.
WHAT'S THAT?

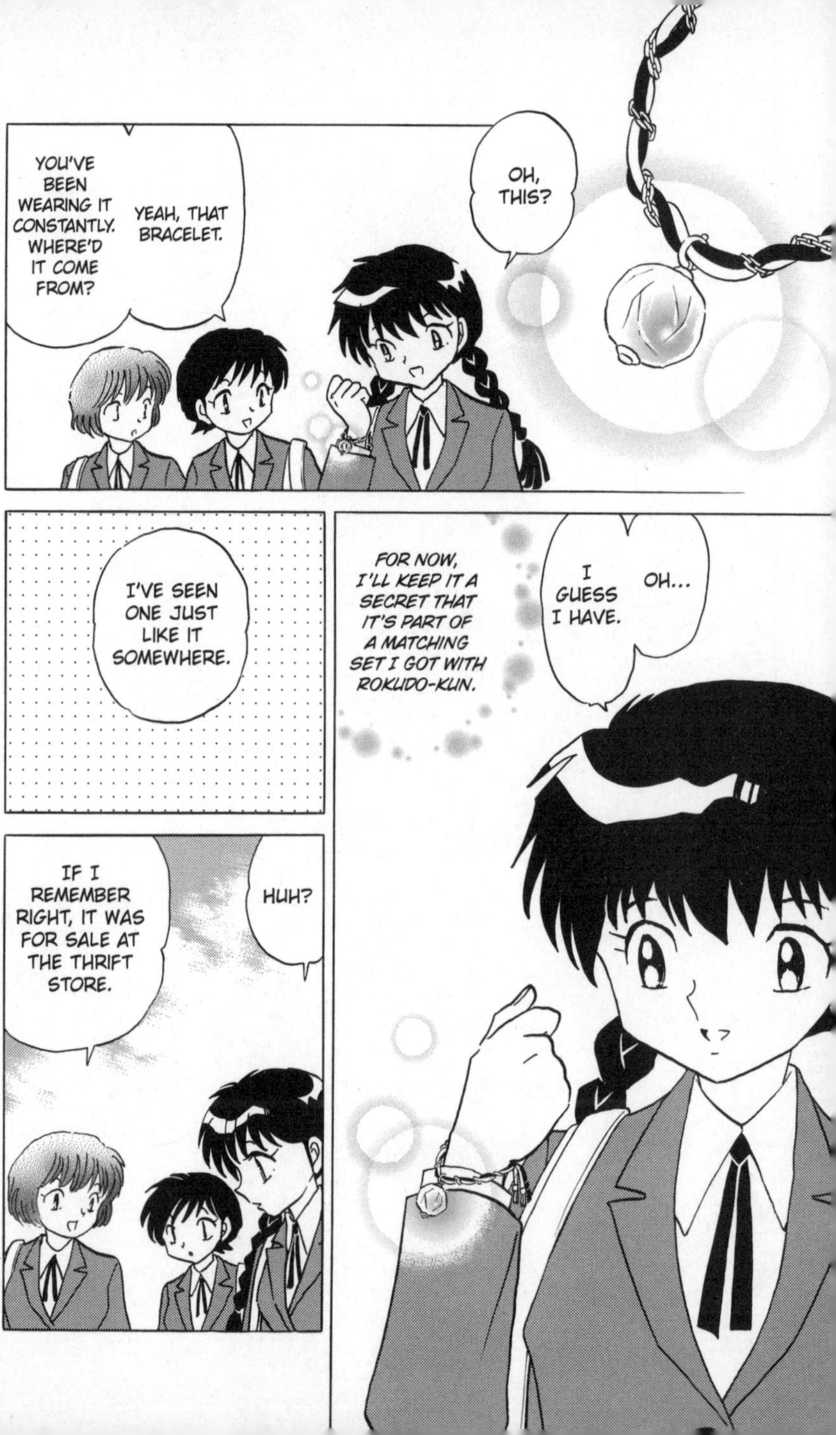
OH, THIS?
YEAH, THAT BRACELET.
YOU'VE BEEN WEARING IT CONSTANTLY. WHERE'D IT COME FROM?
OH...
I GUESS I HAVE.
FOR NOW, I'LL KEEP IT A SECRET THAT IT'S PART OF A MATCHING SET I GOT WITH ROKUDO-KUN.
I'VE SEEN ONE JUST LIKE IT SOMEWHERE.
HUH?
IF I REMEMBER RIGHT, IT WAS FOR SALE AT THE THRIFT STORE.

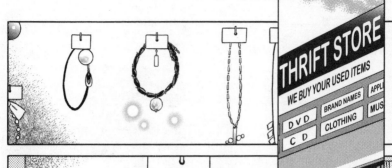

THRIFT STORE
WE BUY YOUR USED ITEMS

| D V D | BRAND NAMES | APPL |
| C D | CLOTHING | MUS |

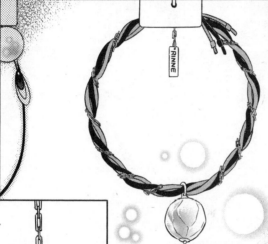

RINNE

Sign: Accessories

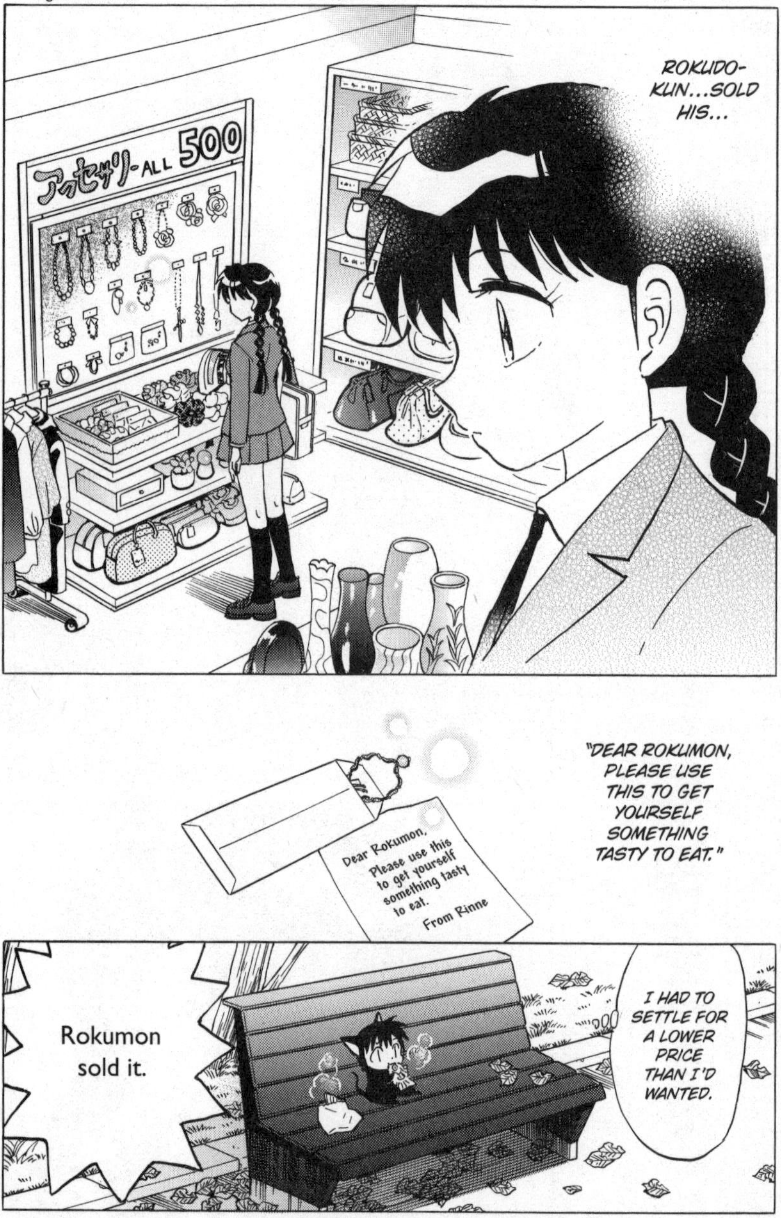
アクセサリー ALL 500
ROKUDO-KUN...SOLD HIS...
"DEAR ROKUMON, PLEASE USE THIS TO GET YOURSELF SOMETHING TASTY TO EAT."
Dear Rokumon, Please use this to get yourself something tasty to eat. From Rinne
I HAD TO SETTLE FOR A LOWER PRICE THAN I'D WANTED.
Rokumon sold it.

CHAPTER 392: FORCE OF HABIT

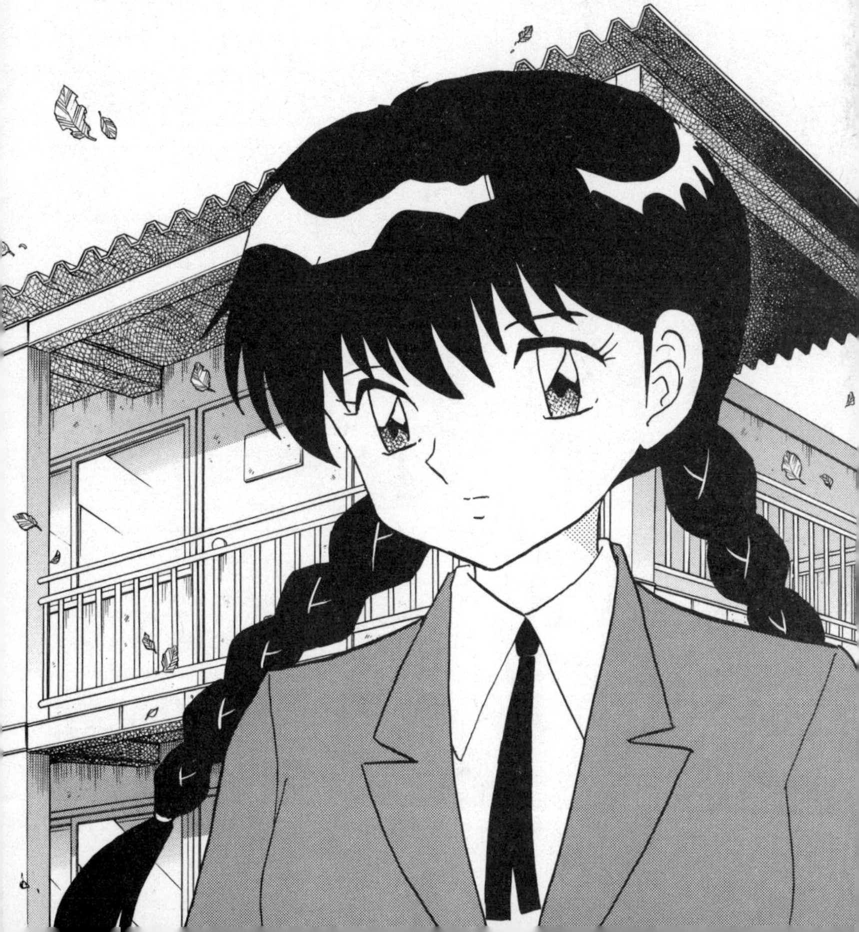

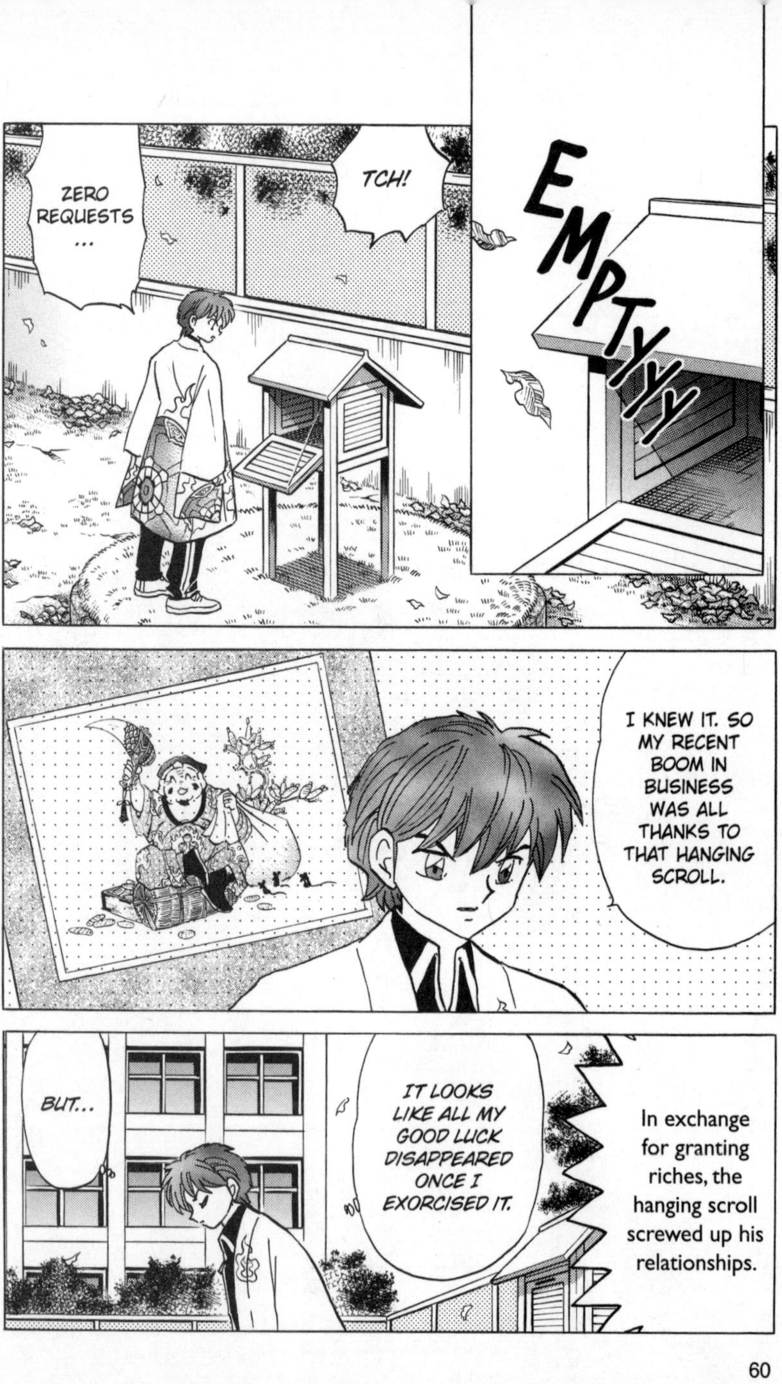
EMPTYYY
TCH!
ZERO REQUESTS ...
I KNEW IT. SO MY RECENT BOOM IN BUSINESS WAS ALL THANKS TO THAT HANGING SCROLL.
In exchange for granting riches, the hanging scroll screwed up his relationships.
IT LOOKS LIKE ALL MY GOOD LUCK DISAPPEARED ONCE I EXORCISED IT.
BUT...

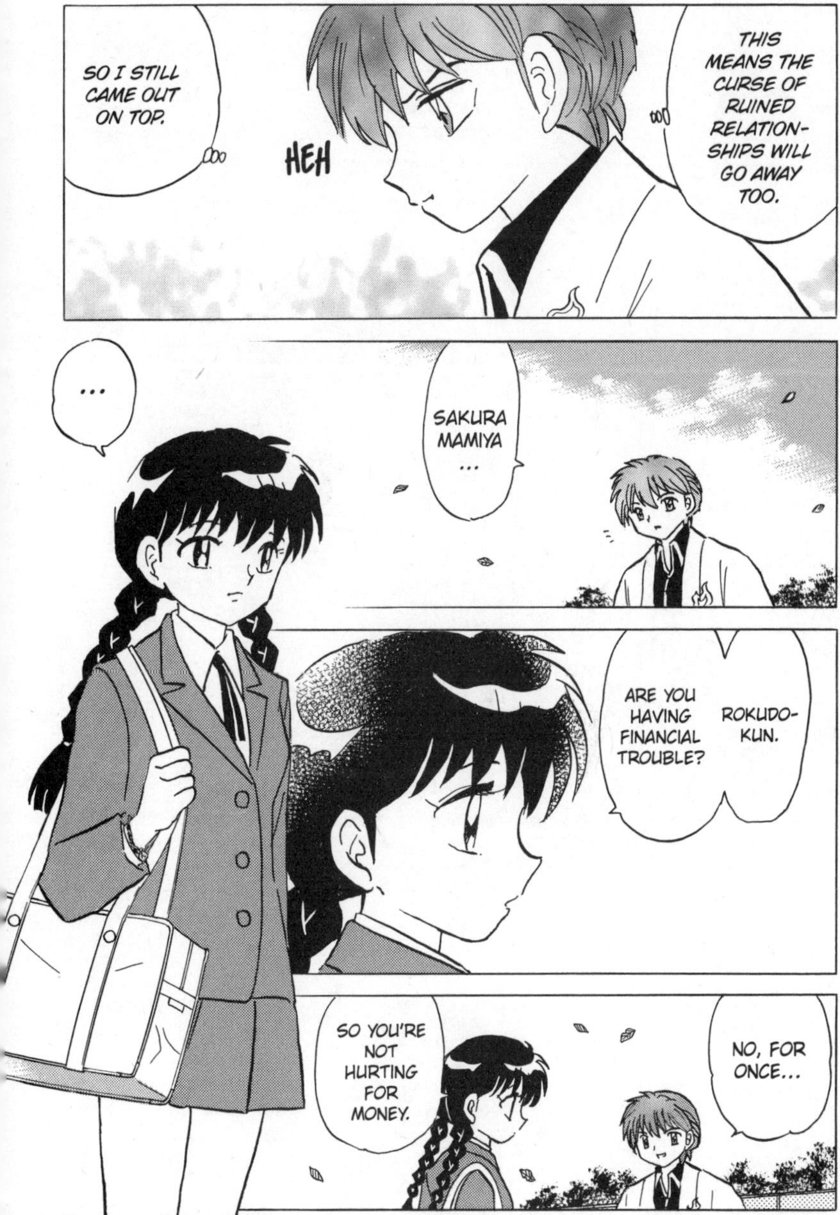
THIS MEANS THE CURSE OF RUINED RELATION-SHIPS WILL GO AWAY TOO.
HEH
SO I STILL CAME OUT ON TOP.
SAKURA MAMIYA ...
ROKUDO-KUN.
ARE YOU HAVING FINANCIAL TROUBLE?
NO, FOR ONCE...
SO YOU'RE NOT HURTING FOR MONEY.
...

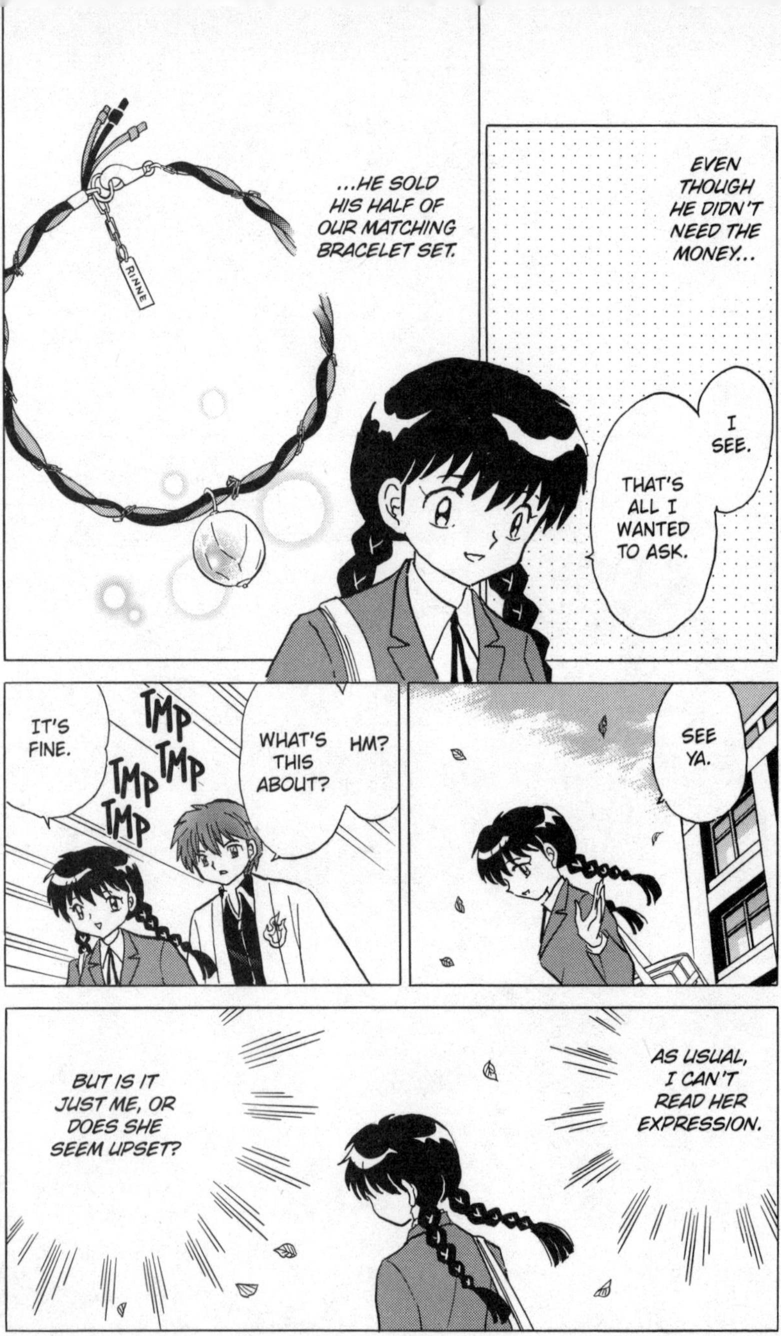
EVEN THOUGH HE DIDN'T NEED THE MONEY...
I SEE.
THAT'S ALL I WANTED TO ASK.
RINNE
...HE SOLD HIS HALF OF OUR MATCHING BRACELET SET.
SEE YA.
HM?
WHAT'S THIS ABOUT?
TMP TMP TMP TMP
IT'S FINE.
AS USUAL, I CAN'T READ HER EXPRESSION.
BUT IS IT JUST ME, OR DOES SHE SEEM UPSET?

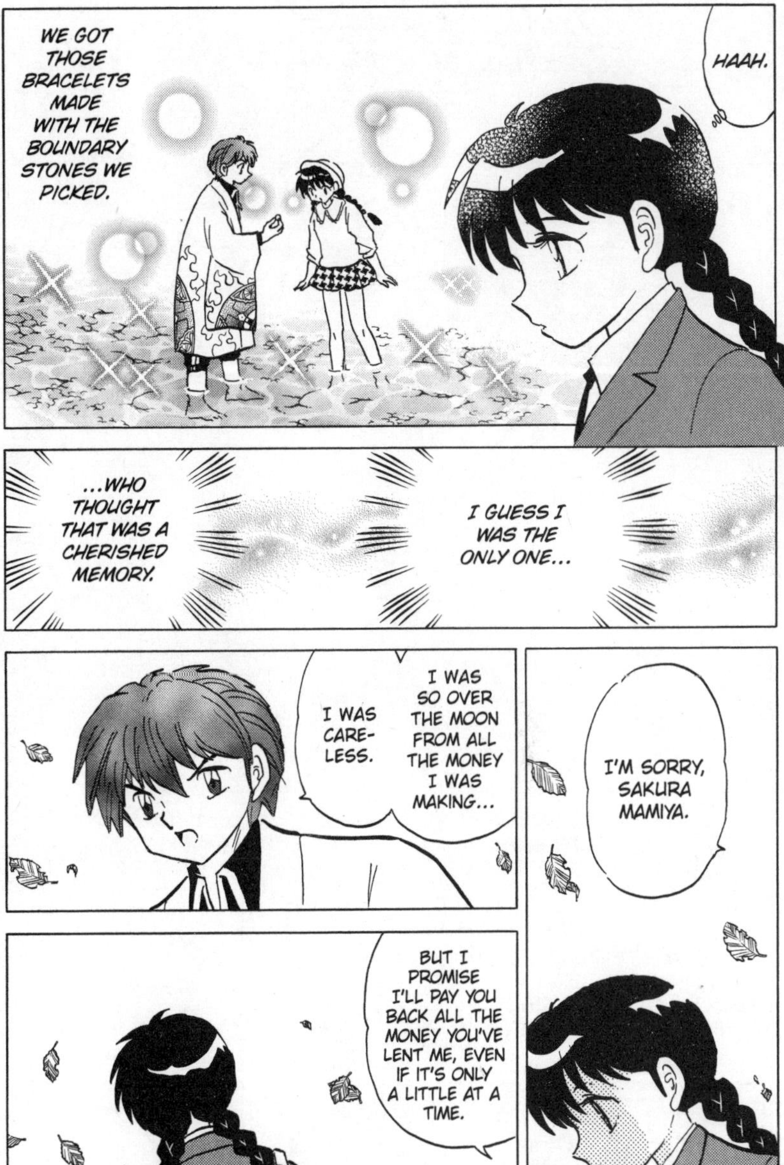
HAAH.
WE GOT THOSE BRACELETS MADE WITH THE BOUNDARY STONES WE PICKED.
I GUESS I WAS THE ONLY ONE...
...WHO THOUGHT THAT WAS A CHERISHED MEMORY.
I'M SORRY, SAKURA MAMIYA.
I WAS SO OVER THE MOON FROM ALL THE MONEY I WAS MAKING...
I WAS CARE-LESS.
BUT I PROMISE I'LL PAY YOU BACK ALL THE MONEY YOU'VE LENT ME, EVEN IF IT'S ONLY A LITTLE AT A TIME.

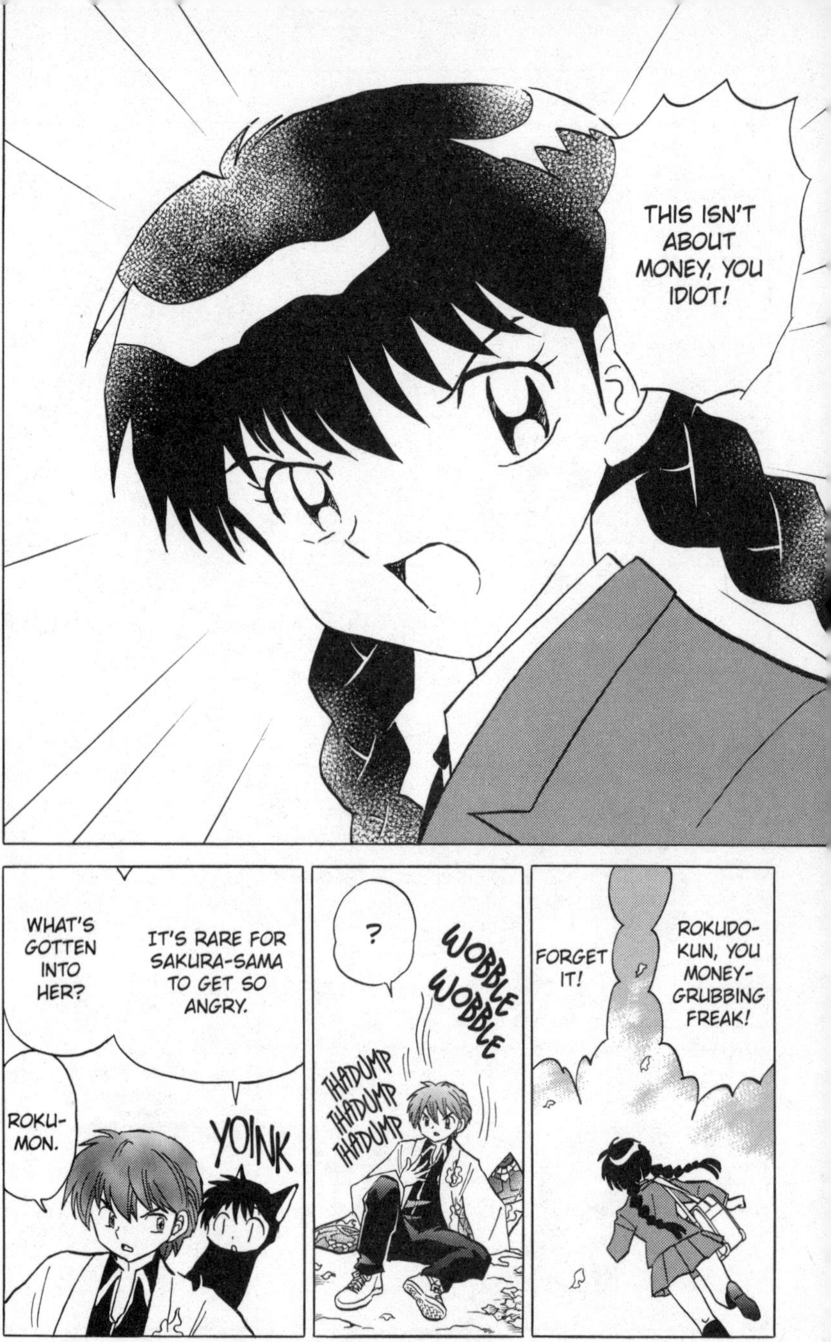

THIS ISN'T ABOUT MONEY, YOU IDIOT!
ROKUDO-KUN, YOU MONEY-GRUBBING FREAK!
FORGET IT!
?
WOBBLE WOBBLE
THADUMP THADUMP THADUMP
IT'S RARE FOR SAKURA-SAMA TO GET SO ANGRY.
WHAT'S GOTTEN INTO HER?
YOINK
ROKU-MON.

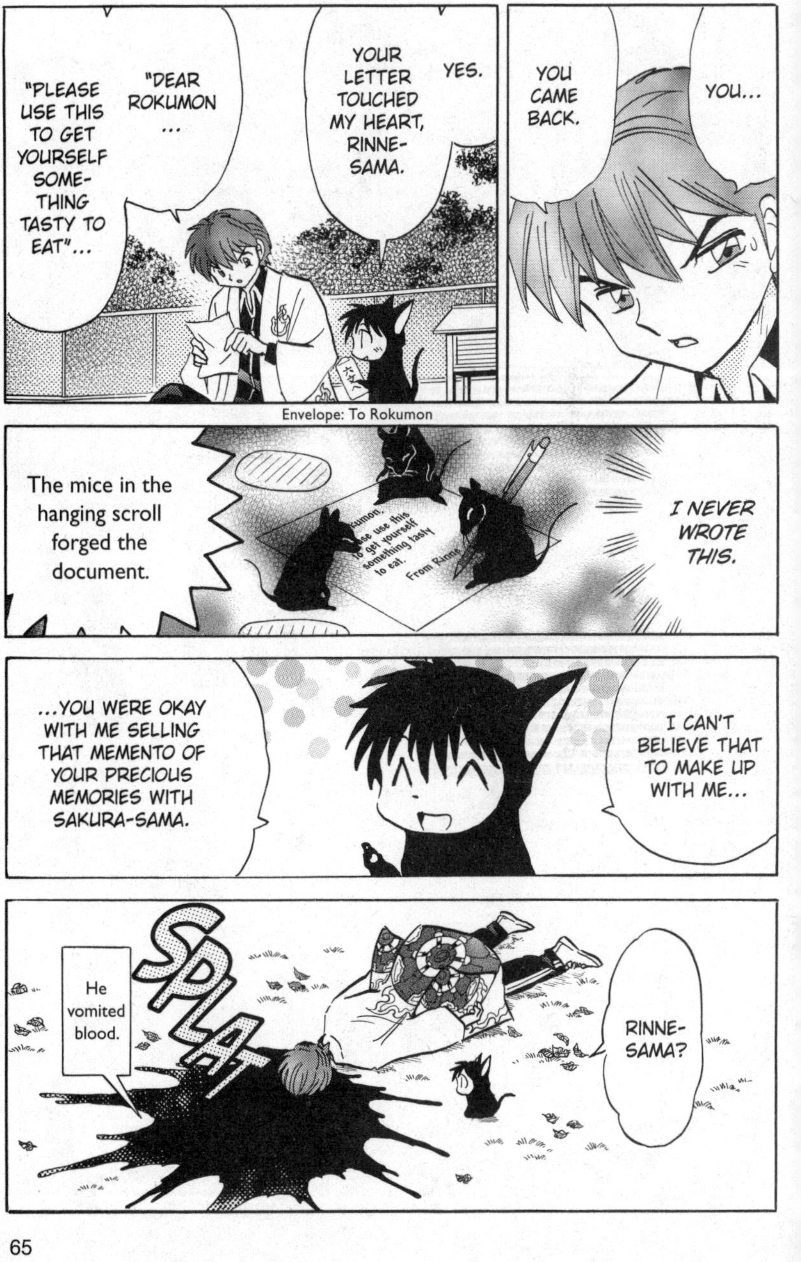
YOU...
YOU CAME BACK.
YES.
YOUR LETTER TOUCHED MY HEART, RINNE-SAMA.
"DEAR ROKUMON ...
"PLEASE USE THIS TO GET YOURSELF SOME-THING TASTY TO EAT"...
Envelope: To Rokumon
I NEVER WROTE THIS.
The mice in the hanging scroll forged the document.
I CAN'T BELIEVE THAT TO MAKE UP WITH ME...
...YOU WERE OKAY WITH ME SELLING THAT MEMENTO OF YOUR PRECIOUS MEMORIES WITH SAKURA-SAMA.
RINNE-SAMA?
SPLAT
He vomited blood.

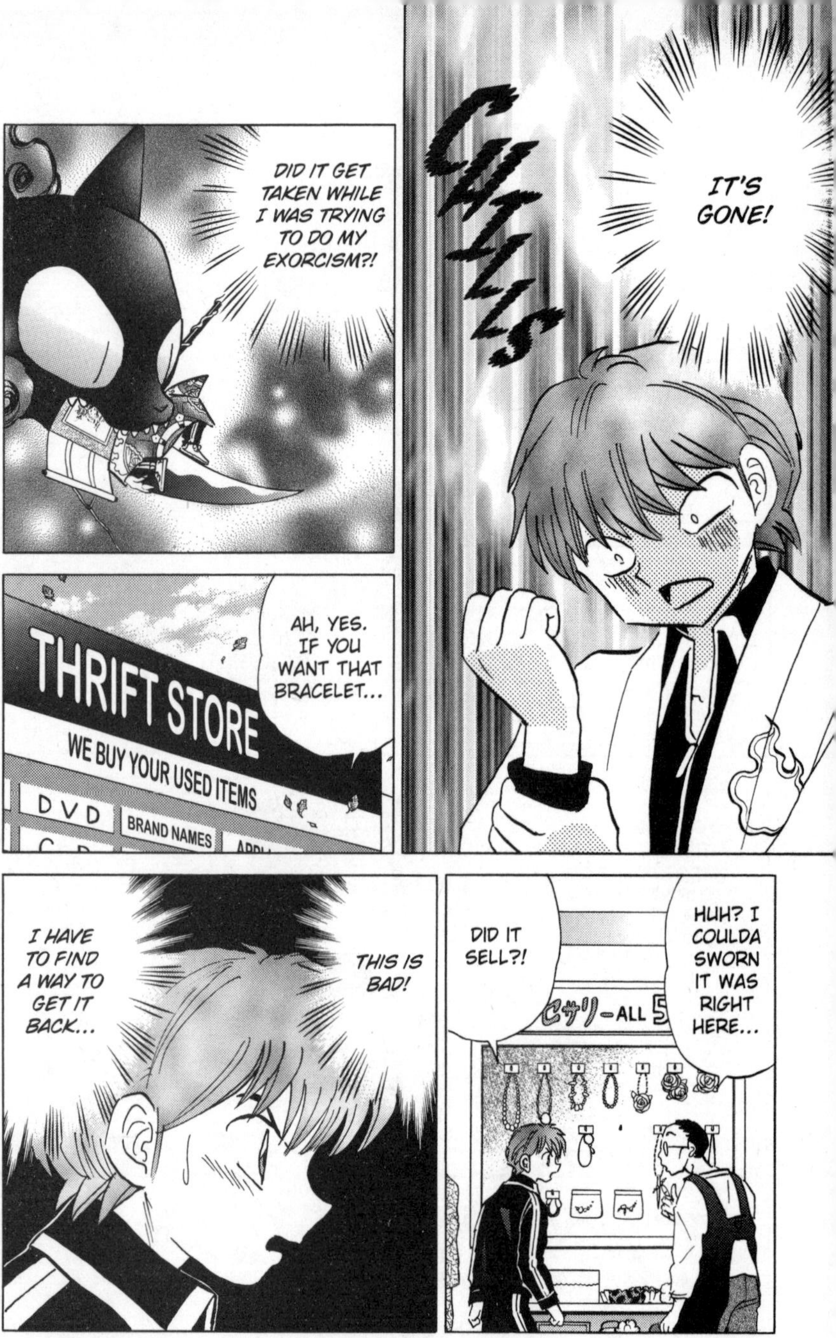
CHILLS
IT'S GONE!
DID IT GET TAKEN WHILE I WAS TRYING TO DO MY EXORCISM?!
AH, YES. IF YOU WANT THAT BRACELET...
THRIFT STORE
WE BUY YOUR USED ITEMS
DVD
BRAND NAMES
HUH? I COULDA SWORN IT WAS RIGHT HERE...
DID IT SELL?!
THIS IS BAD!
I HAVE TO FIND A WAY TO GET IT BACK...

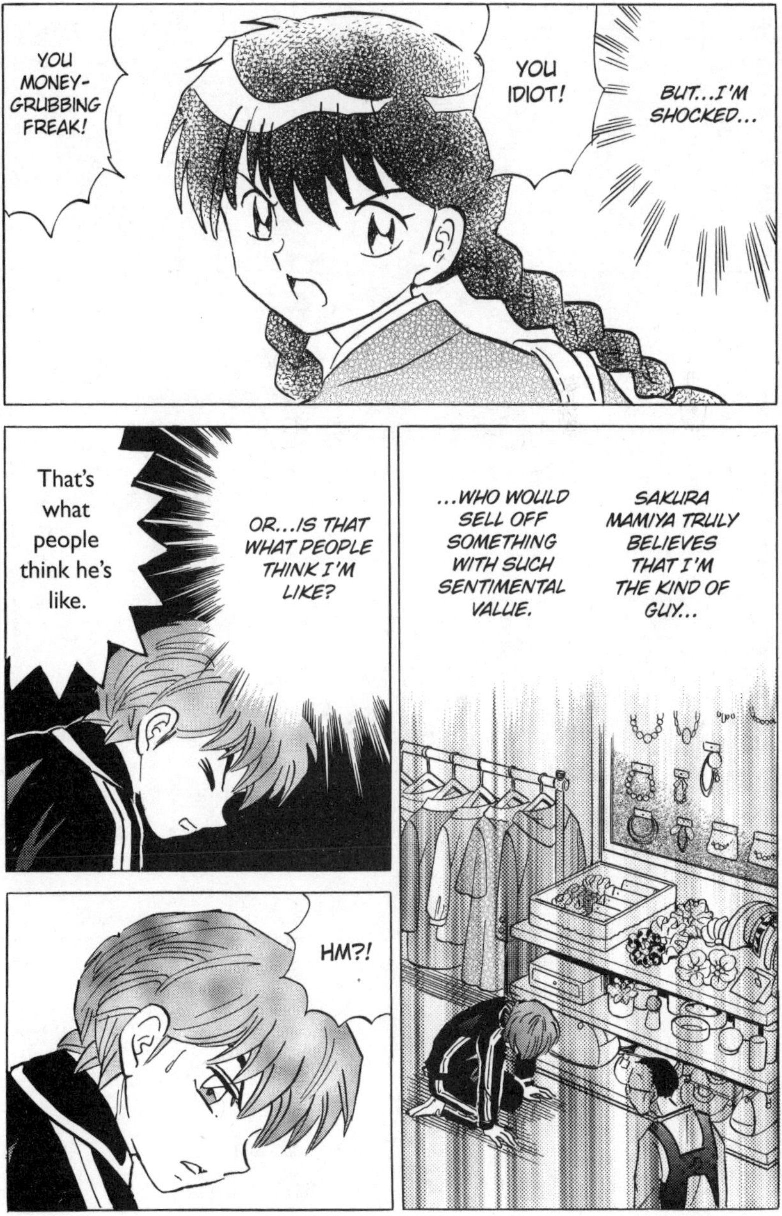
BUT...I'M SHOCKED...
YOU IDIOT!
YOU MONEY-GRUBBING FREAK!
SAKURA MAMIYA TRULY BELIEVES THAT I'M THE KIND OF GUY...
...WHO WOULD SELL OFF SOMETHING WITH SUCH SENTIMENTAL VALUE.
OR...IS THAT WHAT PEOPLE THINK I'M LIKE?
That's what people think he's like.
HM?!

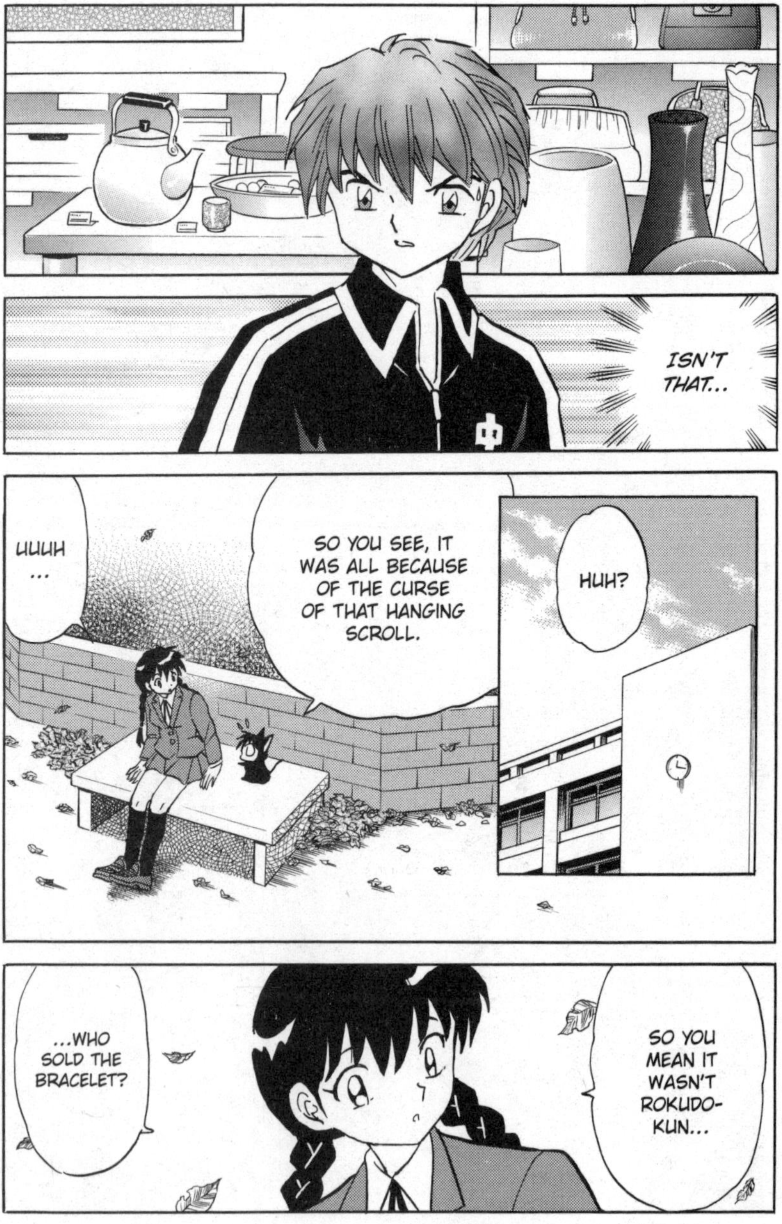
ISN'T THAT...
HUH?
SO YOU SEE, IT WAS ALL BECAUSE OF THE CURSE OF THAT HANGING SCROLL.
UUUH ...
SO YOU MEAN IT WASN'T ROKUDO-KUN...
...WHO SOLD THE BRACELET?

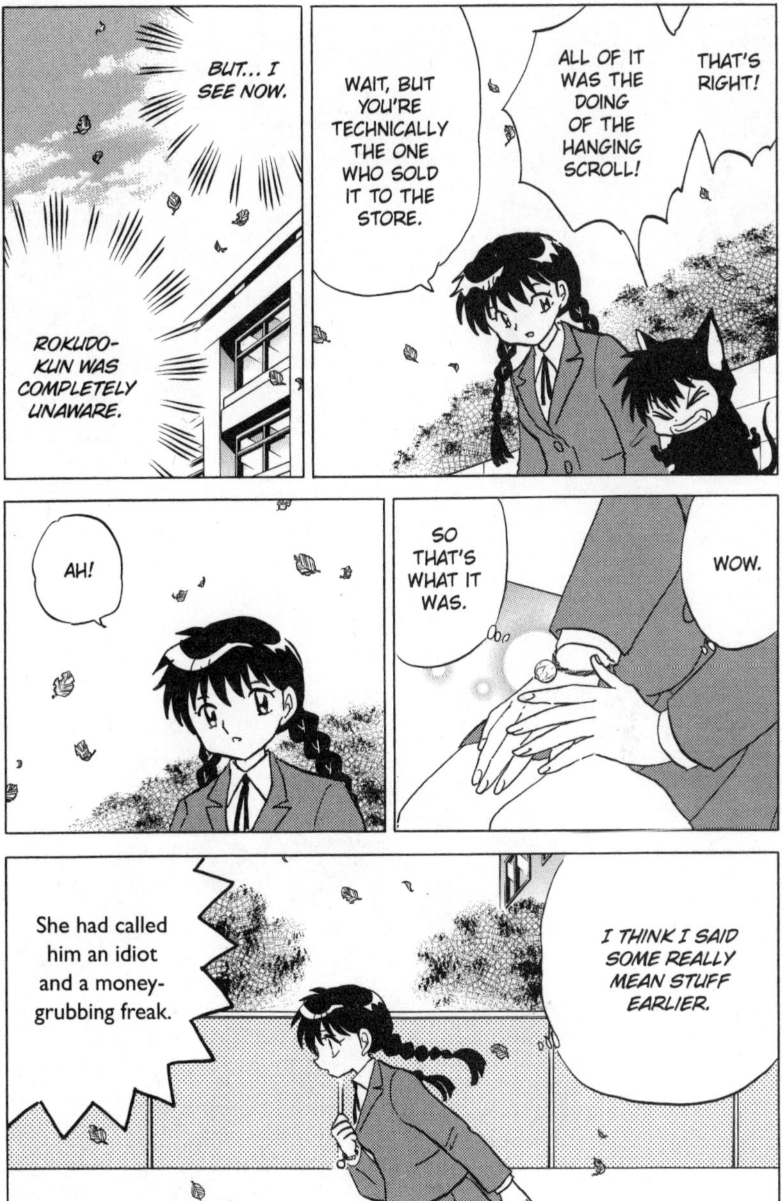
THAT'S RIGHT!
ALL OF IT WAS THE DOING OF THE HANGING SCROLL!
WAIT, BUT YOU'RE TECHNICALLY THE ONE WHO SOLD IT TO THE STORE.
BUT... I SEE NOW.
ROKUDO-KUN WAS COMPLETELY UNAWARE.
WOW.
SO THAT'S WHAT IT WAS.
AH!
I THINK I SAID SOME REALLY MEAN STUFF EARLIER.
She had called him an idiot and a money-grubbing freak.

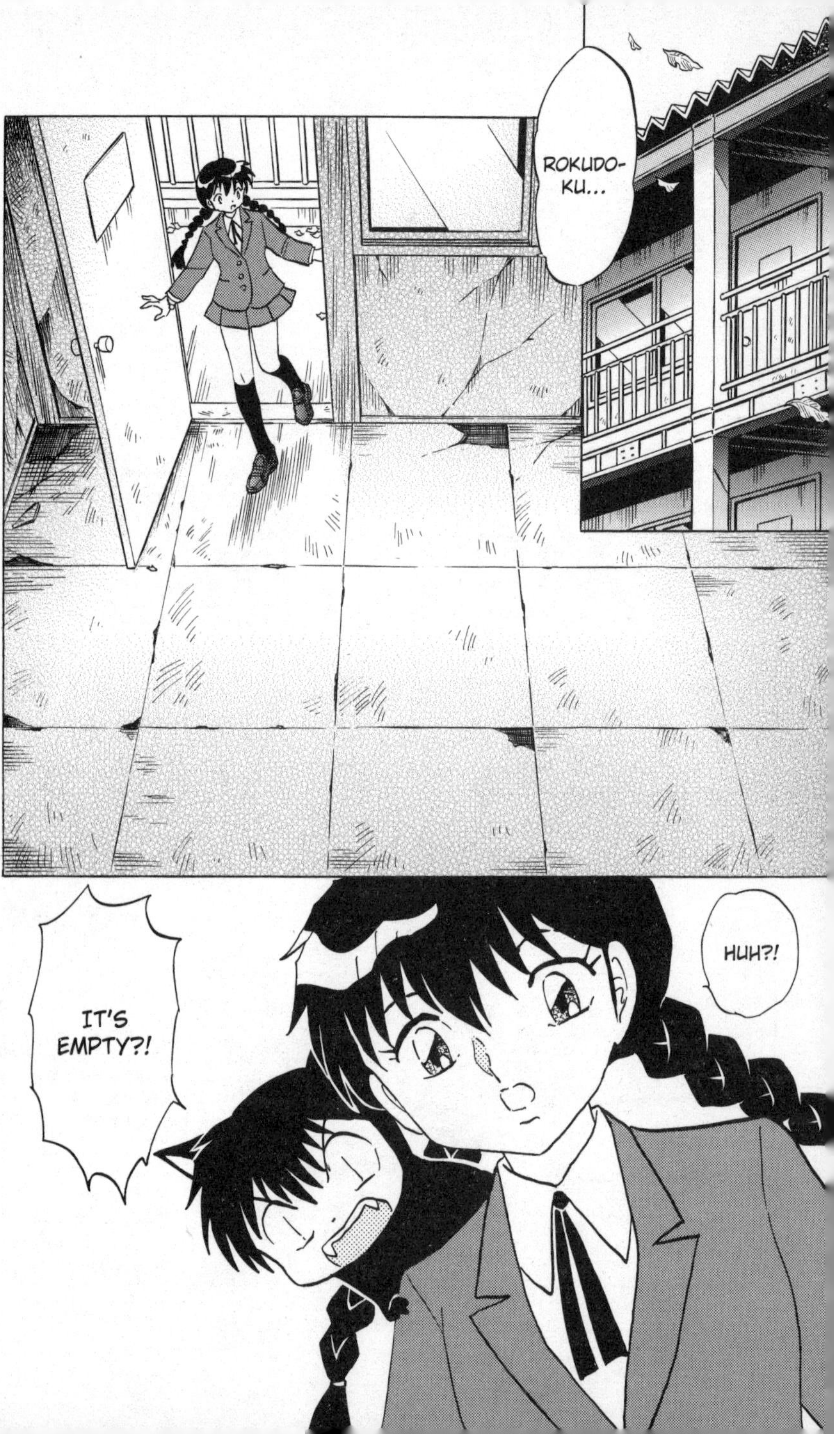
ROKUDO-KU...
HUH?!
IT'S EMPTY?!

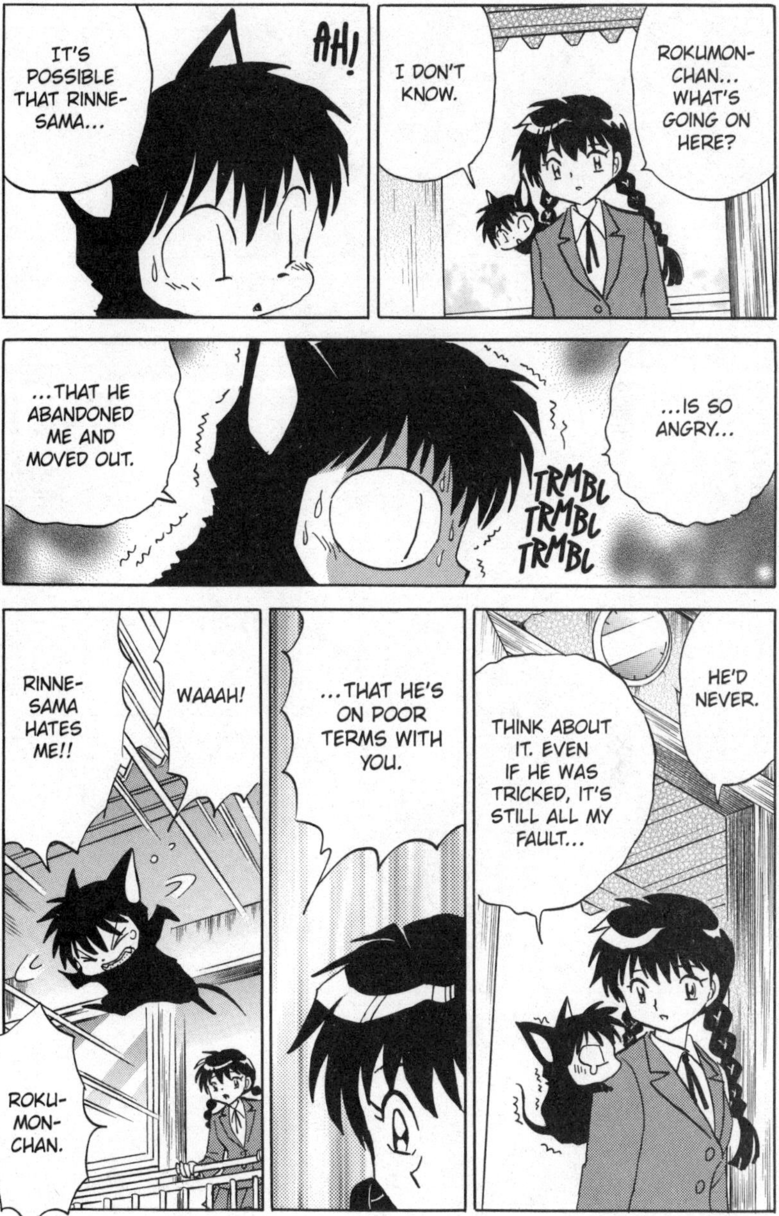
ROKUMON-CHAN... WHAT'S GOING ON HERE?
I DON'T KNOW.
AH!
IT'S POSSIBLE THAT RINNE-SAMA...
...IS SO ANGRY...
TRMBL TRMBL TRMBL
...THAT HE ABANDONED ME AND MOVED OUT.
HE'D NEVER.
THINK ABOUT IT. EVEN IF HE WAS TRICKED, IT'S STILL ALL MY FAULT...
...THAT HE'S ON POOR TERMS WITH YOU.
WAAAH!
RINNE-SAMA HATES ME!!
ROKU-MON-CHAN.

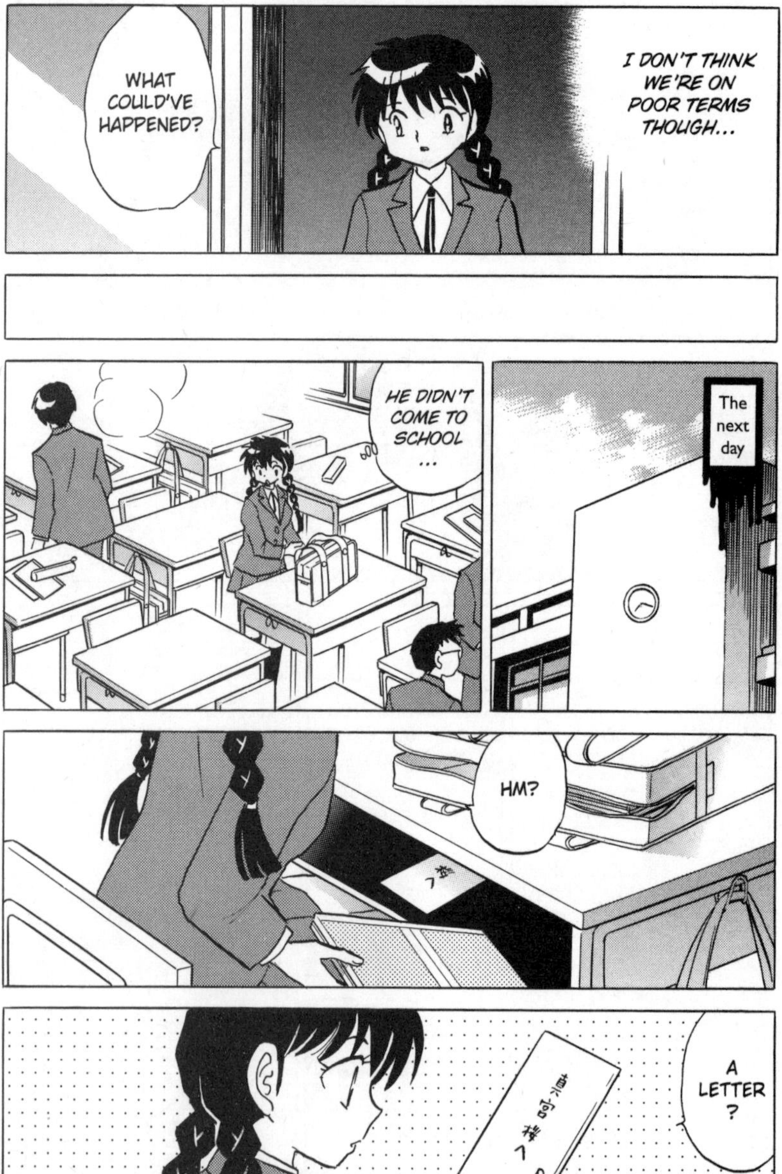
I DON'T THINK WE'RE ON POOR TERMS THOUGH...
WHAT COULD'VE HAPPENED?
The next day
HE DIDN'T COME TO SCHOOL ...
HM?
A LETTER ?
Envelope: To Sakura Mamiya

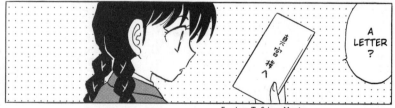

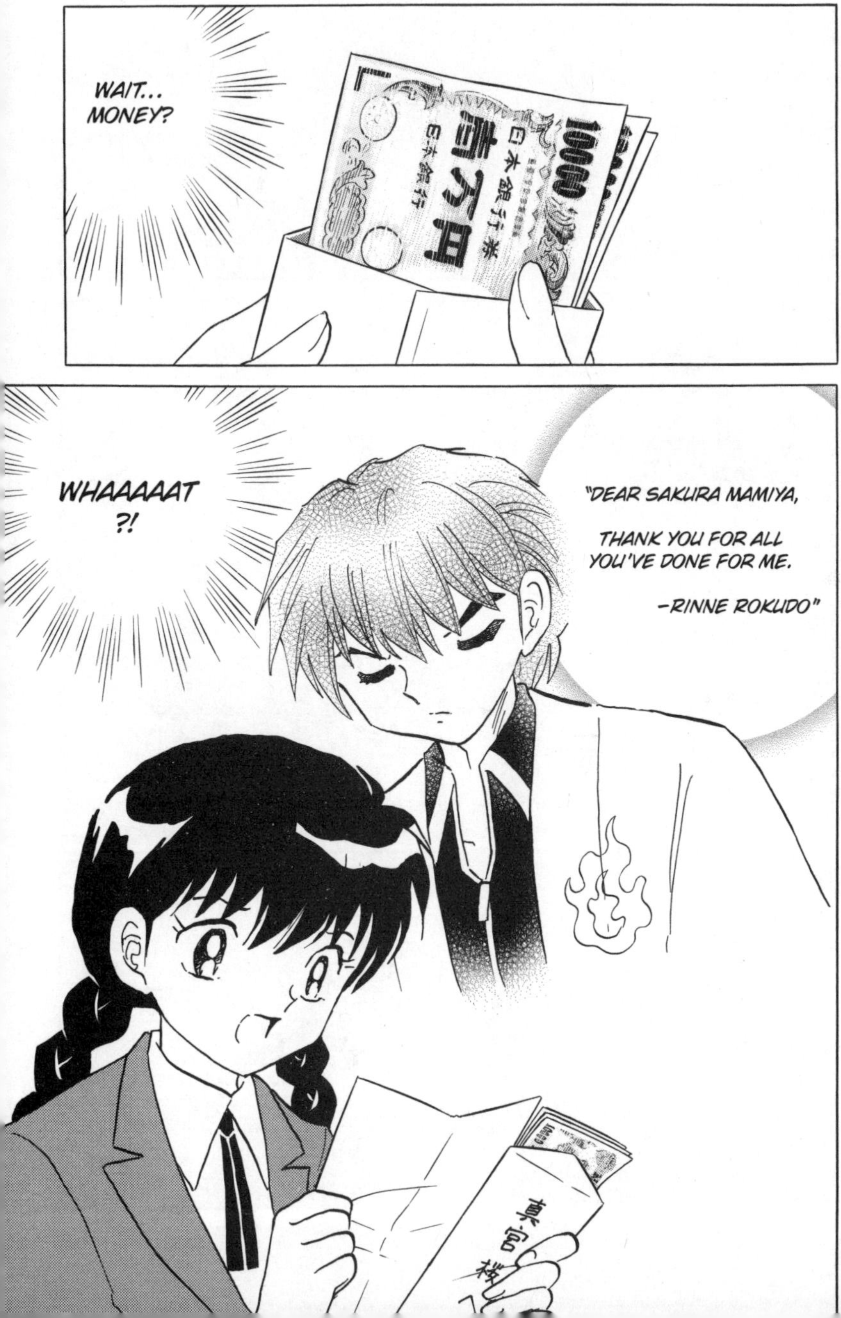
WAIT... MONEY?
"DEAR SAKURA MAMIYA,
THANK YOU FOR ALL YOU'VE DONE FOR ME.
-RINNE ROKUDO"
WHAAAAAT ?!

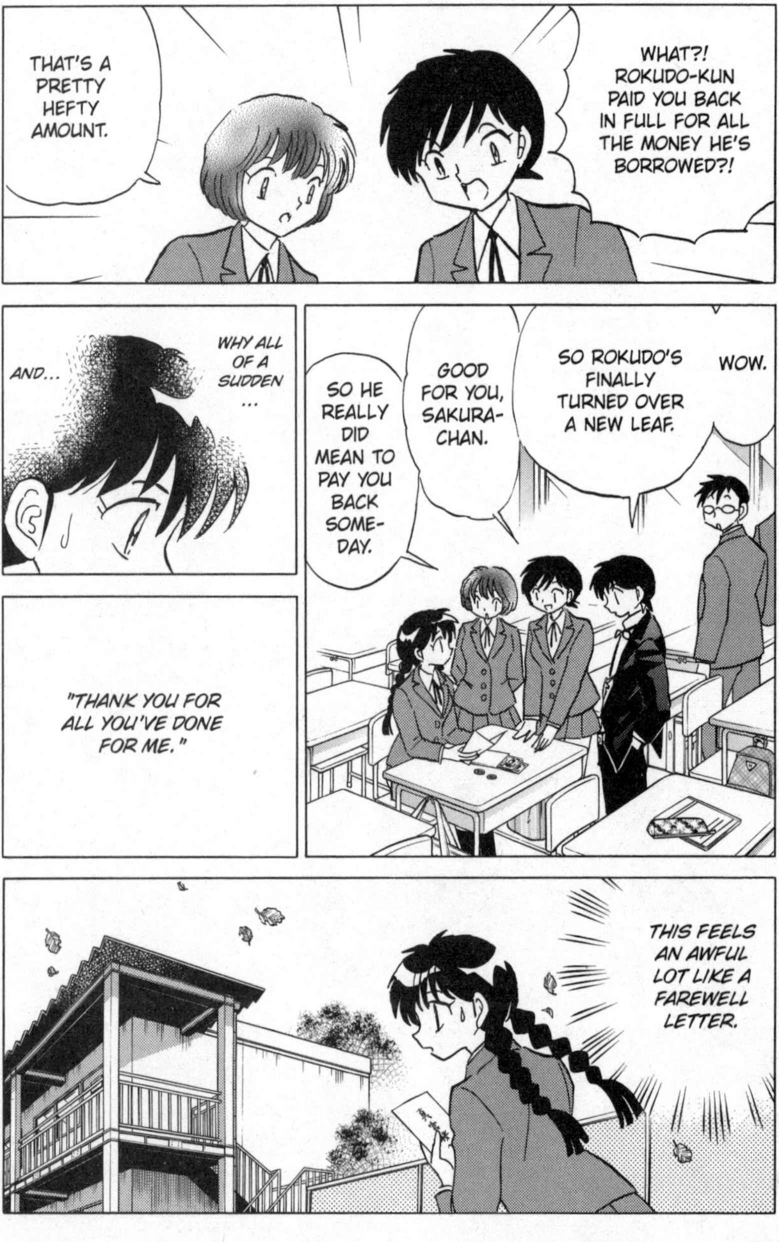
WHAT?! ROKUDO-KUN PAID YOU BACK IN FULL FOR ALL THE MONEY HE'S BORROWED?!
THAT'S A PRETTY HEFTY AMOUNT.
WOW.
SO ROKUDO'S FINALLY TURNED OVER A NEW LEAF.
GOOD FOR YOU, SAKURA-CHAN.
SO HE REALLY DID MEAN TO PAY YOU BACK SOME-DAY.
WHY ALL OF A SUDDEN ...
AND...
"THANK YOU FOR ALL YOU'VE DONE FOR ME."
THIS FEELS AN AWFUL LOT LIKE A FAREWELL LETTER.

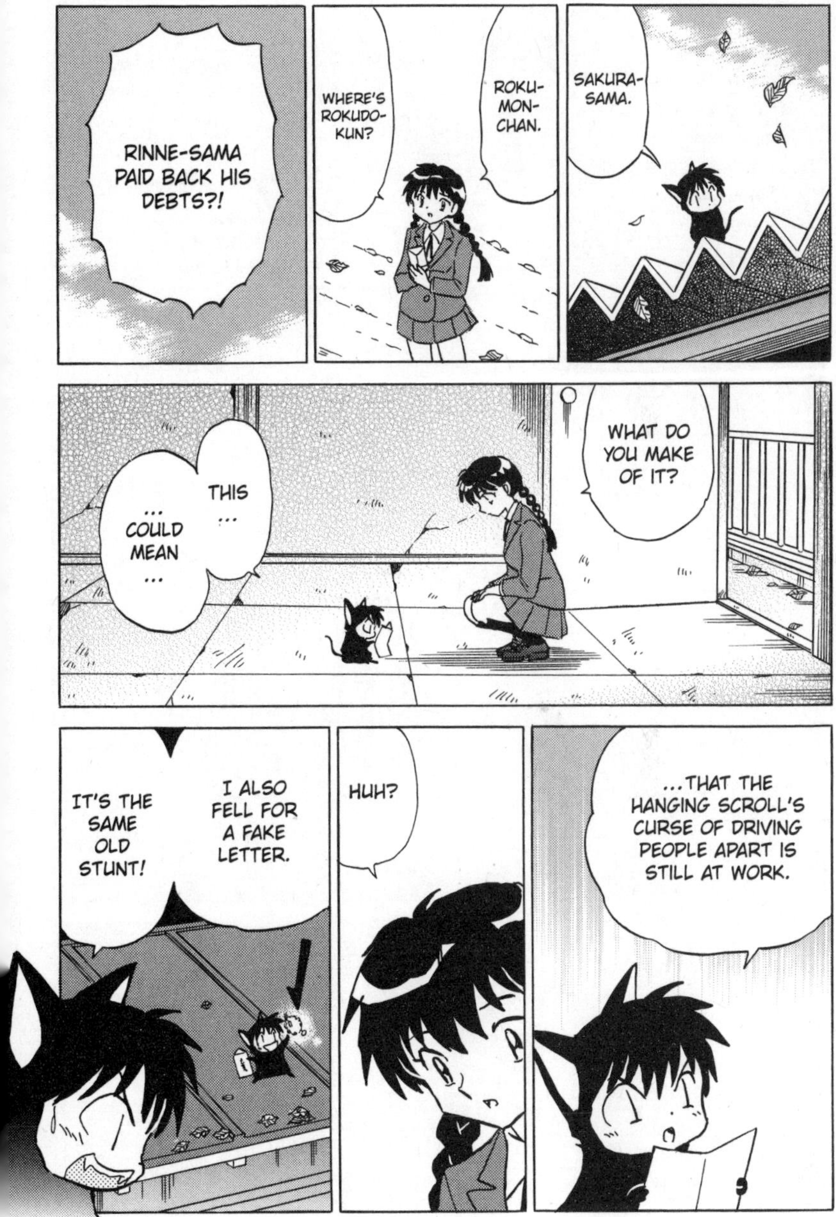
SAKURA-SAMA.
ROKU-MON-CHAN.
WHERE'S ROKUDO-KUN?
RINNE-SAMA PAID BACK HIS DEBTS?!
WHAT DO YOU MAKE OF IT?
THIS ... ... COULD MEAN ...
...THAT THE HANGING SCROLL'S CURSE OF DRIVING PEOPLE APART IS STILL AT WORK.
HUH?
I ALSO FELL FOR A FAKE LETTER.
IT'S THE SAME OLD STUNT!

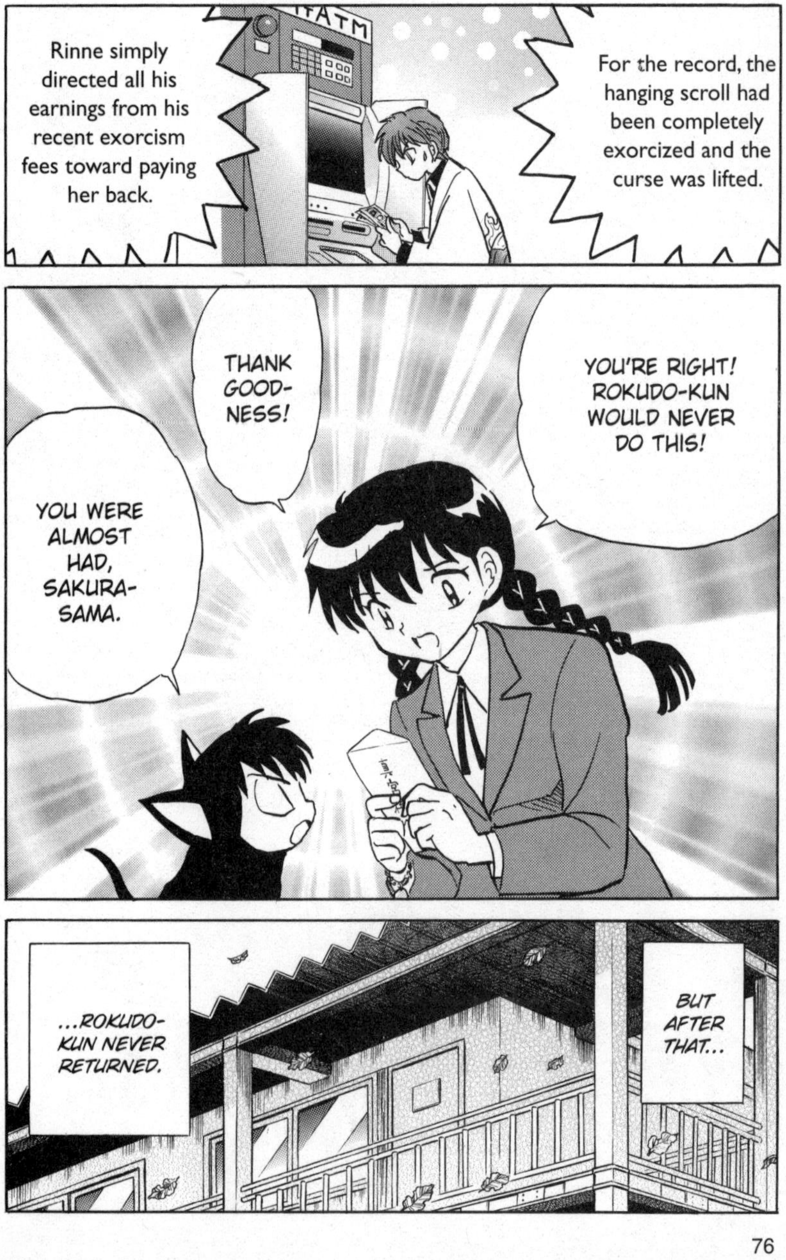
For the record, the hanging scroll had been completely exorcized and the curse was lifted.
Rinne simply directed all his earnings from his recent exorcism fees toward paying her back.
ATM
YOU'RE RIGHT! ROKUDO-KUN WOULD NEVER DO THIS!
THANK GOOD-NESS!
YOU WERE ALMOST HAD, SAKURA-SAMA.
BUT AFTER THAT...
...ROKUDO-KUN NEVER RETURNED.

CHAPTER 393: THE TERRIBLE PLAN

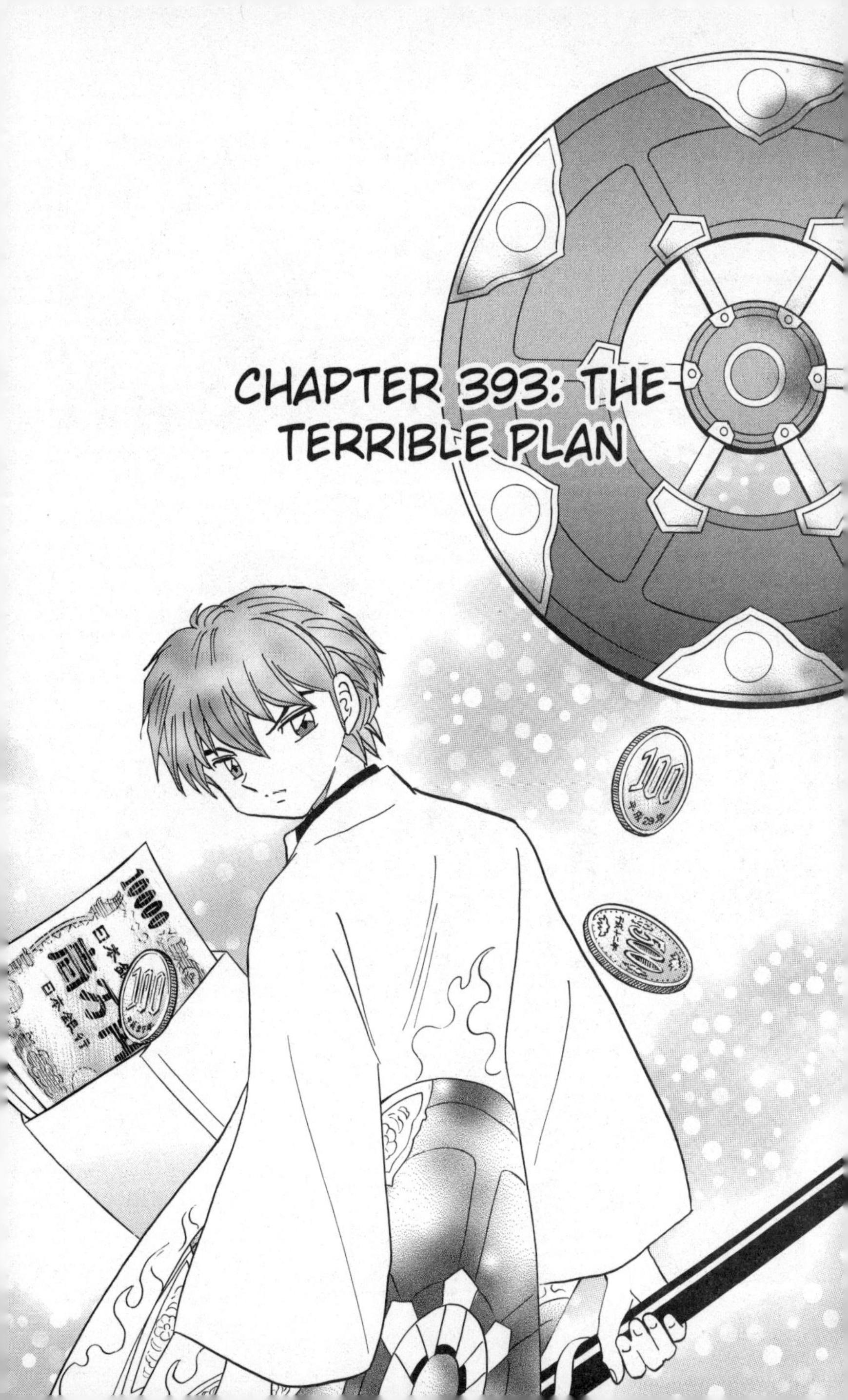

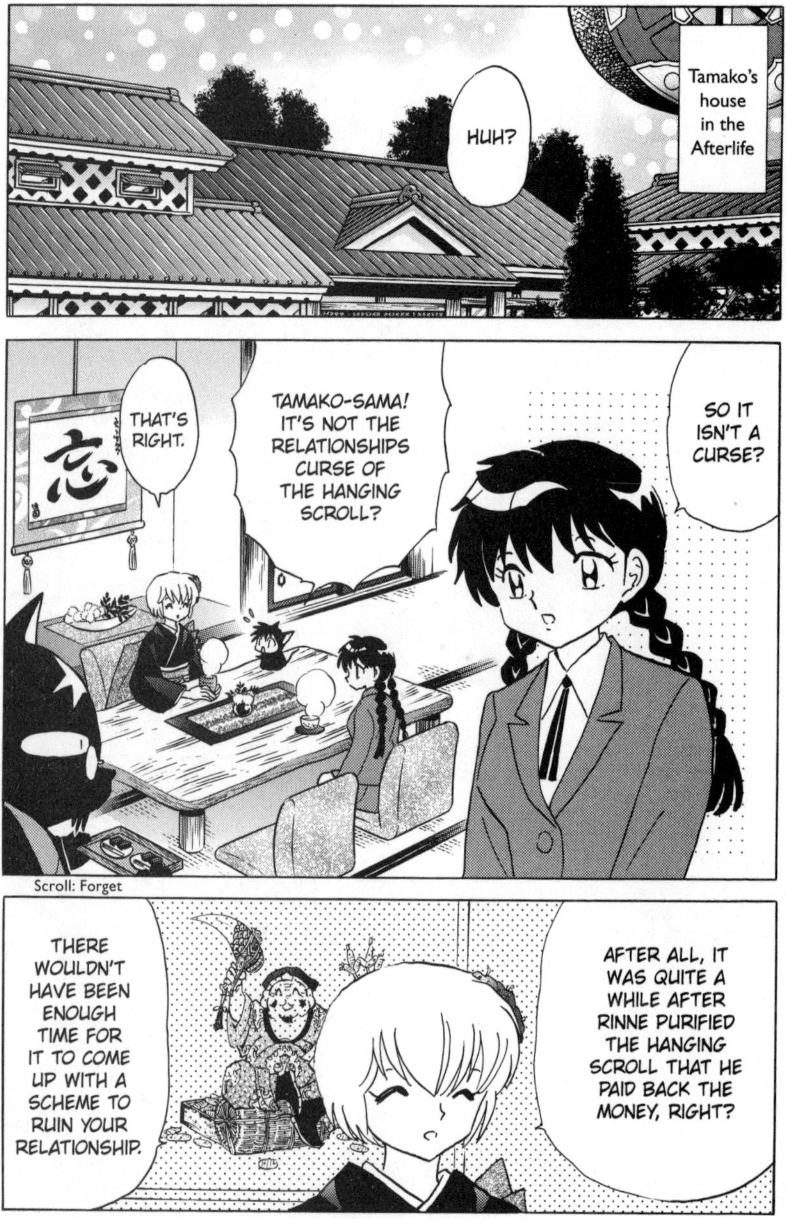
Tamako's house in the Afterlife
HUH?
SO IT ISN'T A CURSE?
TAMAKO-SAMA! IT'S NOT THE RELATIONSHIPS CURSE OF THE HANGING SCROLL?
THAT'S RIGHT.
AFTER ALL, IT WAS QUITE A WHILE AFTER RINNE PURIFIED THE HANGING SCROLL THAT HE PAID BACK THE MONEY, RIGHT?
THERE WOULDN'T HAVE BEEN ENOUGH TIME FOR IT TO COME UP WITH A SCHEME TO RUIN YOUR RELATIONSHIP.
Scroll: Forget

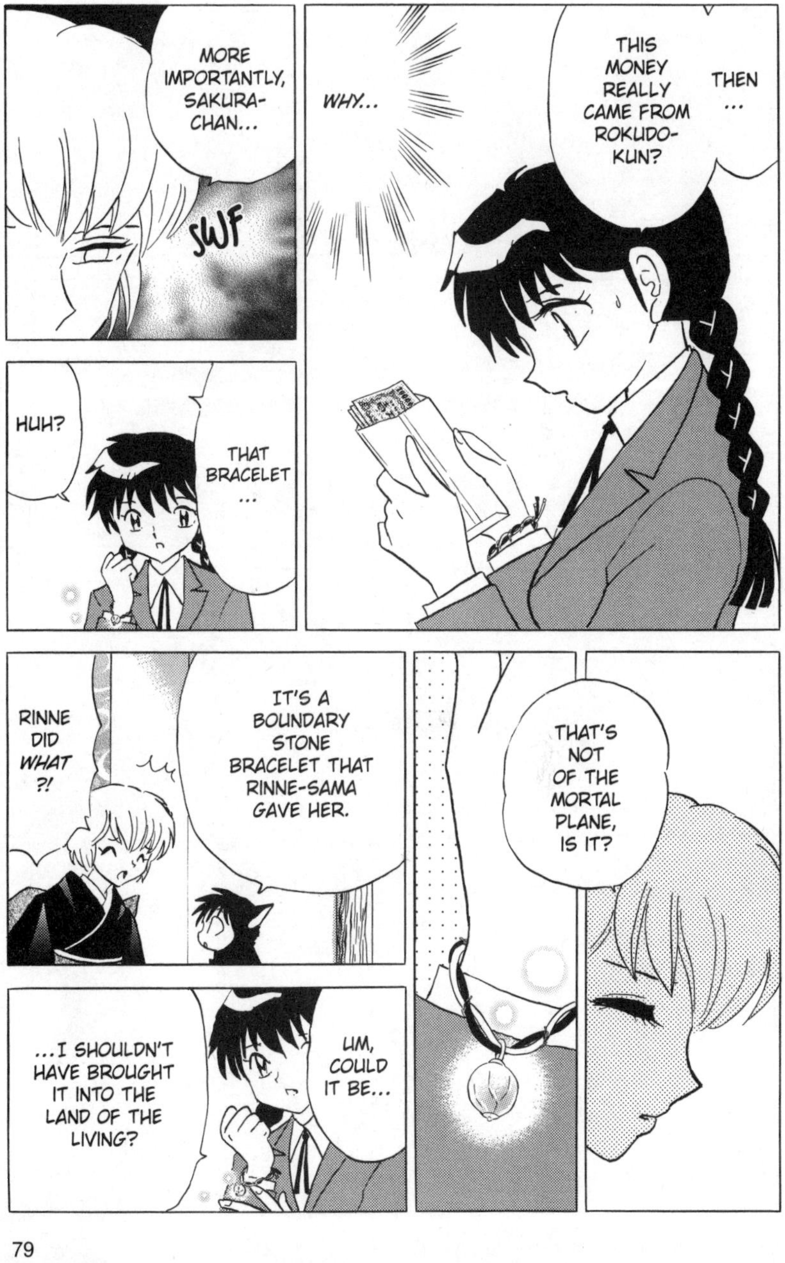
THEN ...
THIS MONEY REALLY CAME FROM ROKUDO-KUN?
WHY...
MORE IMPORTANTLY, SAKURA-CHAN...
SWF
THAT BRACELET ...
HUH?
THAT'S NOT OF THE MORTAL PLANE, IS IT?
IT'S A BOUNDARY STONE BRACELET THAT RINNE-SAMA GAVE HER.
RINNE DID WHAT?!
UM, COULD IT BE...
...I SHOULDN'T HAVE BROUGHT IT INTO THE LAND OF THE LIVING?

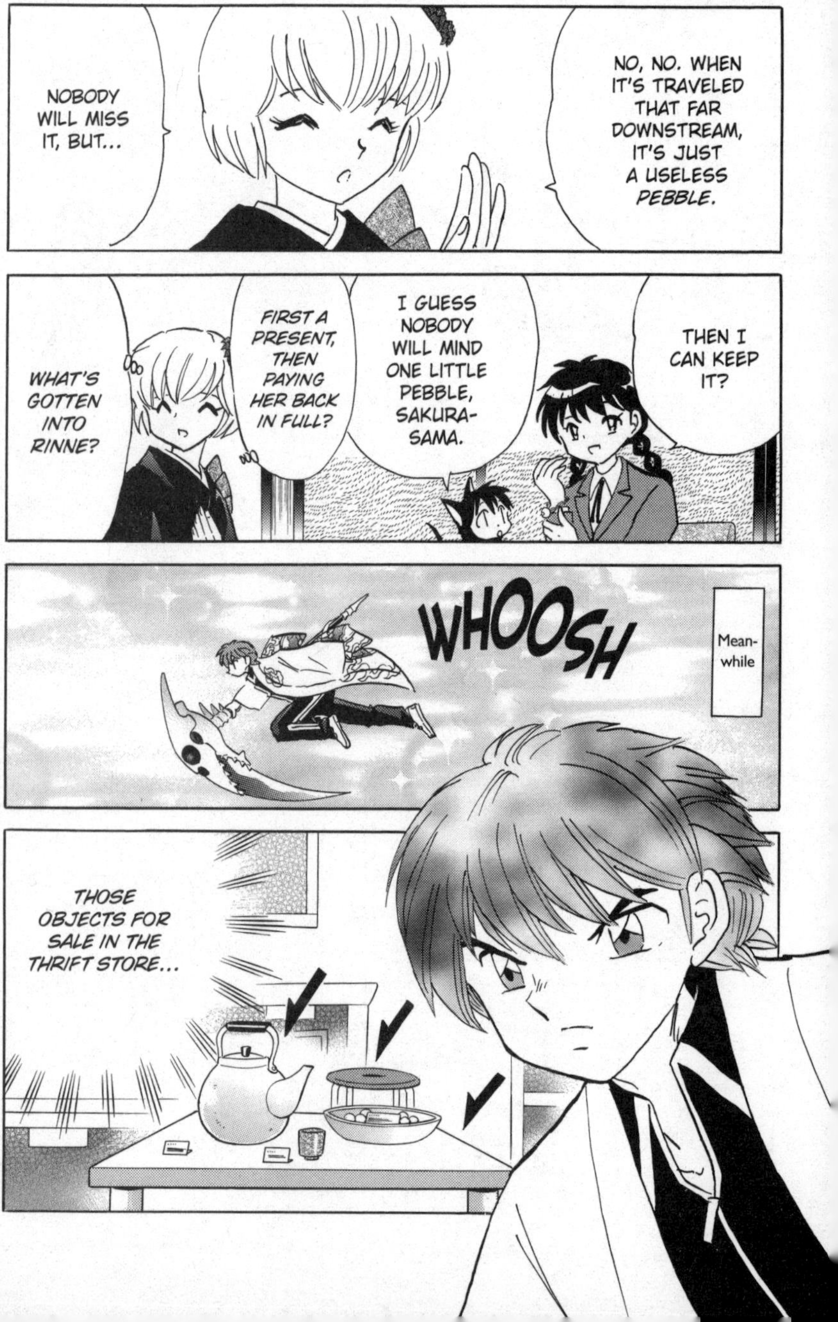
NO, NO. WHEN IT'S TRAVELED THAT FAR DOWNSTREAM, IT'S JUST A USELESS *PEBBLE*.
NOBODY WILL MISS IT, BUT...
THEN I CAN KEEP IT?
I GUESS NOBODY WILL MIND ONE LITTLE PEBBLE, SAKURA-SAMA.
FIRST A PRESENT, THEN PAYING HER BACK IN FULL?
WHAT'S GOTTEN INTO RINNE?
Mean-while
WHOOSH
THOSE OBJECTS FOR SALE IN THE THRIFT STORE...

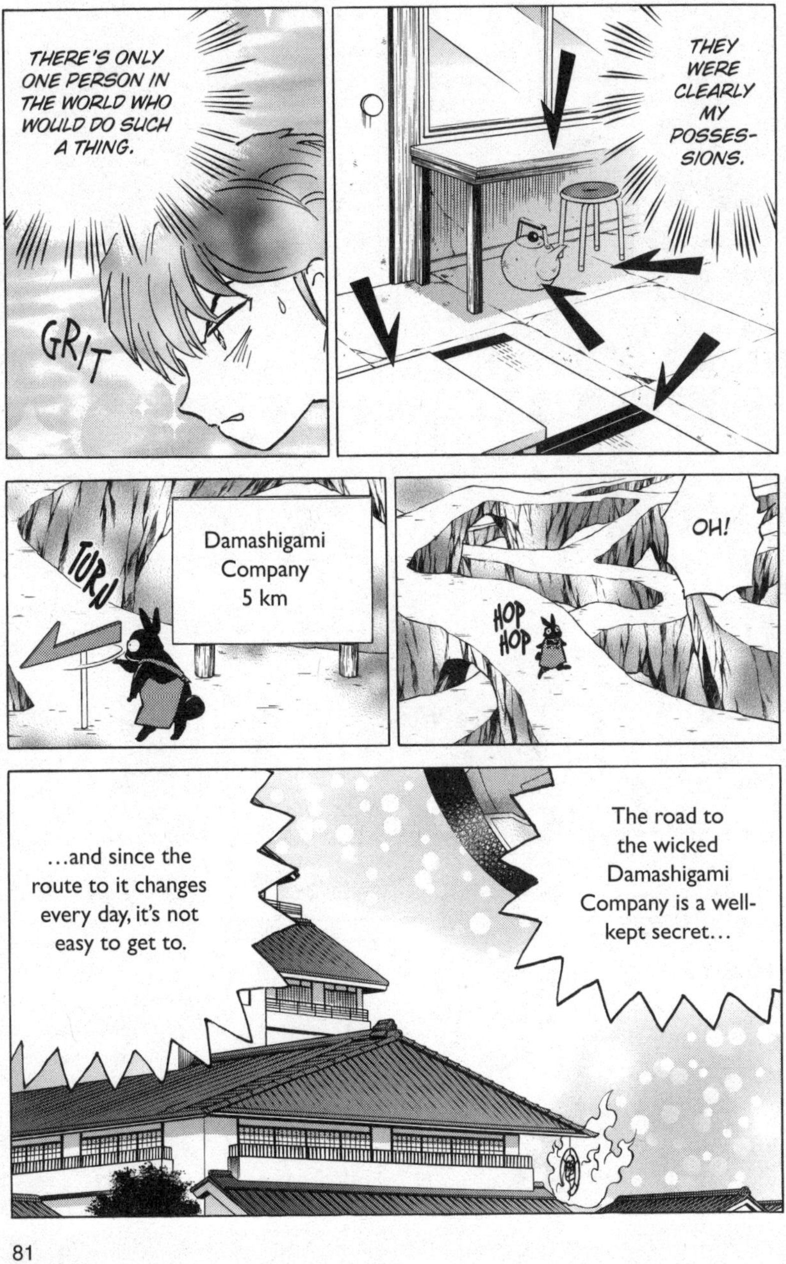
THEY WERE CLEARLY MY POSSES-SIONS.
THERE'S ONLY ONE PERSON IN THE WORLD WHO WOULD DO SUCH A THING.
GRIT
OH!
HOP HOP
Damashigami Company 5 km
TURN
The road to the wicked Damashigami Company is a well-kept secret…
…and since the route to it changes every day, it's not easy to get to.

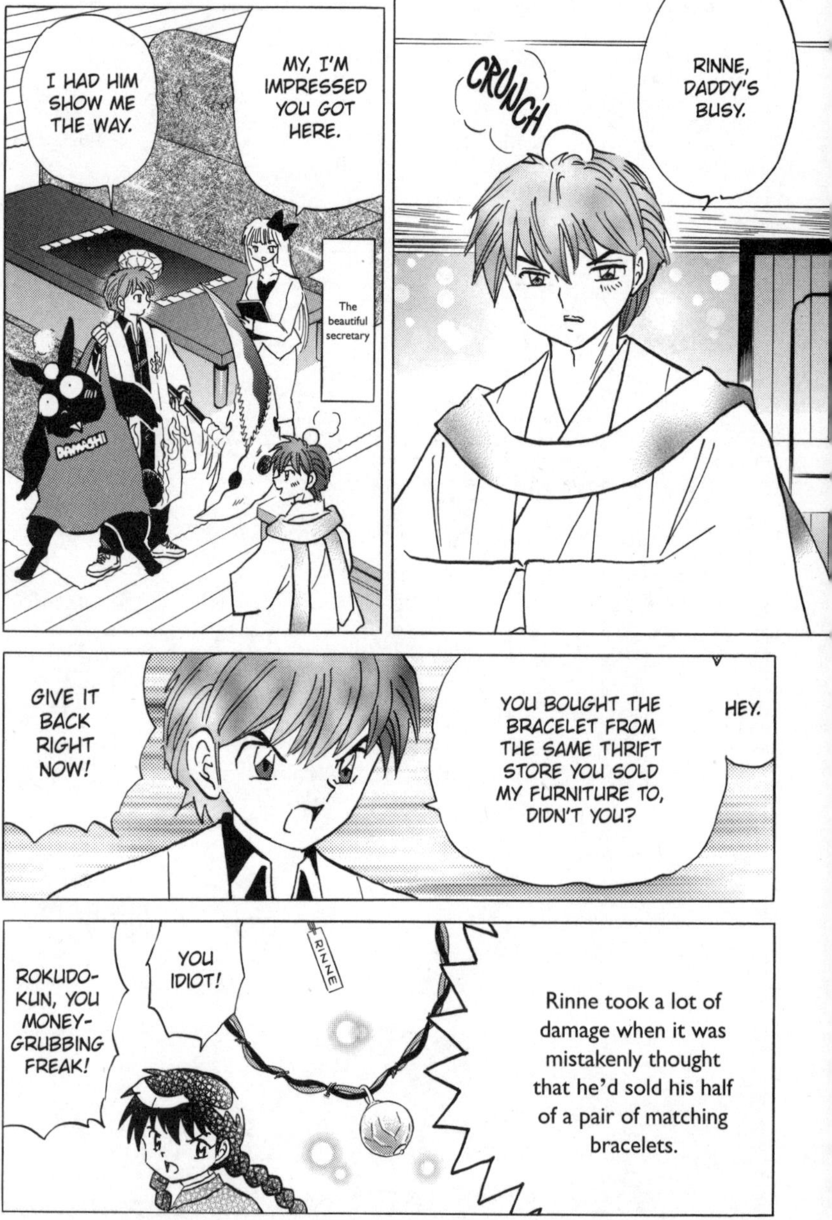
RINNE, DADDY'S BUSY.
CRUNCH
MY, I'M IMPRESSED YOU GOT HERE.
I HAD HIM SHOW ME THE WAY.
The beautiful secretary
DAMASHI
HEY.
YOU BOUGHT THE BRACELET FROM THE SAME THRIFT STORE YOU SOLD MY FURNITURE TO, DIDN'T YOU?
GIVE IT BACK RIGHT NOW!
Rinne took a lot of damage when it was mistakenly thought that he'd sold his half of a pair of matching bracelets.
RINNE
YOU IDIOT!
ROKUDO-KUN, YOU MONEY-GRUBBING FREAK!

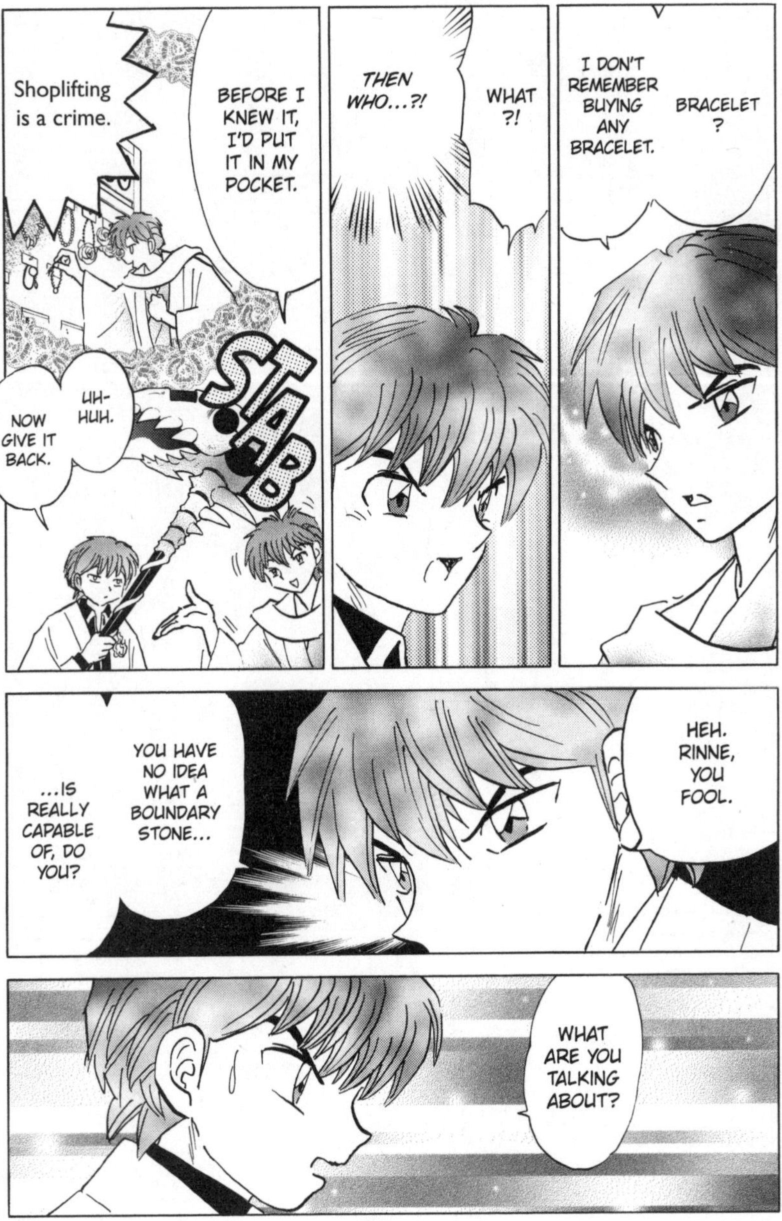
BRACELET ?
I DON'T REMEMBER BUYING ANY BRACELET.
WHAT ?!
THEN WHO...?!
BEFORE I KNEW IT, I'D PUT IT IN MY POCKET.
Shoplifting is a crime.
UH-HUH.
NOW GIVE IT BACK.
STAB
HEH. RINNE, YOU FOOL.
YOU HAVE NO IDEA WHAT A BOUNDARY STONE...
...IS REALLY CAPABLE OF, DO YOU?
WHAT ARE YOU TALKING ABOUT?

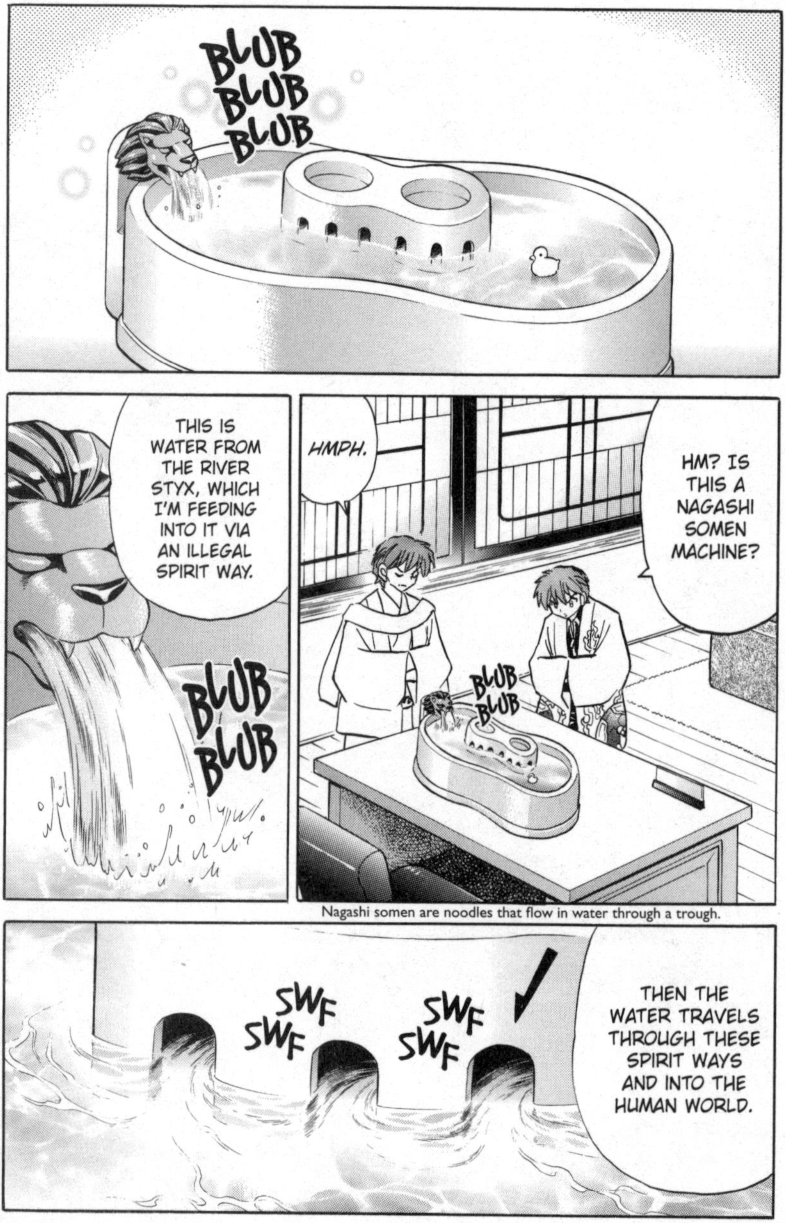
BLUB
BLUB
BLUB
HM? IS THIS A NAGASHI SOMEN MACHINE?
HMPH.
BLUB
BLUB
THIS IS WATER FROM THE RIVER STYX, WHICH I'M FEEDING INTO IT VIA AN ILLEGAL SPIRIT WAY.
BLUB
BLUB
THEN THE WATER TRAVELS THROUGH THESE SPIRIT WAYS AND INTO THE HUMAN WORLD.
SWF
SWF
SWF
SWF

Nagashi somen are noodles that flow in water through a trough.

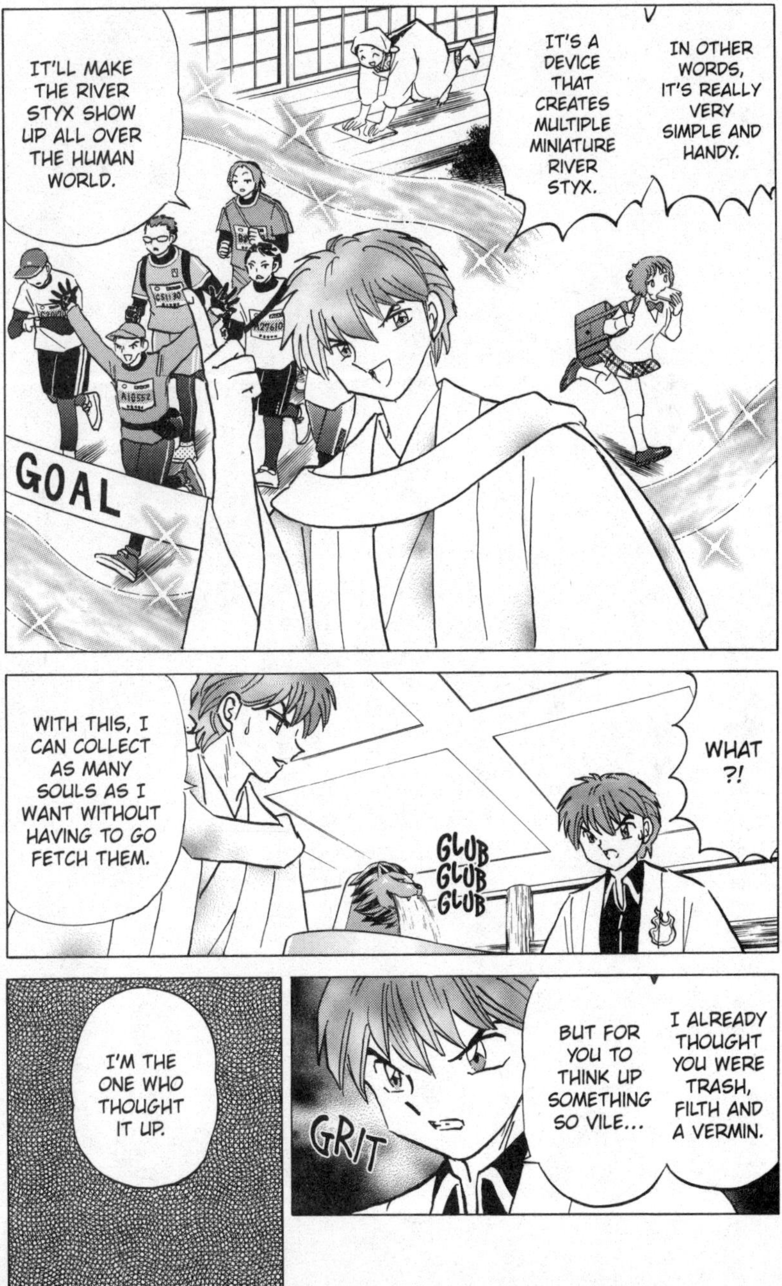
IN OTHER WORDS, IT'S REALLY VERY SIMPLE AND HANDY.
IT'S A DEVICE THAT CREATES MULTIPLE MINIATURE RIVER STYX.
IT'LL MAKE THE RIVER STYX SHOW UP ALL OVER THE HUMAN WORLD.
GOAL
WHAT?!
GLUB GLUB GLUB
WITH THIS, I CAN COLLECT AS MANY SOULS AS I WANT WITHOUT HAVING TO GO FETCH THEM.
I ALREADY THOUGHT YOU WERE TRASH, FILTH AND A VERMIN.
BUT FOR YOU TO THINK UP SOMETHING SO VILE...
GRIT
I'M THE ONE WHO THOUGHT IT UP.

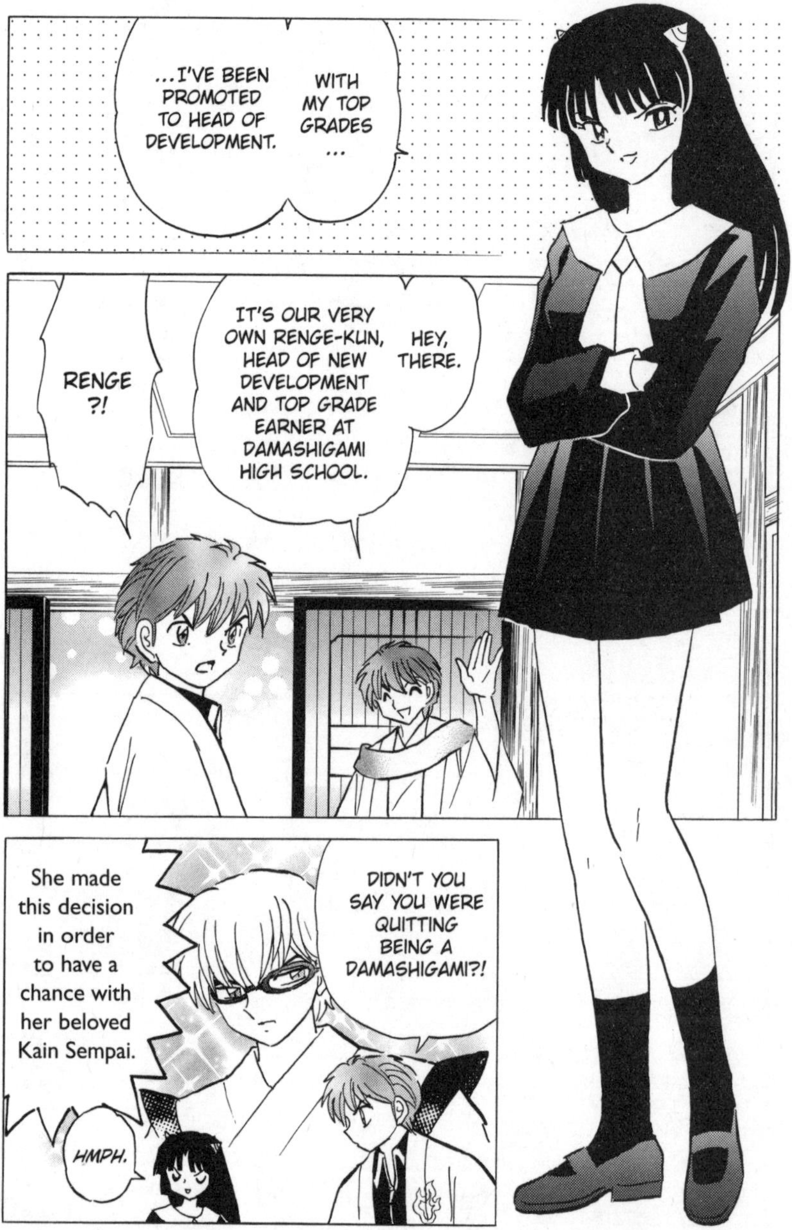
WITH MY TOP GRADES ...
...I'VE BEEN PROMOTED TO HEAD OF DEVELOPMENT.
HEY, THERE.
IT'S OUR VERY OWN RENGE-KUN, HEAD OF NEW DEVELOPMENT AND TOP GRADE EARNER AT DAMASHIGAMI HIGH SCHOOL.
RENGE ?!
DIDN'T YOU SAY YOU WERE QUITTING BEING A DAMASHIGAMI?!
She made this decision in order to have a chance with her beloved Kain Sempai.
HMPH.

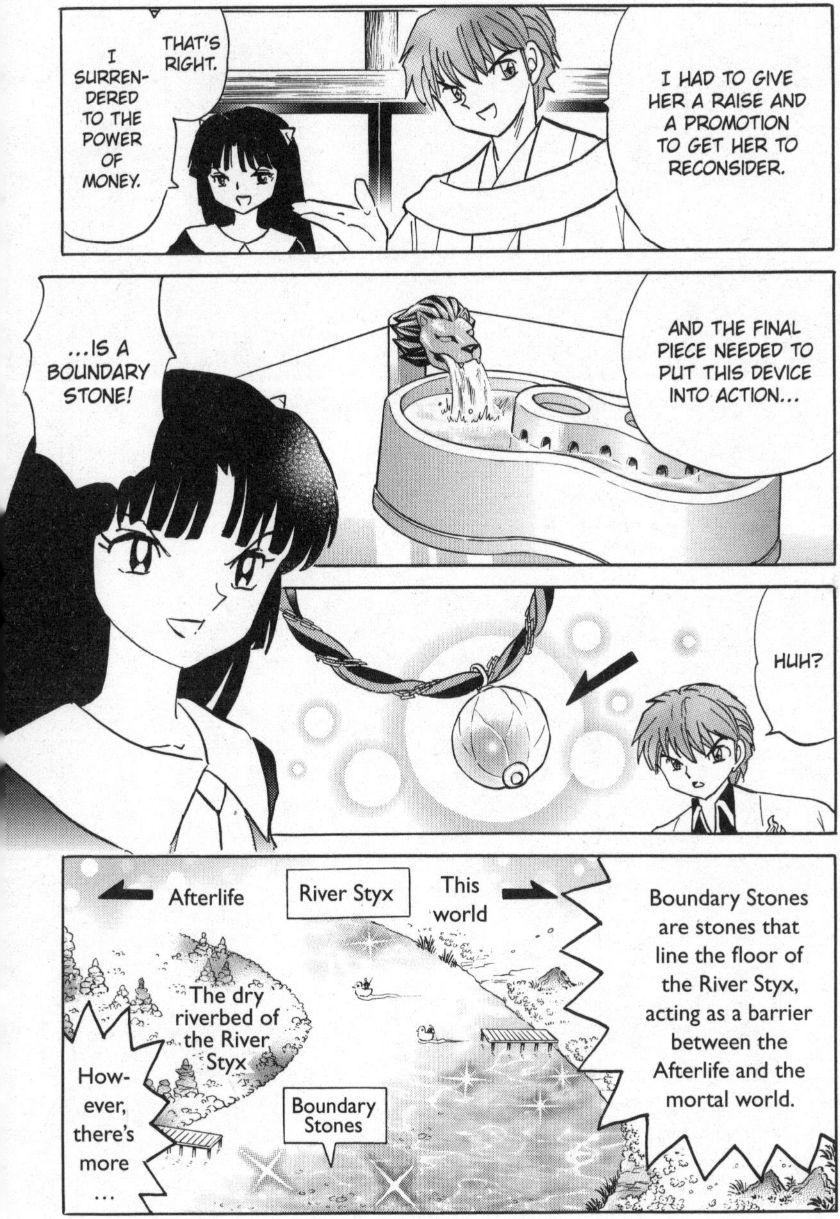
I HAD TO GIVE HER A RAISE AND A PROMOTION TO GET HER TO RECONSIDER.
THAT'S RIGHT.
I SURRENDERED TO THE POWER OF MONEY.
AND THE FINAL PIECE NEEDED TO PUT THIS DEVICE INTO ACTION...
...IS A BOUNDARY STONE!
HUH?
Boundary Stones are stones that line the floor of the River Styx, acting as a barrier between the Afterlife and the mortal world.
This world
River Styx
Afterlife
The dry riverbed of the River Styx
Boundary Stones
How-ever, there's more...

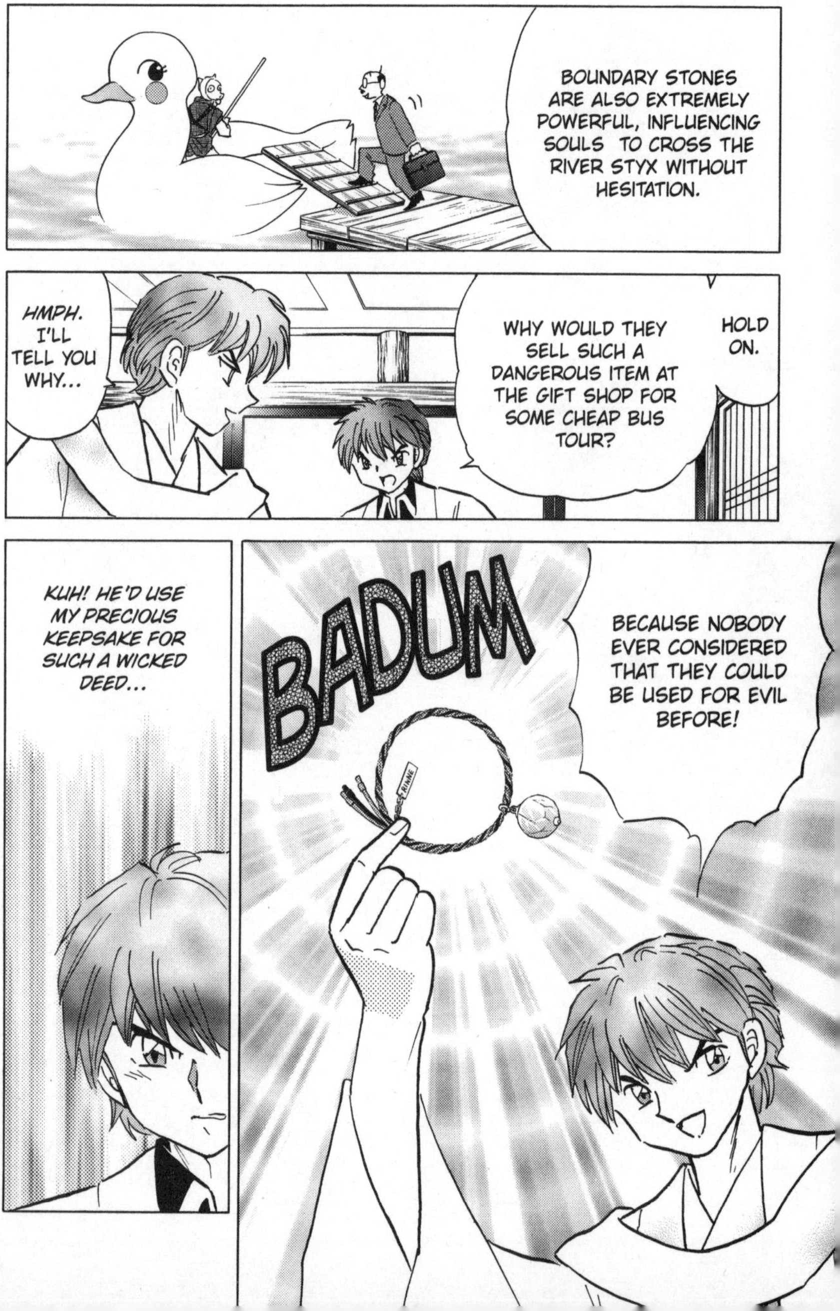
BOUNDARY STONES ARE ALSO EXTREMELY POWERFUL, INFLUENCING SOULS TO CROSS THE RIVER STYX WITHOUT HESITATION.
HOLD ON.
WHY WOULD THEY SELL SUCH A DANGEROUS ITEM AT THE GIFT SHOP FOR SOME CHEAP BUS TOUR?
HMPH. I'LL TELL YOU WHY...
BECAUSE NOBODY EVER CONSIDERED THAT THEY COULD BE USED FOR EVIL BEFORE!
BADUM
RINNE
KUH! HE'D USE MY PRECIOUS KEEPSAKE FOR SUCH A WICKED DEED...

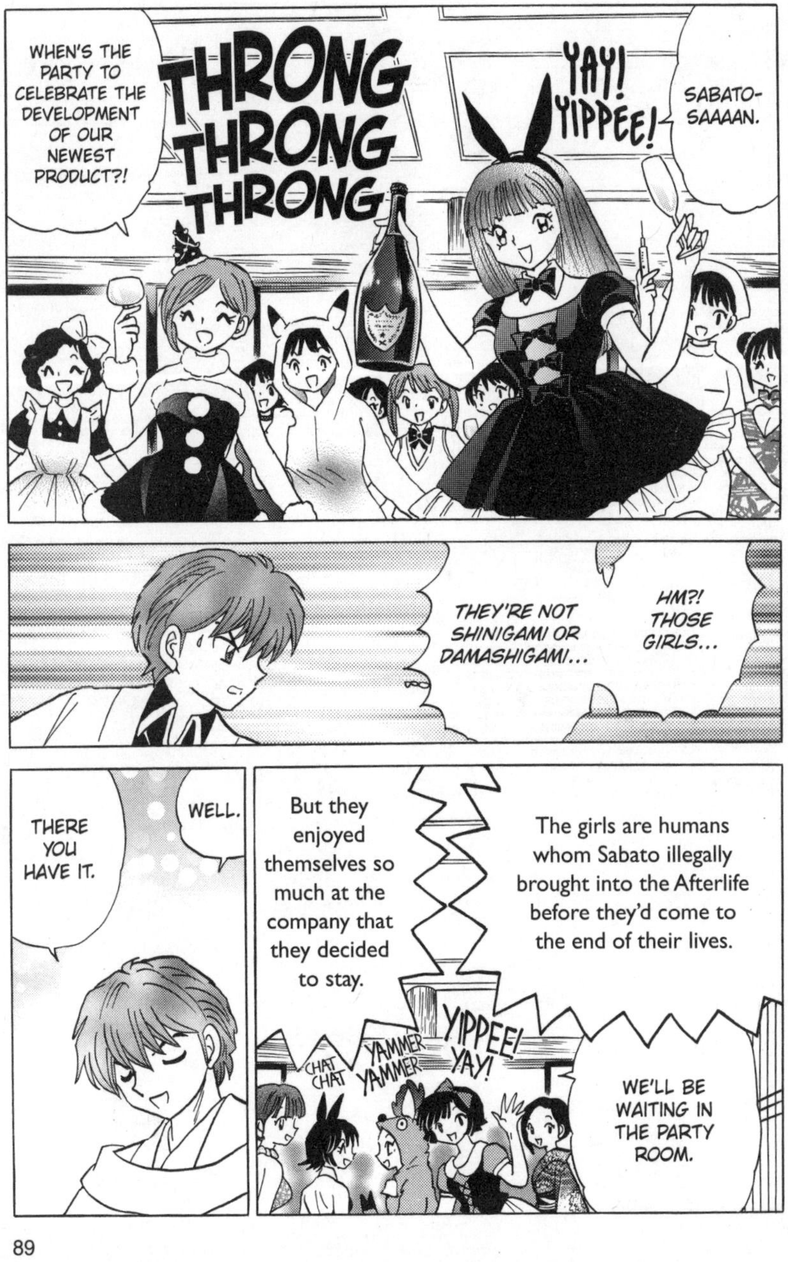
SABATO-SAAAAN.
YAY! YIPPEE!
THRONG THRONG THRONG
WHEN'S THE PARTY TO CELEBRATE THE DEVELOPMENT OF OUR NEWEST PRODUCT?!
HM?! THOSE GIRLS...
THEY'RE NOT SHINIGAMI OR DAMASHIGAMI...
The girls are humans whom Sabato illegally brought into the Afterlife before they'd come to the end of their lives.
But they enjoyed themselves so much at the company that they decided to stay.
YIPPEE! YAY!
YAMMER YAMMER
CHAT CHAT
WE'LL BE WAITING IN THE PARTY ROOM.
WELL.
THERE YOU HAVE IT.

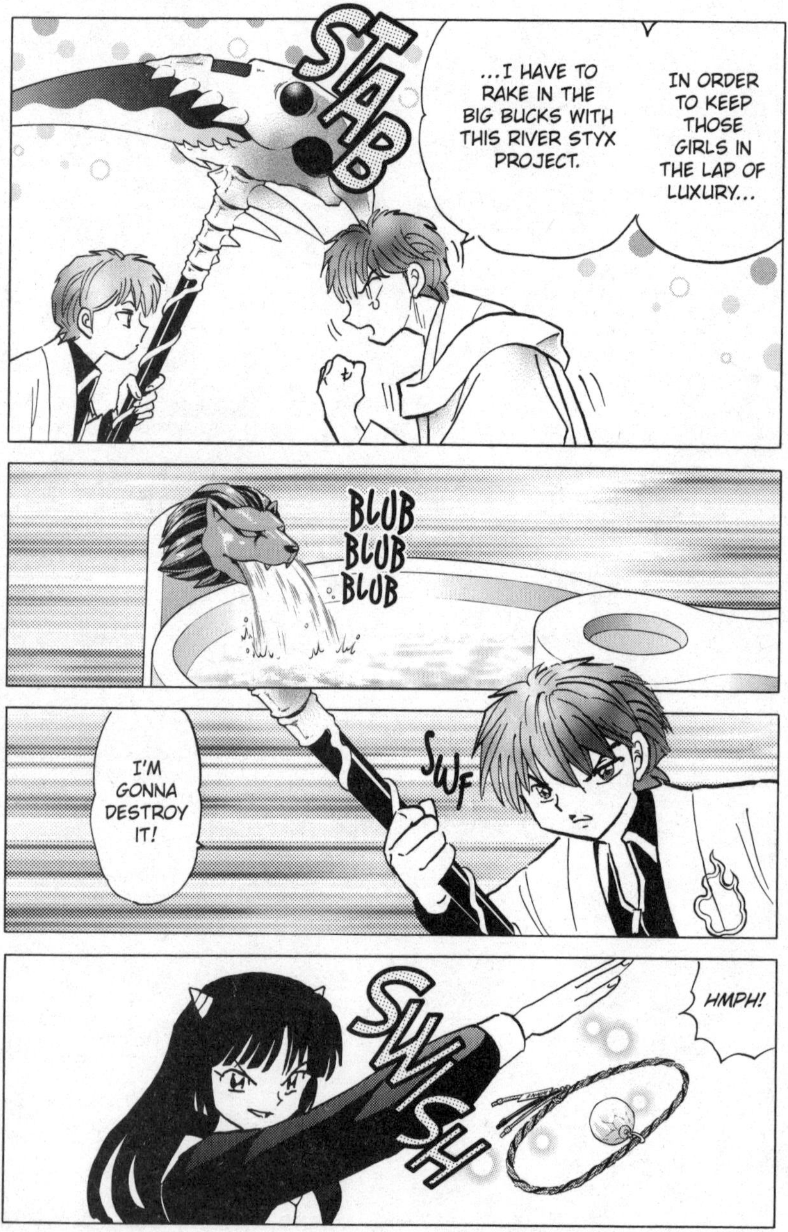
IN ORDER TO KEEP THOSE GIRLS IN THE LAP OF LUXURY...
...I HAVE TO RAKE IN THE BIG BUCKS WITH THIS RIVER STYX PROJECT.
STAB
BLUB BLUB BLUB
SWF
I'M GONNA DESTROY IT!
HMPH!
SWISH

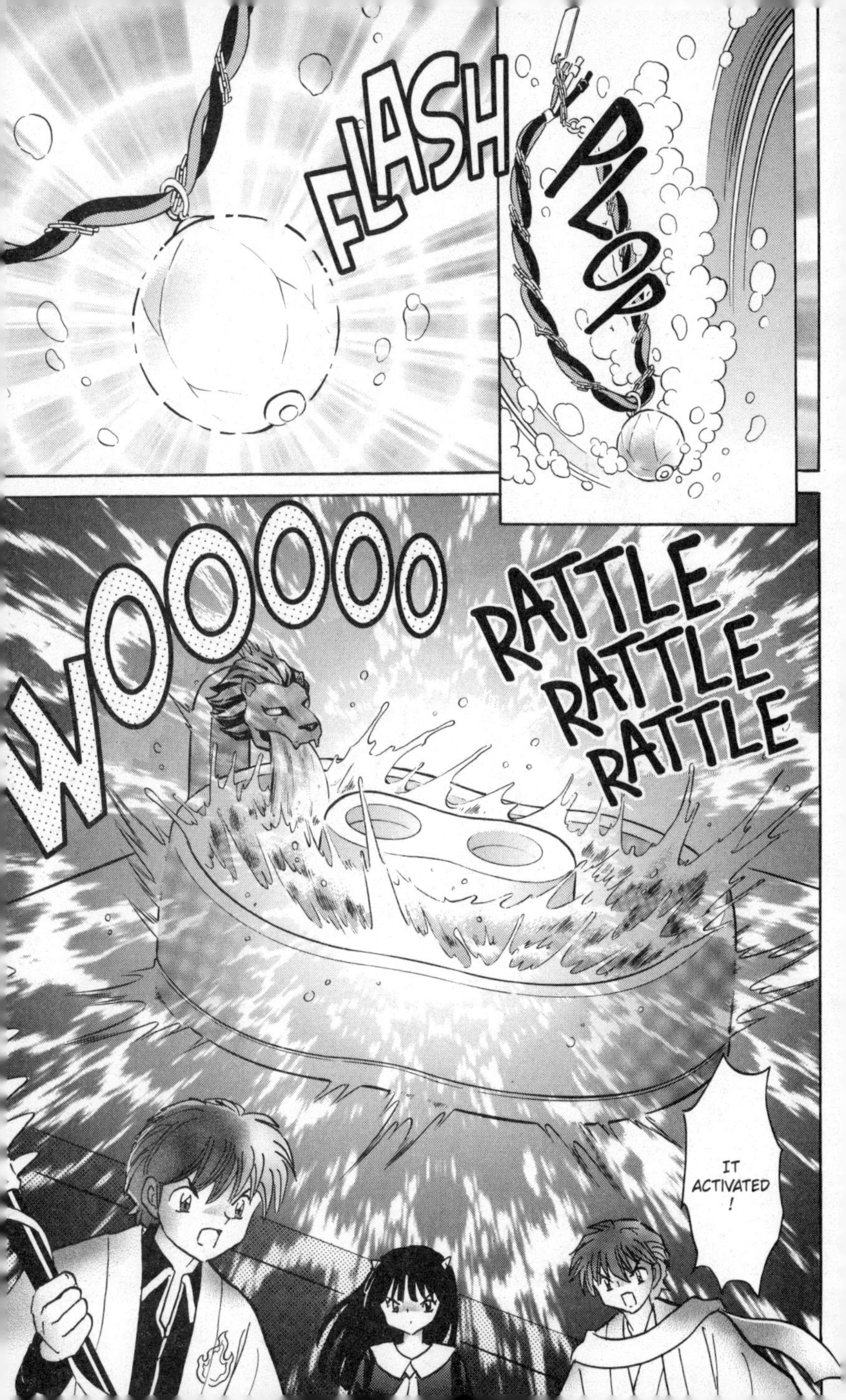
PLOP
FLASH
WOOOOOO
RATTLE RATTLE RATTLE
IT ACTIVATED!

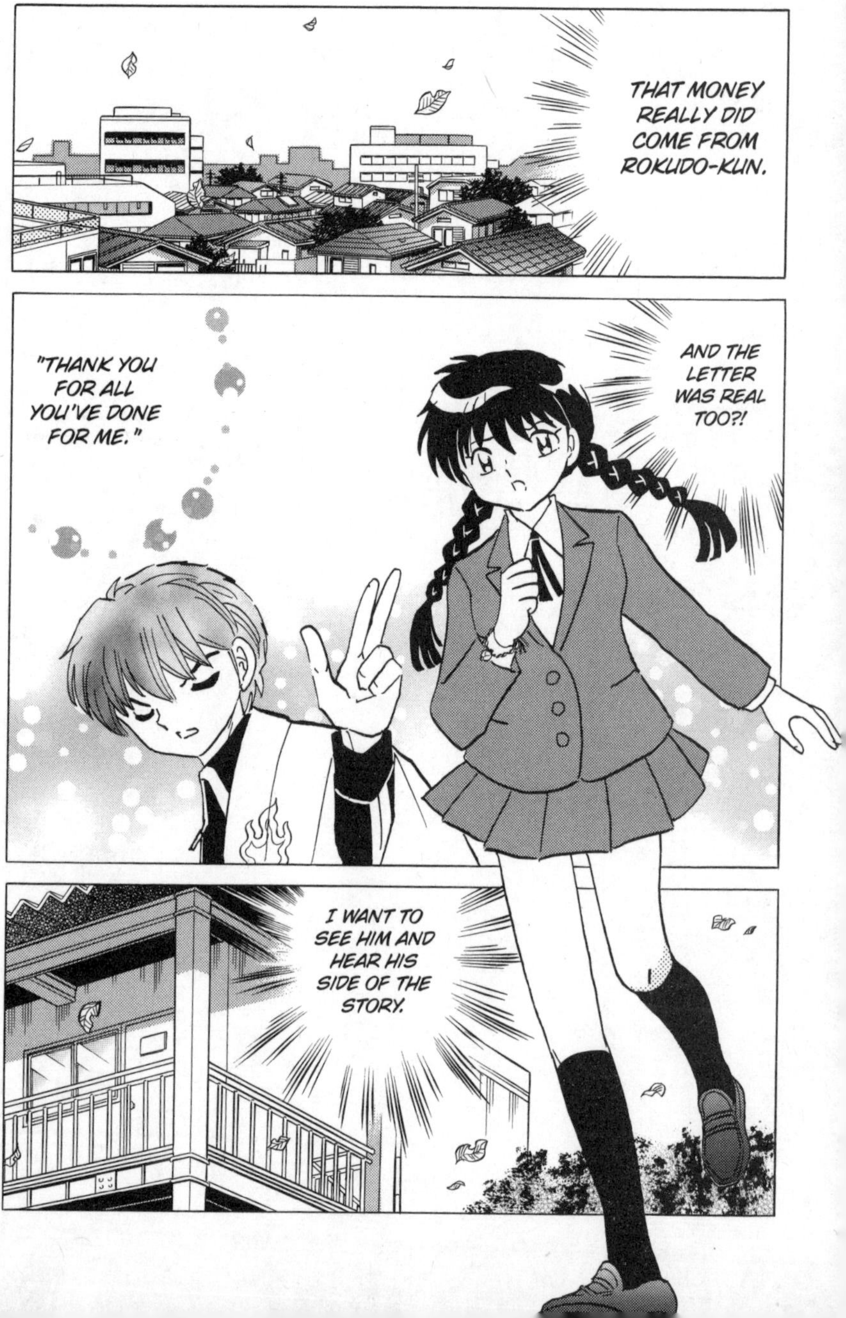
THAT MONEY REALLY DID COME FROM ROKUDO-KUN.
AND THE LETTER WAS REAL TOO?!
"THANK YOU FOR ALL YOU'VE DONE FOR ME."
I WANT TO SEE HIM AND HEAR HIS SIDE OF THE STORY.

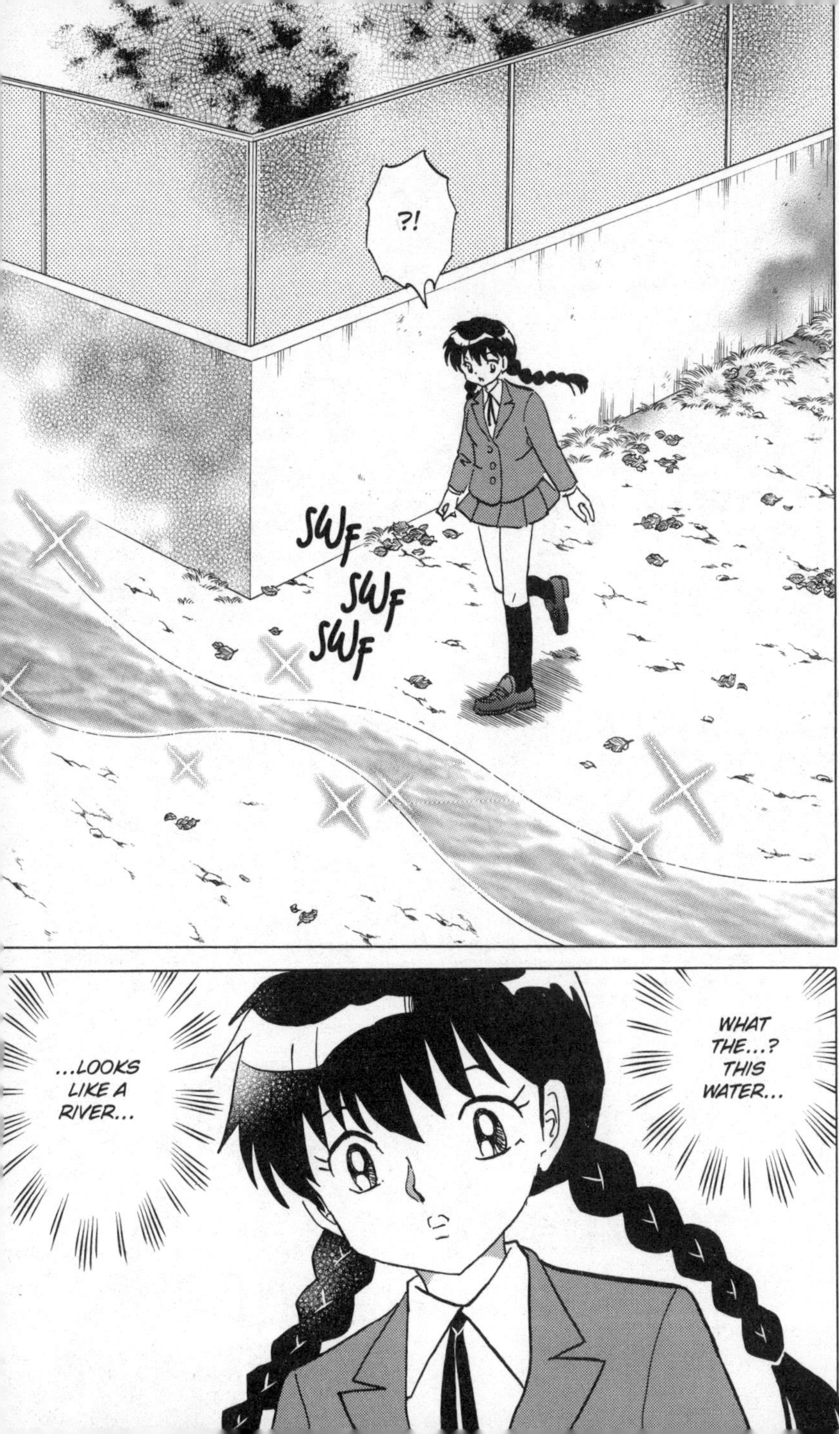
?!
SWF SWF SWF
WHAT THE…? THIS WATER…
…LOOKS LIKE A RIVER…

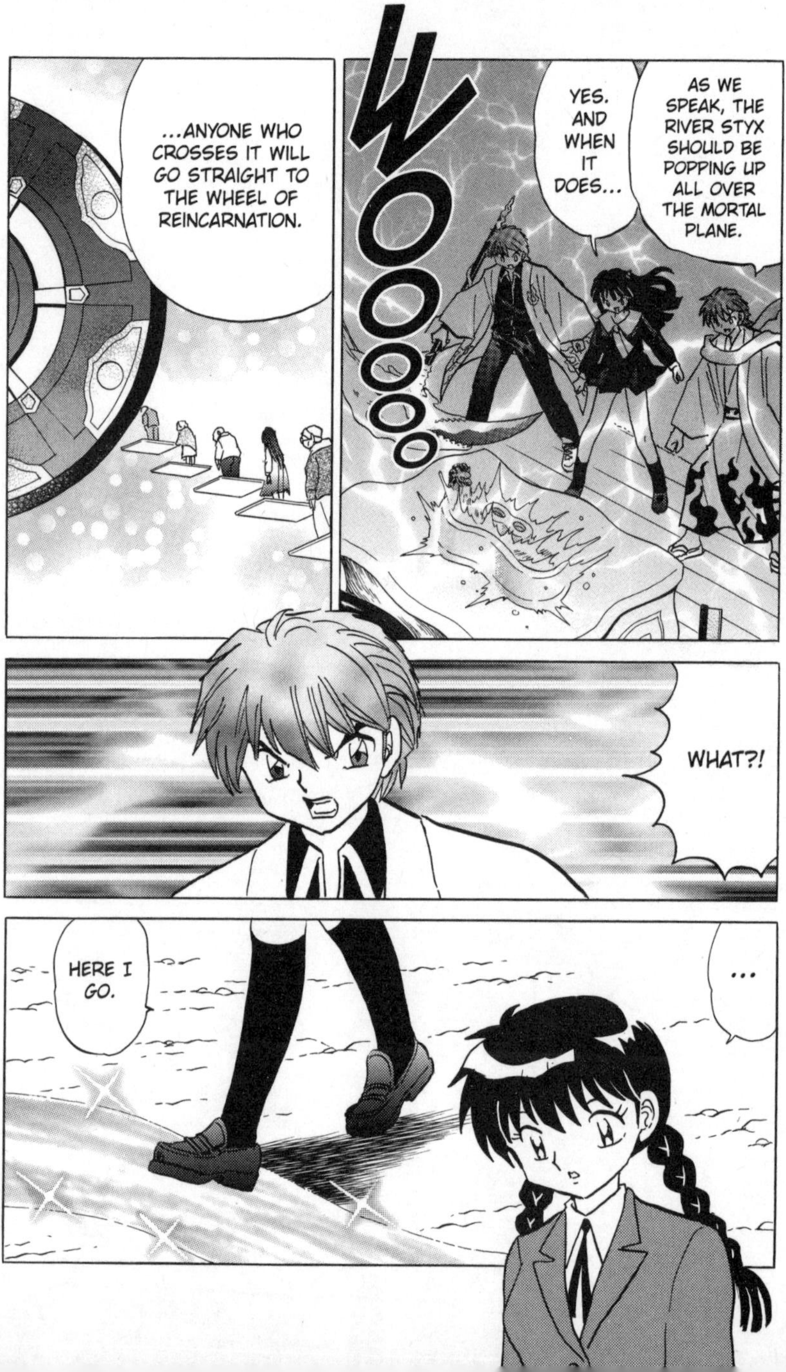
WOOOOOOO
AS WE SPEAK, THE RIVER STYX SHOULD BE POPPING UP ALL OVER THE MORTAL PLANE.
YES. AND WHEN IT DOES...
...ANYONE WHO CROSSES IT WILL GO STRAIGHT TO THE WHEEL OF REINCARNATION.
WHAT?!
...
HERE I GO.

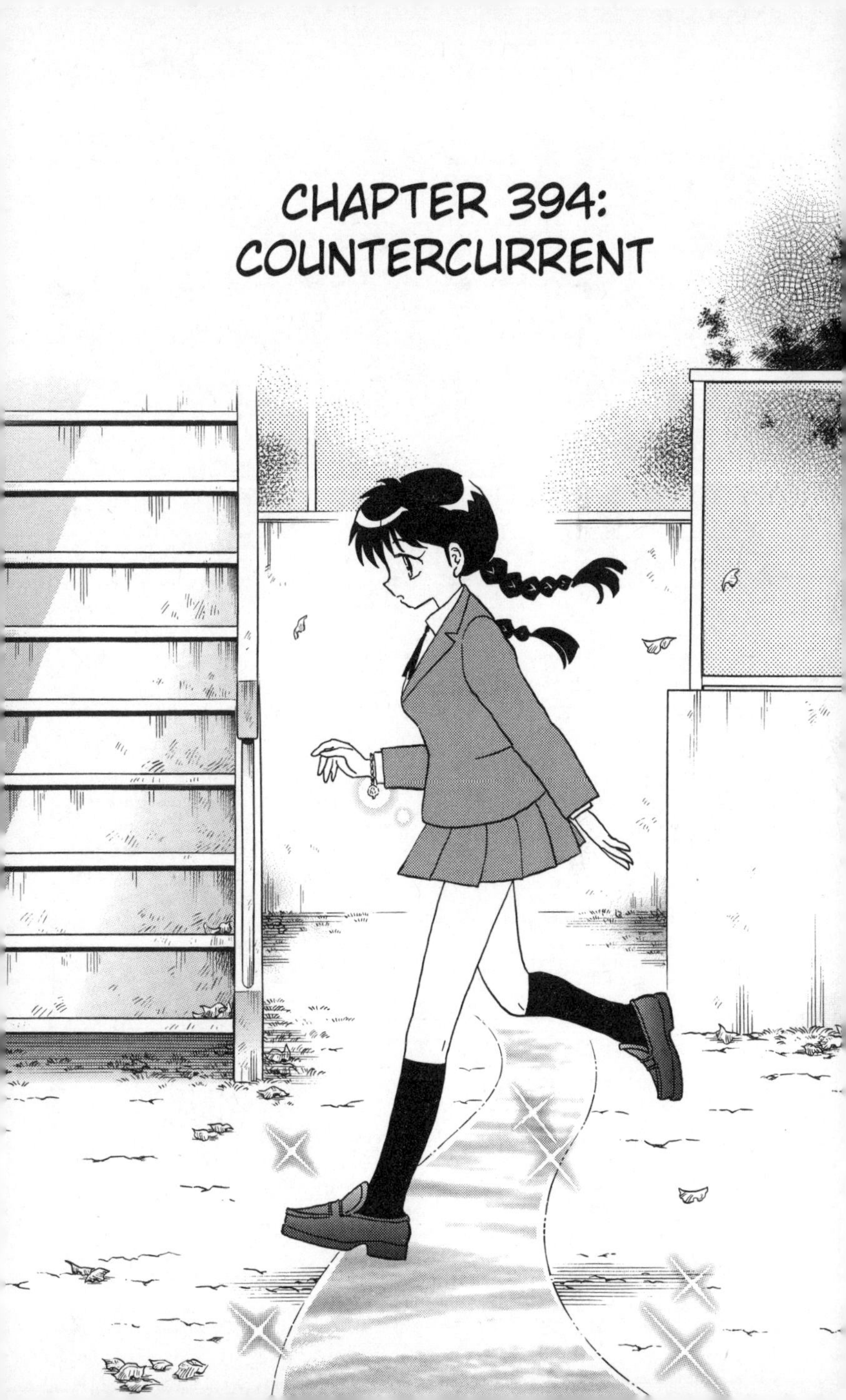
CHAPTER 394:
COUNTERCURRENT

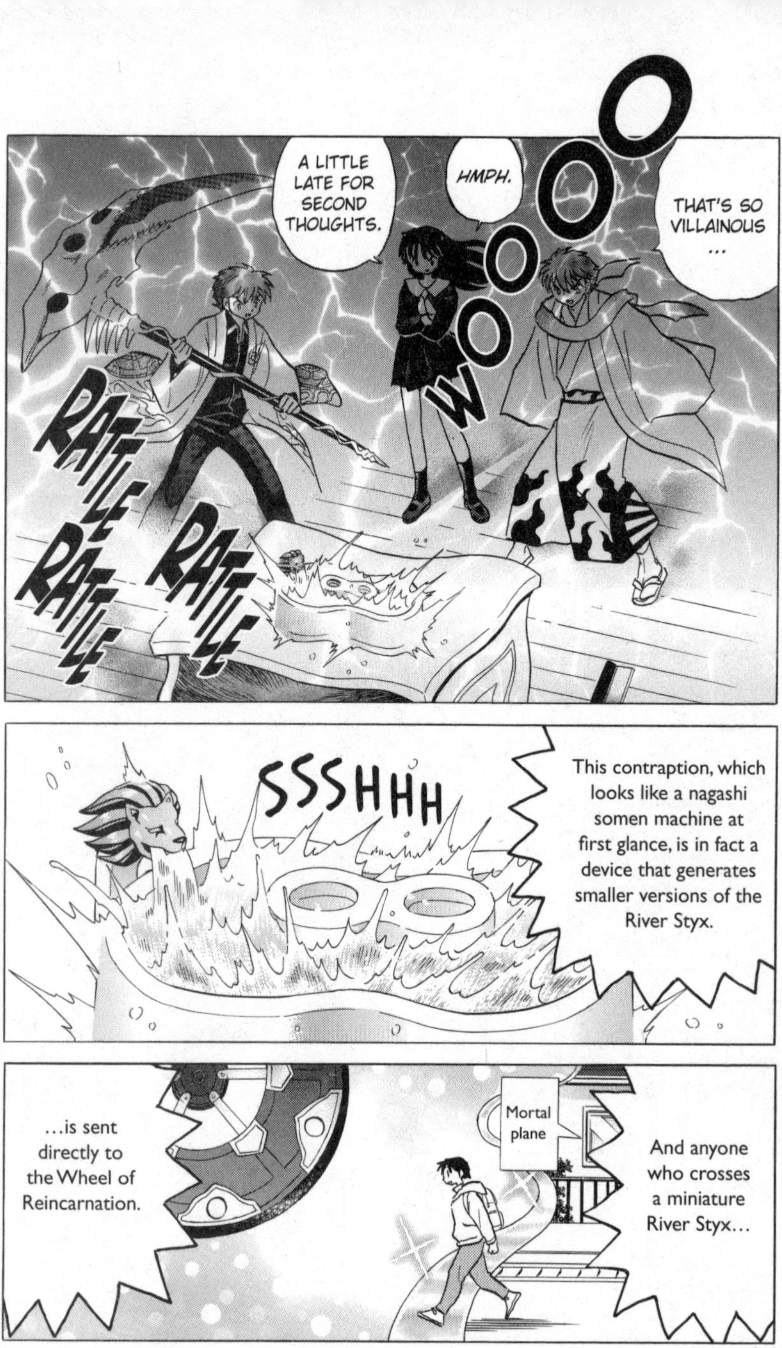
THAT'S SO VILLAINOUS ...
WOOOOOO
HMPH.
A LITTLE LATE FOR SECOND THOUGHTS.
RATTLE
RATTLE
RATTLE
This contraption, which looks like a nagashi somen machine at first glance, is in fact a device that generates smaller versions of the River Styx.
SSSHHH
And anyone who crosses a miniature River Styx…
Mortal plane
…is sent directly to the Wheel of Reincarnation.

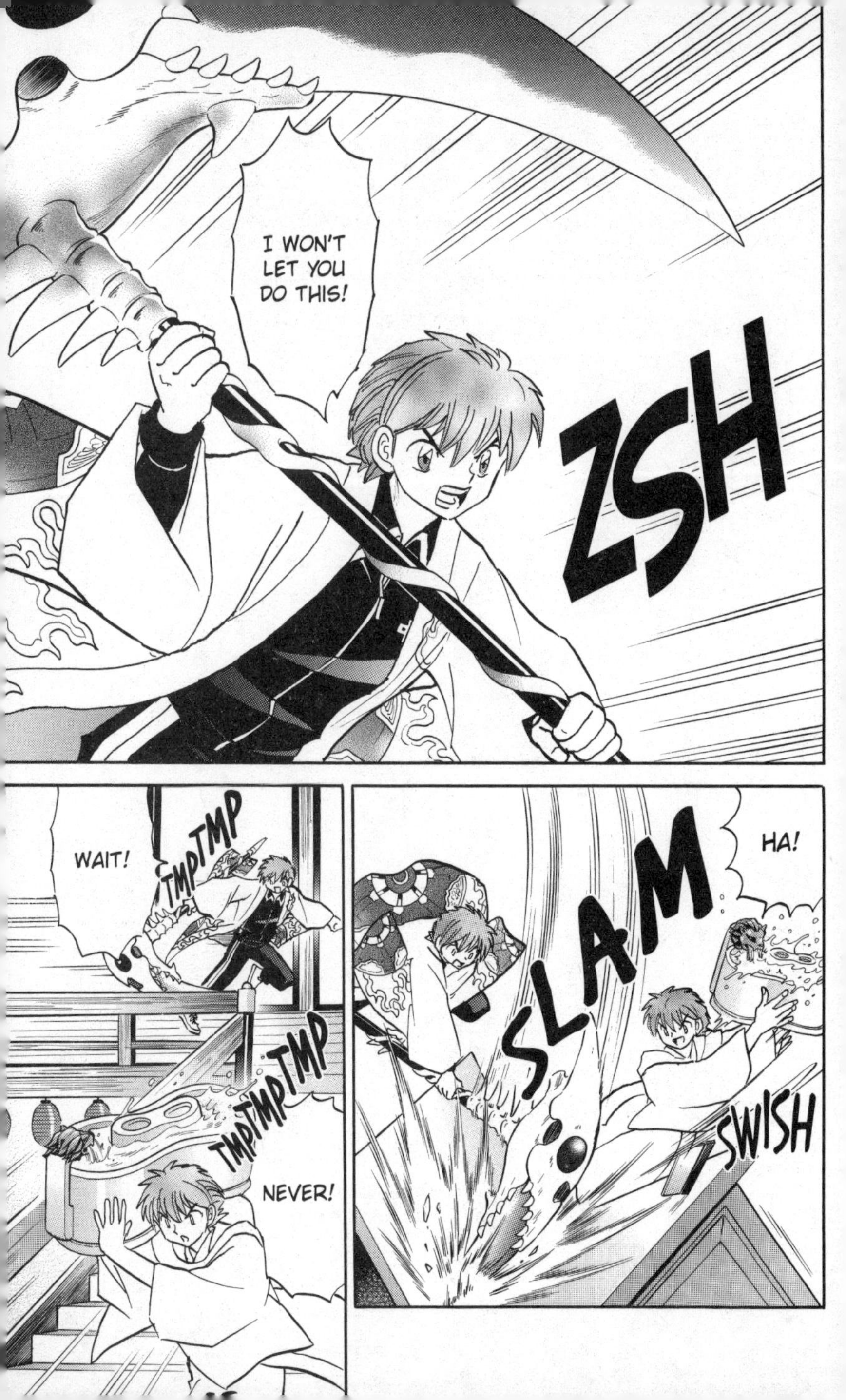
I WON'T LET YOU DO THIS!
ZSH
HA!
SLAM
SWISH
TMPTMP
WAIT!
TMPTMPTMP
NEVER!

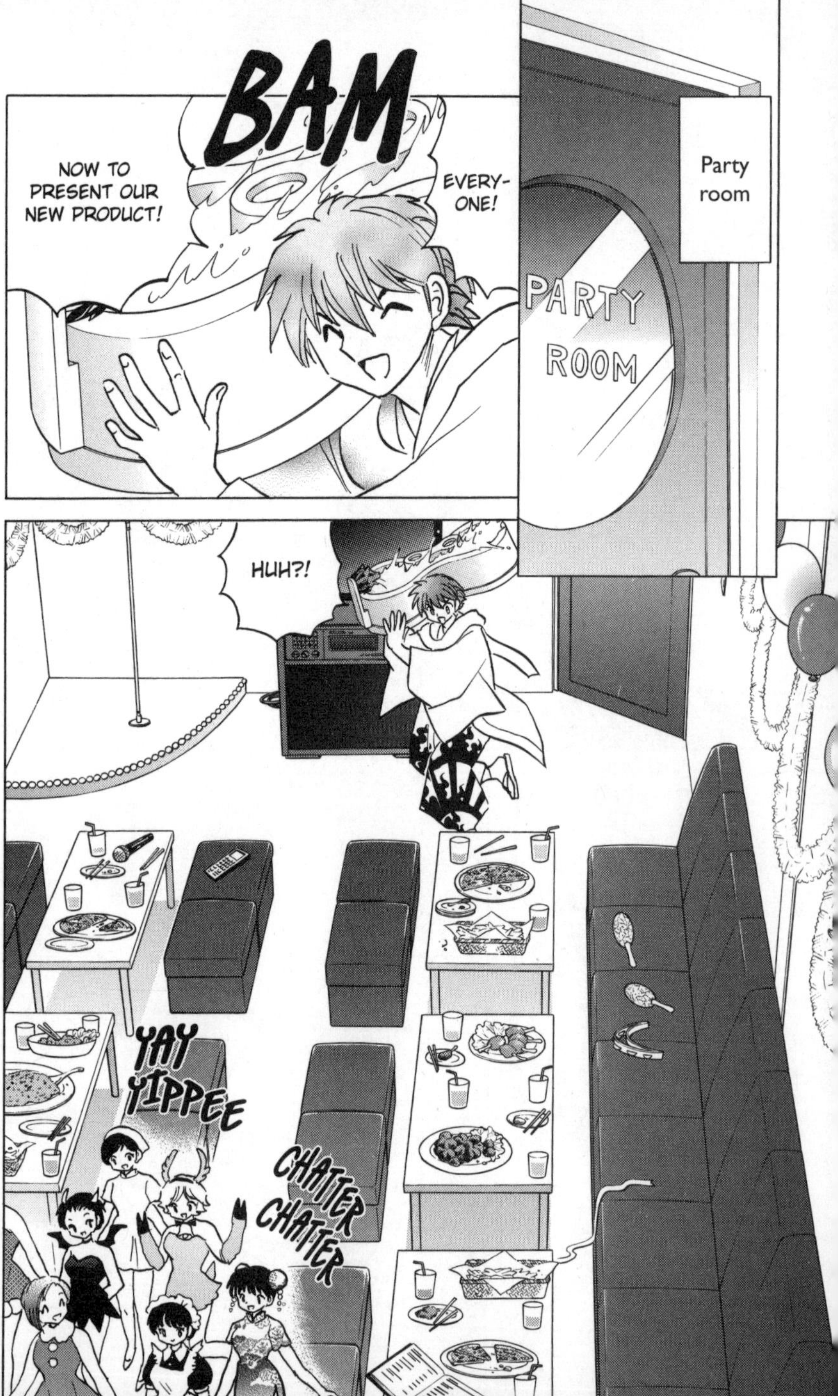
Party room
PARTY ROOM
BAM
EVERY-ONE!
NOW TO PRESENT OUR NEW PRODUCT!
HUH?!
YAY YIPPEE
CHATTER CHATTER

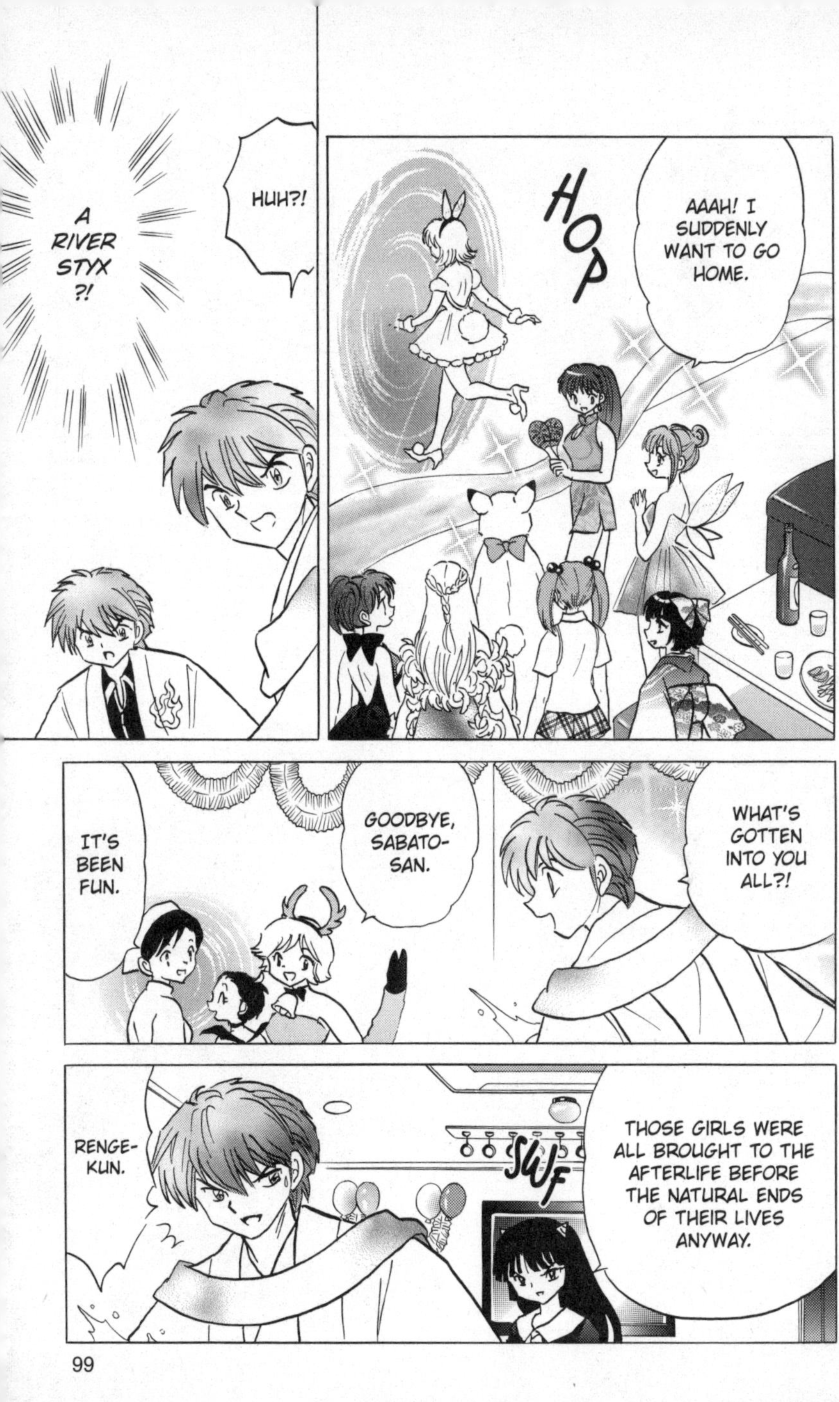
AAAH! I SUDDENLY WANT TO GO HOME.
HOP
HUH?!
A RIVER STYX ?!
WHAT'S GOTTEN INTO YOU ALL?!
GOODBYE, SABATO-SAN.
IT'S BEEN FUN.
THOSE GIRLS WERE ALL BROUGHT TO THE AFTERLIFE BEFORE THE NATURAL ENDS OF THEIR LIVES ANYWAY.
SWF
RENGE-KUN.

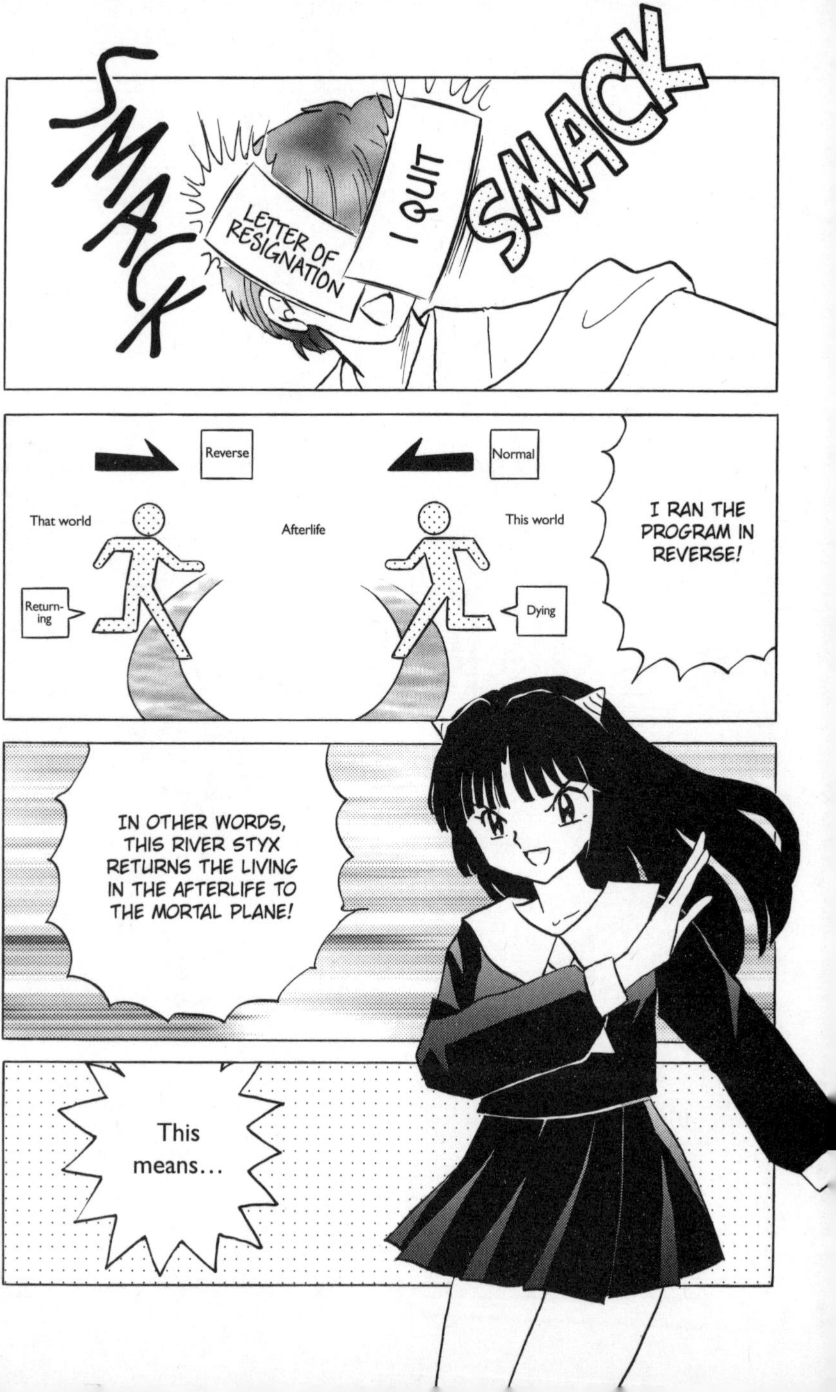
SMACK
I QUIT
LETTER OF RESIGNATION
SMACK
I RAN THE PROGRAM IN REVERSE!
Normal
Reverse
This world
Afterlife
That world
Dying
Return-ing
IN OTHER WORDS, THIS RIVER STYX RETURNS THE LIVING IN THE AFTERLIFE TO THE MORTAL PLANE!
This means…

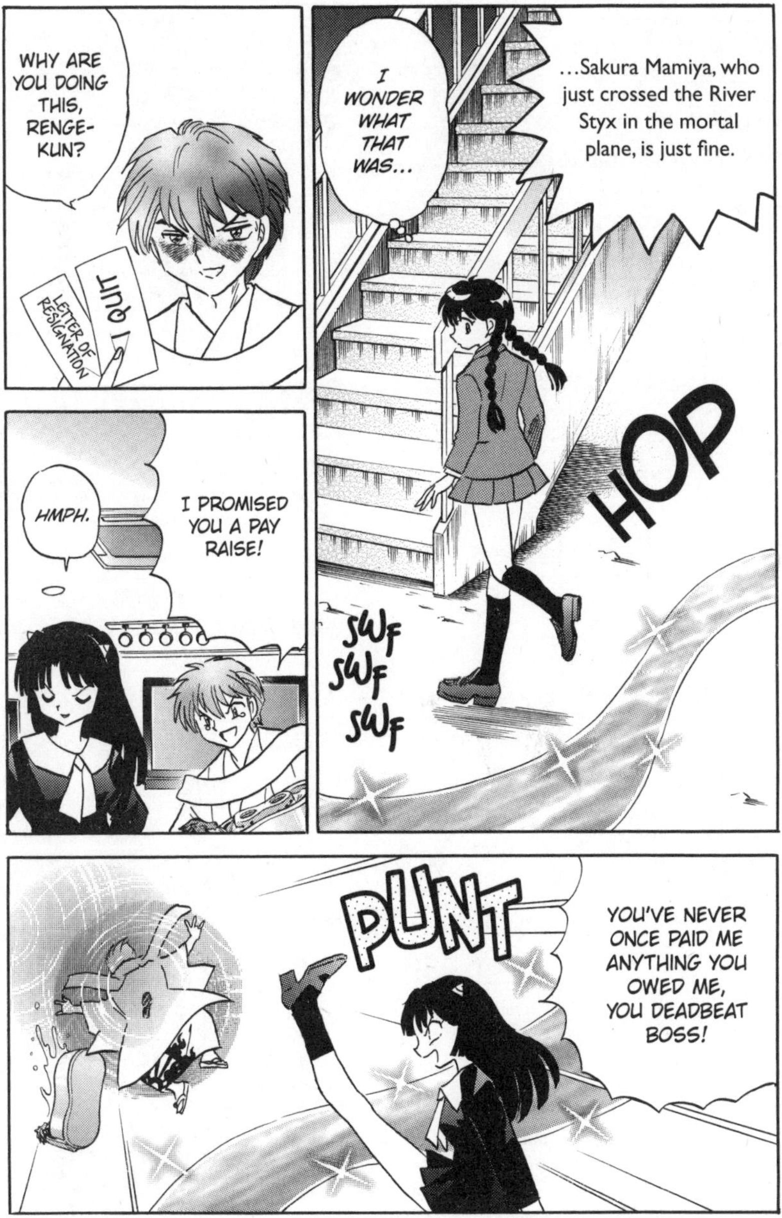
...Sakura Mamiya, who just crossed the River Styx in the mortal plane, is just fine.
I WONDER WHAT THAT WAS...
HOP
SWF SWF SWF
WHY ARE YOU DOING THIS, RENGE-KUN?
I QUIT
LETTER OF RESIGNATION
I PROMISED YOU A PAY RAISE!
HMPH.
YOU'VE NEVER ONCE PAID ME ANYTHING YOU OWED ME, YOU DEADBEAT BOSS!
PUNT

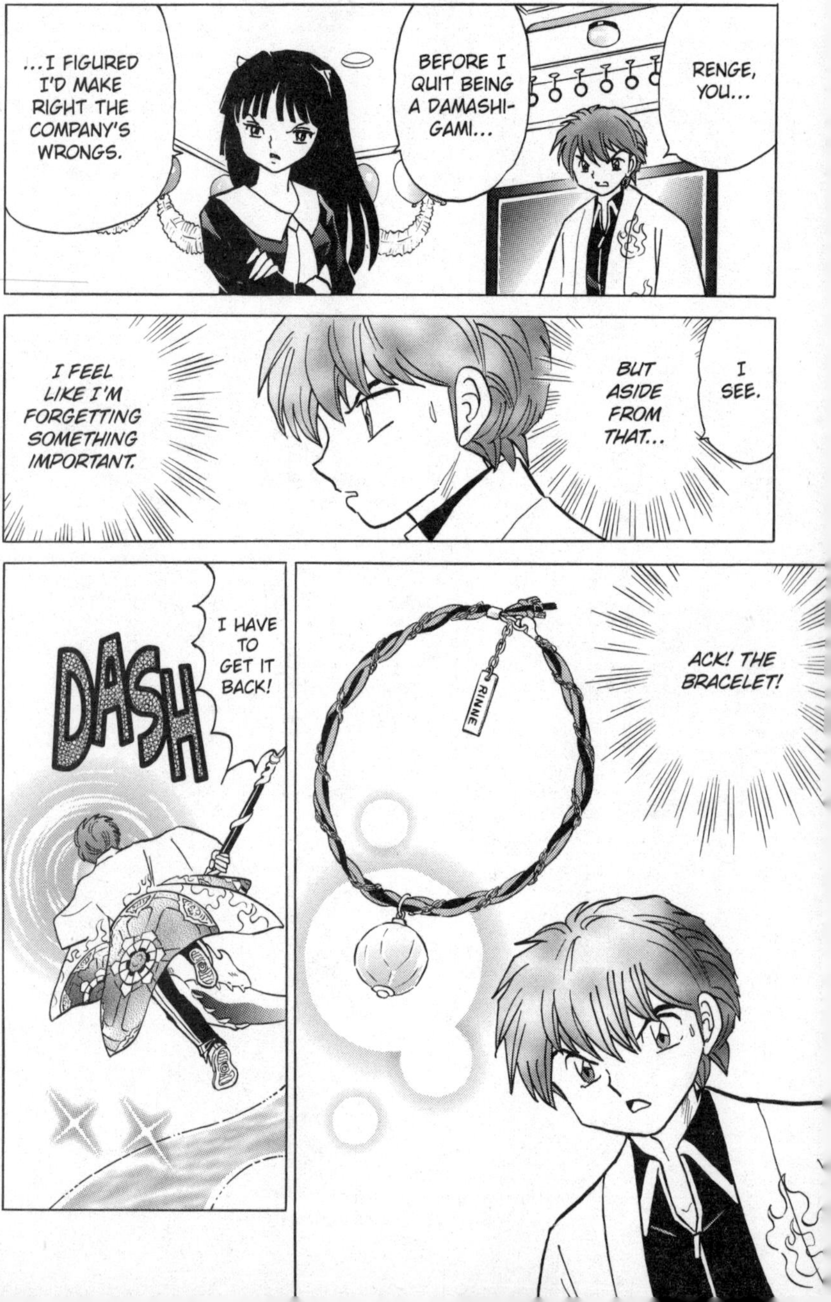

RENGE, YOU...
BEFORE I QUIT BEING A DAMASHI-GAMI...
...I FIGURED I'D MAKE RIGHT THE COMPANY'S WRONGS.
I SEE.
BUT ASIDE FROM THAT...
I FEEL LIKE I'M FORGETTING SOMETHING IMPORTANT.
ACK! THE BRACELET!
RINNE
I HAVE TO GET IT BACK!
DASH

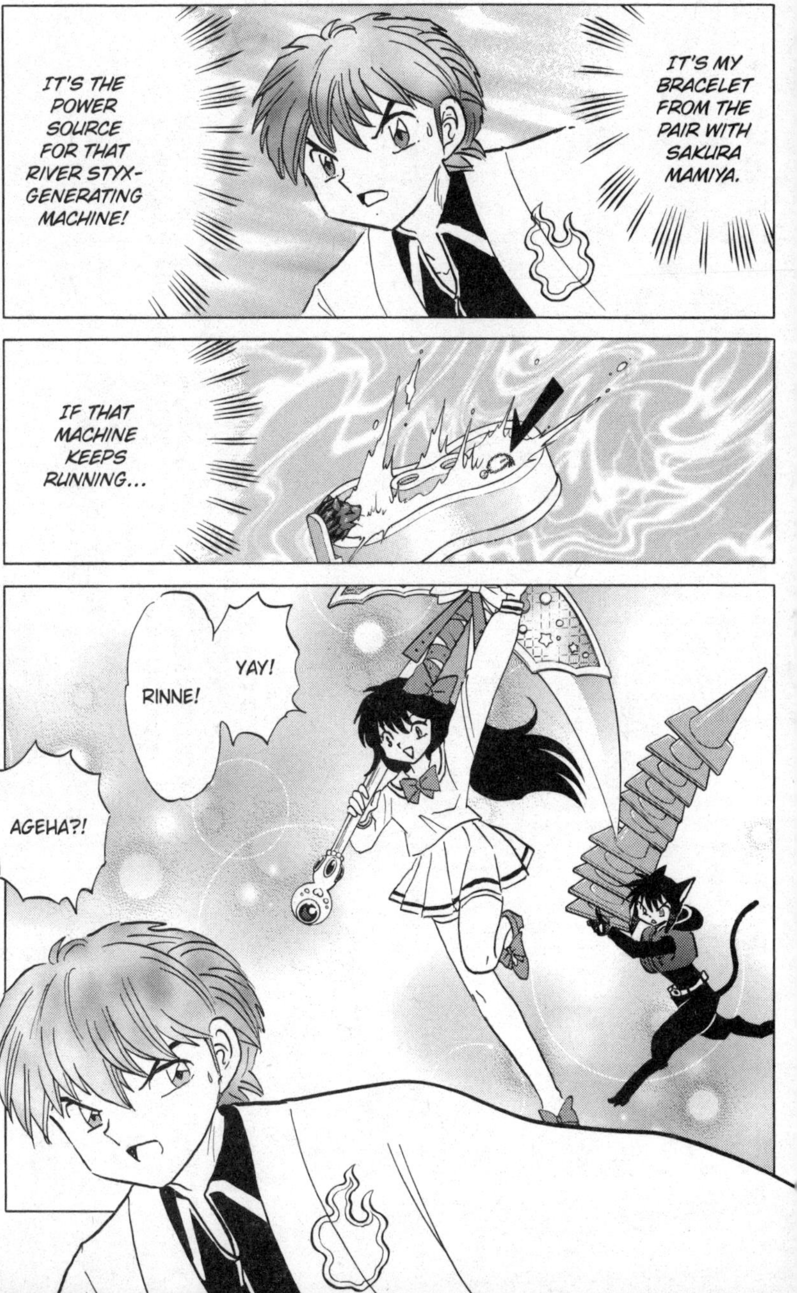
IT'S MY BRACELET FROM THE PAIR WITH SAKURA MAMIYA.
IT'S THE POWER SOURCE FOR THAT RIVER STYX-GENERATING MACHINE!
IF THAT MACHINE KEEPS RUNNING...
YAY!
RINNE!
AGEHA?!

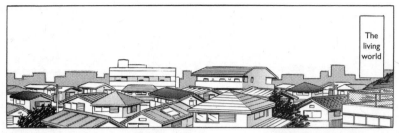

The living world

HM?

CROWD CROWD

WAHOO!

SPIRITS ?!

KOFF KOFF KOFF!

POOF

DIVINE ASHES!

IT SEEMS THE SPIRITS OF THE DEAD ARE FLOWING BACK INTO THE MORTAL PLANE.

THE ENTIRE SHINIGAMI BOYS' CLUB HAS BEEN SENT TO STOP THEM.

I KNEW IT.

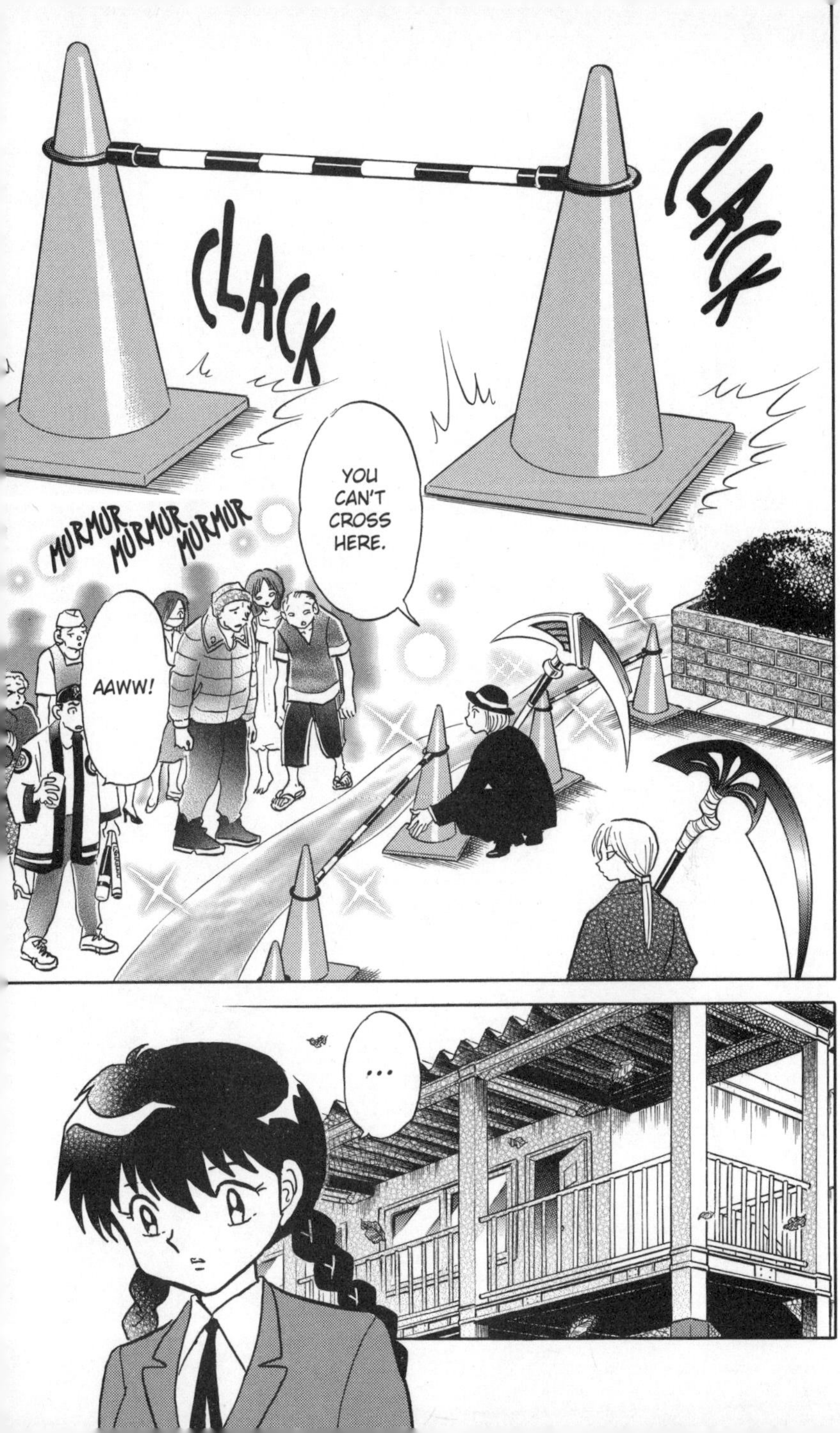
CLACK
CLACK
YOU CAN'T CROSS HERE.
MURMUR MURMUR MURMUR
AAWW!
...

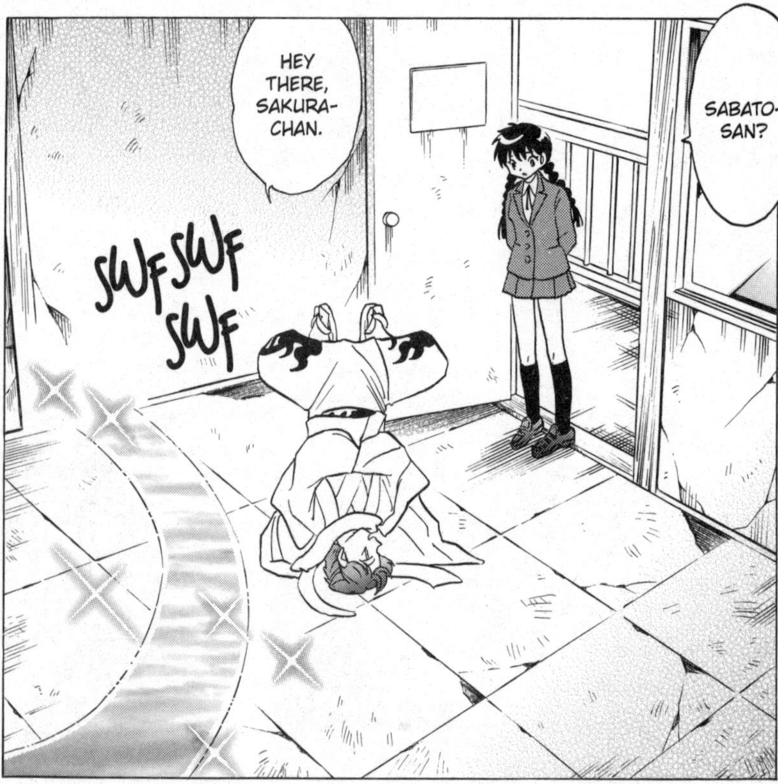
SABATO-SAN?
HEY THERE, SAKURA-CHAN.
SWF SWF SWF

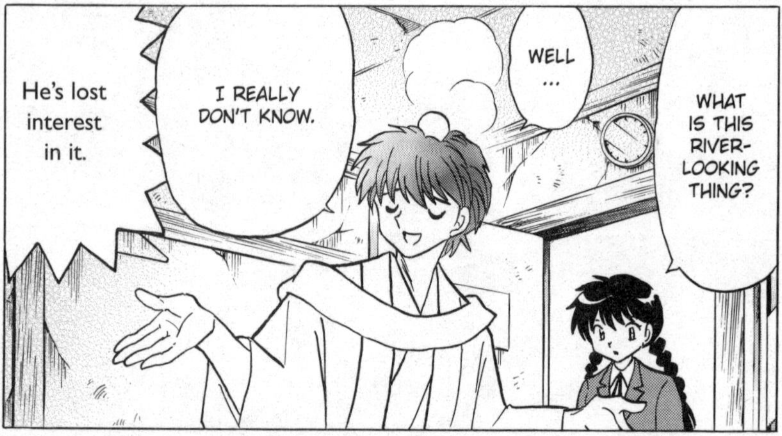
WHAT IS THIS RIVER-LOOKING THING?
WELL ...
I REALLY DON'T KNOW.
He's lost interest in it.

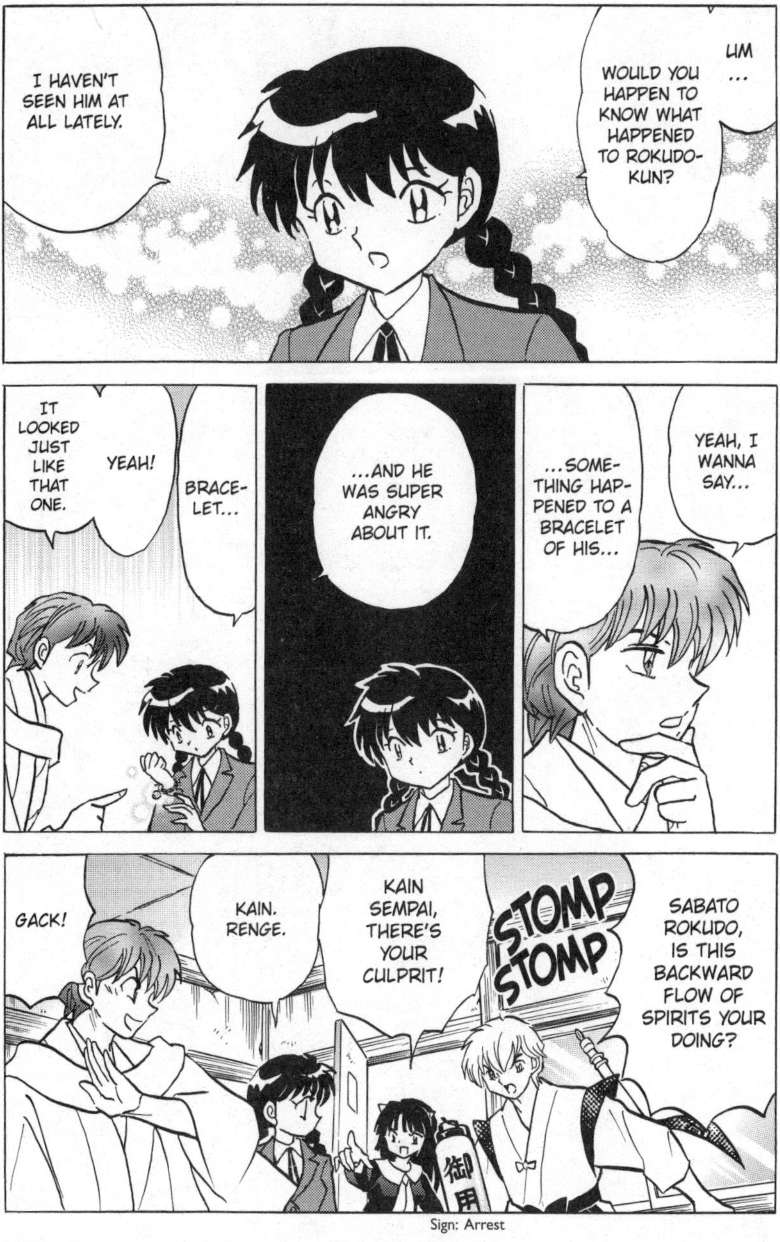
UM ...
WOULD YOU HAPPEN TO KNOW WHAT HAPPENED TO ROKUDO-KUN?
I HAVEN'T SEEN HIM AT ALL LATELY.
YEAH, I WANNA SAY...
...SOMETHING HAPPENED TO A BRACELET OF HIS...
...AND HE WAS SUPER ANGRY ABOUT IT.
BRACELET...
YEAH!
IT LOOKED JUST LIKE THAT ONE.
SABATO ROKUDO, IS THIS BACKWARD FLOW OF SPIRITS YOUR DOING?
STOMP
STOMP
KAIN SEMPAI, THERE'S YOUR CULPRIT!
KAIN. RENGE.
GACK!
御用
Sign: Arrest

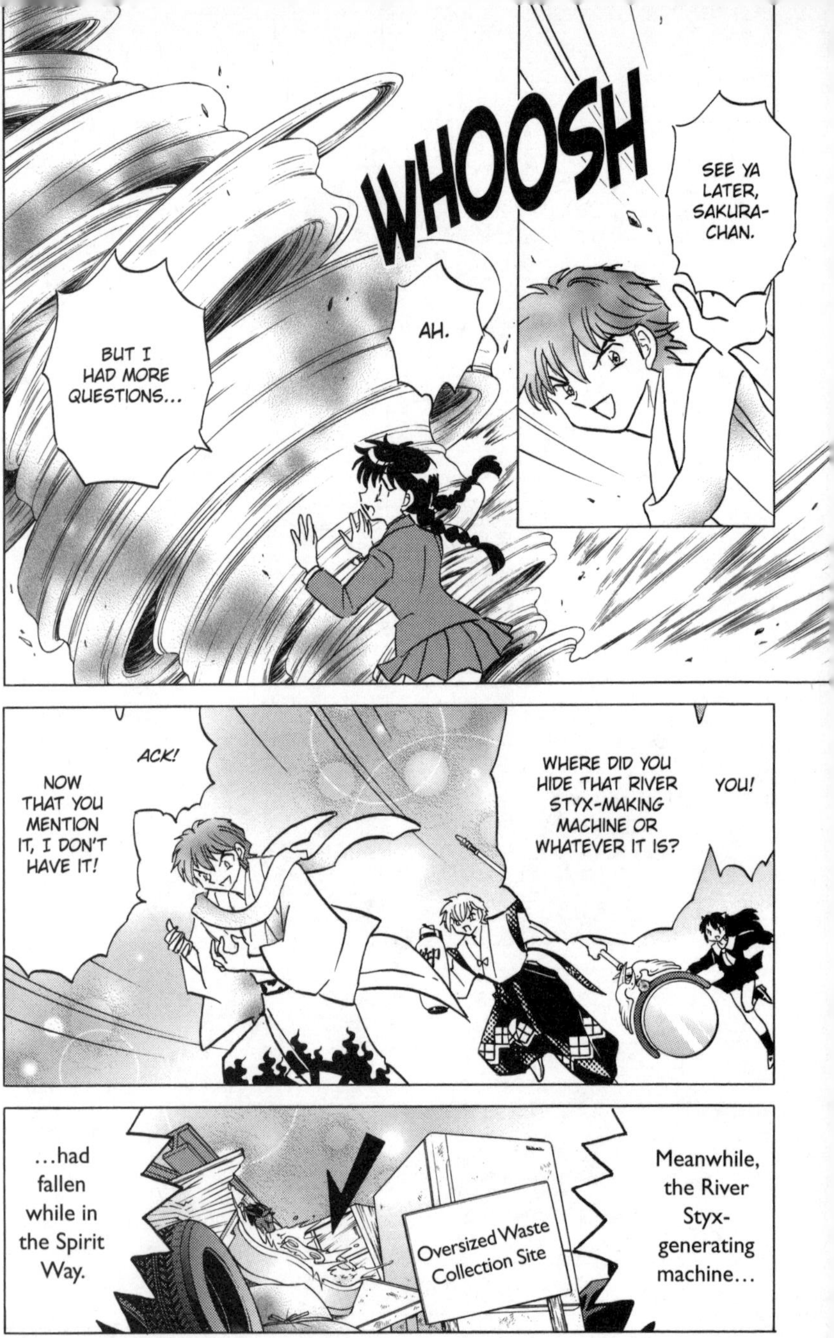
SEE YA LATER, SAKURA-CHAN.
WHOOSH
AH.
BUT I HAD MORE QUESTIONS...
YOU!
WHERE DID YOU HIDE THAT RIVER STYX-MAKING MACHINE OR WHATEVER IT IS?
ACK!
NOW THAT YOU MENTION IT, I DON'T HAVE IT!
Meanwhile, the River Styx-generating machine…
Oversized Waste Collection Site
…had fallen while in the Spirit Way.

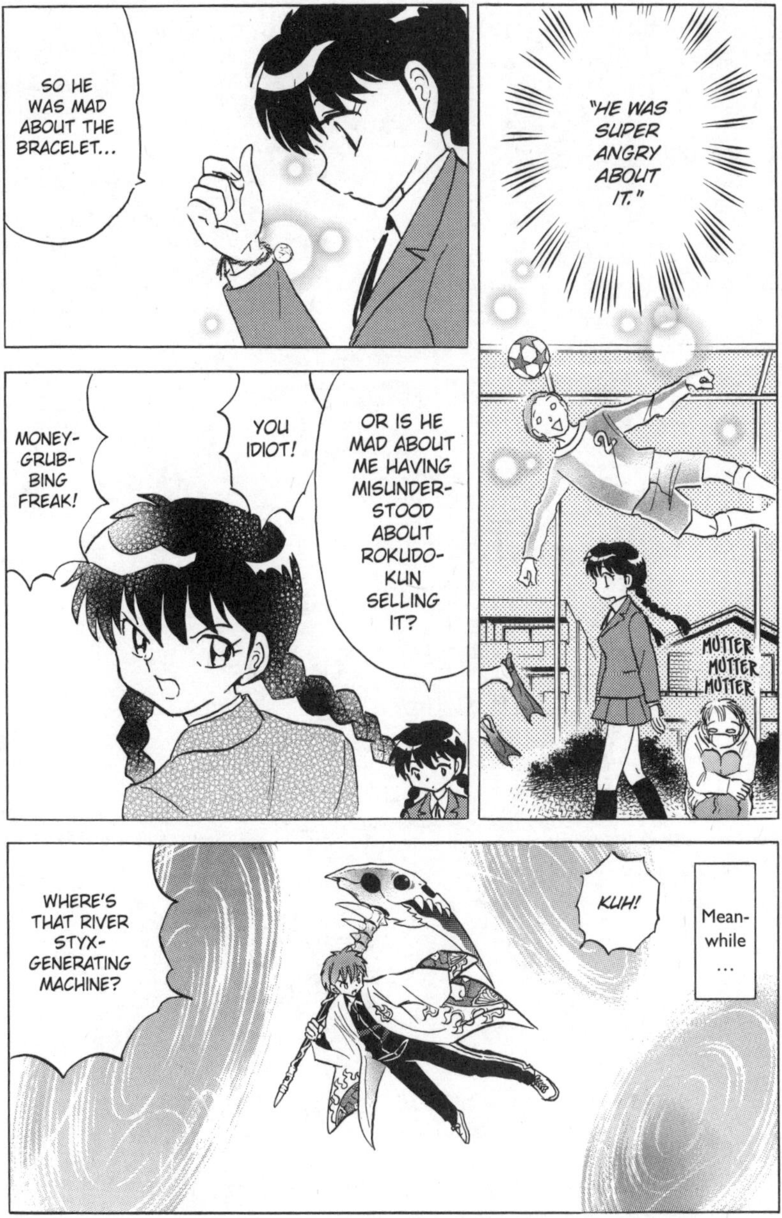

"HE WAS SUPER ANGRY ABOUT IT."
MUTTER MUTTER MUTTER
SO HE WAS MAD ABOUT THE BRACELET...
OR IS HE MAD ABOUT ME HAVING MISUNDERSTOOD ABOUT ROKUDO-KUN SELLING IT?
YOU IDIOT!
MONEY-GRUBBING FREAK!
Meanwhile...
KUH!
WHERE'S THAT RIVER STYX-GENERATING MACHINE?

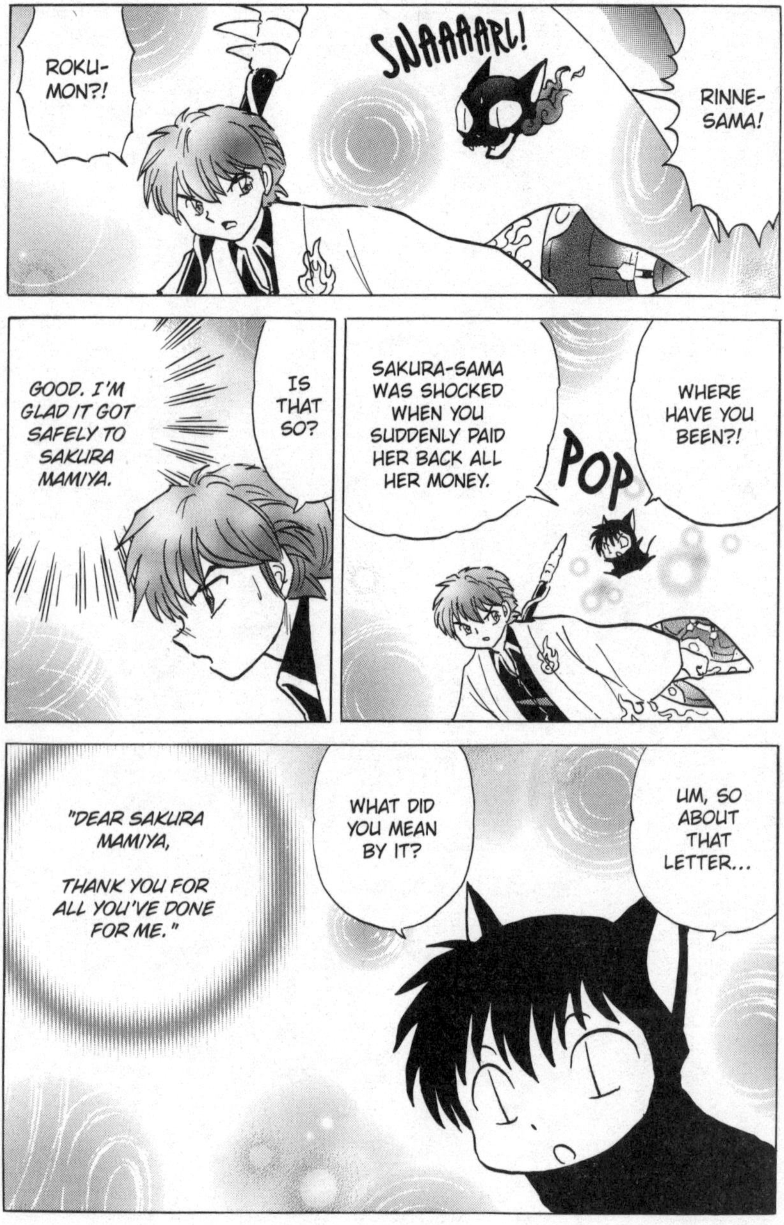
RINNE-SAMA!
SNAAAARL!
ROKU-MON?!
WHERE HAVE YOU BEEN?!
POP
SAKURA-SAMA WAS SHOCKED WHEN YOU SUDDENLY PAID HER BACK ALL HER MONEY.
IS THAT SO?
GOOD. I'M GLAD IT GOT SAFELY TO SAKURA MAMIYA.
UM, SO ABOUT THAT LETTER...
WHAT DID YOU MEAN BY IT?
"DEAR SAKURA MAMIYA,
THANK YOU FOR ALL YOU'VE DONE FOR ME."

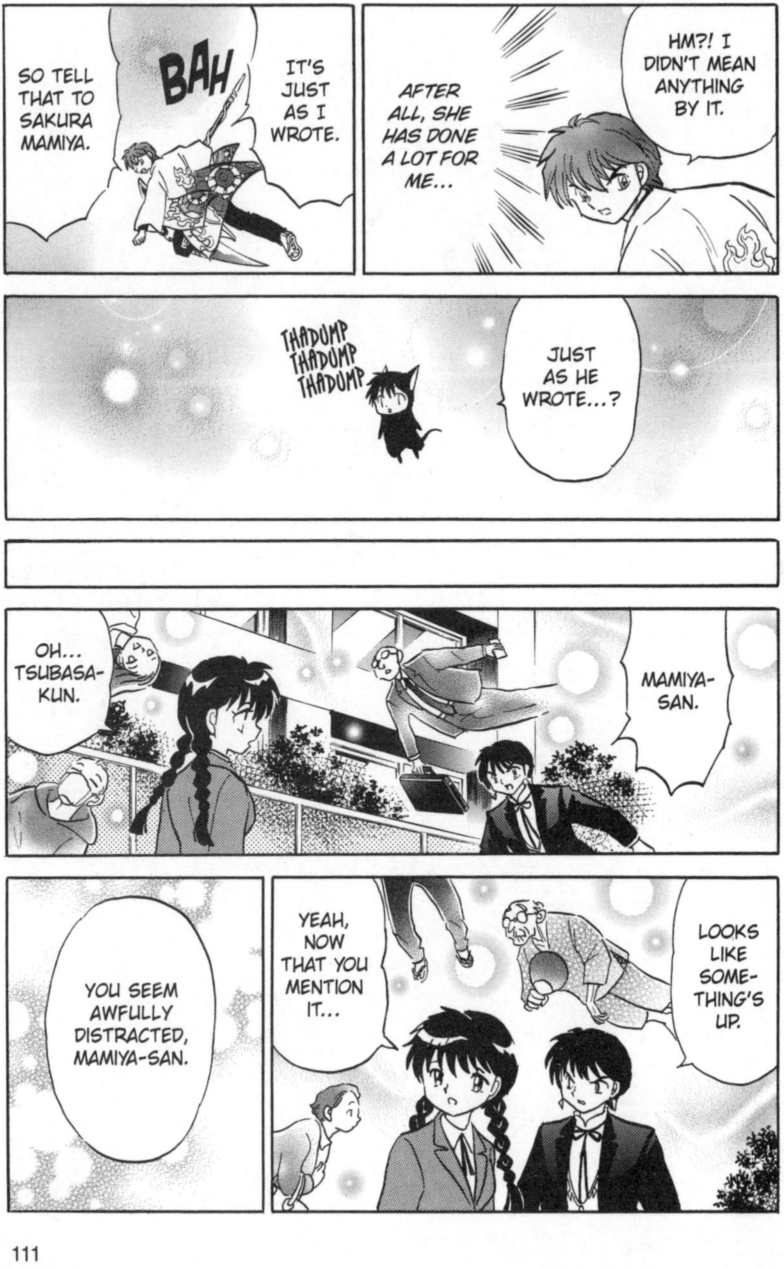
HM?! I DIDN'T MEAN ANYTHING BY IT.
AFTER ALL, SHE HAS DONE A LOT FOR ME...
IT'S JUST AS I WROTE.
BAH
SO TELL THAT TO SAKURA MAMIYA.
JUST AS HE WROTE...?
THADUMP THADUMP THADUMP
MAMIYA-SAN.
OH... TSUBASA-KUN.
LOOKS LIKE SOME-THING'S UP.
YEAH, NOW THAT YOU MENTION IT...
YOU SEEM AWFULLY DISTRACTED, MAMIYA-SAN.

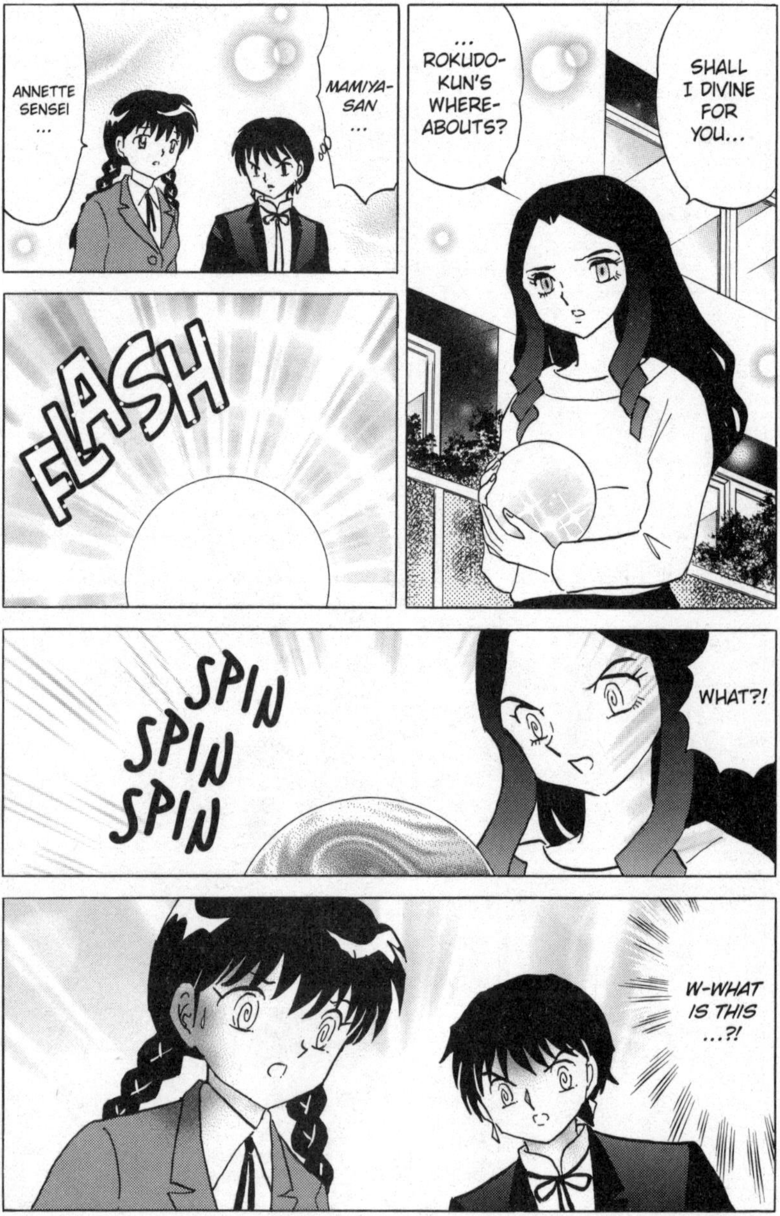
SHALL I DIVINE FOR YOU...
... ROKUDO-KUN'S WHERE-ABOUTS?
MAMIYA-SAN ...
ANNETTE SENSEI ...
FLASH
WHAT?!
SPIN SPIN SPIN
W-WHAT IS THIS ...?!

CHAPTER 395: THE OTHER BOUNDARY STONE

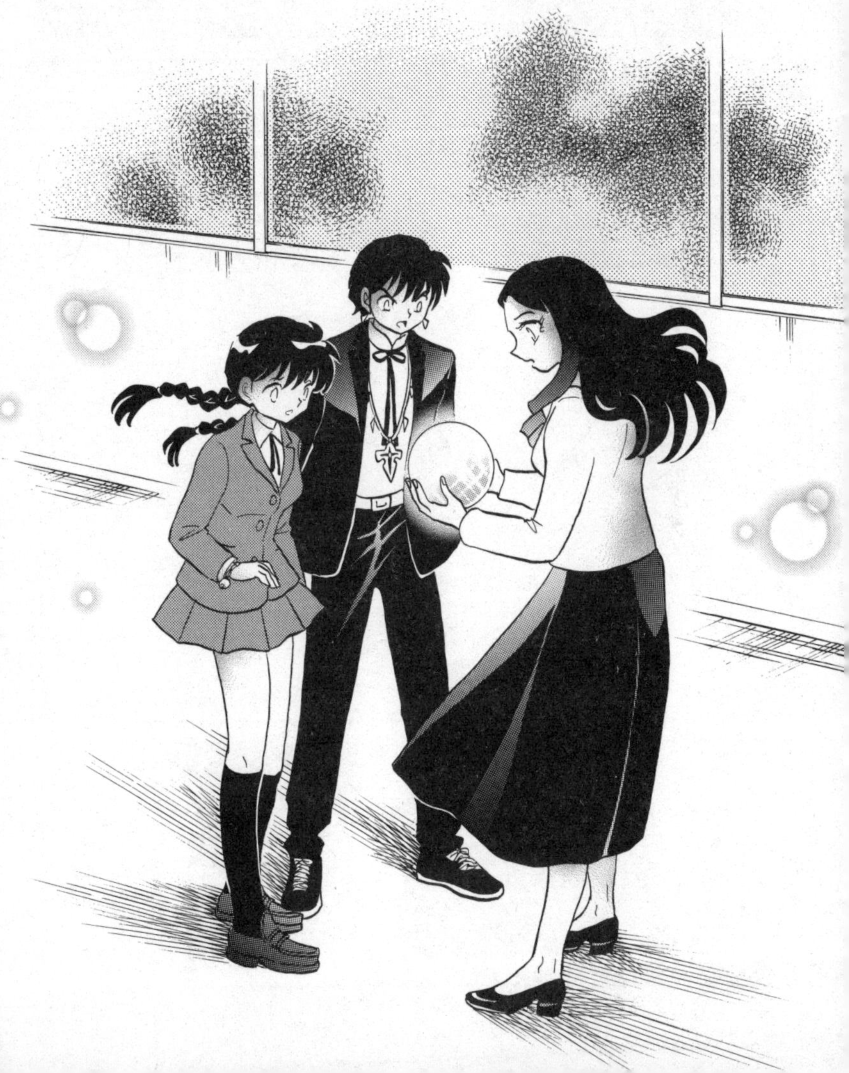

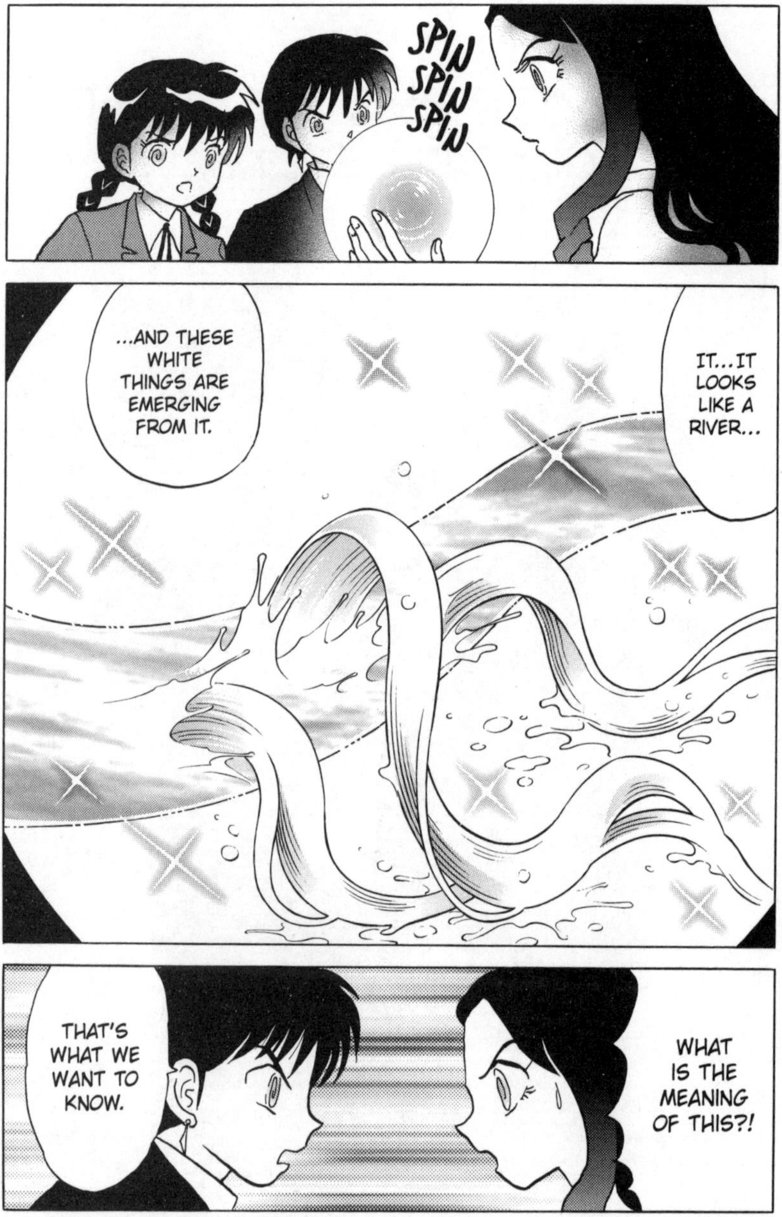
SPIN SPIN SPIN
IT...IT LOOKS LIKE A RIVER...
...AND THESE WHITE THINGS ARE EMERGING FROM IT.
WHAT IS THE MEANING OF THIS?!
THAT'S WHAT WE WANT TO KNOW.

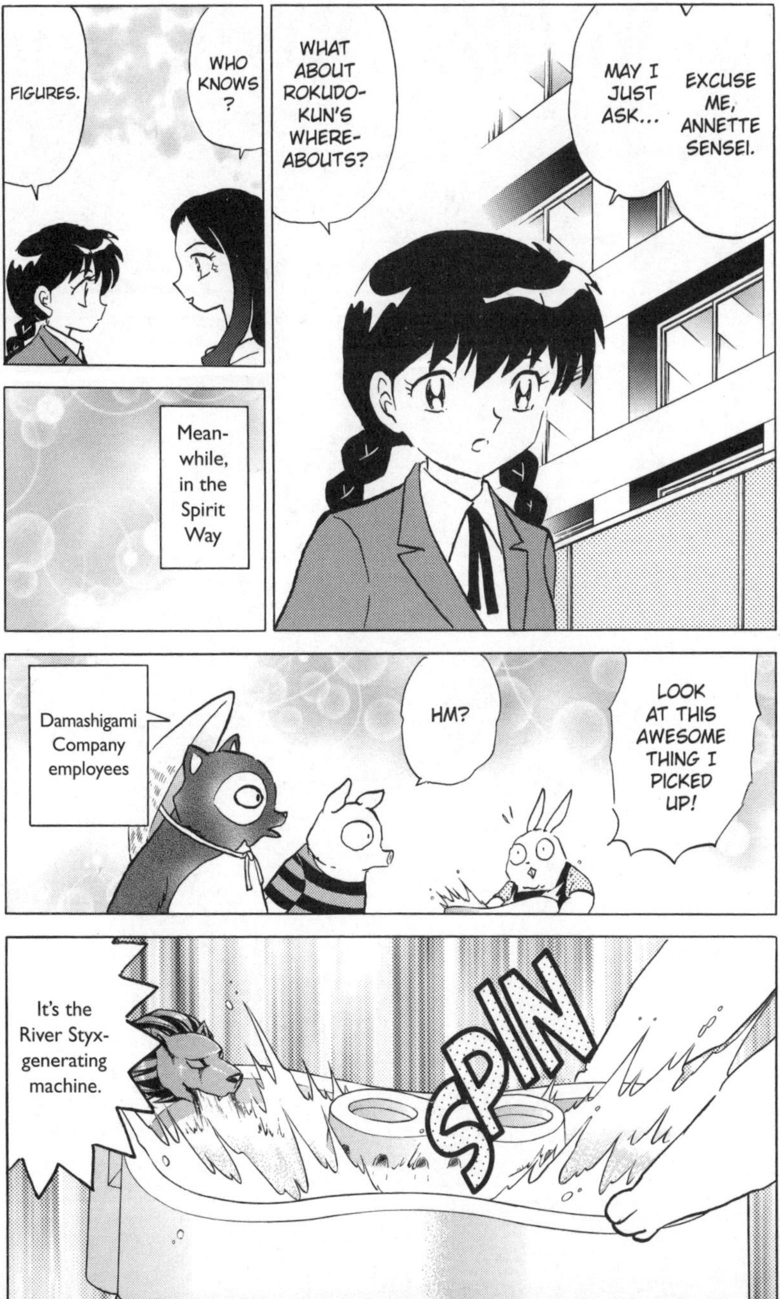
EXCUSE ME, ANNETTE SENSEI.
MAY I JUST ASK...
WHAT ABOUT ROKUDO-KUN'S WHEREABOUTS?
WHO KNOWS?
FIGURES.
Meanwhile, in the Spirit Way
LOOK AT THIS AWESOME THING I PICKED UP!
HM?
Damashigami Company employees
SPIN
It's the River Styx-generating machine.

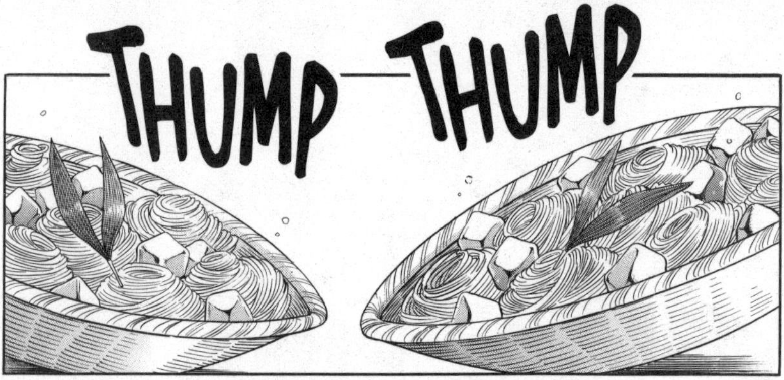
THUMP THUMP

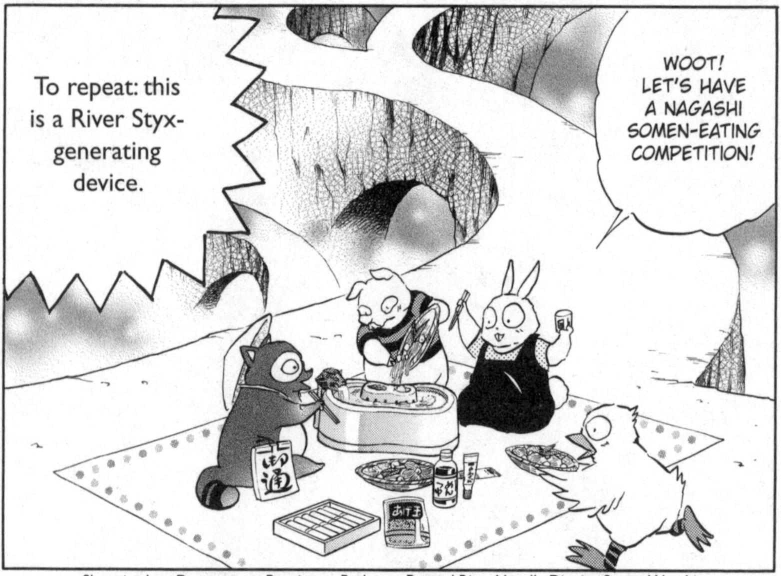
WOOT! LET'S HAVE A NAGASHI SOMEN-EATING COMPETITION!
To repeat: this is a River Styx-generating device.

Shopping bag: Downstream Boutique Packages: Popped Rice, Noodle Dipping Sauce, Wasabi

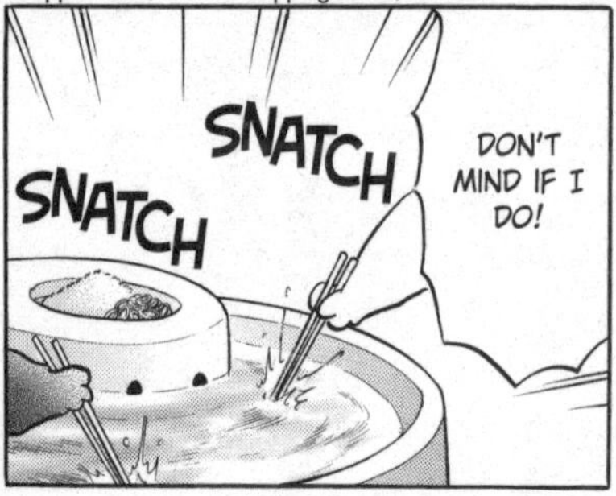
DON'T MIND IF I DO!
SNATCH
SNATCH

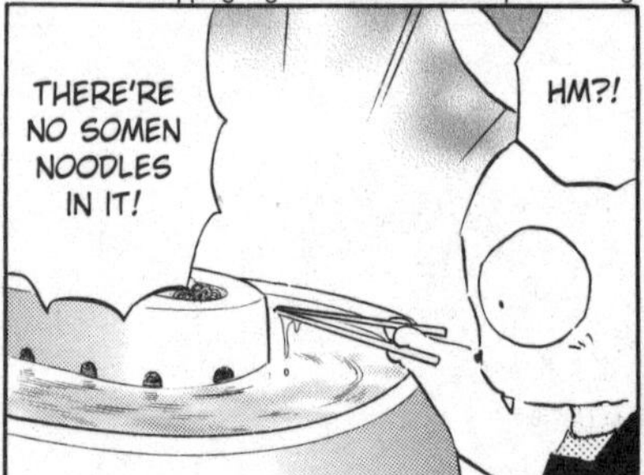
HM?!
THERE'RE NO SOMEN NOODLES IN IT!

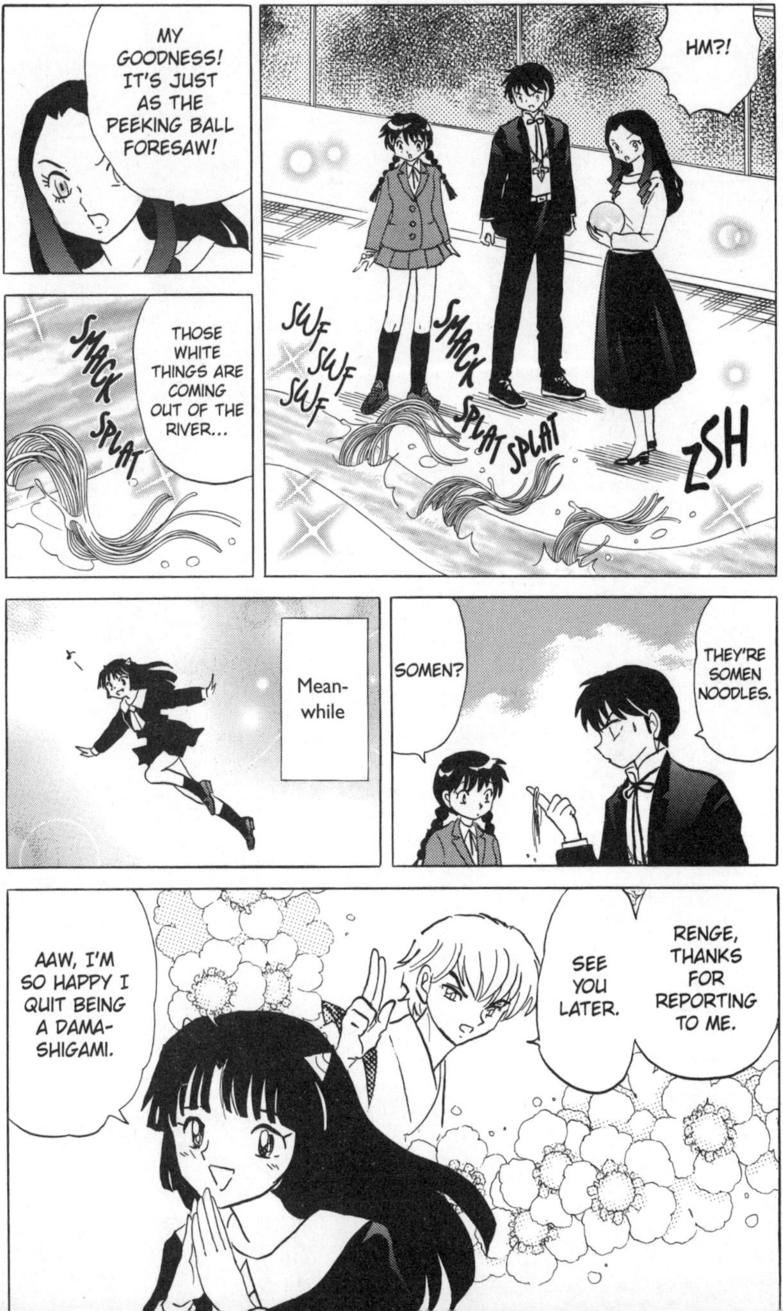
HM?!
SMACK
SWF SWF SWF
ZSH
SPLAT SPLAT
MY GOODNESS! IT'S JUST AS THE PEEKING BALL FORESAW!
THOSE WHITE THINGS ARE COMING OUT OF THE RIVER...
SMACK
SPLAT
THEY'RE SOMEN NOODLES.
SOMEN?
Mean-while
RENGE, THANKS FOR REPORTING TO ME.
SEE YOU LATER.
AAW, I'M SO HAPPY I QUIT BEING A DAMA-SHIGAMI.

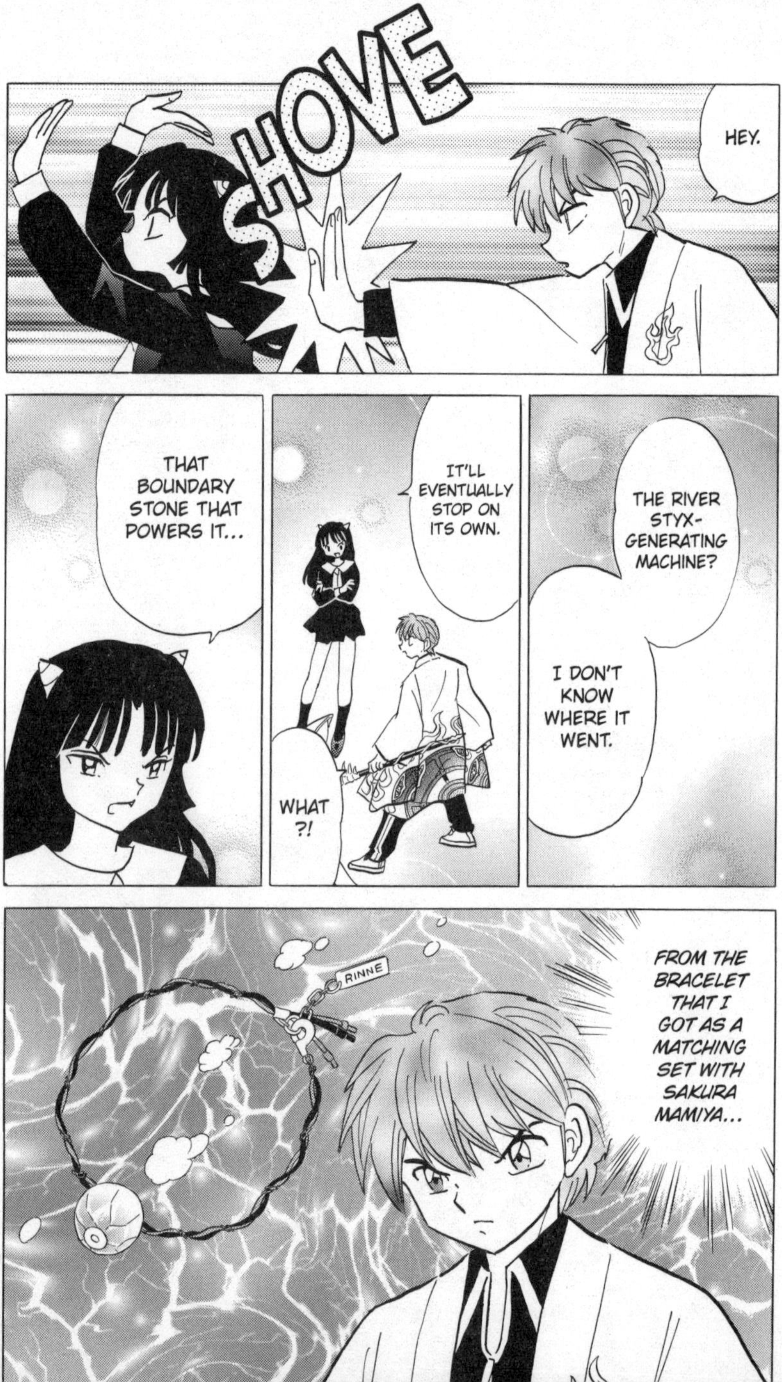
HEY.
SHOVE
THE RIVER STYX-GENERATING MACHINE?
I DON'T KNOW WHERE IT WENT.
IT'LL EVENTUALLY STOP ON ITS OWN.
WHAT?!
THAT BOUNDARY STONE THAT POWERS IT...
FROM THE BRACELET THAT I GOT AS A MATCHING SET WITH SAKURA MAMIYA...
RINNE

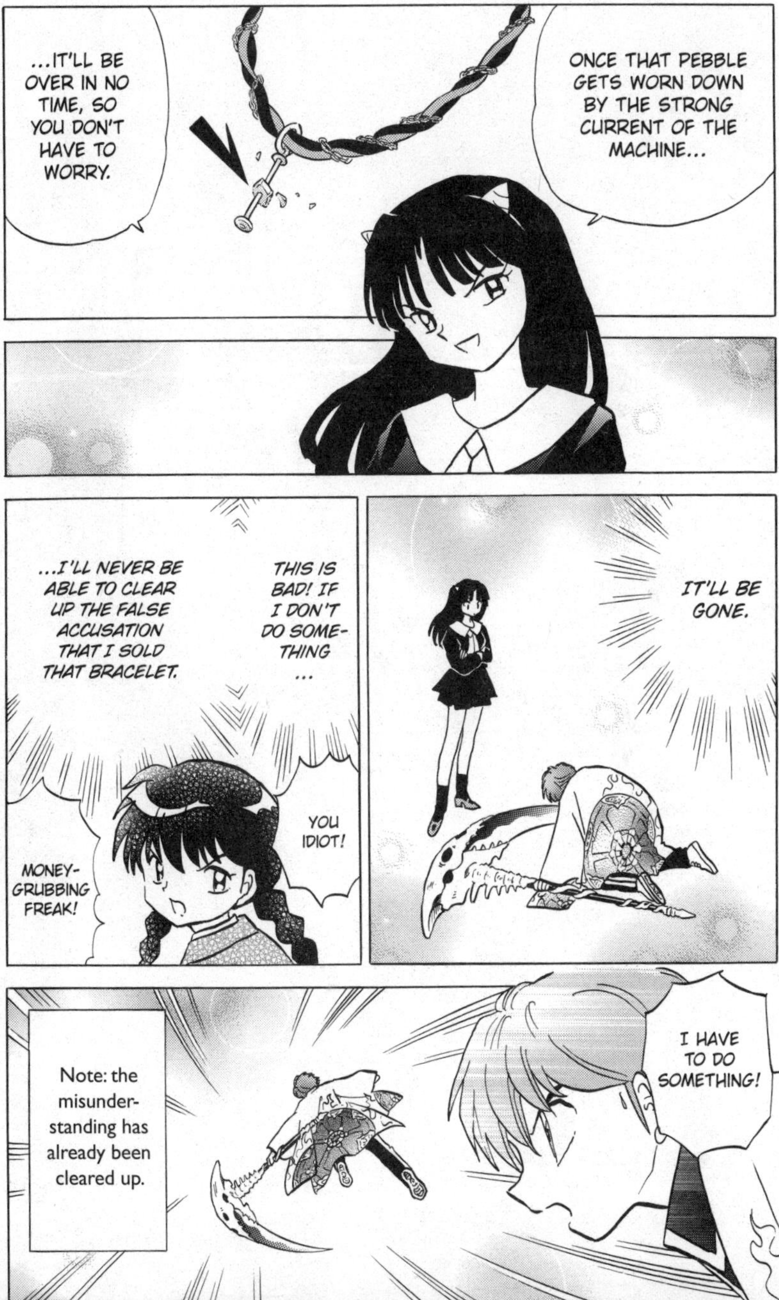
ONCE THAT PEBBLE GETS WORN DOWN BY THE STRONG CURRENT OF THE MACHINE...
...IT'LL BE OVER IN NO TIME, SO YOU DON'T HAVE TO WORRY.
IT'LL BE GONE.
THIS IS BAD! IF I DON'T DO SOMETHING...
...I'LL NEVER BE ABLE TO CLEAR UP THE FALSE ACCUSATION THAT I SOLD THAT BRACELET.
YOU IDIOT!
MONEY-GRUBBING FREAK!
I HAVE TO DO SOMETHING!
Note: the misunderstanding has already been cleared up.

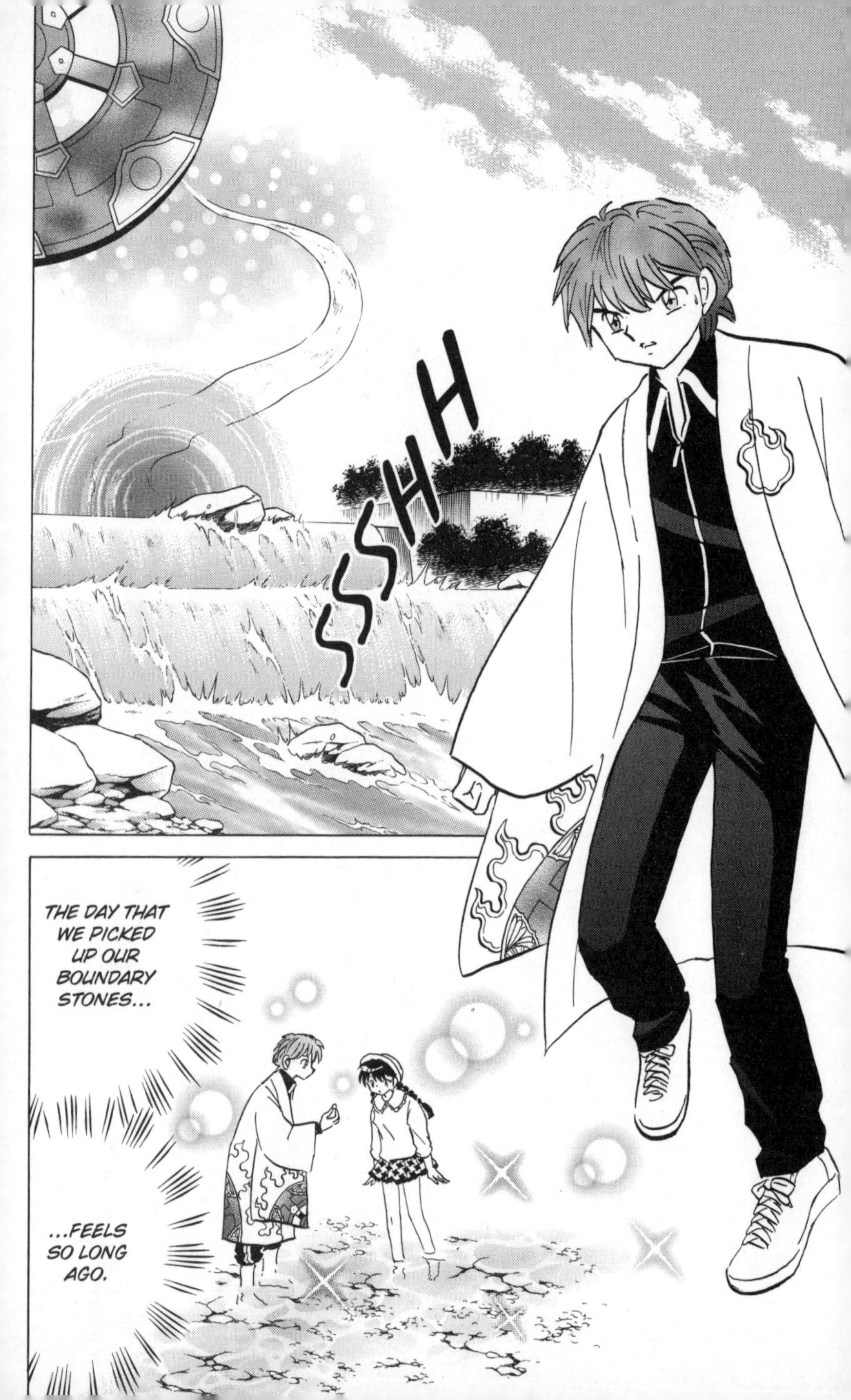
SSSHH
THE DAY THAT WE PICKED UP OUR BOUNDARY STONES...
...FEELS SO LONG AGO.

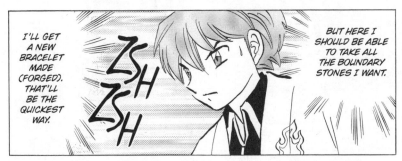

BUT HERE I SHOULD BE ABLE TO TAKE ALL THE BOUNDARY STONES I WANT.
ZSH ZSH
I'LL GET A NEW BRACELET MADE (FORGED). THAT'LL BE THE QUICKEST WAY.
THUMP
AREA CLOSED
THUMP
NO ENTERING THE RIVERBED!
鎖
AH, YOU SEE, THE DEVICE HAS BEEN PUT IN REVERSE.
I'LL HAVE IT FIXED IN NO TIME.
道具機器
修理
Sign: Appliances and Repairs

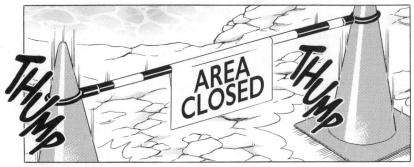

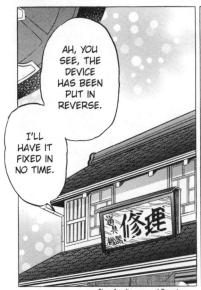

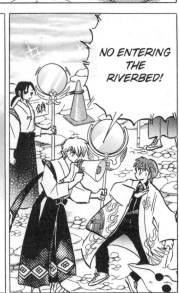

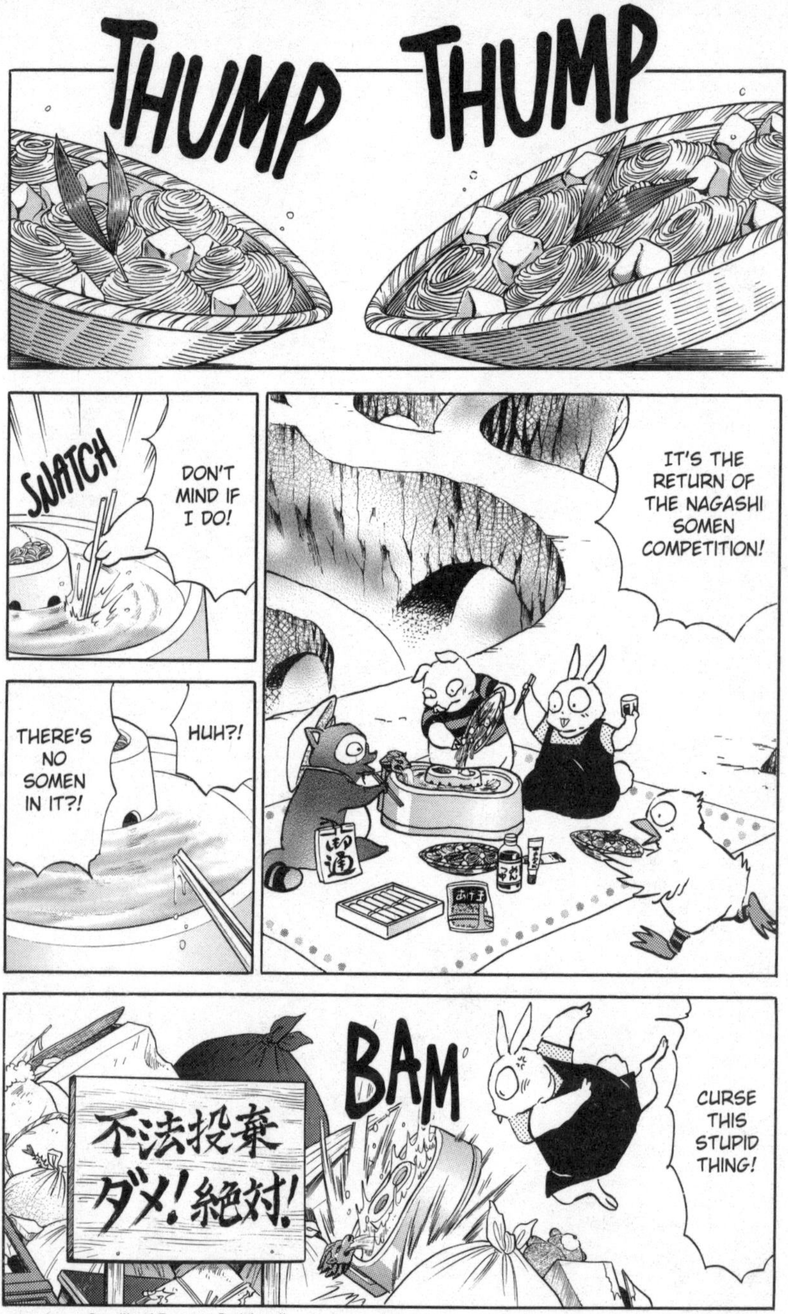
THUMP THUMP
IT'S THE RETURN OF THE NAGASHI SOMEN COMPETITION!
DON'T MIND IF I DO!
SWATCH
HUH?!
THERE'S NO SOMEN IN IT?!
CURSE THIS STUPID THING!
BAM
不法投棄
ダメ！絶対！

Sign: Illegal Dumping Prohibited!

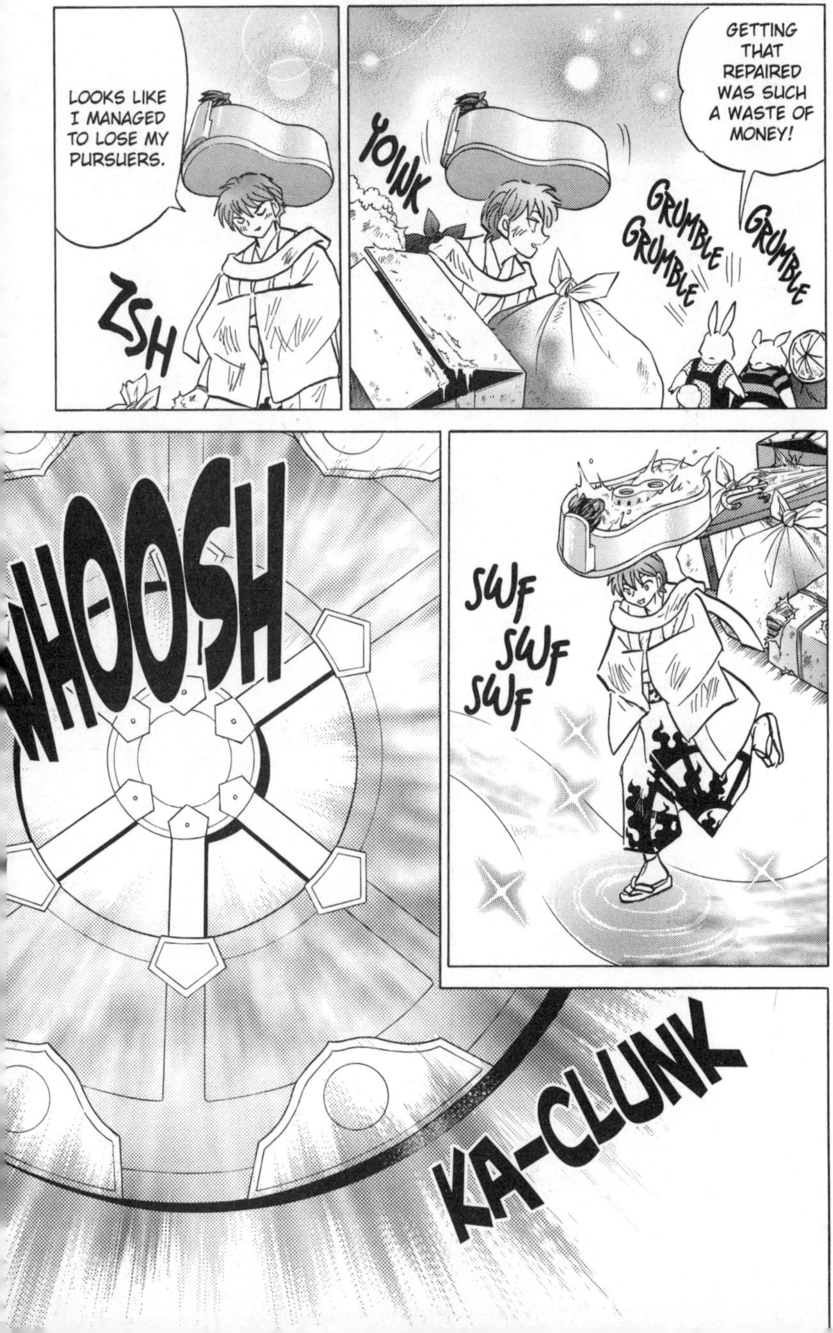
GETTING THAT REPAIRED WAS SUCH A WASTE OF MONEY!
GRUMBLE
GRUMBLE GRUMBLE
YOINK
LOOKS LIKE I MANAGED TO LOSE MY PURSUERS.
ZSH
SWF SWF SWF
KA-CLUNK
WHOOSH

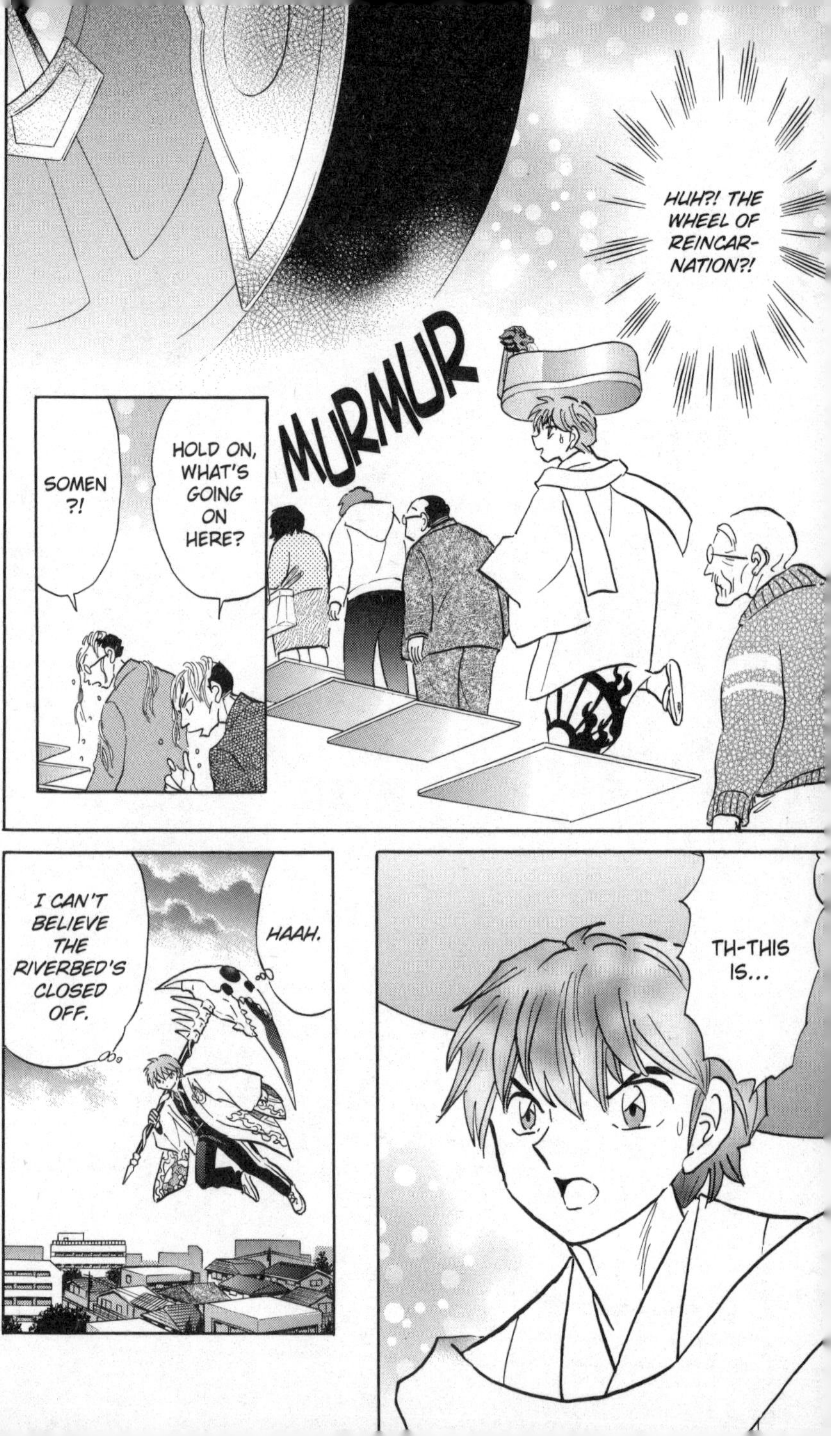
HUH?! THE WHEEL OF REINCARNATION?!
MURMUR
HOLD ON, WHAT'S GOING ON HERE?
SOMEN ?!
TH-THIS IS...
HAAH.
I CAN'T BELIEVE THE RIVERBED'S CLOSED OFF.

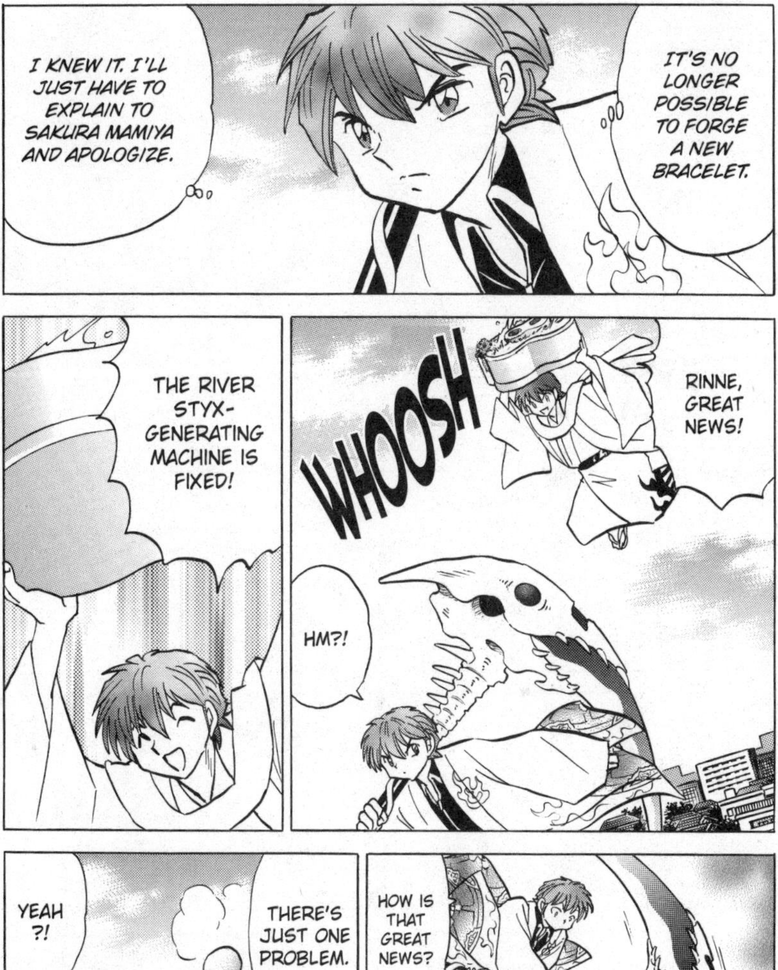
IT'S NO LONGER POSSIBLE TO FORGE A NEW BRACELET.
I KNEW IT. I'LL JUST HAVE TO EXPLAIN TO SAKURA MAMIYA AND APOLOGIZE.
RINNE, GREAT NEWS!
WHOOSH
HM?!
THE RIVER STYX-GENERATING MACHINE IS FIXED!
HOW IS THAT GREAT NEWS?
STAB
THERE'S JUST ONE PROBLEM.
YEAH ?!

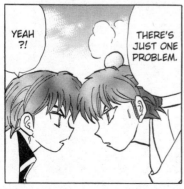

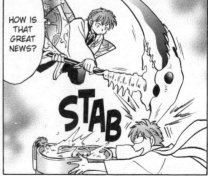

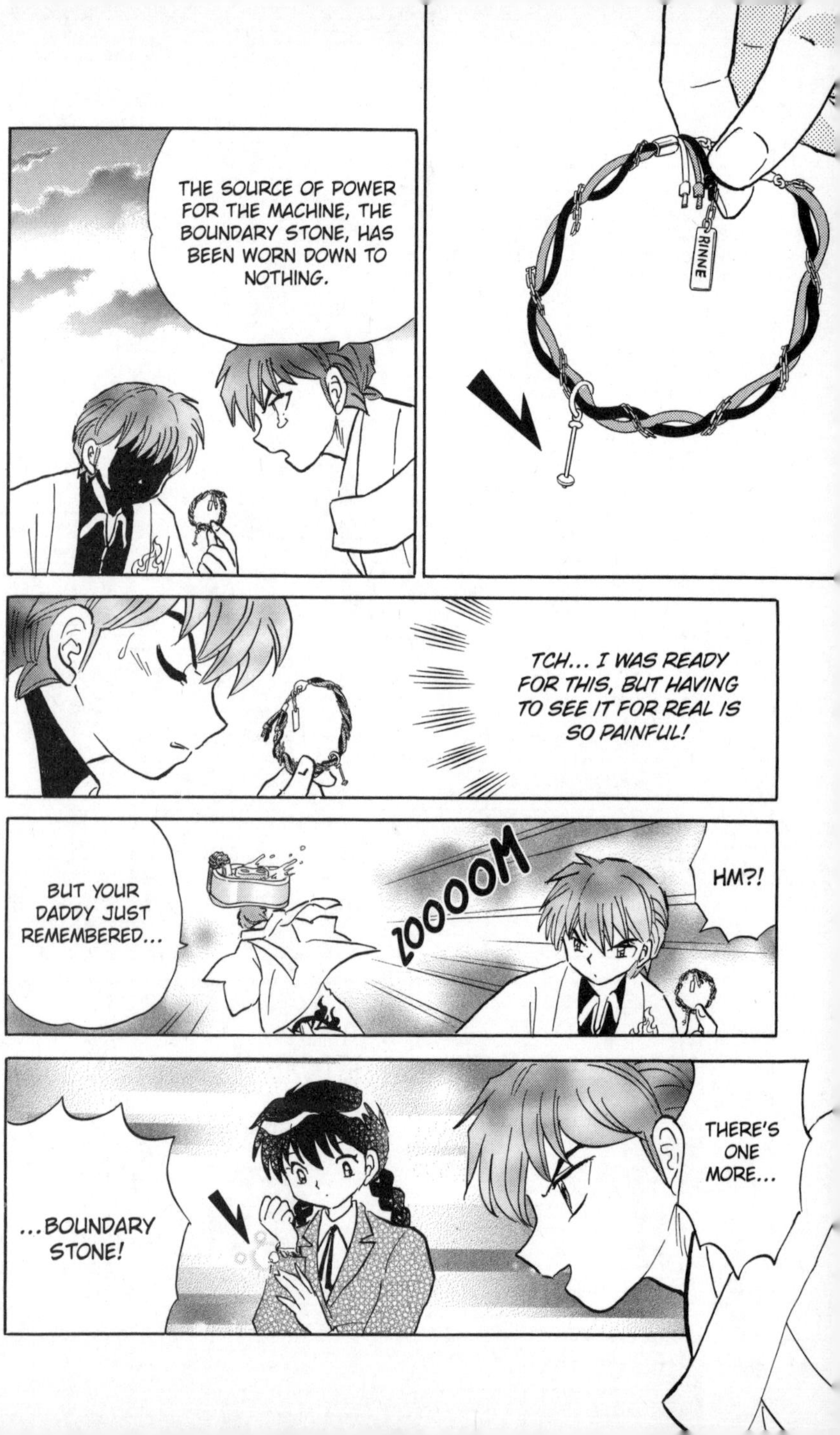
RINNE
THE SOURCE OF POWER FOR THE MACHINE, THE BOUNDARY STONE, HAS BEEN WORN DOWN TO NOTHING.
TCH... I WAS READY FOR THIS, BUT HAVING TO SEE IT FOR REAL IS SO PAINFUL!
HM?!
ZOOOOM
BUT YOUR DADDY JUST REMEMBERED...
THERE'S ONE MORE...
...BOUNDARY STONE!

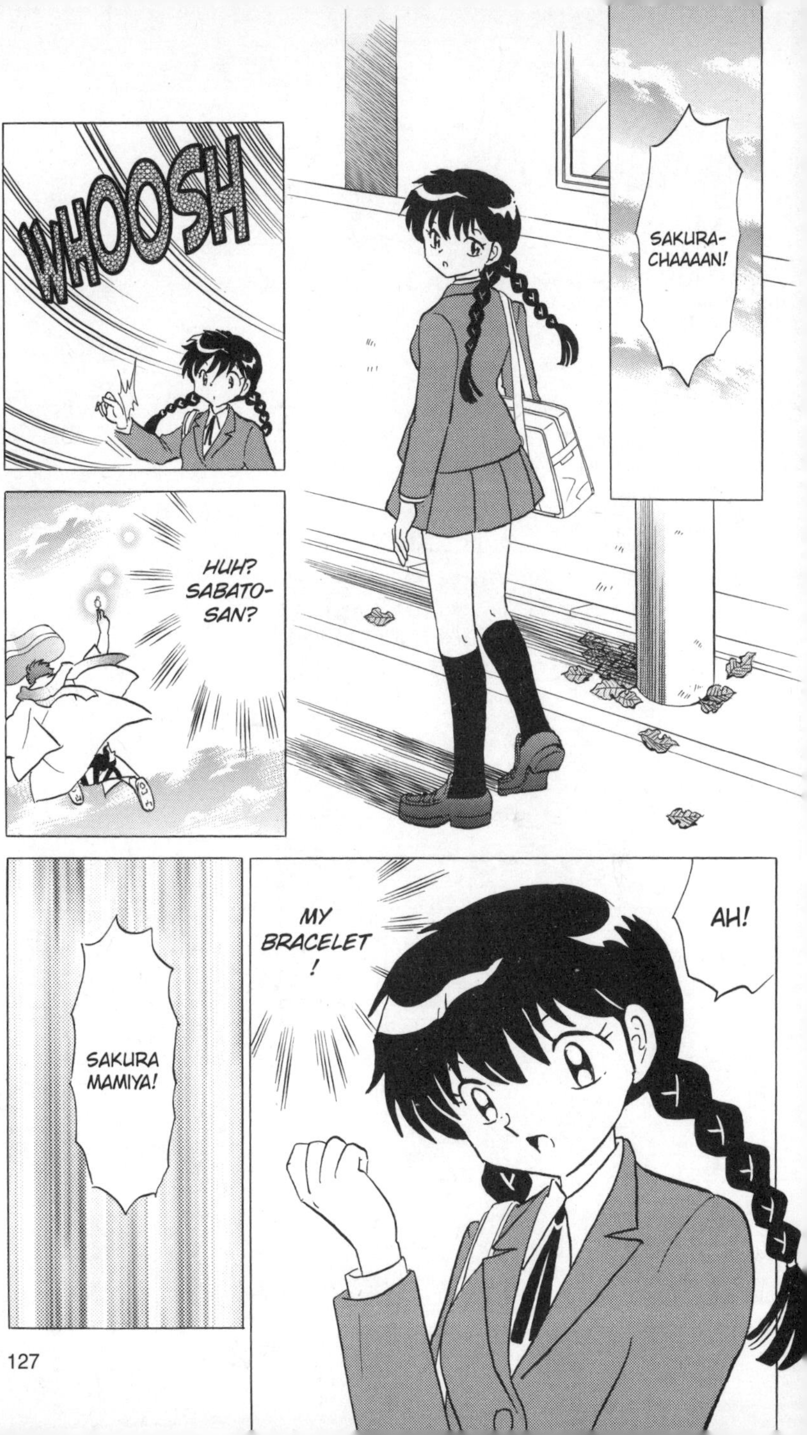
SAKURA-CHAAAAN!
WHOOSH
HUH? SABATO-SAN?
AH!
MY BRACELET!
SAKURA MAMIYA!

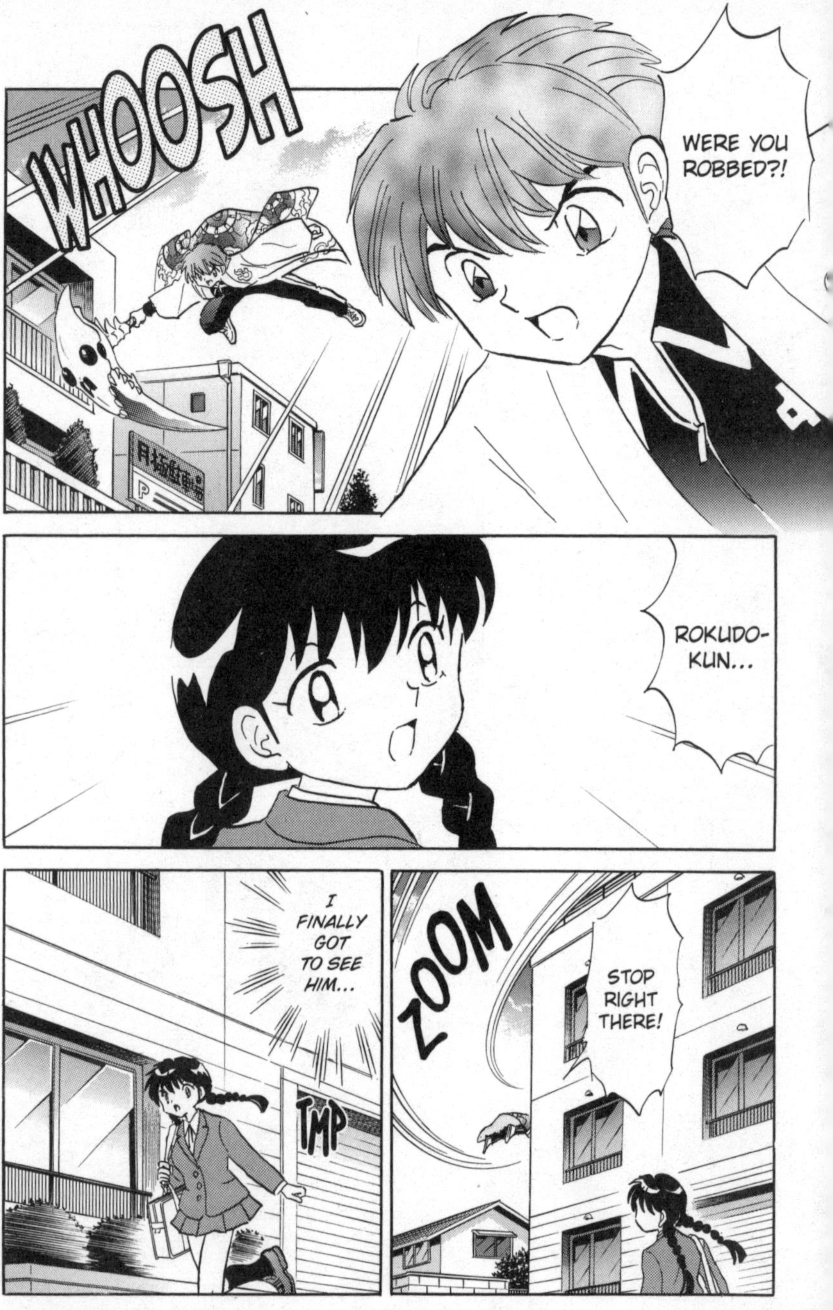
WERE YOU ROBBED?!
WHOOSH
ROKUDO-KUN...
STOP RIGHT THERE!
ZOOM
I FINALLY GOT TO SEE HIM...
TMP

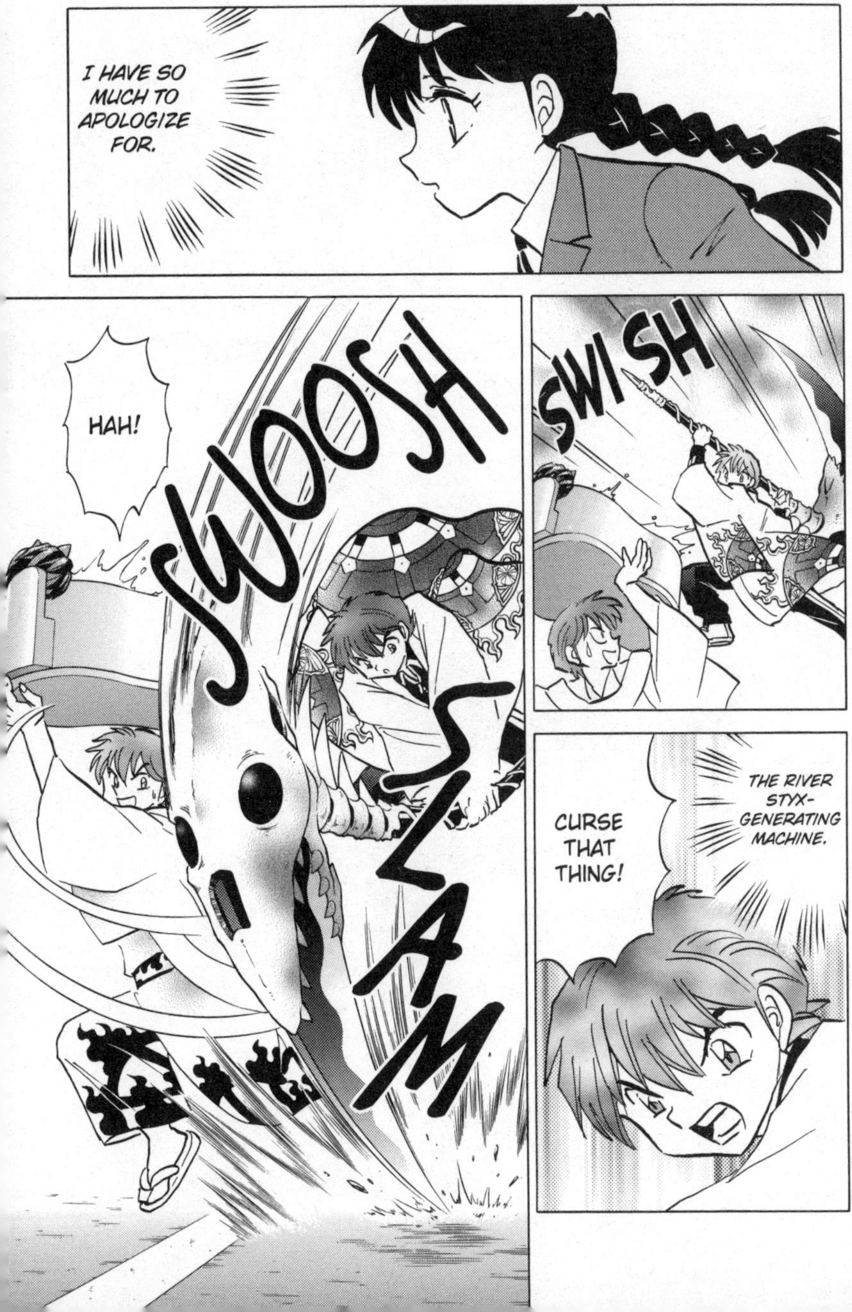
I HAVE SO MUCH TO APOLOGIZE FOR.
SWISH
THE RIVER STYX-GENERATING MACHINE.
CURSE THAT THING!
HAH!
SWOOSH
SLAM

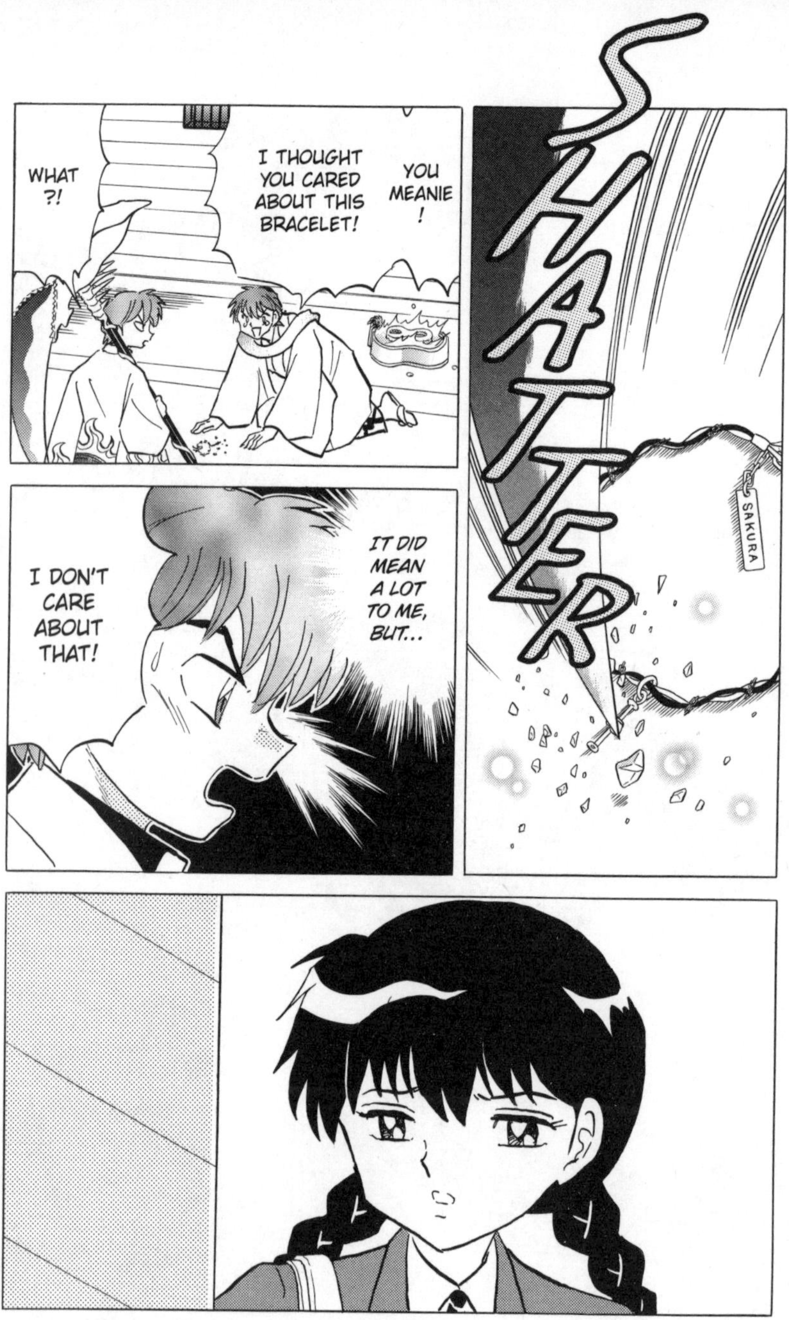
SHATTER
SAKURA
WHAT ?!
I THOUGHT YOU CARED ABOUT THIS BRACELET!
YOU MEANIE!
IT DID MEAN A LOT TO ME, BUT...
I DON'T CARE ABOUT THAT!

CHAPTER 396: FAREWELL, ROKUDO-KUN

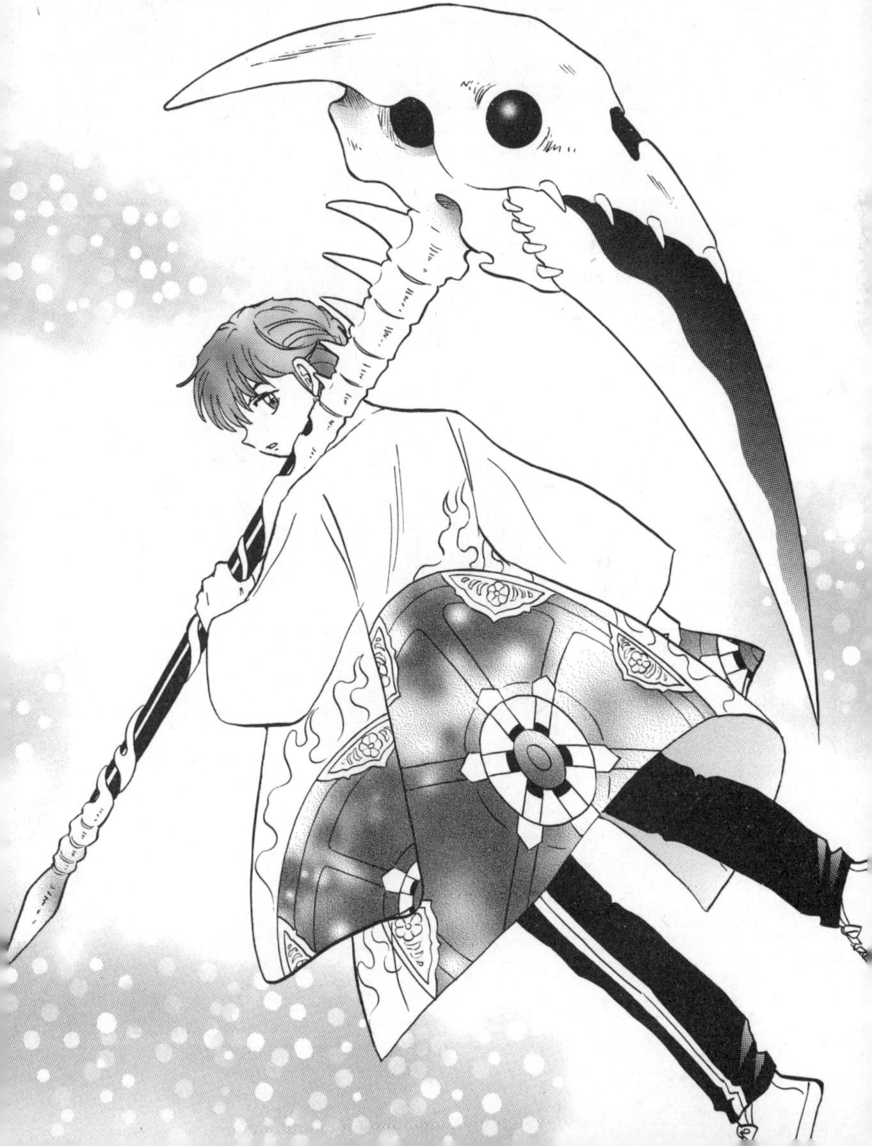

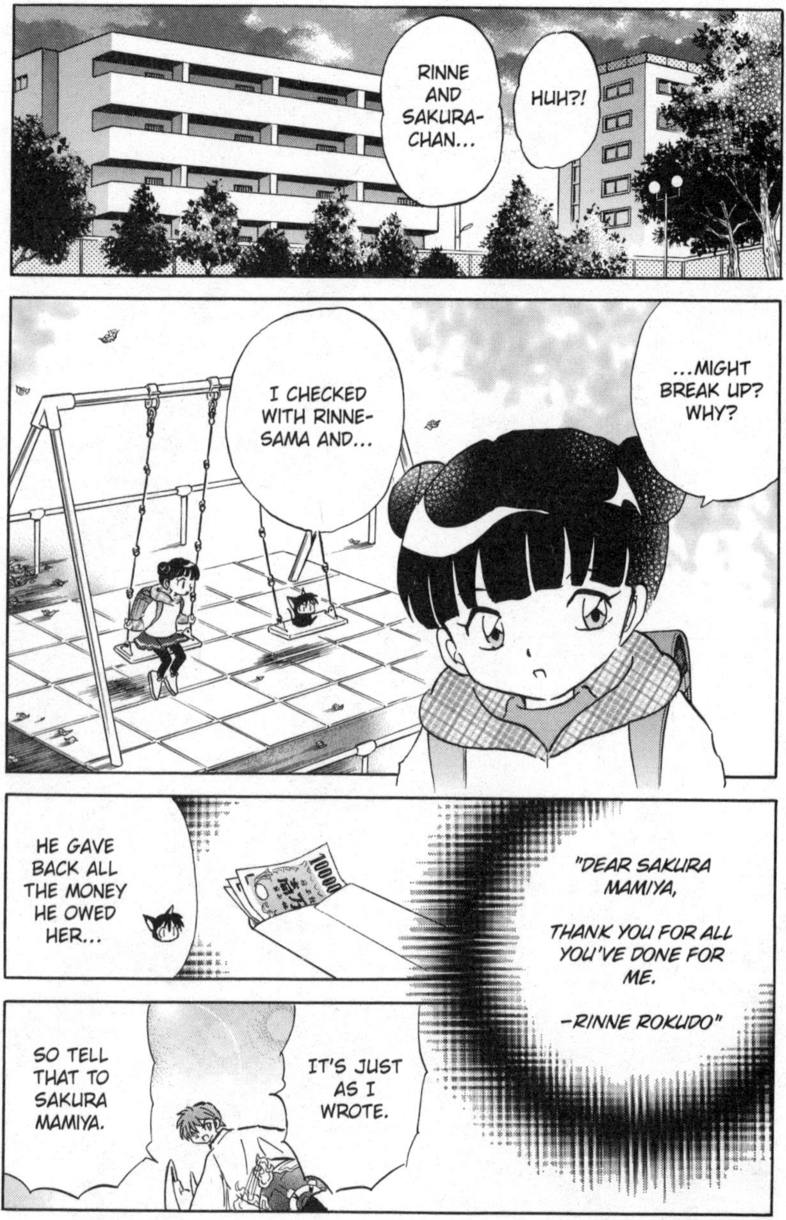
HUH?!
RINNE AND SAKURA-CHAN...
...MIGHT BREAK UP? WHY?
I CHECKED WITH RINNE-SAMA AND...
"DEAR SAKURA MAMIYA,
THANK YOU FOR ALL YOU'VE DONE FOR ME.
-RINNE ROKUDO"
HE GAVE BACK ALL THE MONEY HE OWED HER...
IT'S JUST AS I WROTE.
SO TELL THAT TO SAKURA MAMIYA.

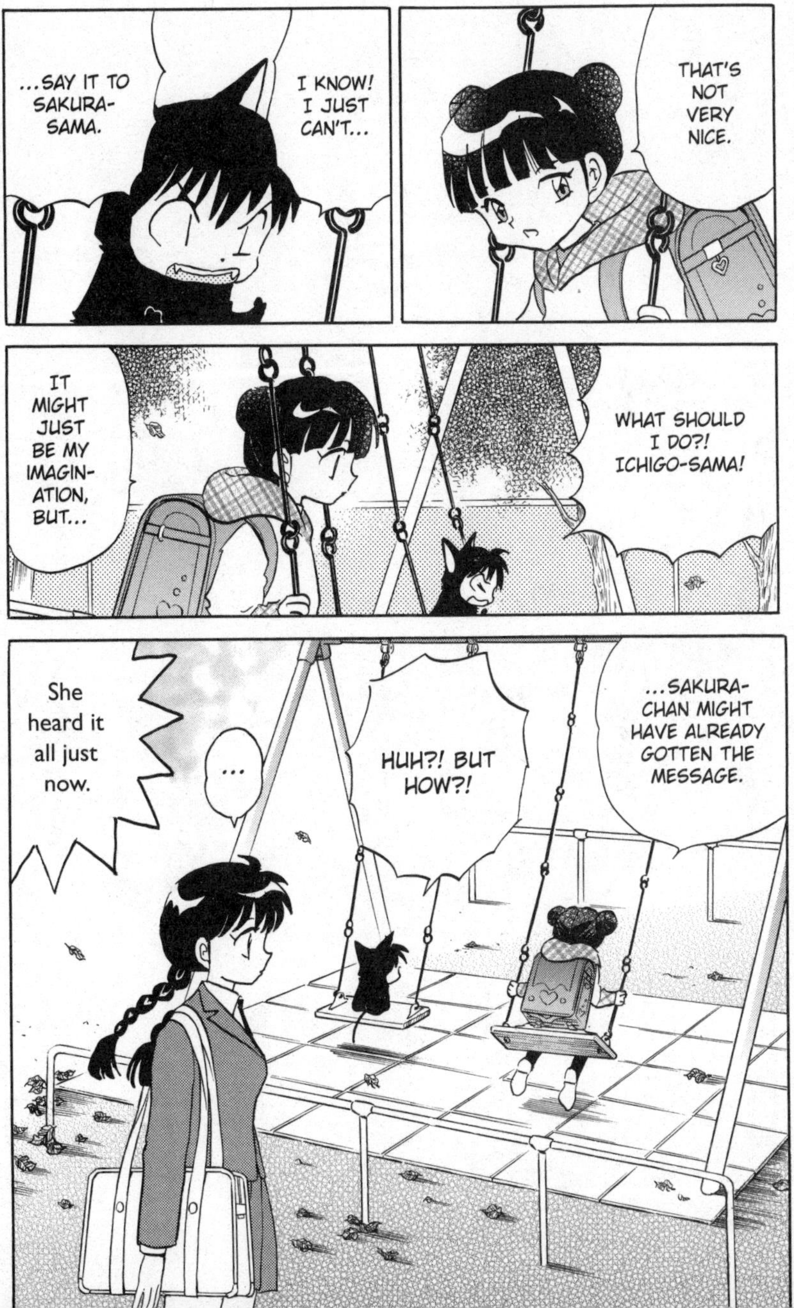
THAT'S NOT VERY NICE.
I KNOW! I JUST CAN'T...
...SAY IT TO SAKURA-SAMA.
WHAT SHOULD I DO?! ICHIGO-SAMA!
IT MIGHT JUST BE MY IMAGINATION, BUT...
...SAKURA-CHAN MIGHT HAVE ALREADY GOTTEN THE MESSAGE.
HUH?! BUT HOW?!
...
She heard it all just now.

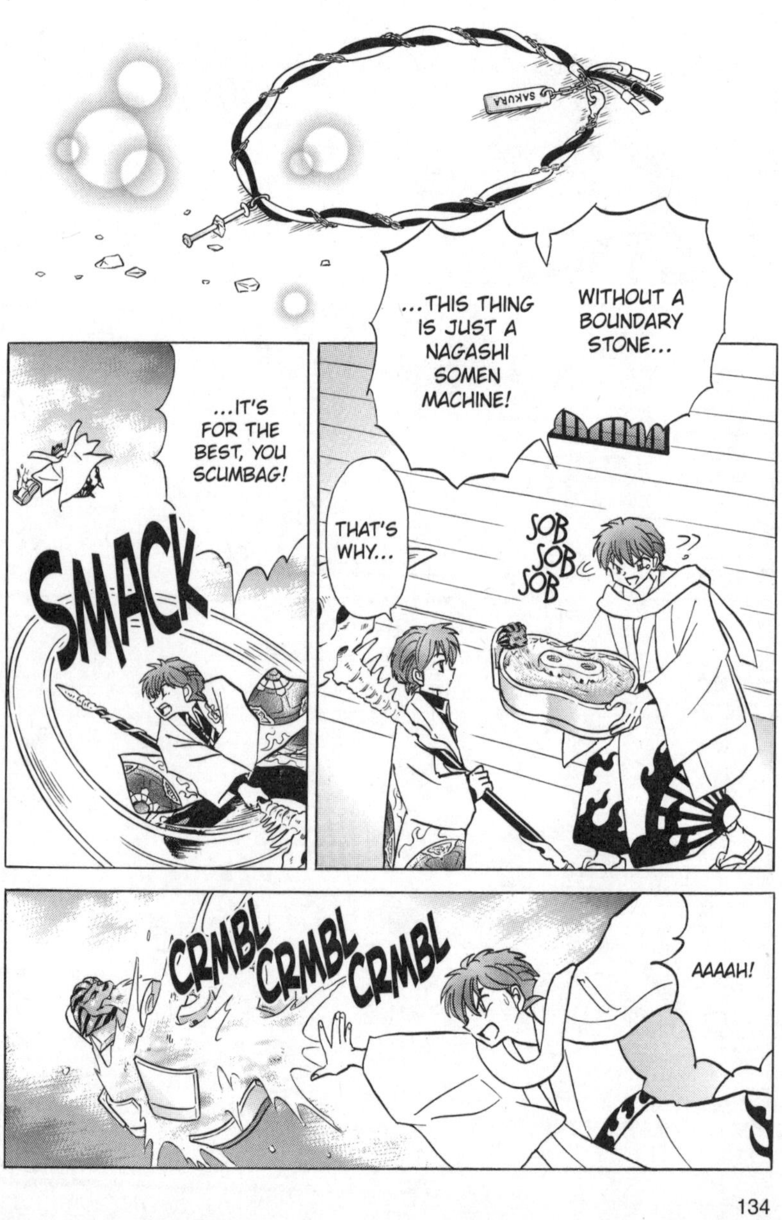
SAKURA
WITHOUT A BOUNDARY STONE...
...THIS THING IS JUST A NAGASHI SOMEN MACHINE!
SOB SOB SOB
THAT'S WHY...
...IT'S FOR THE BEST, YOU SCUMBAG!
SMACK
CRMBL CRMBL CRMBL
AAAAH!

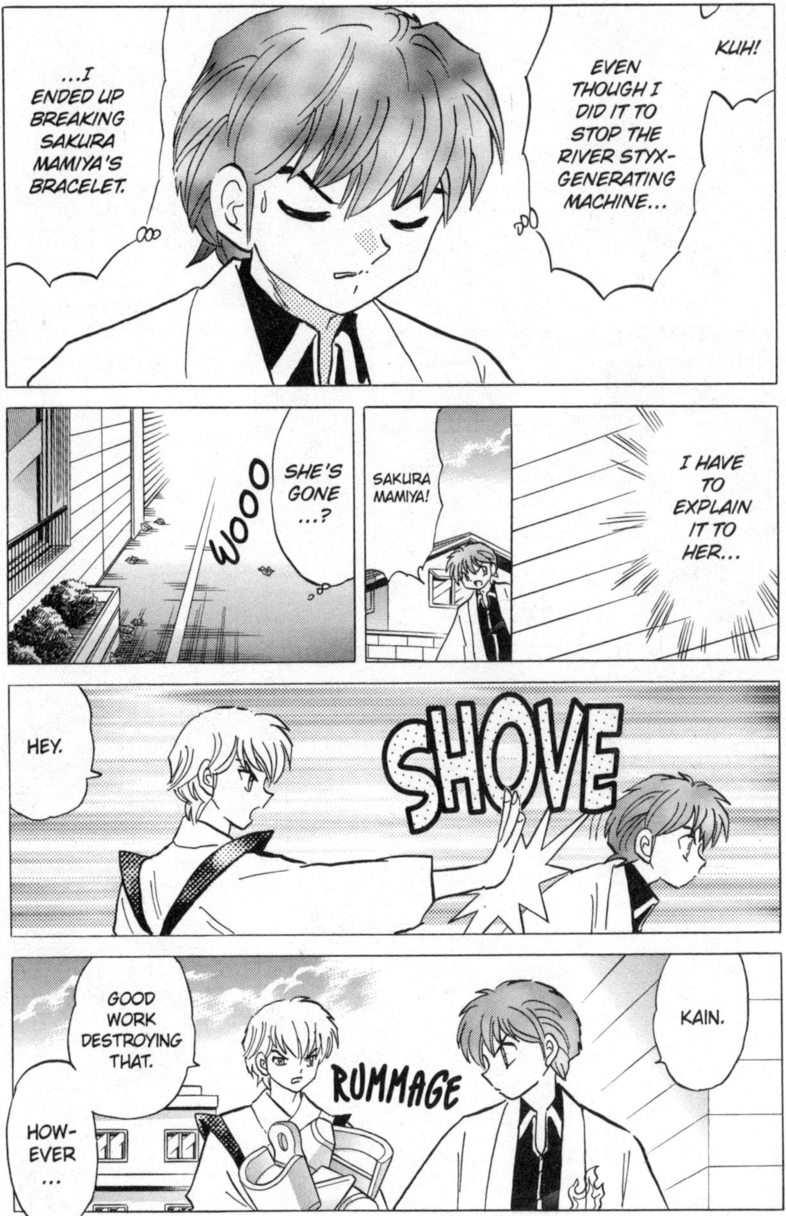
KUH!
EVEN THOUGH I DID IT TO STOP THE RIVER STYX-GENERATING MACHINE...
...I ENDED UP BREAKING SAKURA MAMIYA'S BRACELET.
I HAVE TO EXPLAIN IT TO HER...
SAKURA MAMIYA!
SHE'S GONE ...?
WOOO
SHOVE
HEY.
KAIN.
RUMMAGE
GOOD WORK DESTROYING THAT.
HOW-EVER ...

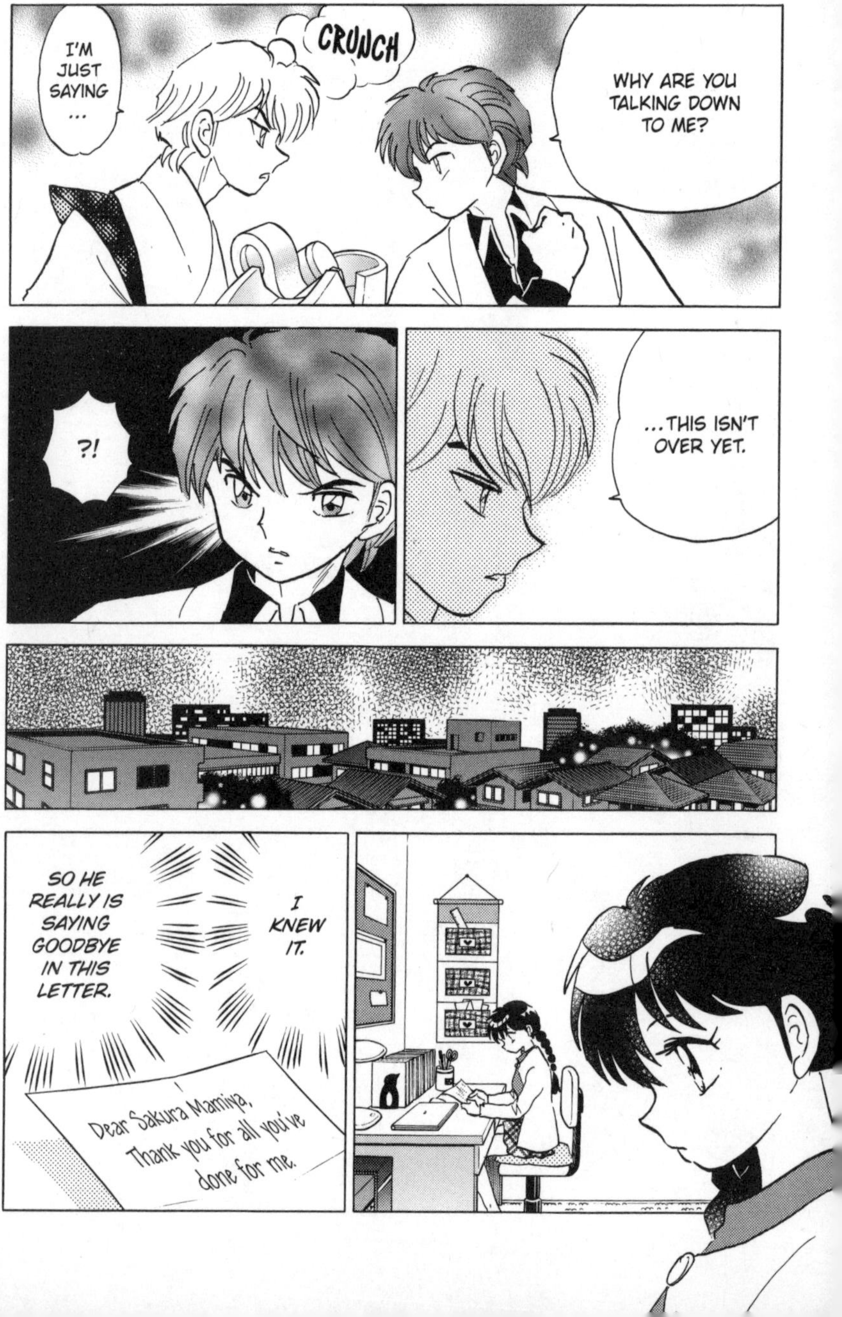
WHY ARE YOU TALKING DOWN TO ME?
CRUNCH
I'M JUST SAYING ...
...THIS ISN'T OVER YET.
?!
I KNEW IT.
SO HE REALLY IS SAYING GOODBYE IN THIS LETTER.
Dear Sakura Mamiya,
Thank you for all you've done for me.

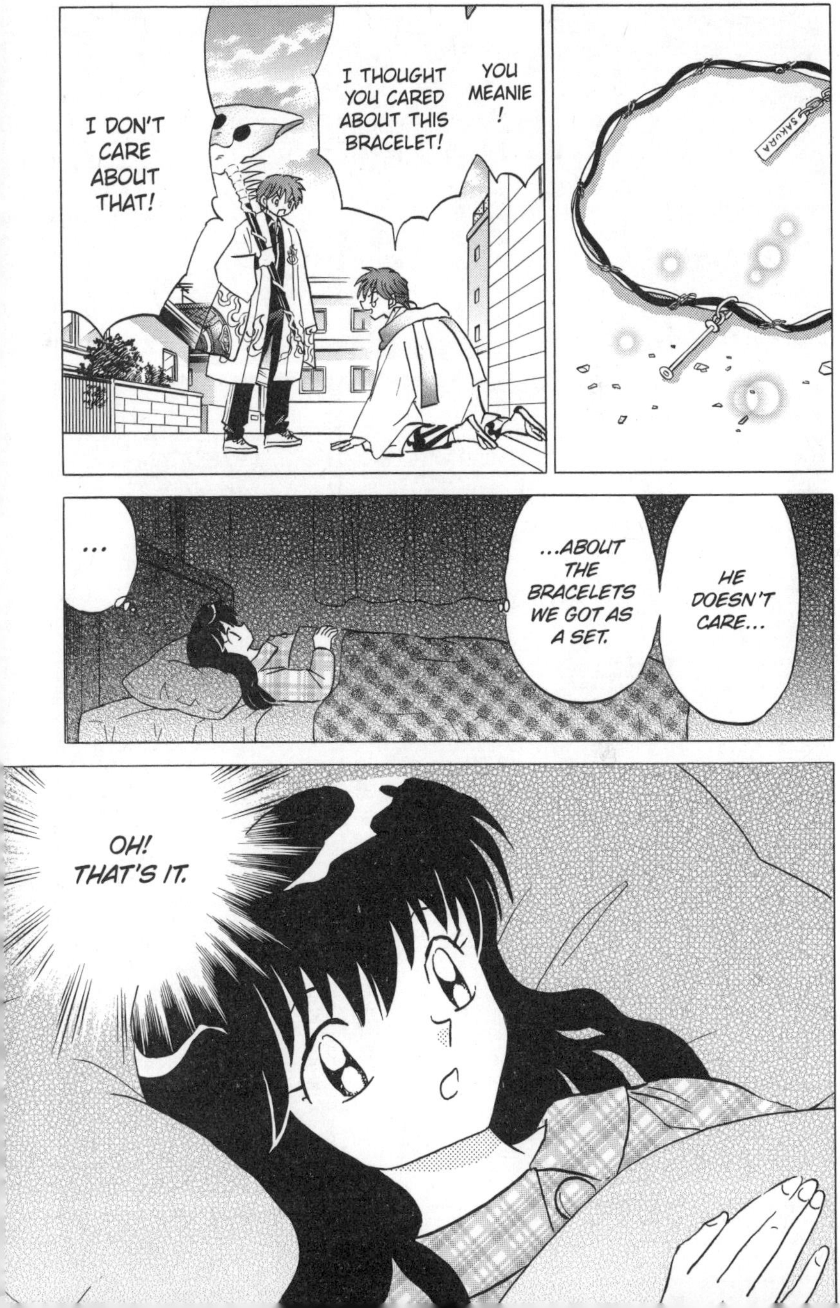
SAKURA
YOU MEANIE!
I THOUGHT YOU CARED ABOUT THIS BRACELET!
I DON'T CARE ABOUT THAT!
HE DOESN'T CARE...
...ABOUT THE BRACELETS WE GOT AS A SET.
...
OH! THAT'S IT.

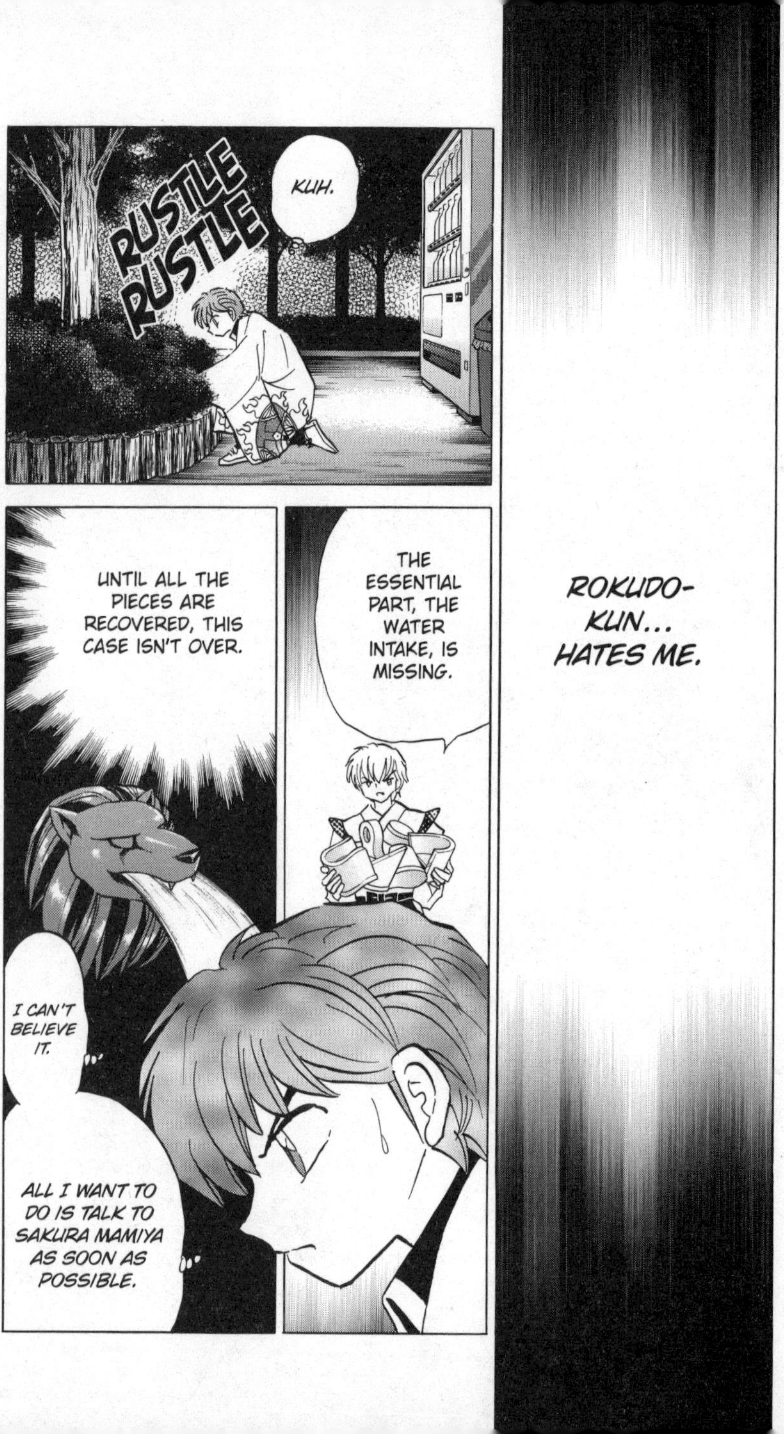
ROKUDO-KUN... HATES ME.
RUSTLE RUSTLE
KUH.
THE ESSENTIAL PART, THE WATER INTAKE, IS MISSING.
UNTIL ALL THE PIECES ARE RECOVERED, THIS CASE ISN'T OVER.
I CAN'T BELIEVE IT.
ALL I WANT TO DO IS TALK TO SAKURA MAMIYA AS SOON AS POSSIBLE.

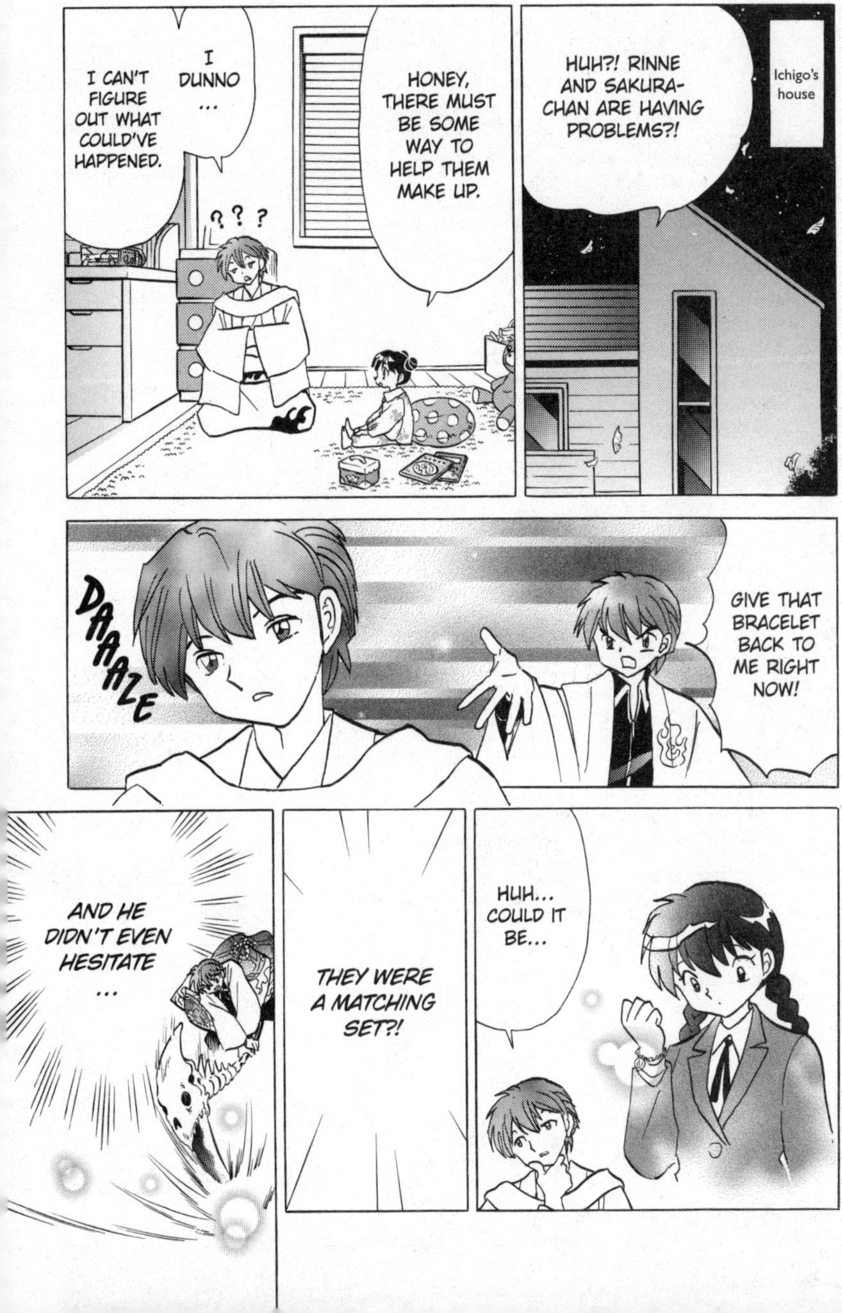
Ichigo's house
HUH?! RINNE AND SAKURA-CHAN ARE HAVING PROBLEMS?!
HONEY, THERE MUST BE SOME WAY TO HELP THEM MAKE UP.
I DUNNO...
I CAN'T FIGURE OUT WHAT COULD'VE HAPPENED.
? ? ?
GIVE THAT BRACELET BACK TO ME RIGHT NOW!
DAAAZE
HUH... COULD IT BE...
THEY WERE A MATCHING SET?!
AND HE DIDN'T EVEN HESITATE...

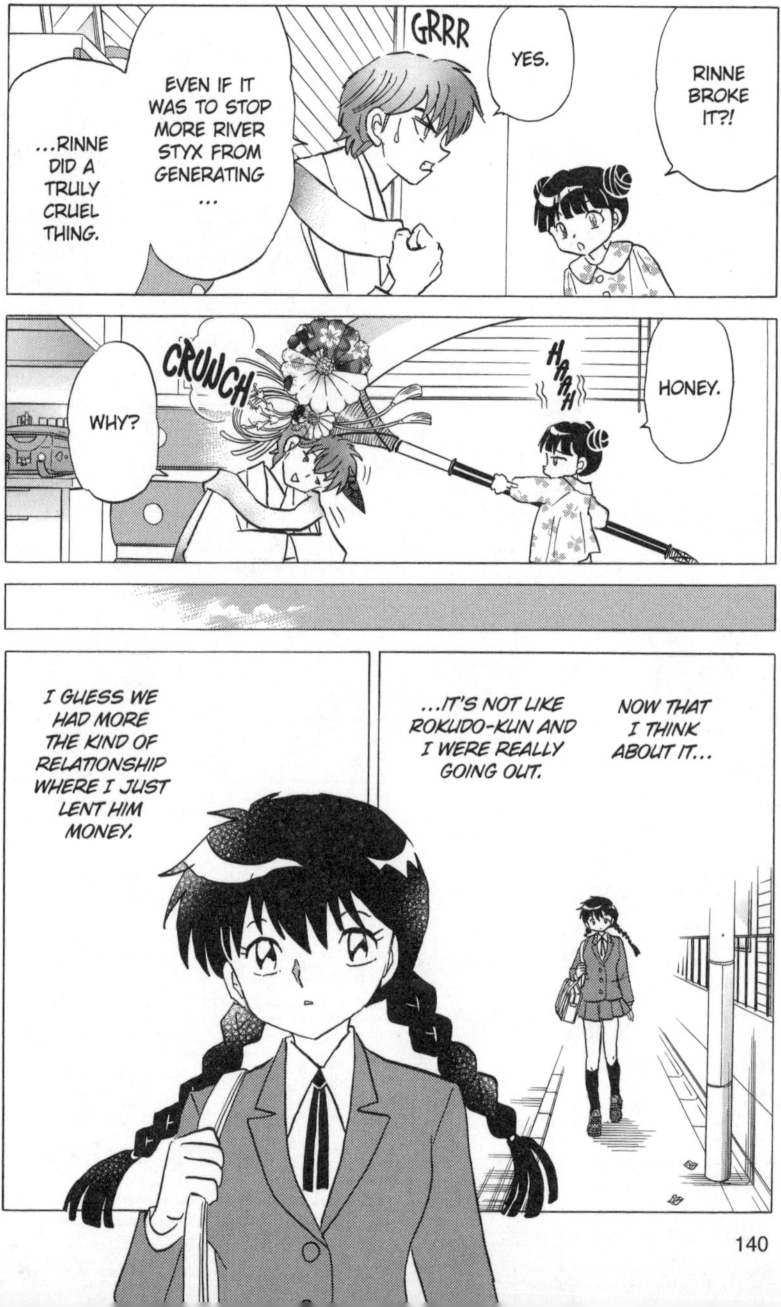
RINNE BROKE IT?!
YES.
GRRR
EVEN IF IT WAS TO STOP MORE RIVER STYX FROM GENERATING ...
...RINNE DID A TRULY CRUEL THING.
HONEY.
HAAH
CRUNCH
WHY?
NOW THAT I THINK ABOUT IT...
...IT'S NOT LIKE ROKUDO-KUN AND I WERE REALLY GOING OUT.
I GUESS WE HAD MORE THE KIND OF RELATIONSHIP WHERE I JUST LENT HIM MONEY.

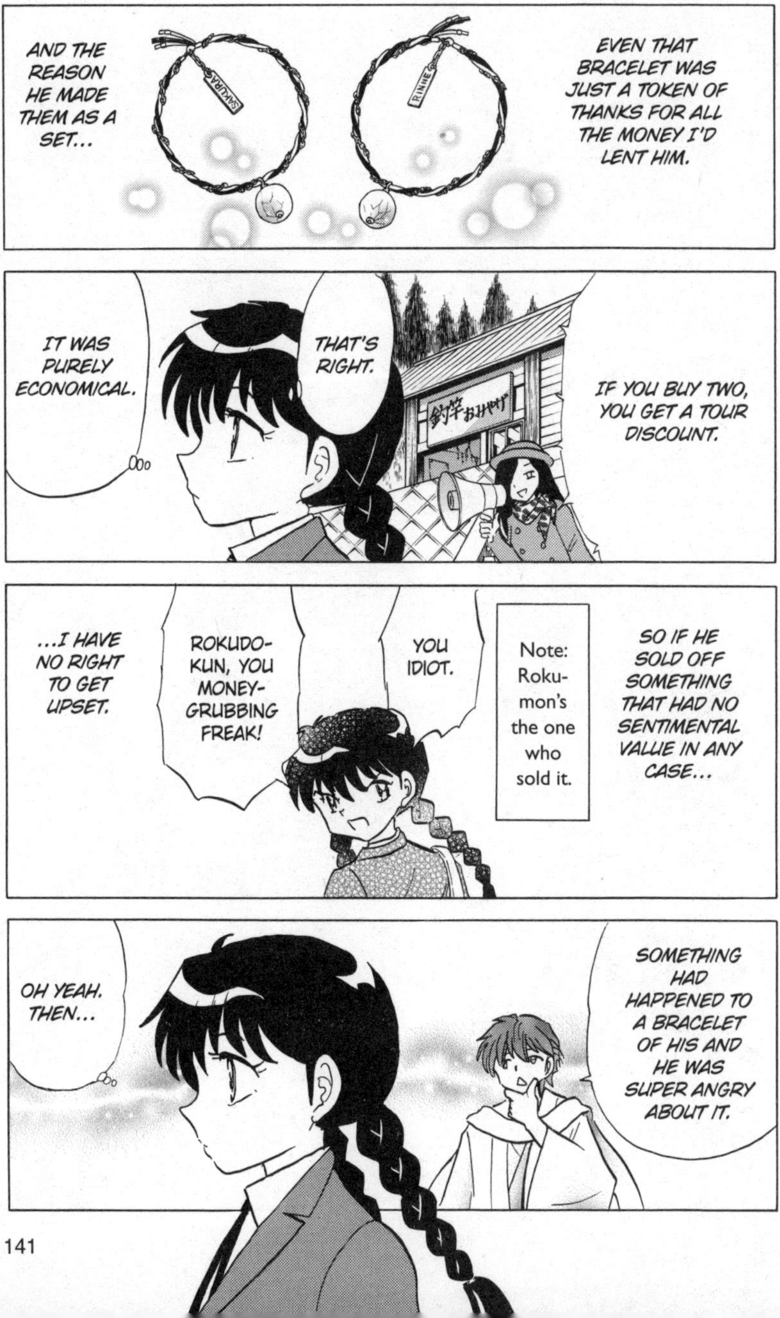
EVEN THAT BRACELET WAS JUST A TOKEN OF THANKS FOR ALL THE MONEY I'D LENT HIM.
RINNE
SAKURA
AND THE REASON HE MADE THEM AS A SET...
IF YOU BUY TWO, YOU GET A TOUR DISCOUNT.
釣竿おみやげ
THAT'S RIGHT.
IT WAS PURELY ECONOMICAL.
SO IF HE SOLD OFF SOMETHING THAT HAD NO SENTIMENTAL VALUE IN ANY CASE...
Note: Rokumon's the one who sold it.
YOU IDIOT.
ROKUDO-KUN, YOU MONEY-GRUBBING FREAK!
...I HAVE NO RIGHT TO GET UPSET.
SOMETHING HAD HAPPENED TO A BRACELET OF HIS AND HE WAS SUPER ANGRY ABOUT IT.
OH YEAH. THEN...

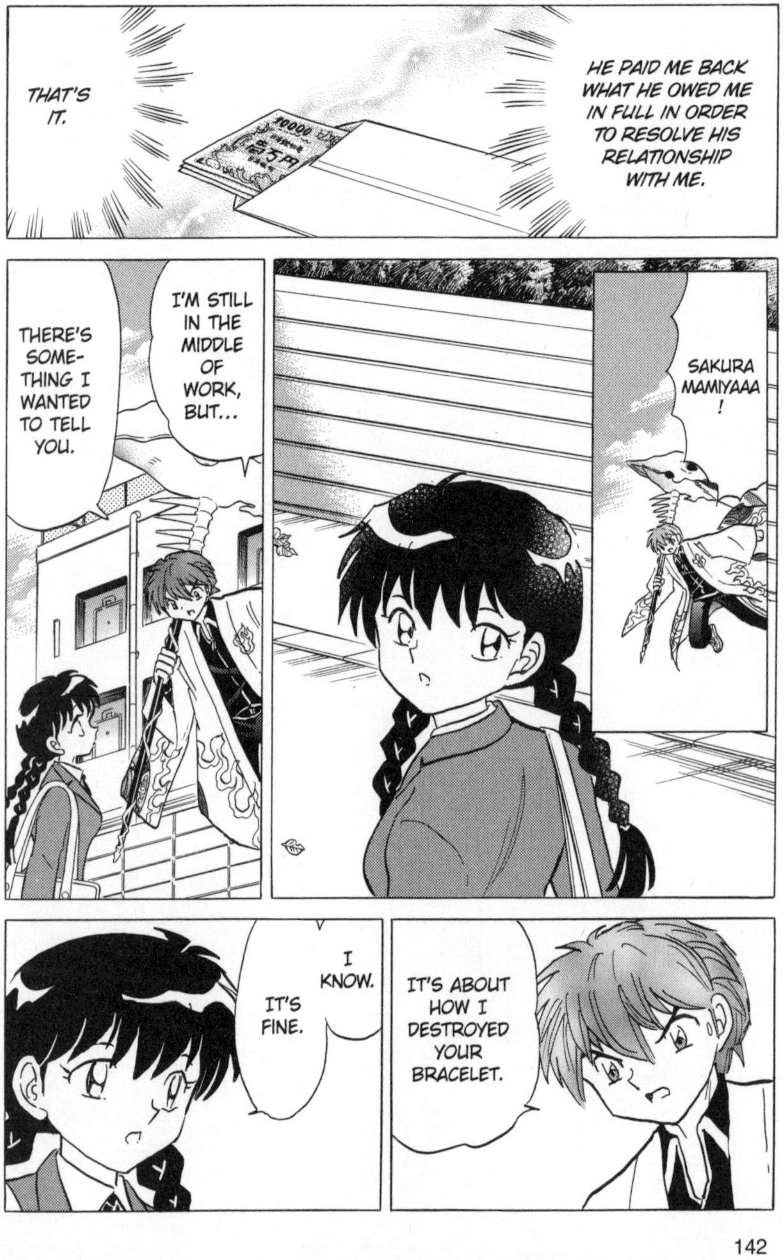
HE PAID ME BACK WHAT HE OWED ME IN FULL IN ORDER TO RESOLVE HIS RELATIONSHIP WITH ME.
THAT'S IT.
SAKURA MAMIYAAA!
I'M STILL IN THE MIDDLE OF WORK, BUT...
THERE'S SOMETHING I WANTED TO TELL YOU.
IT'S ABOUT HOW I DESTROYED YOUR BRACELET.
I KNOW.
IT'S FINE.

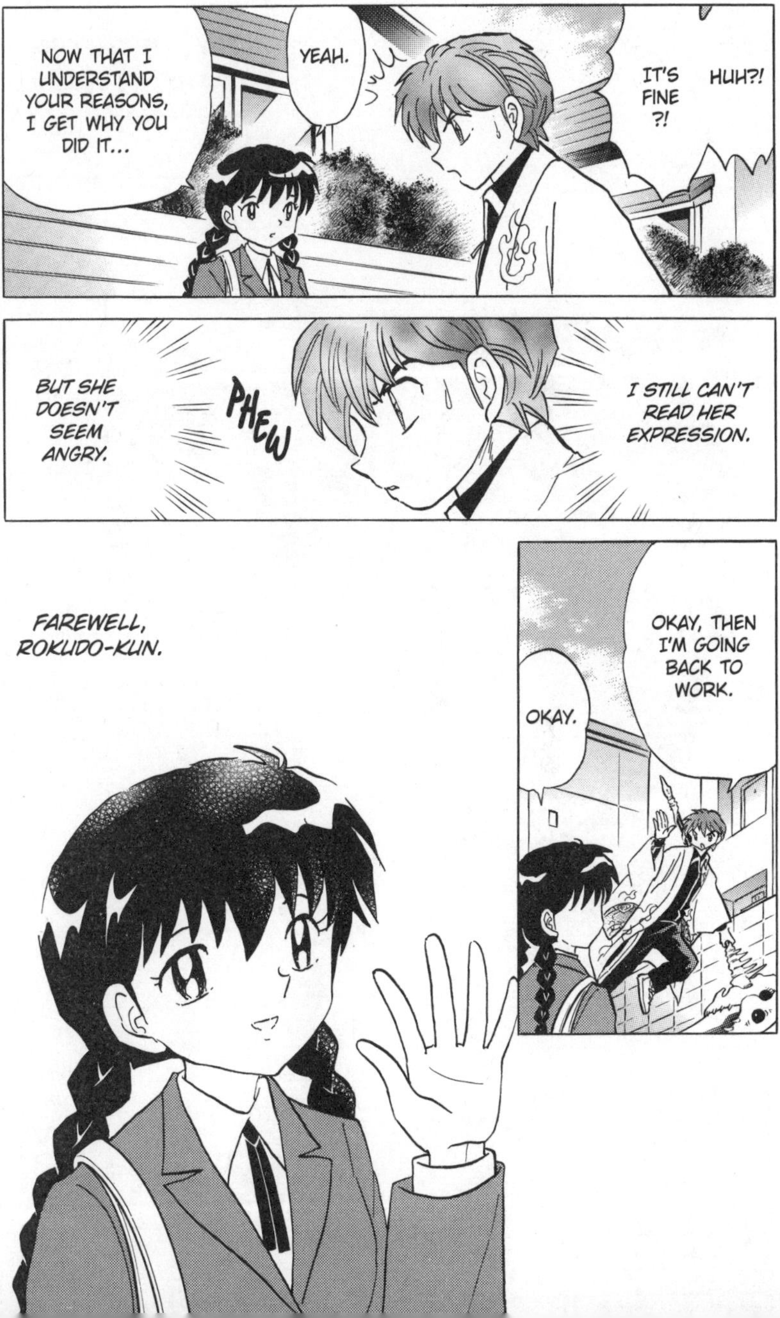
HUH?!
IT'S FINE ?!
YEAH.
NOW THAT I UNDERSTAND YOUR REASONS, I GET WHY YOU DID IT...
I STILL CAN'T READ HER EXPRESSION.
PHEW
BUT SHE DOESN'T SEEM ANGRY.
OKAY, THEN I'M GOING BACK TO WORK.
OKAY.
FAREWELL, ROKUDO-KUN.

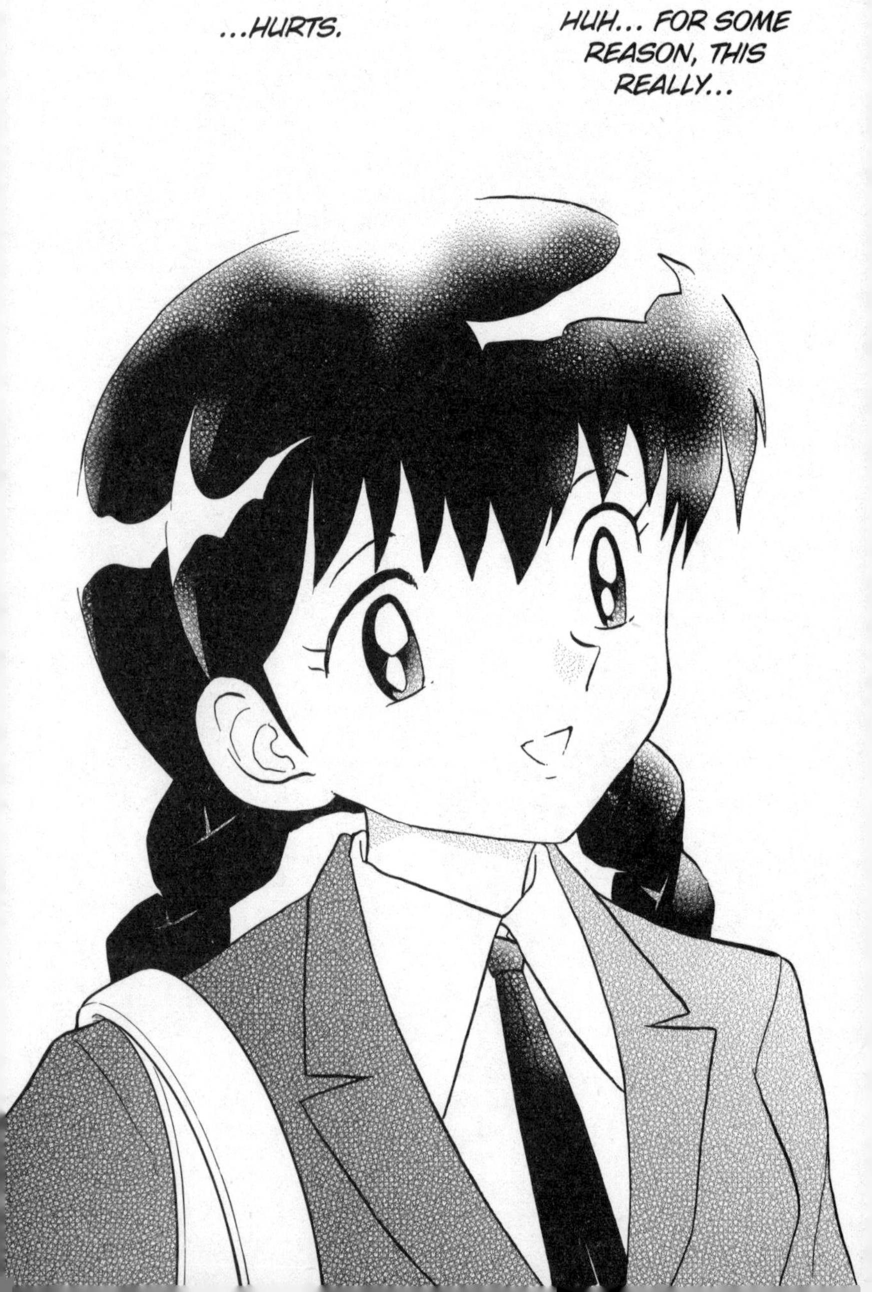
HUH... FOR SOME REASON, THIS REALLY...
...HURTS.

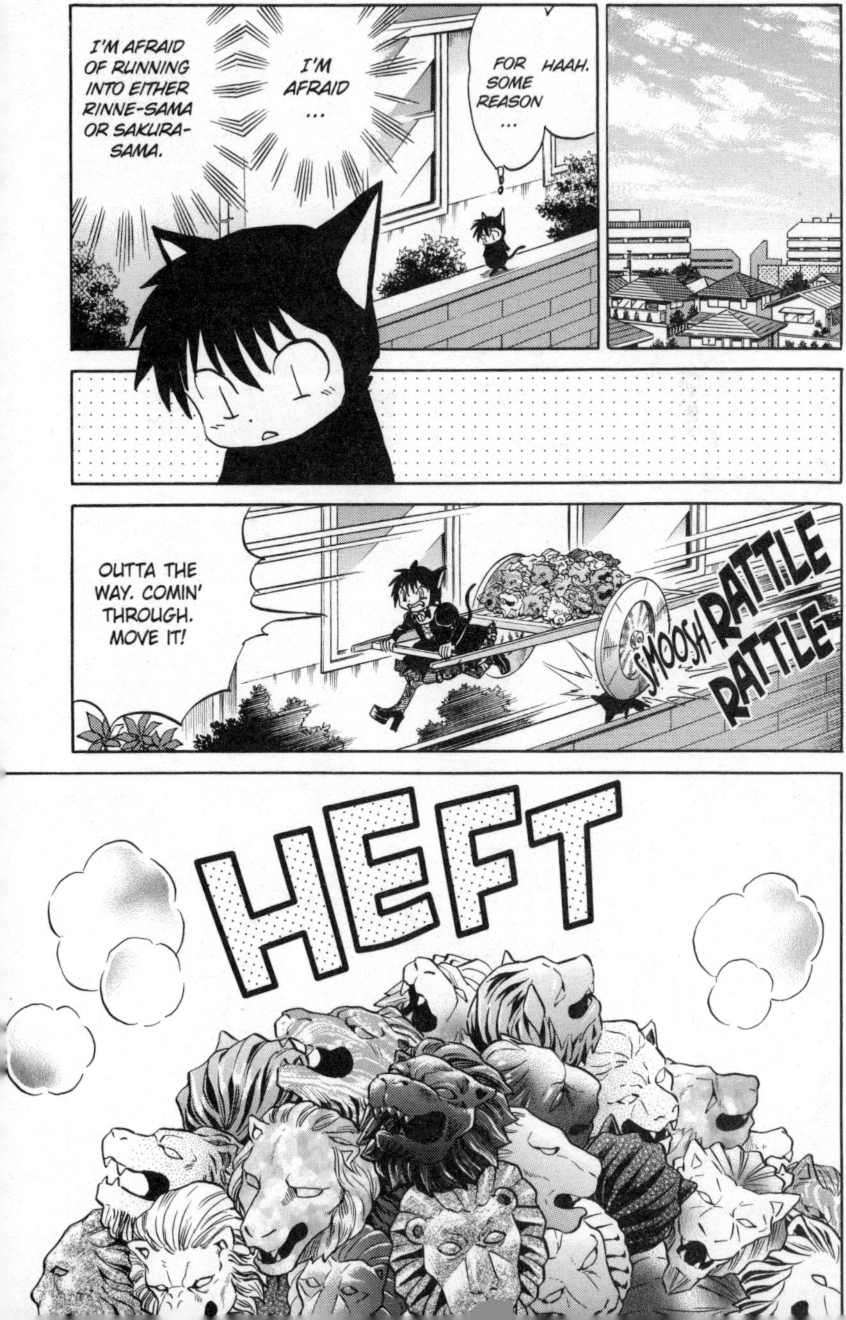
HAAH.
FOR SOME REASON ...
I'M AFRAID ...
I'M AFRAID OF RUNNING INTO EITHER RINNE-SAMA OR SAKURA-SAMA.
RATTLE RATTLE
SMOOSH
OUTTA THE WAY. COMIN' THROUGH. MOVE IT!
HEFT

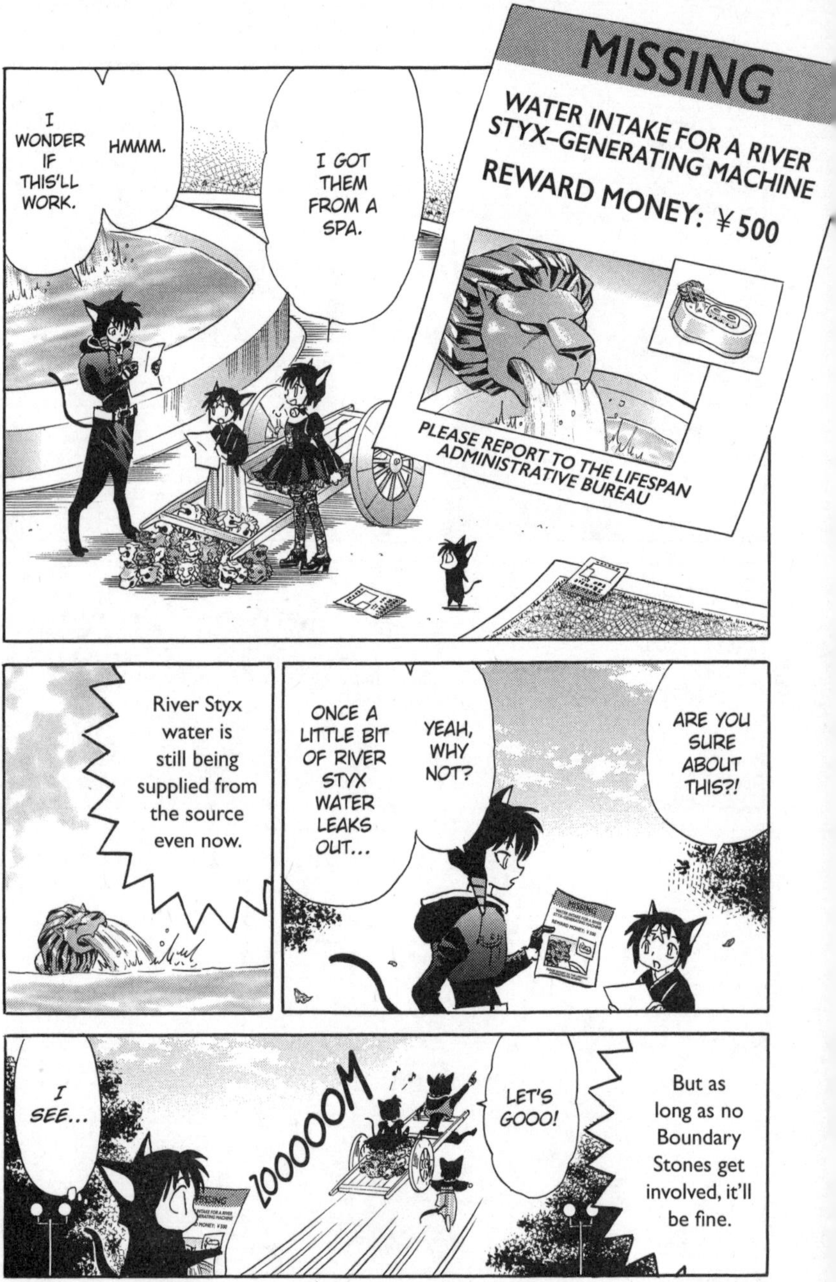
MISSING
WATER INTAKE FOR A RIVER STYX–GENERATING MACHINE
REWARD MONEY: ¥500
PLEASE REPORT TO THE LIFESPAN ADMINISTRATIVE BUREAU
I GOT THEM FROM A SPA.
HMMM.
I WONDER IF THIS'LL WORK.
ARE YOU SURE ABOUT THIS?!
YEAH, WHY NOT?
ONCE A LITTLE BIT OF RIVER STYX WATER LEAKS OUT…
River Styx water is still being supplied from the source even now.
But as long as no Boundary Stones get involved, it'll be fine.
LET'S GOOO!
ZOOOOOM
I SEE…

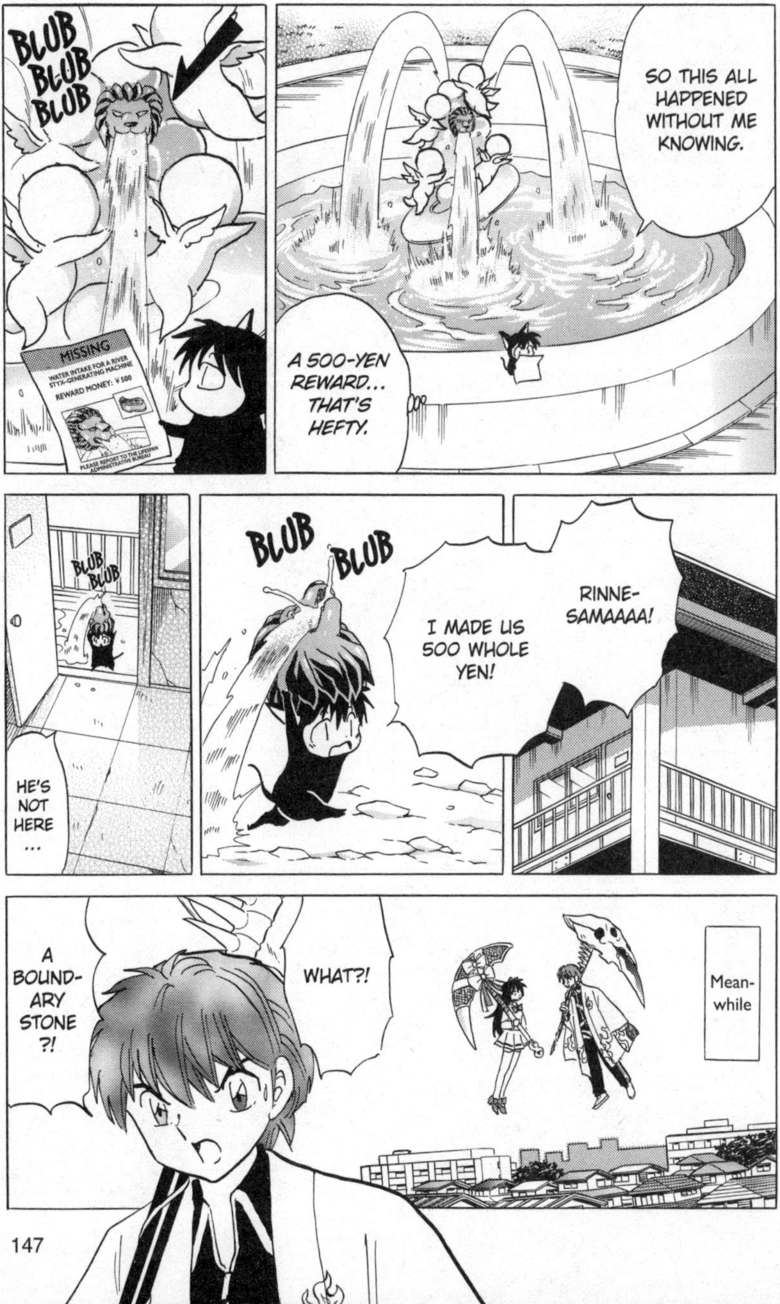
SO THIS ALL HAPPENED WITHOUT ME KNOWING.
A 500-YEN REWARD... THAT'S HEFTY.
BLUB BLUB BLUB
MISSING
WATER INTAKE FOR A RIVER STYX-GENERATING MACHINE
REWARD MONEY: ¥500
PLEASE REPORT TO THE LIFESPAN ADMINISTRATIVE BUREAU
RINNE-SAMAAAA!
BLUB BLUB
I MADE US 500 WHOLE YEN!
BLUB BLUB
HE'S NOT HERE...
Mean-while
WHAT?!
A BOUND-ARY STONE?!

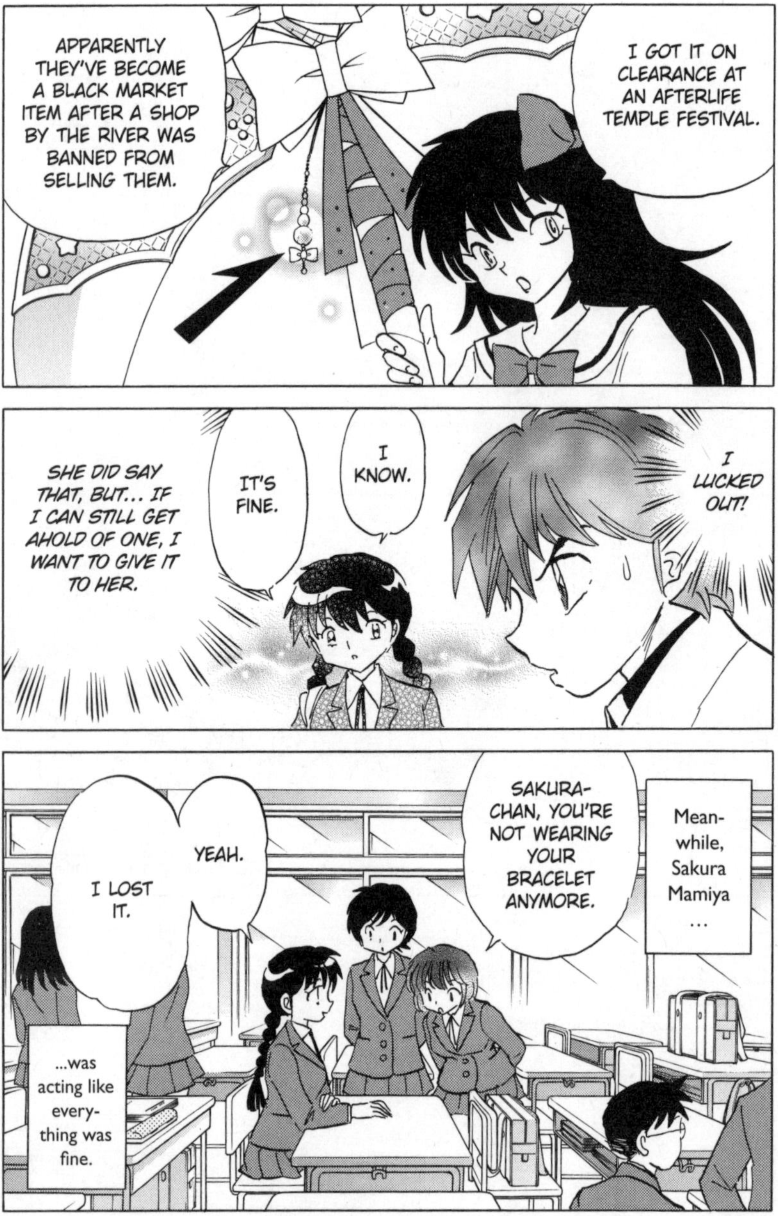
I GOT IT ON CLEARANCE AT AN AFTERLIFE TEMPLE FESTIVAL.
APPARENTLY THEY'VE BECOME A BLACK MARKET ITEM AFTER A SHOP BY THE RIVER WAS BANNED FROM SELLING THEM.
I LUCKED OUT!
I KNOW.
IT'S FINE.
SHE DID SAY THAT, BUT... IF I CAN STILL GET AHOLD OF ONE, I WANT TO GIVE IT TO HER.
Meanwhile, Sakura Mamiya...
SAKURA-CHAN, YOU'RE NOT WEARING YOUR BRACELET ANYMORE.
YEAH.
I LOST IT.
...was acting like everything was fine.

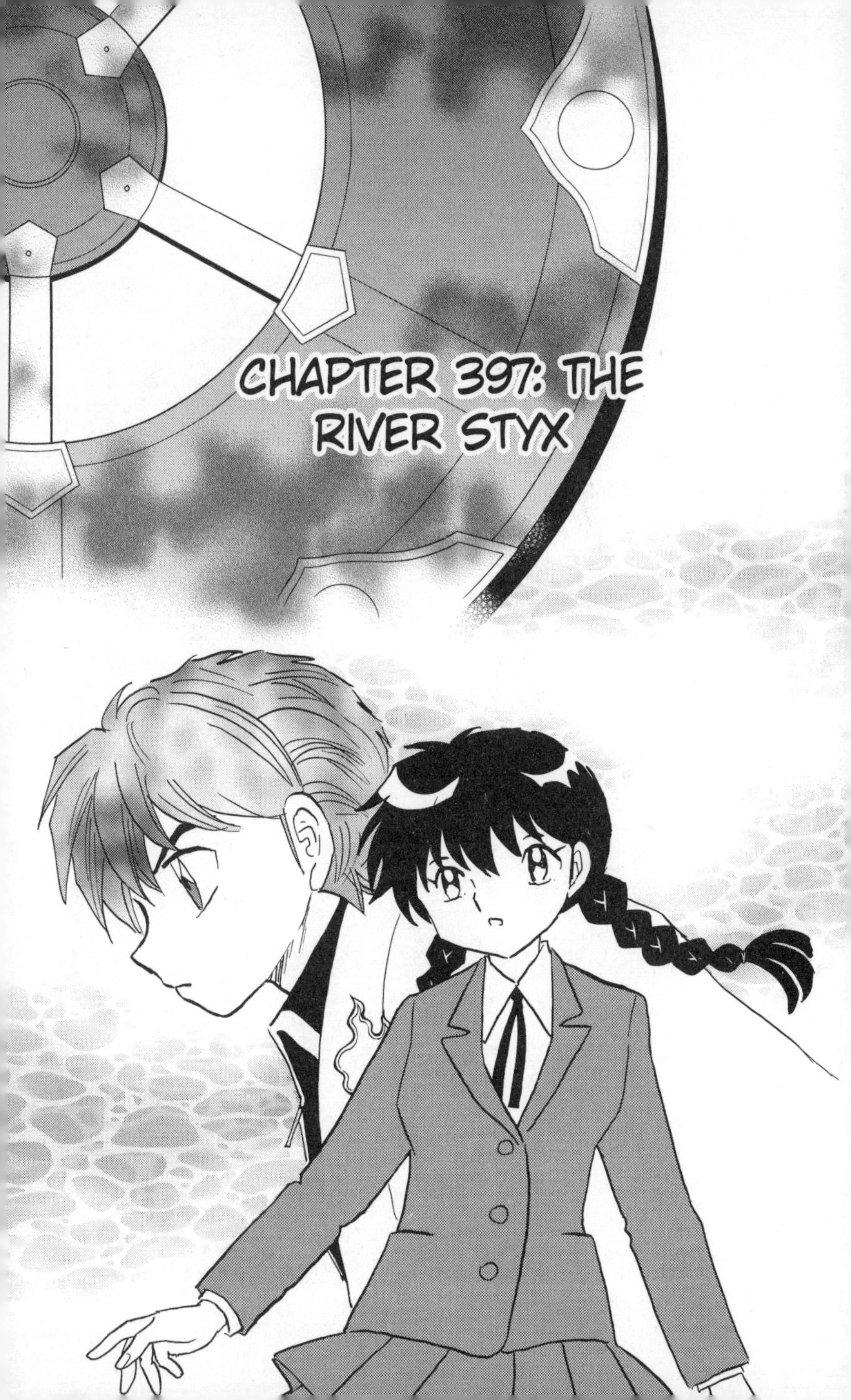
CHAPTER 397: THE RIVER STYX

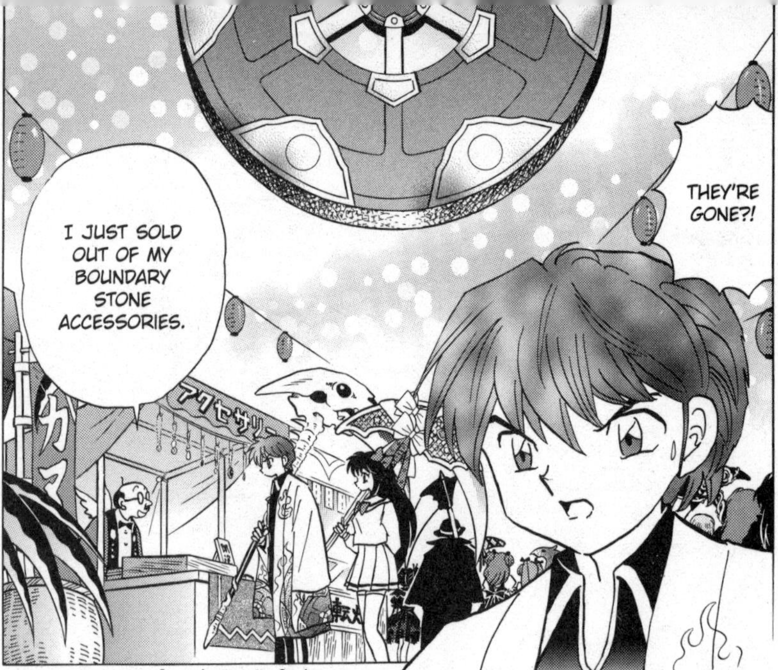
THEY'RE GONE?!
I JUST SOLD OUT OF MY BOUNDARY STONE ACCESSORIES.
Signs: Accessories, Scythes

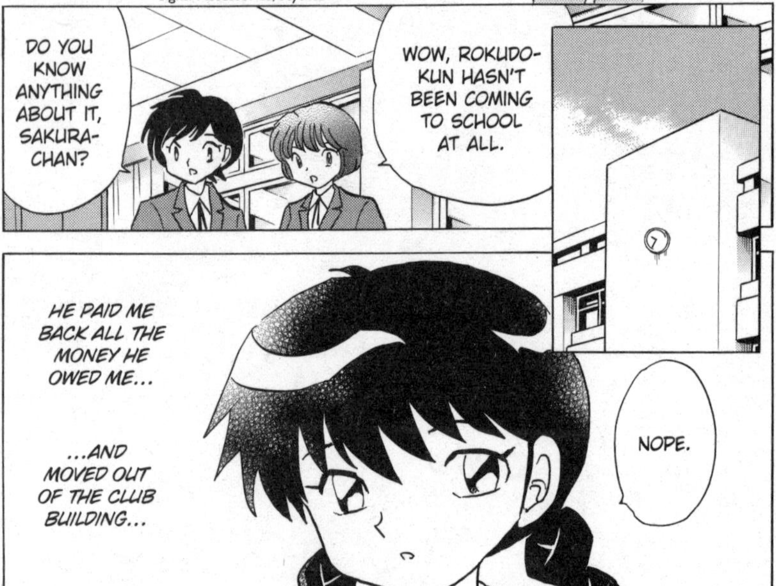
WOW, ROKUDO-KUN HASN'T BEEN COMING TO SCHOOL AT ALL.
DO YOU KNOW ANYTHING ABOUT IT, SAKURA-CHAN?
NOPE.
HE PAID ME BACK ALL THE MONEY HE OWED ME...
...AND MOVED OUT OF THE CLUB BUILDING...

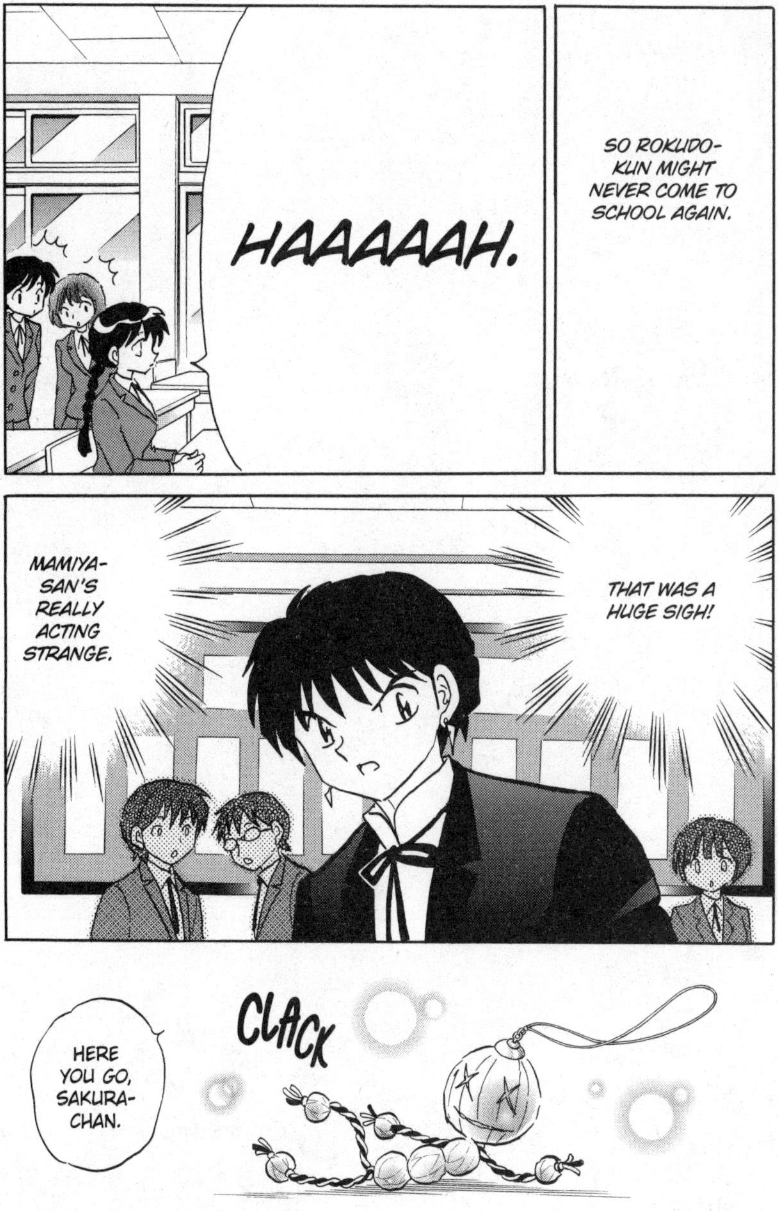
SO ROKUDO-KUN MIGHT NEVER COME TO SCHOOL AGAIN.
HAAAAAH.
THAT WAS A HUGE SIGH!
MAMIYA-SAN'S REALLY ACTING STRANGE.
CLACK
HERE YOU GO, SAKURA-CHAN.

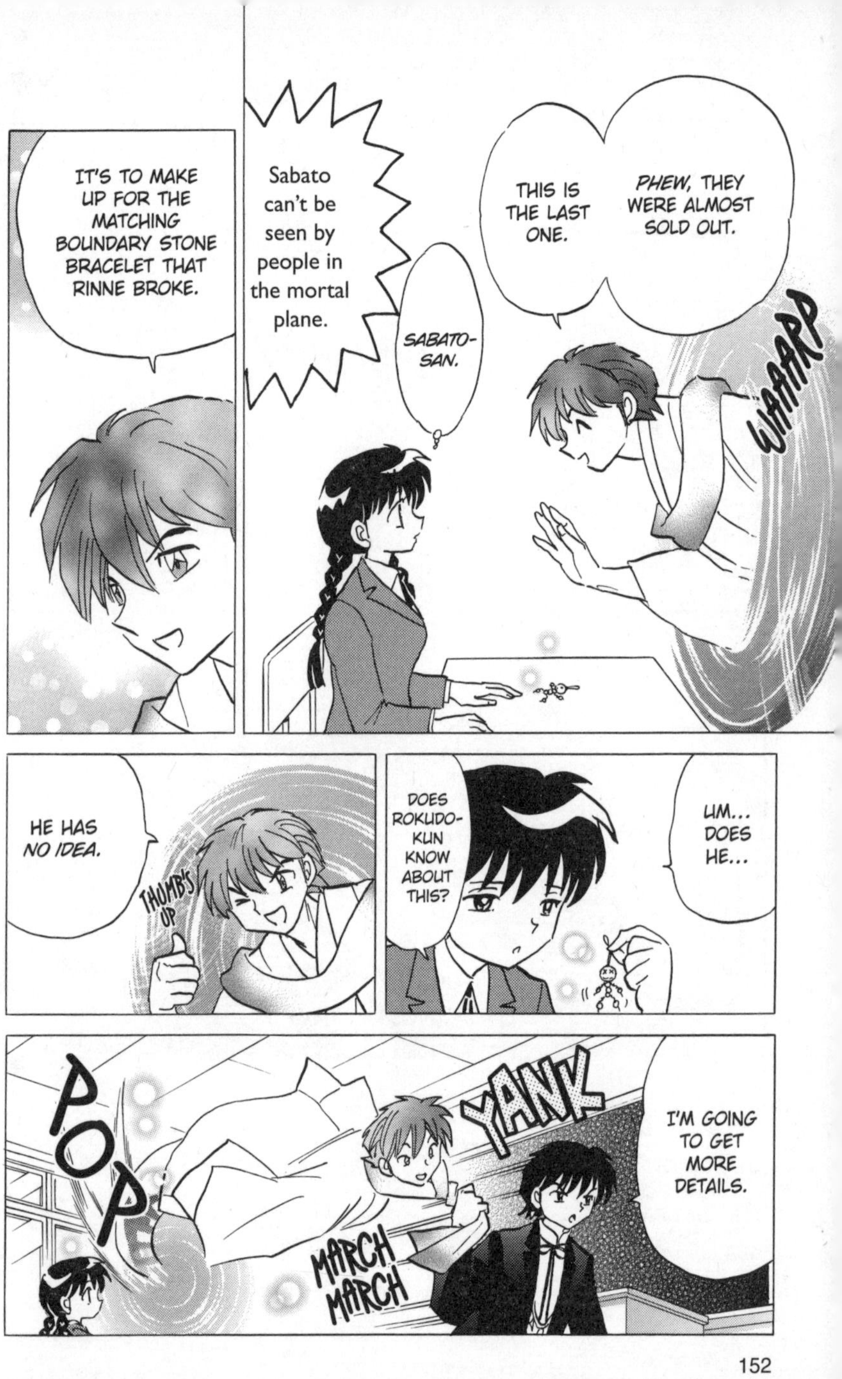

PHEW, THEY WERE ALMOST SOLD OUT.
THIS IS THE LAST ONE.
Sabato can't be seen by people in the mortal plane.
SABATO-SAN.
WAARP
IT'S TO MAKE UP FOR THE MATCHING BOUNDARY STONE BRACELET THAT RINNE BROKE.
UM... DOES HE...
DOES ROKUDO-KUN KNOW ABOUT THIS?
HE HAS NO IDEA.
THUMB'S UP
I'M GOING TO GET MORE DETAILS.
YANK
POP
MARCH MARCH

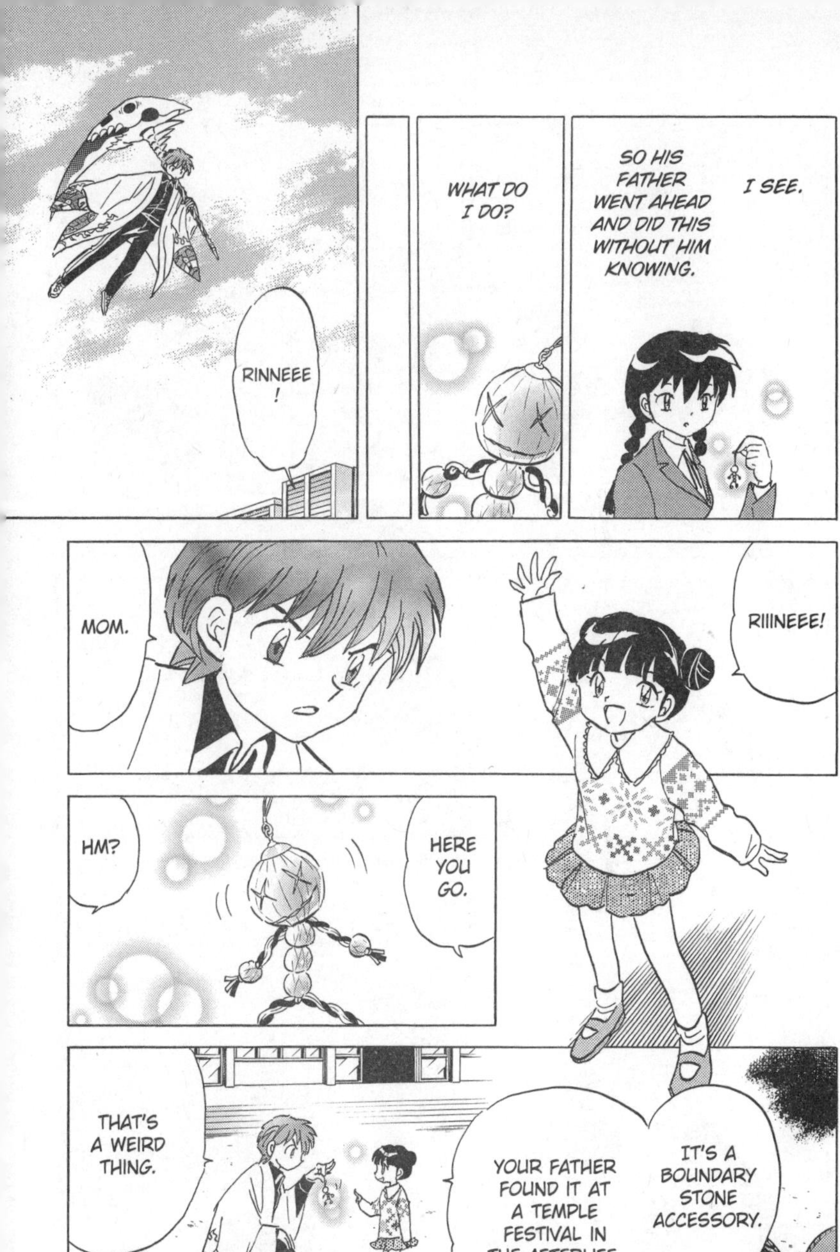
I SEE.
SO HIS FATHER WENT AHEAD AND DID THIS WITHOUT HIM KNOWING.
WHAT DO I DO?
RINNEEE!
RIIINEEE!
MOM.
HERE YOU GO.
HM?
IT'S A BOUNDARY STONE ACCESSORY.
YOUR FATHER FOUND IT AT A TEMPLE FESTIVAL IN THE AFTERLIFE.
THAT'S A WEIRD THING.

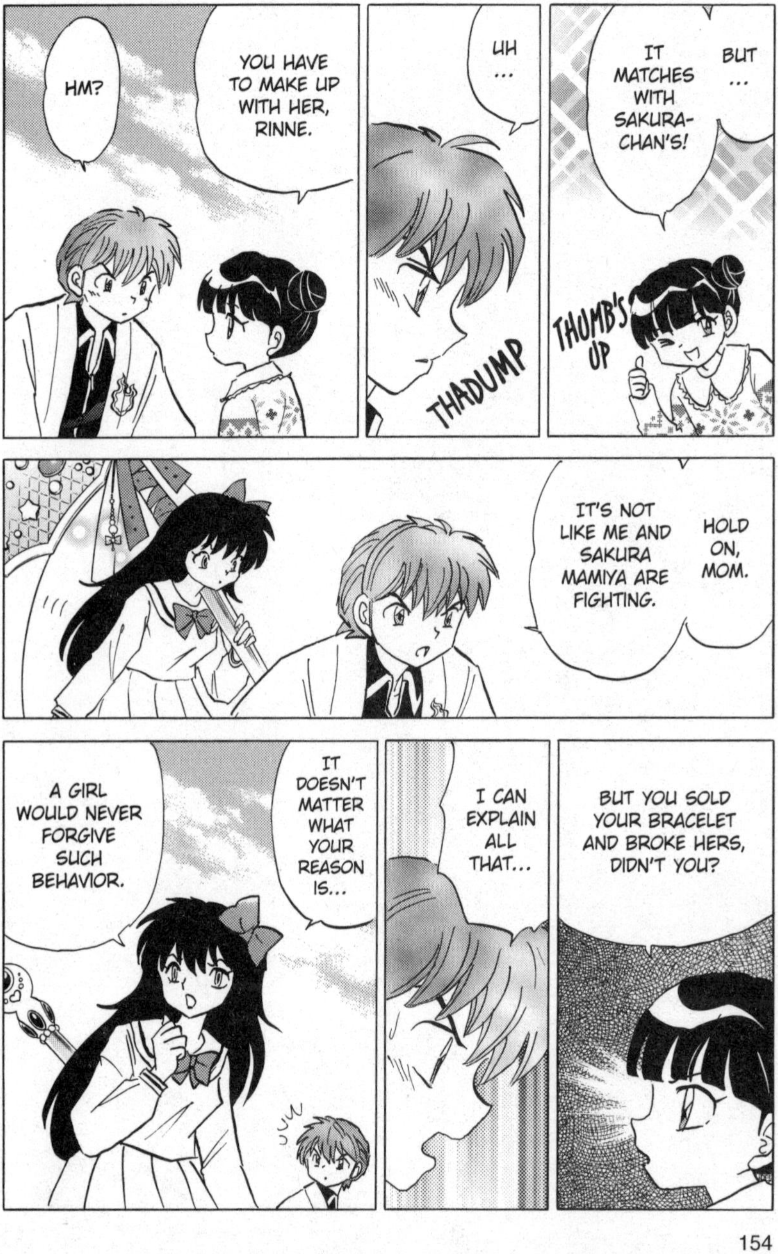
BUT ...
IT MATCHES WITH SAKURA-CHAN'S!
THUMB'S UP
UH ...
THADUMP
YOU HAVE TO MAKE UP WITH HER, RINNE.
HM?
HOLD ON, MOM.
IT'S NOT LIKE ME AND SAKURA MAMIYA ARE FIGHTING.
BUT YOU SOLD YOUR BRACELET AND BROKE HERS, DIDN'T YOU?
I CAN EXPLAIN ALL THAT...
IT DOESN'T MATTER WHAT YOUR REASON IS...
A GIRL WOULD NEVER FORGIVE SUCH BEHAVIOR.

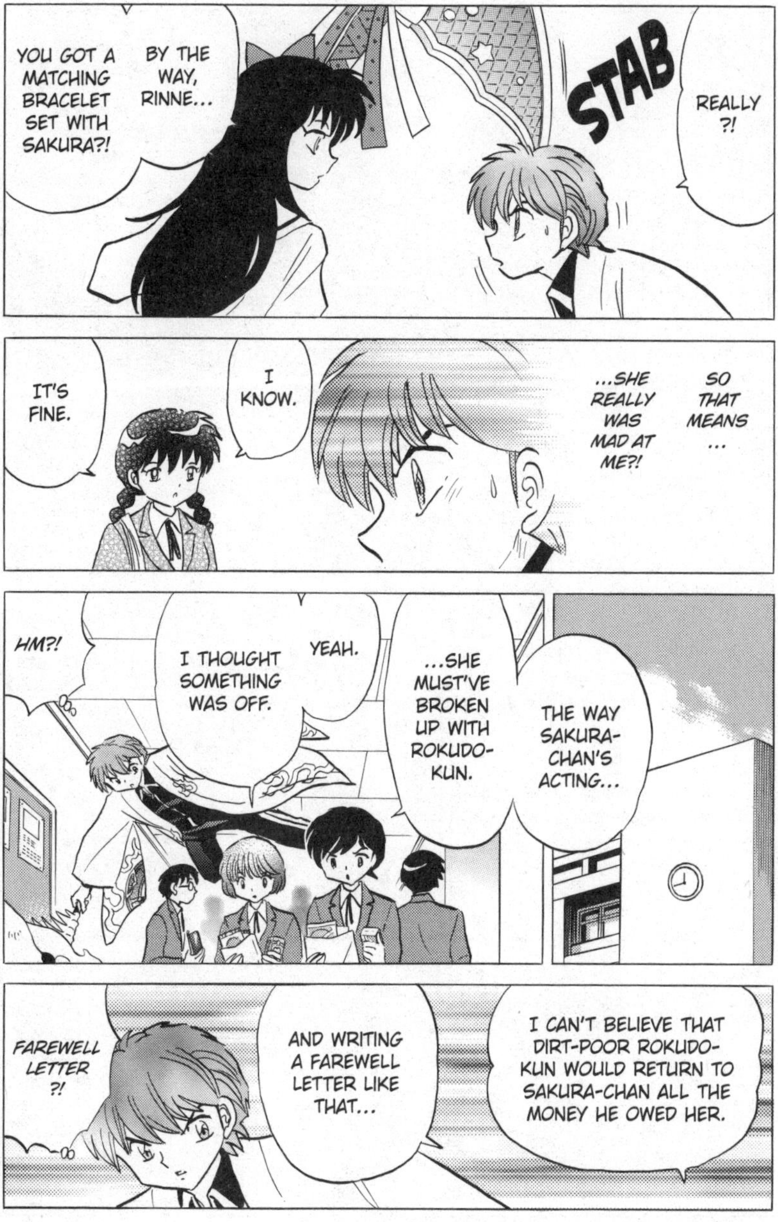
REALLY?!
STAB
BY THE WAY, RINNE...
YOU GOT A MATCHING BRACELET SET WITH SAKURA?!
SO THAT MEANS...
...SHE REALLY WAS MAD AT ME?!
I KNOW.
IT'S FINE.
THE WAY SAKURA-CHAN'S ACTING...
...SHE MUST'VE BROKEN UP WITH ROKUDO-KUN.
YEAH.
I THOUGHT SOMETHING WAS OFF.
HM?!
I CAN'T BELIEVE THAT DIRT-POOR ROKUDO-KUN WOULD RETURN TO SAKURA-CHAN ALL THE MONEY HE OWED HER.
AND WRITING A FAREWELL LETTER LIKE THAT...
FAREWELL LETTER?!

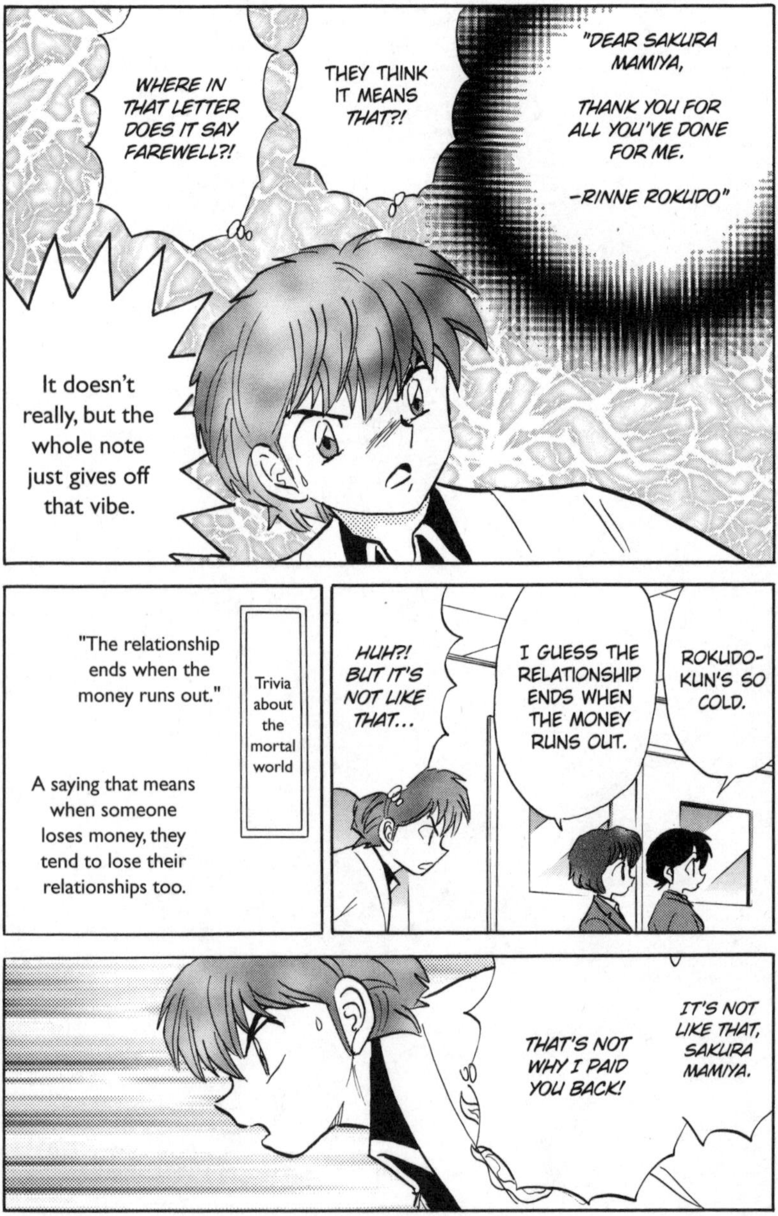
"DEAR SAKURA MAMIYA, THANK YOU FOR ALL YOU'VE DONE FOR ME. -RINNE ROKUDO"
THEY THINK IT MEANS THAT?!
WHERE IN THAT LETTER DOES IT SAY FAREWELL?!
It doesn't really, but the whole note just gives off that vibe.
ROKUDO-KUN'S SO COLD.
I GUESS THE RELATIONSHIP ENDS WHEN THE MONEY RUNS OUT.
HUH?! BUT IT'S NOT LIKE THAT...
Trivia about the mortal world
"The relationship ends when the money runs out."
A saying that means when someone loses money, they tend to lose their relationships too.
IT'S NOT LIKE THAT, SAKURA MAMIYA.
THAT'S NOT WHY I PAID YOU BACK!

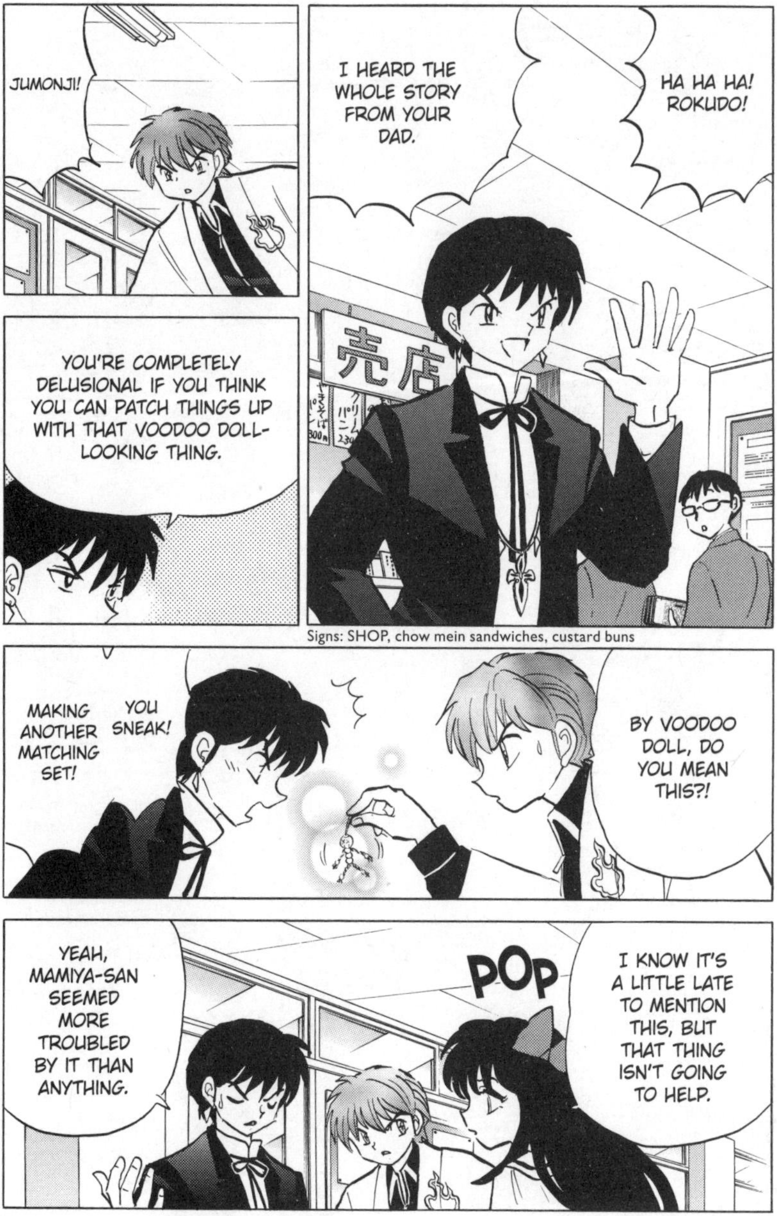
HA HA HA! ROKUDO!
I HEARD THE WHOLE STORY FROM YOUR DAD.
JUMONJI!
YOU'RE COMPLETELY DELUSIONAL IF YOU THINK YOU CAN PATCH THINGS UP WITH THAT VOODOO DOLL-LOOKING THING.
BY VOODOO DOLL, DO YOU MEAN THIS?!
YOU SNEAK!
MAKING ANOTHER MATCHING SET!
I KNOW IT'S A LITTLE LATE TO MENTION THIS, BUT THAT THING ISN'T GOING TO HELP.
POP
YEAH, MAMIYA-SAN SEEMED MORE TROUBLED BY IT THAN ANYTHING.
Signs: SHOP, chow mein sandwiches, custard buns

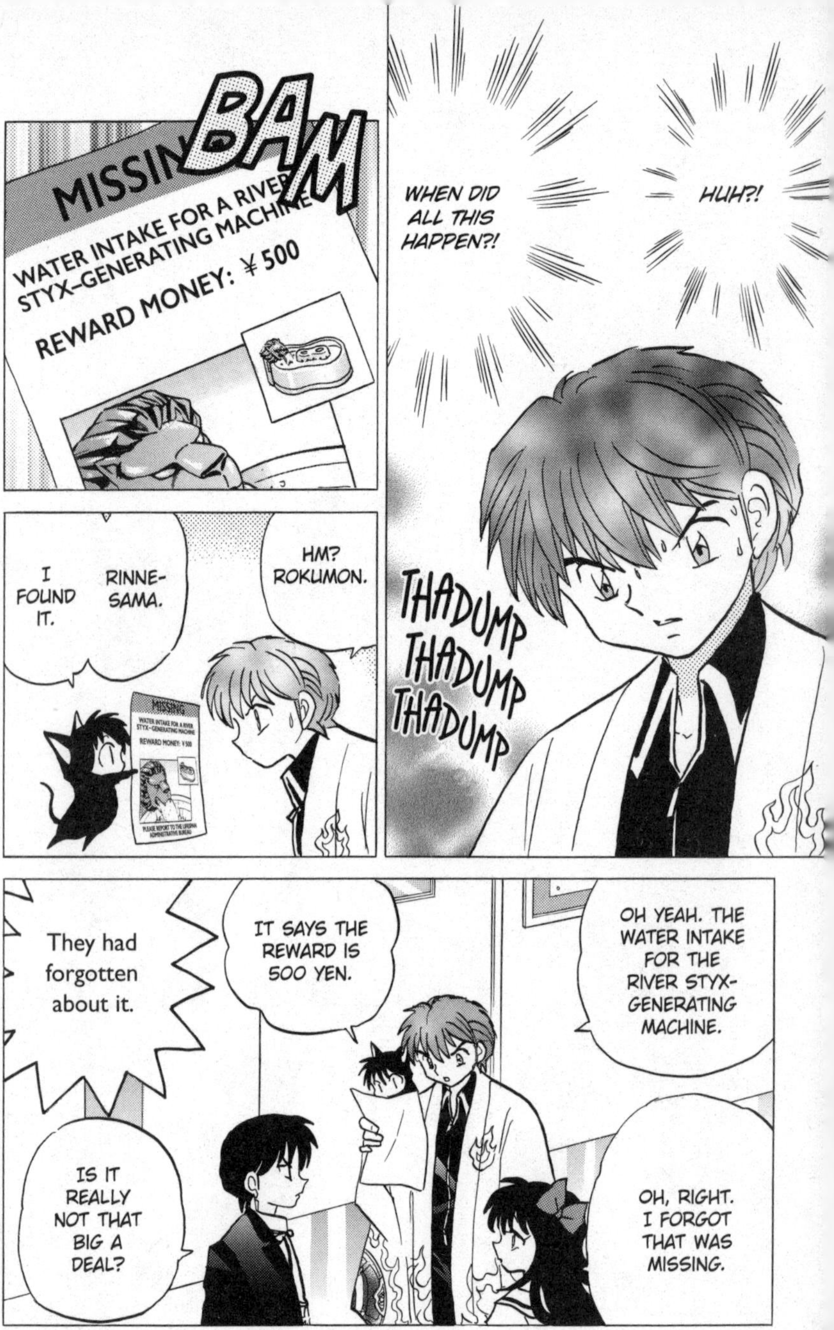
HUH?!
WHEN DID ALL THIS HAPPEN?!
THADUMP THADUMP THADUMP
MISSIN
BAM
WATER INTAKE FOR A RIVER STYX-GENERATING MACHINE
REWARD MONEY: ¥500
HM? ROKUMON.
RINNE-SAMA.
I FOUND IT.
MISSING
WATER INTAKE FOR A RIVER STYX-GENERATING MACHINE
REWARD MONEY: ¥500
PLEASE REPORT TO THE LIFESPAN ADMINISTRATIVE BUREAU
OH YEAH. THE WATER INTAKE FOR THE RIVER STYX-GENERATING MACHINE.
IT SAYS THE REWARD IS 500 YEN.
They had forgotten about it.
OH, RIGHT. I FORGOT THAT WAS MISSING.
IS IT REALLY NOT THAT BIG A DEAL?

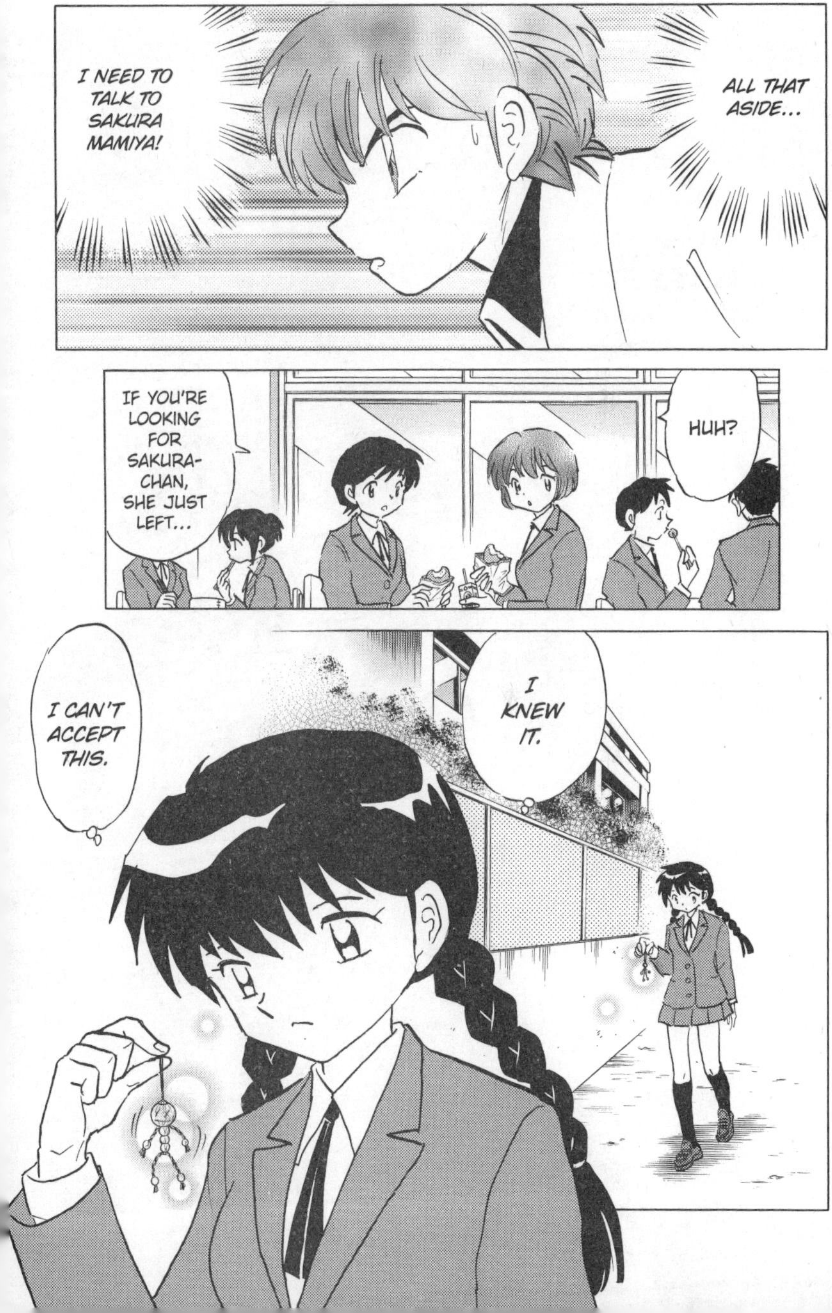
ALL THAT ASIDE...
I NEED TO TALK TO SAKURA MAMIYA!
HUH?
IF YOU'RE LOOKING FOR SAKURA-CHAN, SHE JUST LEFT...
I KNEW IT.
I CAN'T ACCEPT THIS.

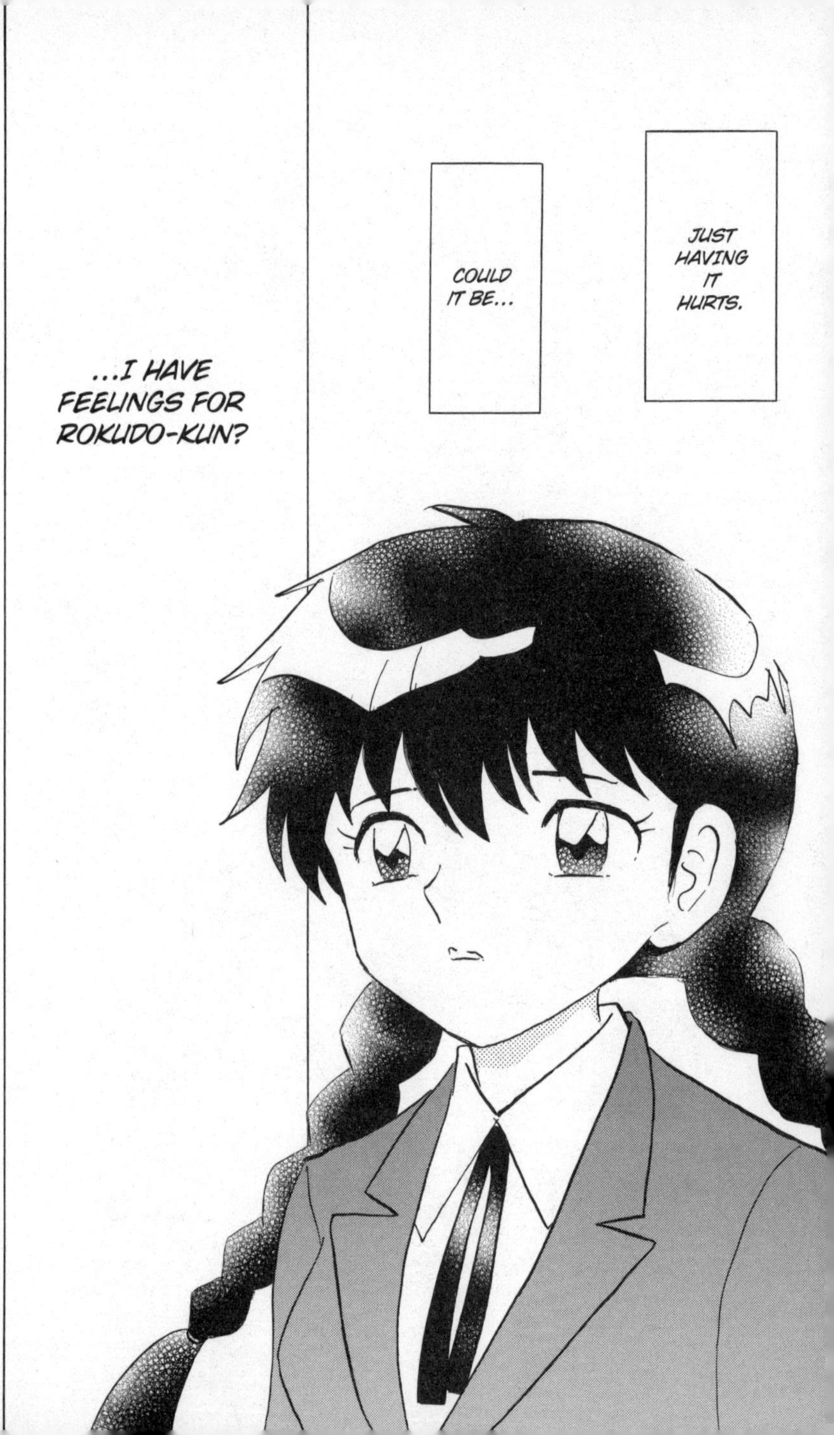
JUST HAVING IT HURTS.
COULD IT BE...
...I HAVE FEELINGS FOR ROKUDO-KUN?

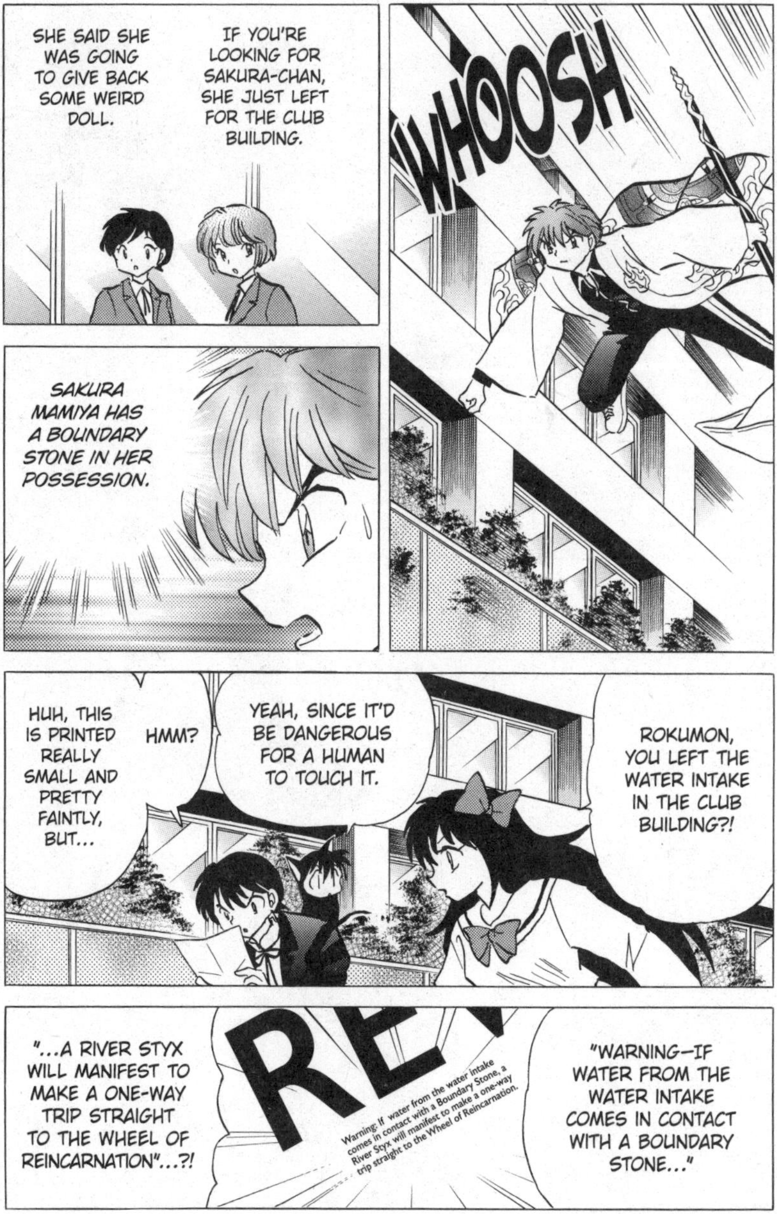
WHOOSH
IF YOU'RE LOOKING FOR SAKURA-CHAN, SHE JUST LEFT FOR THE CLUB BUILDING.
SHE SAID SHE WAS GOING TO GIVE BACK SOME WEIRD DOLL.
SAKURA MAMIYA HAS A BOUNDARY STONE IN HER POSSESSION.
ROKUMON, YOU LEFT THE WATER INTAKE IN THE CLUB BUILDING?!
YEAH, SINCE IT'D BE DANGEROUS FOR A HUMAN TO TOUCH IT.
HMM?
HUH, THIS IS PRINTED REALLY SMALL AND PRETTY FAINTLY, BUT...
"WARNING—IF WATER FROM THE WATER INTAKE COMES IN CONTACT WITH A BOUNDARY STONE..."
RE
Warning: If water from the water intake comes in contact with a Boundary Stone, a River Styx will manifest to make a one-way trip straight to the Wheel of Reincarnation.
"...A RIVER STYX WILL MANIFEST TO MAKE A ONE-WAY TRIP STRAIGHT TO THE WHEEL OF REINCARNATION"...?!

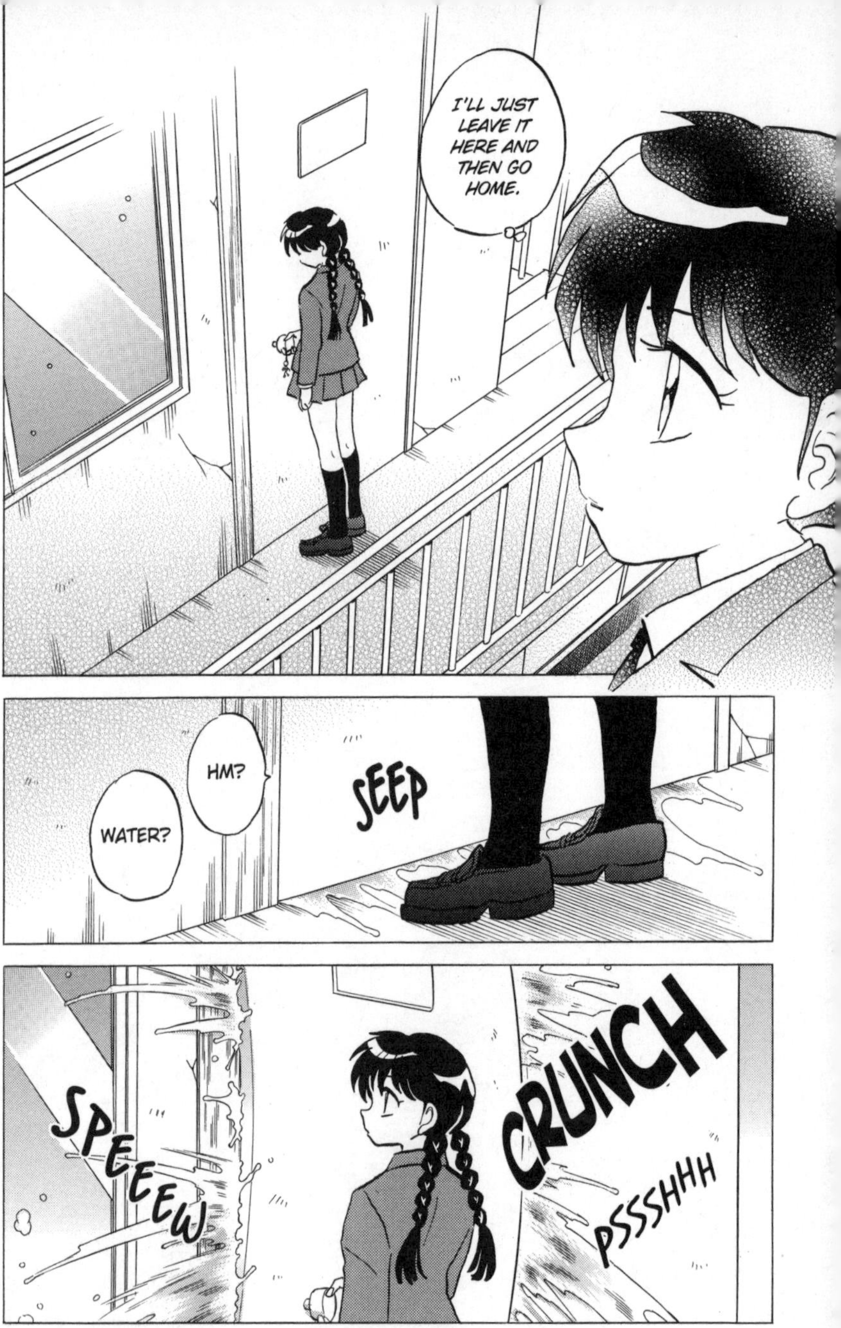
I'LL JUST LEAVE IT HERE AND THEN GO HOME.
SEEP
HM?
WATER?
CRUNCH
PSSSHHH
SPEEEW

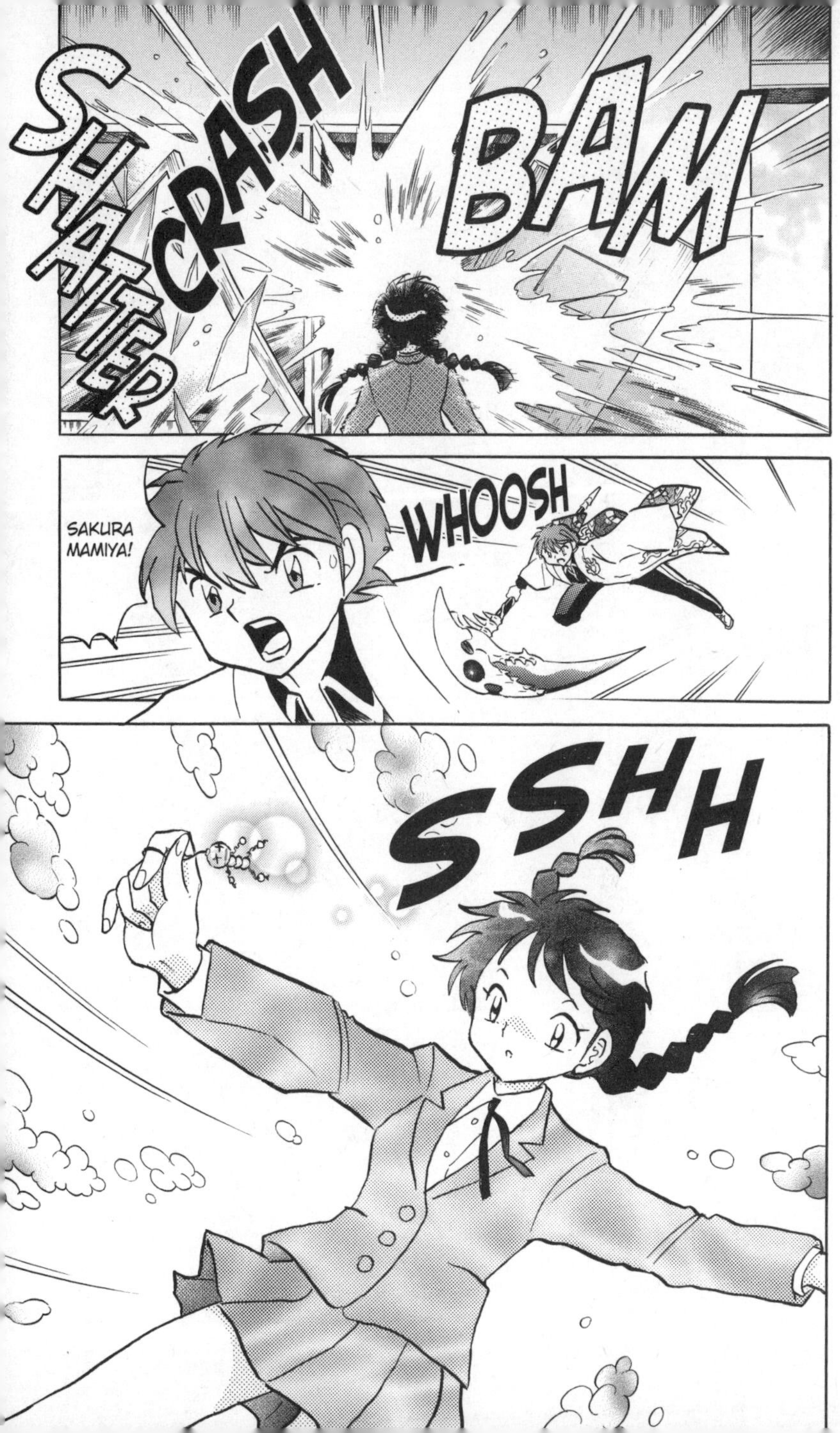
BAM
CRASH
SHATTER
WHOOSH
SAKURA MAMIYA!
SSHH

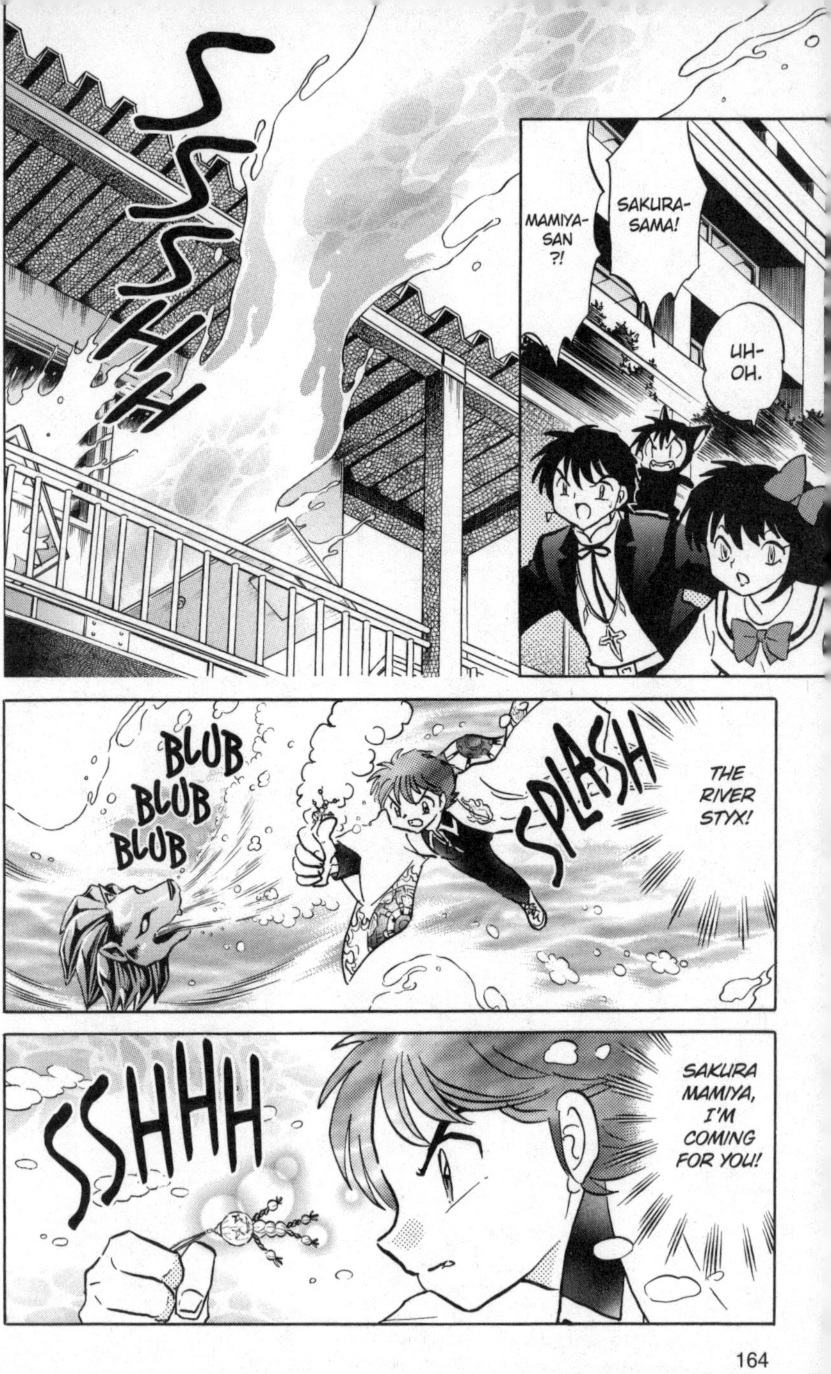
SAKURA-SAMA!
MAMIYA-SAN ?!
UH-OH.
SSSHHH
THE RIVER STYX!
SPLASH
BLUB BLUB BLUB
SAKURA MAMIYA, I'M COMING FOR YOU!
SSHHH

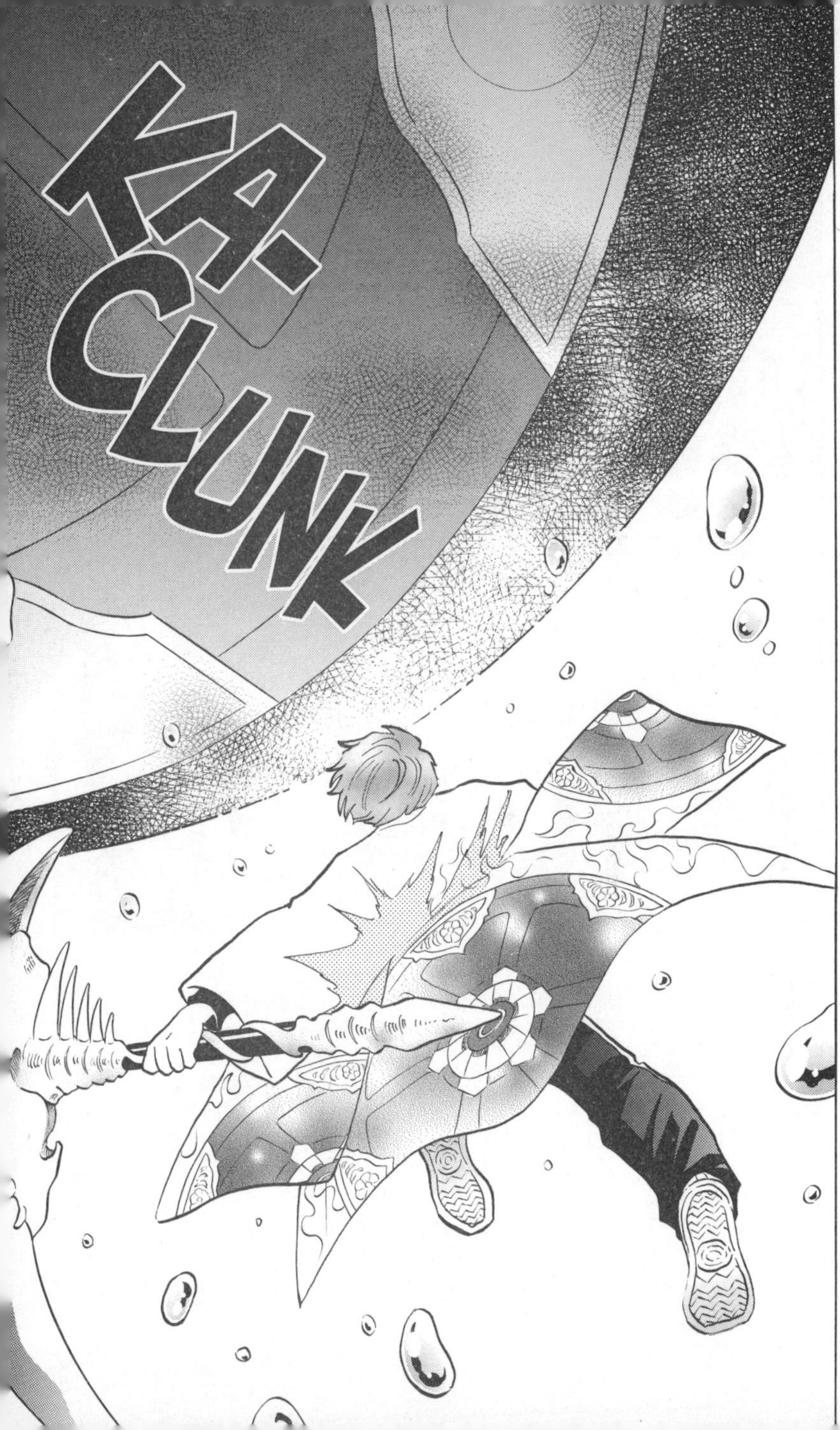
KA-CLUNK

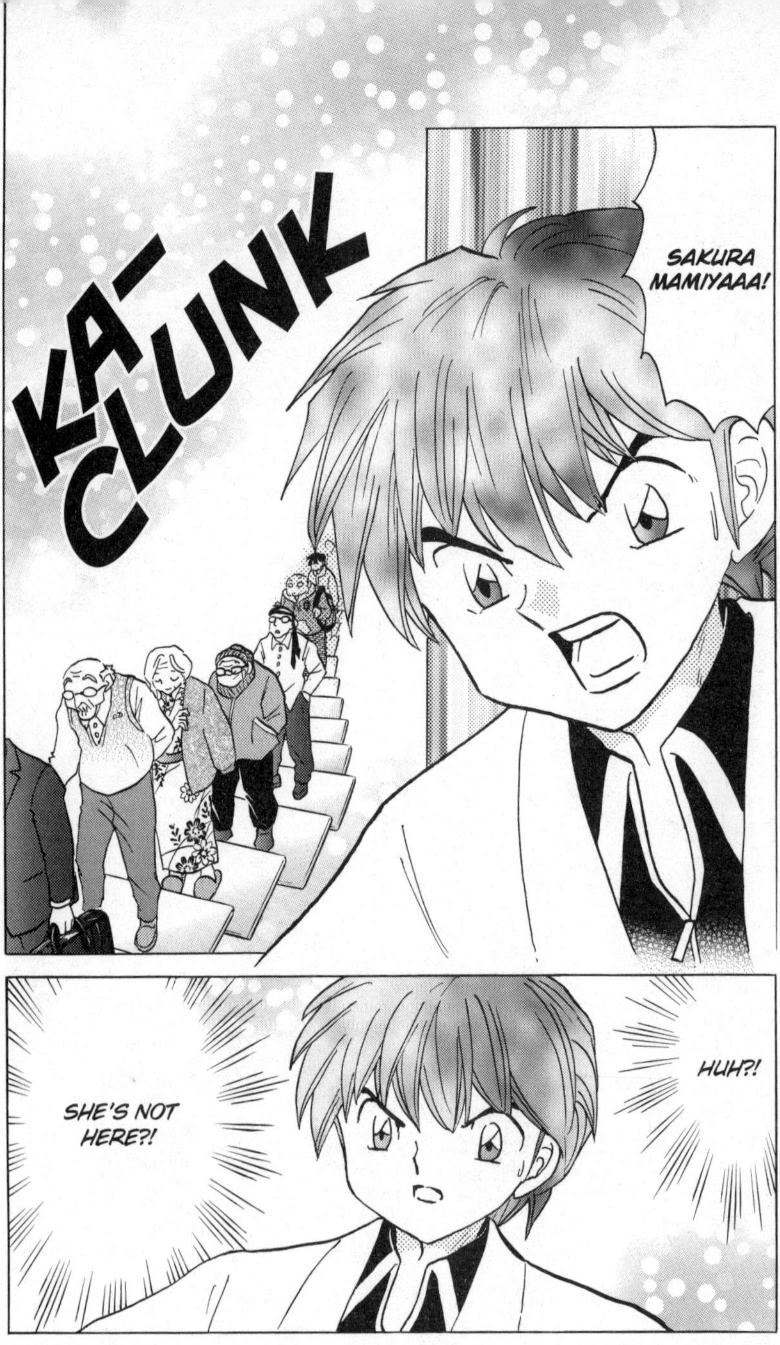
SAKURA MAMIYAAA!
KA-CLUNK
HUH?!
SHE'S NOT HERE?!

FINAL CHAPTER: THE WHEEL OF REINCARNATION

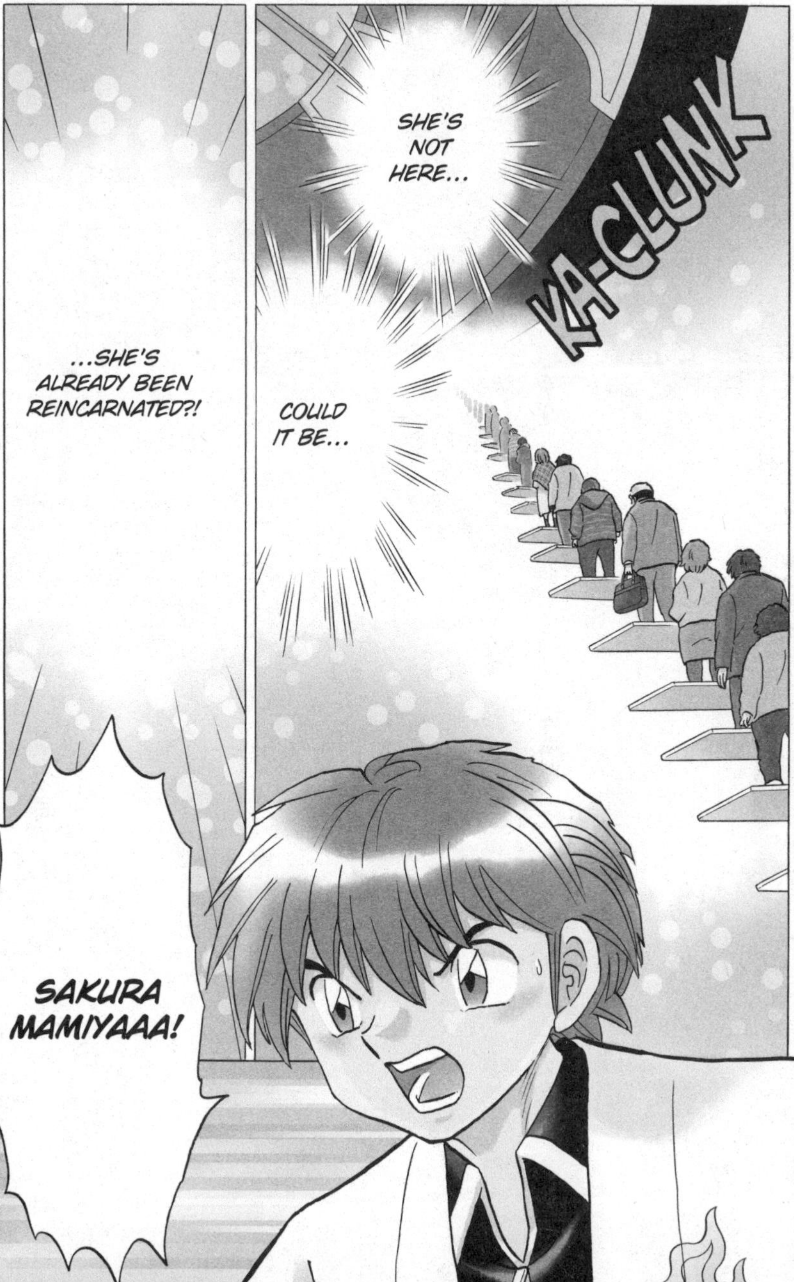
SHE'S NOT HERE...
KA-CLUNK
COULD IT BE...
...SHE'S ALREADY BEEN REINCARNATED?!
SAKURA MAMIYAAA!

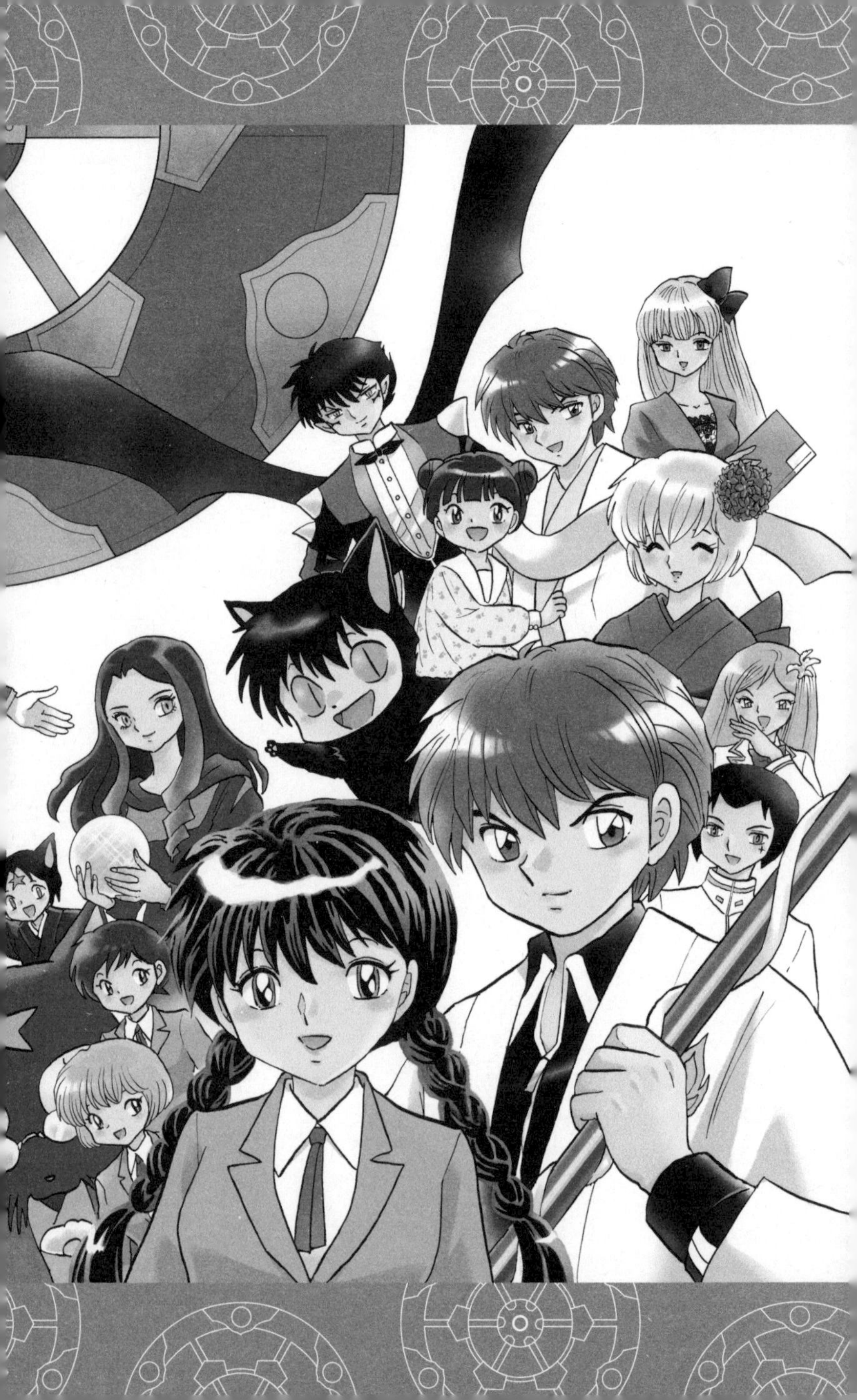

FINAL CHAPTER: THE WHEEL OF REINCARNATION

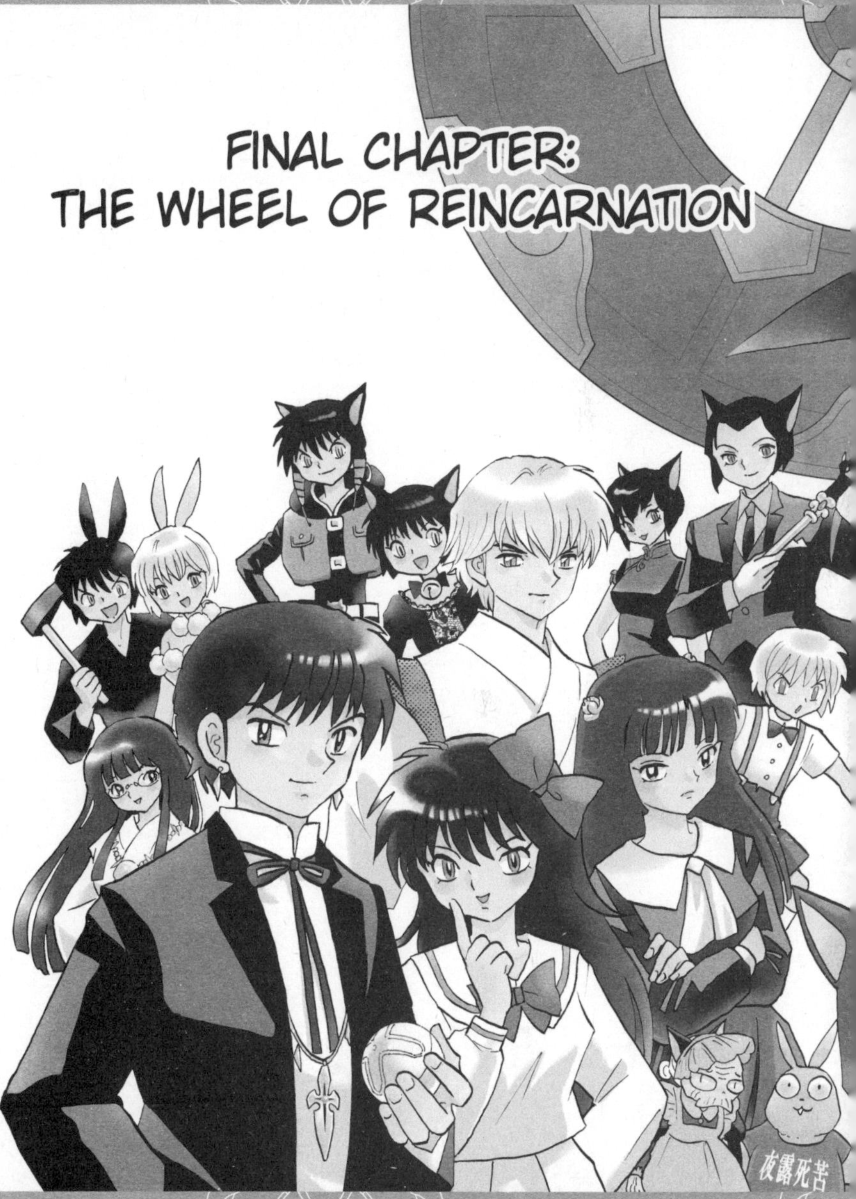
夜露死苦

りんね

RIN-NE

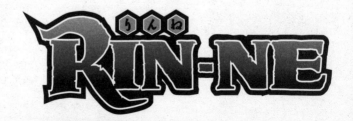

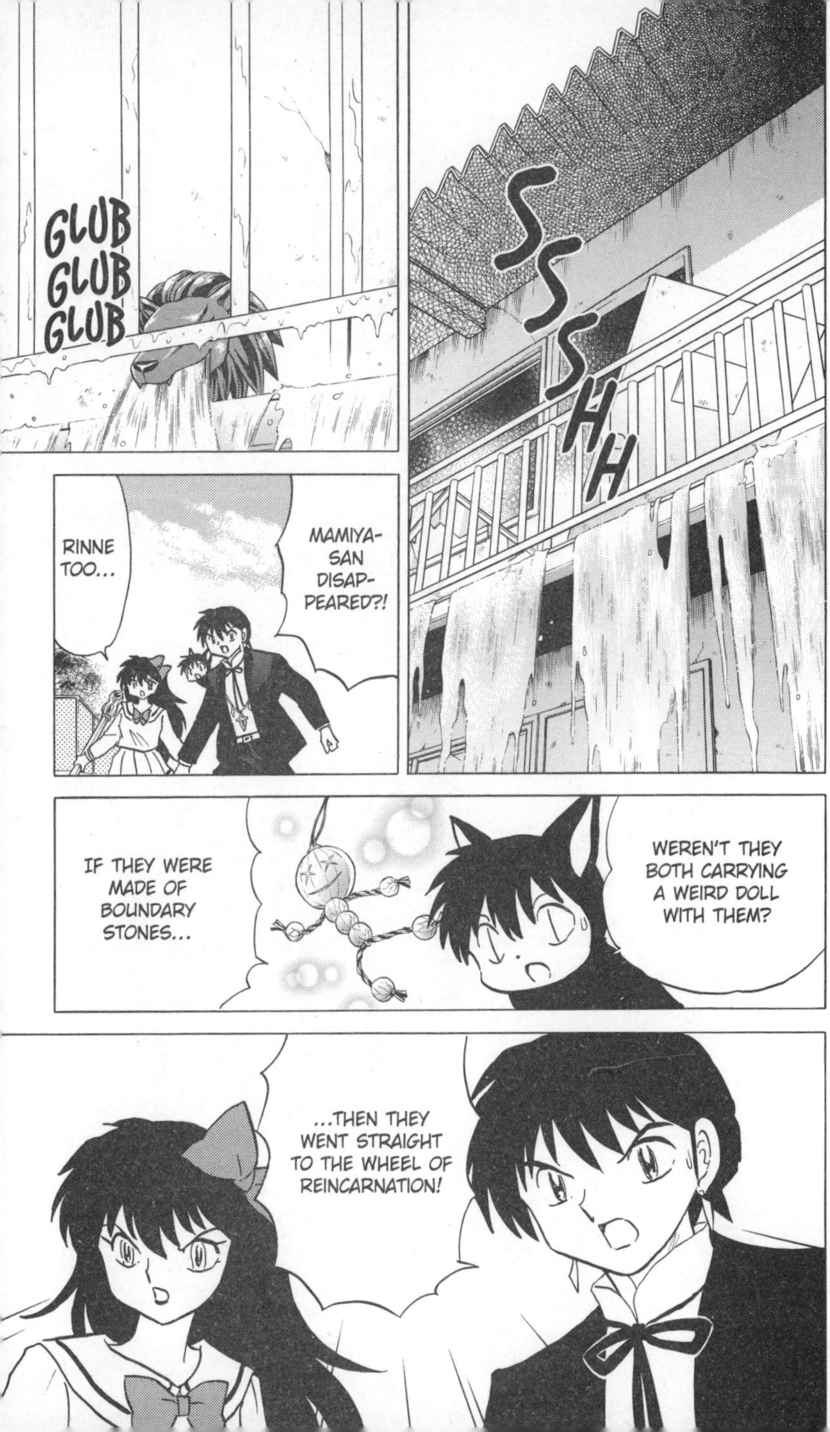
SSSHH
GLUB GLUB GLUB
MAMIYA-SAN DISAPPEARED?!
RINNE TOO...
WEREN'T THEY BOTH CARRYING A WEIRD DOLL WITH THEM?
IF THEY WERE MADE OF BOUNDARY STONES...
...THEN THEY WENT STRAIGHT TO THE WHEEL OF REINCARNATION!

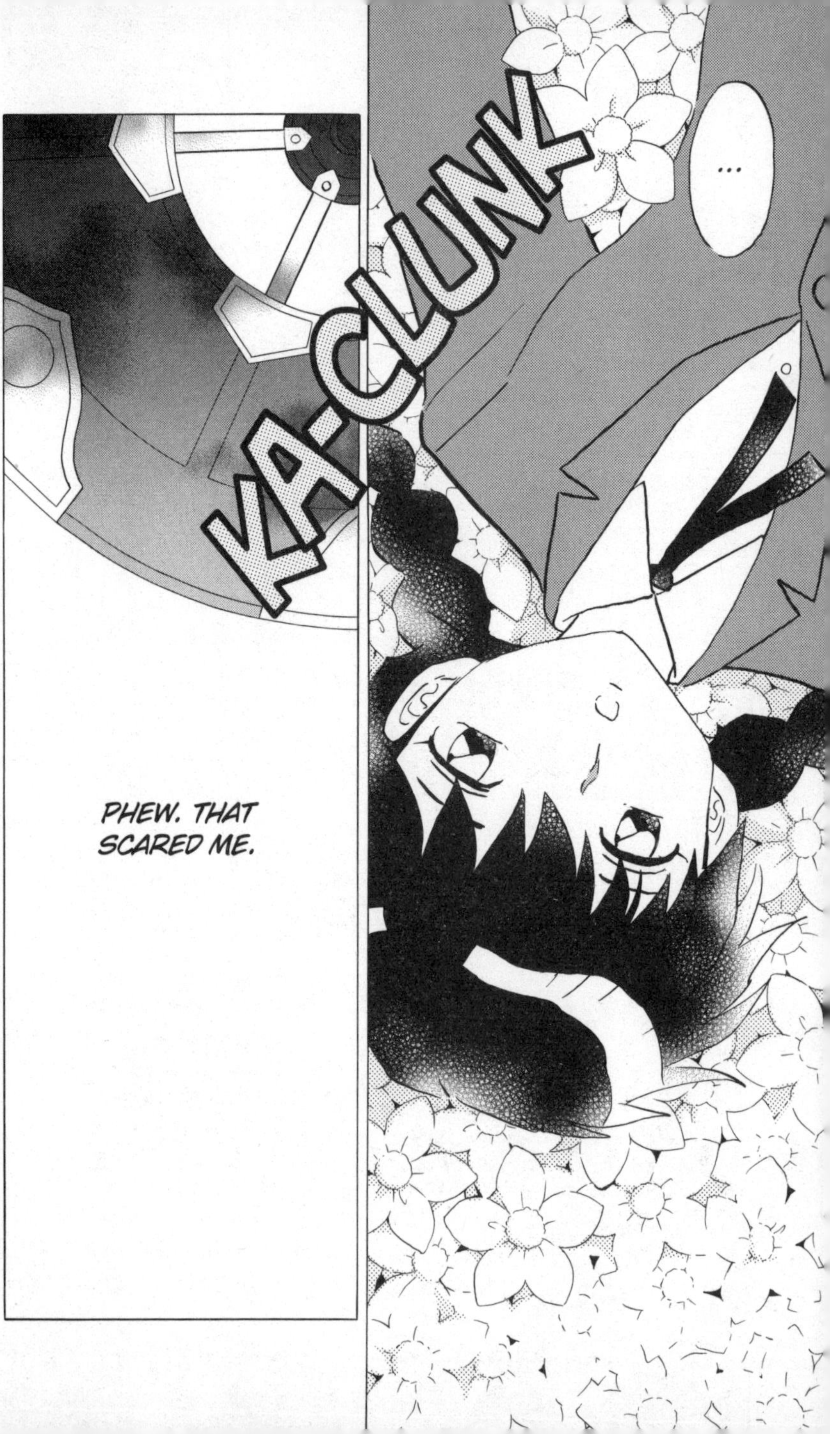
...
KA-CLUNK
PHEW. THAT SCARED ME.

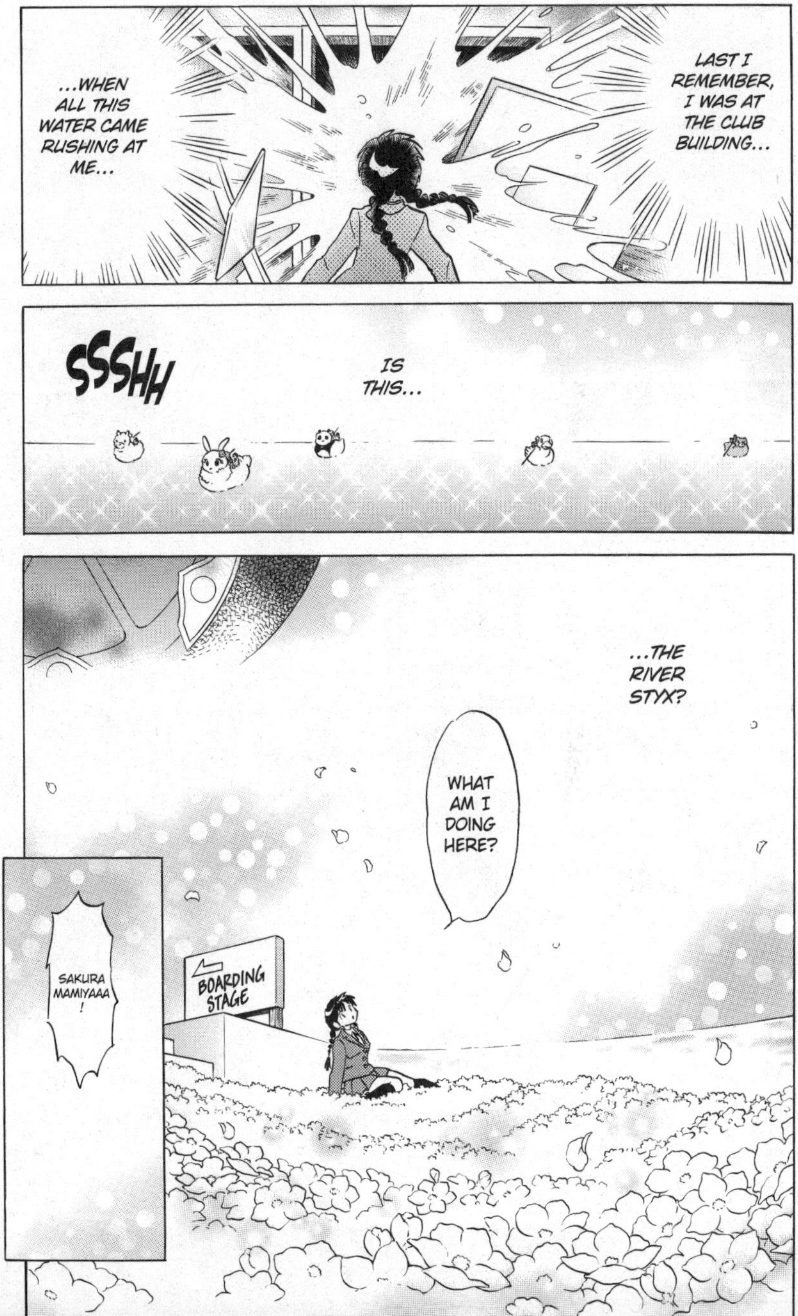
LAST I REMEMBER, I WAS AT THE CLUB BUILDING...
...WHEN ALL THIS WATER CAME RUSHING AT ME...
IS THIS...
SSSHH
...THE RIVER STYX?
WHAT AM I DOING HERE?
BOARDING STAGE
SAKURA MAMIYAAA!

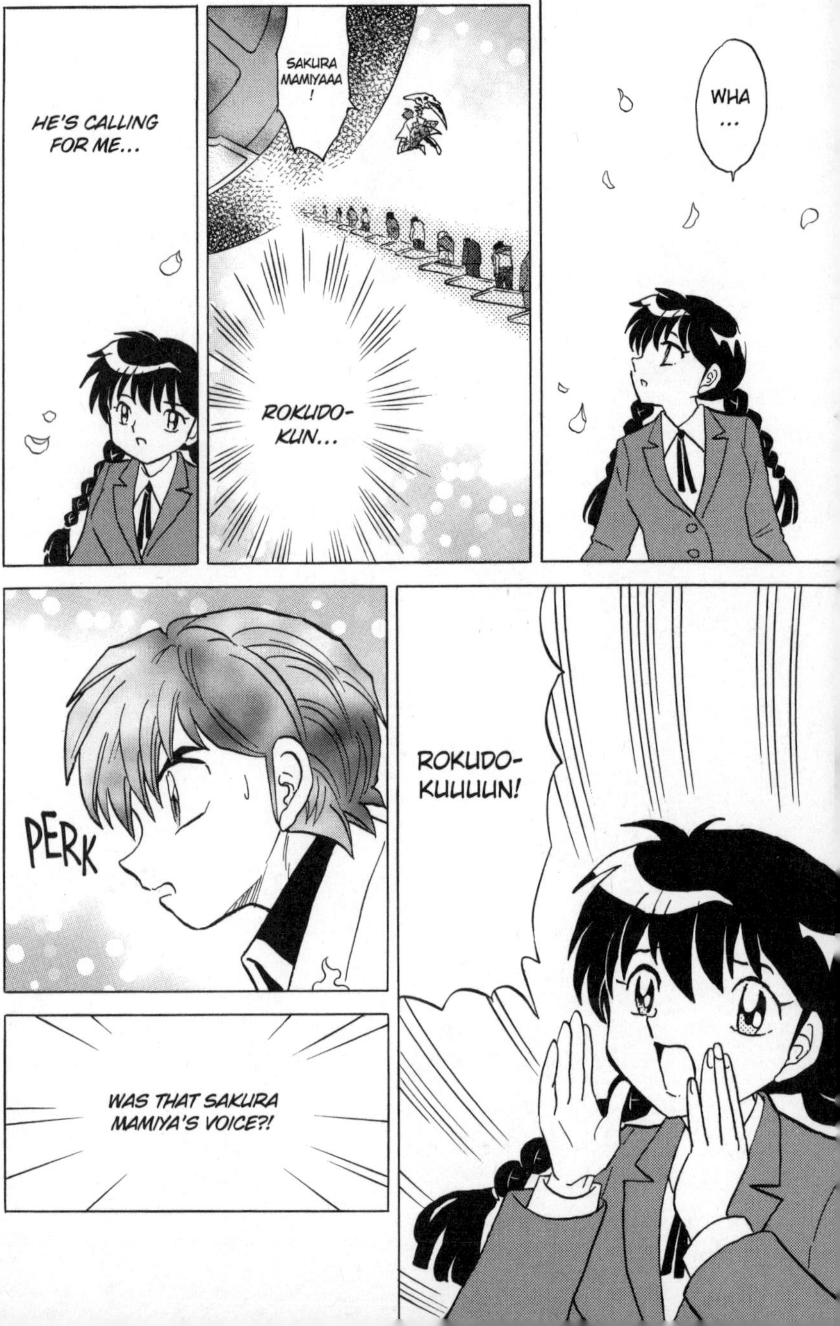
WHA...
SAKURA MAMIYAAA!
ROKUDO-KUN...
HE'S CALLING FOR ME...
ROKUDO-KUUUUN!
PERK
WAS THAT SAKURA MAMIYA'S VOICE?!

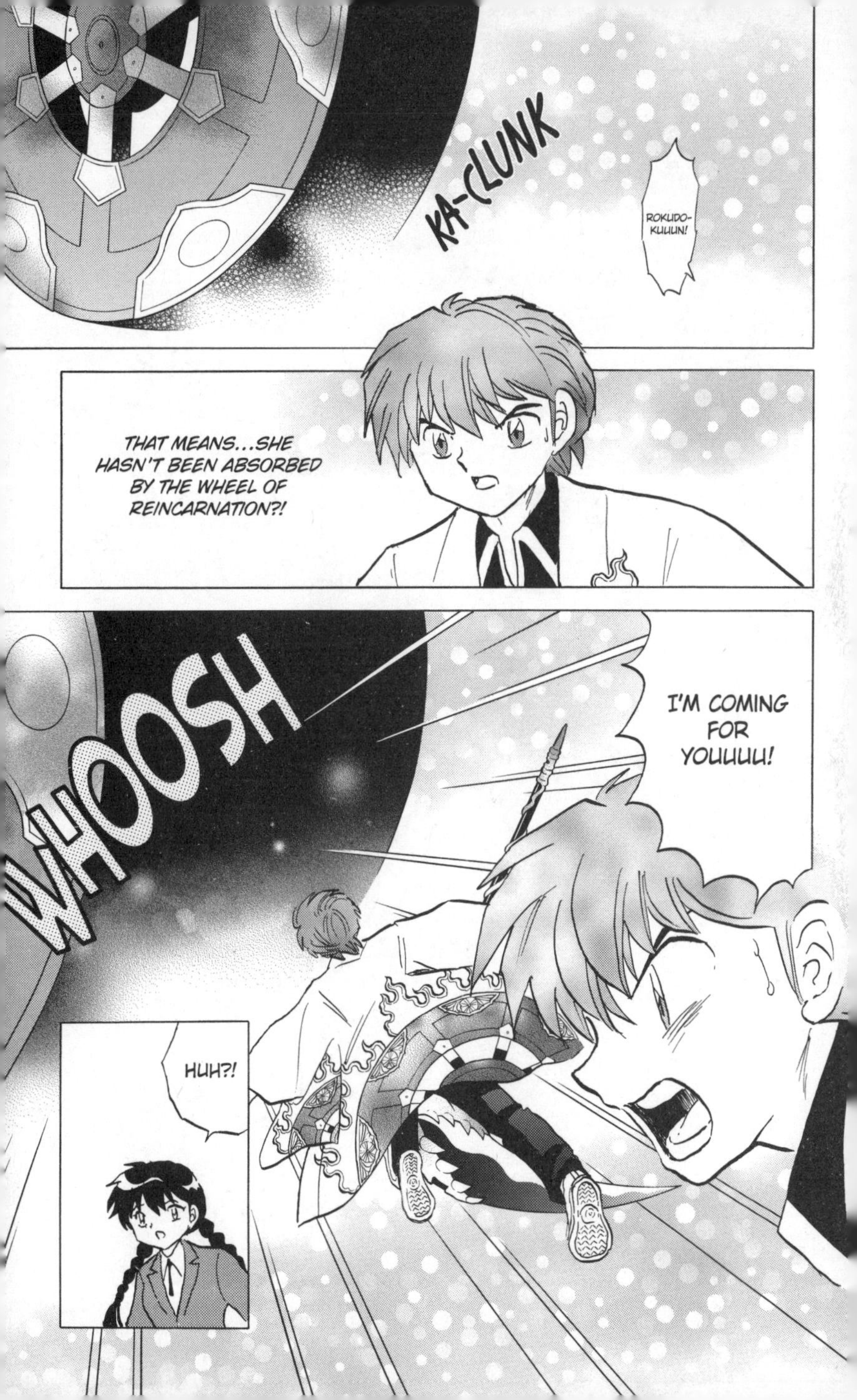
ROKUDO-KUUUN!
KA-CLUNK
THAT MEANS...SHE HASN'T BEEN ABSORBED BY THE WHEEL OF REINCARNATION?!
I'M COMING FOR YOUUUU!
WHOOSH
HUH?!

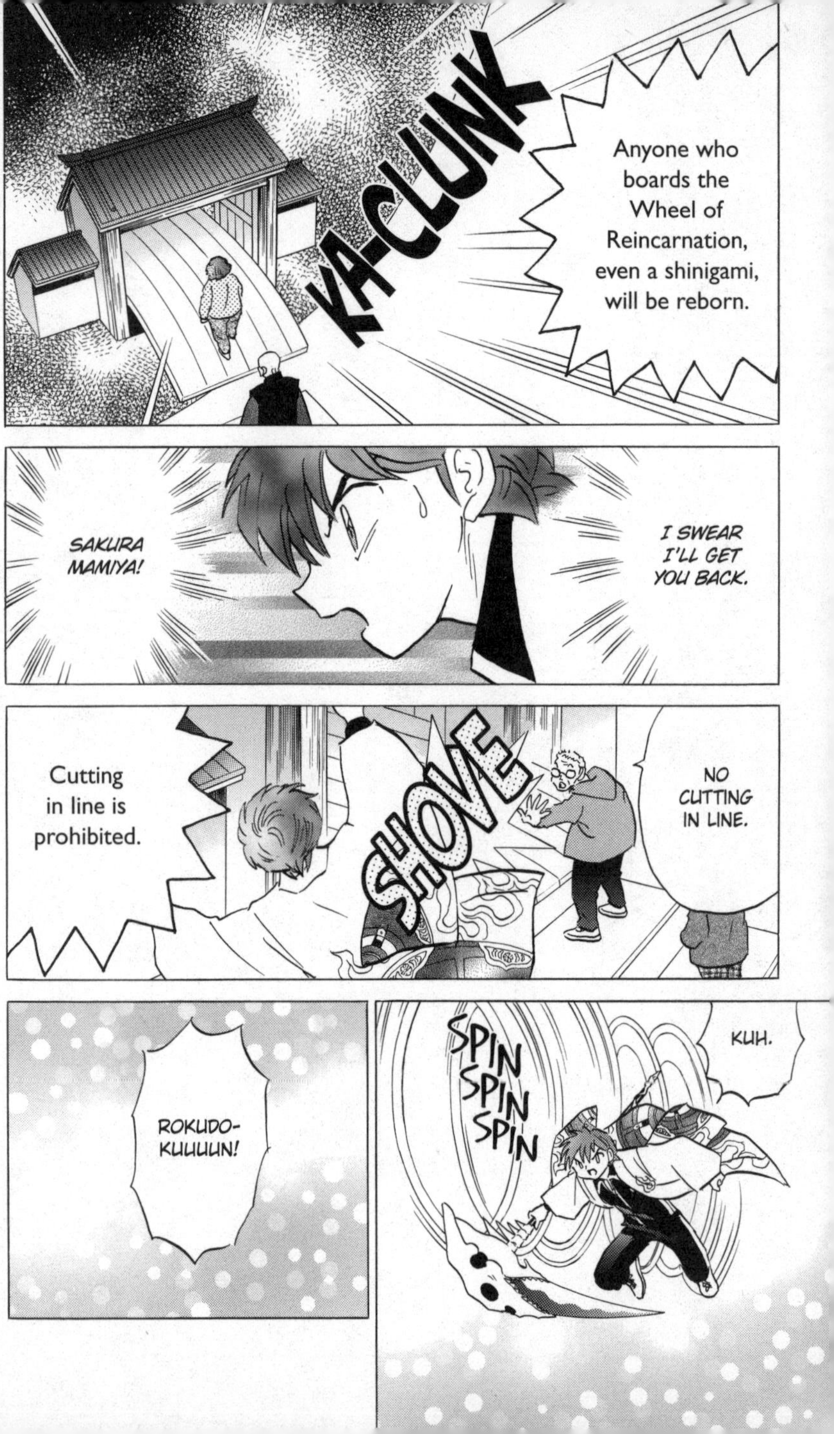
Anyone who boards the Wheel of Reincarnation, even a shinigami, will be reborn.
KA-CLUNK
I SWEAR I'LL GET YOU BACK.
SAKURA MAMIYA!
NO CUTTING IN LINE.
SHOVE
Cutting in line is prohibited.
KUH.
SPIN SPIN SPIN
ROKUDO-KUUUUN!

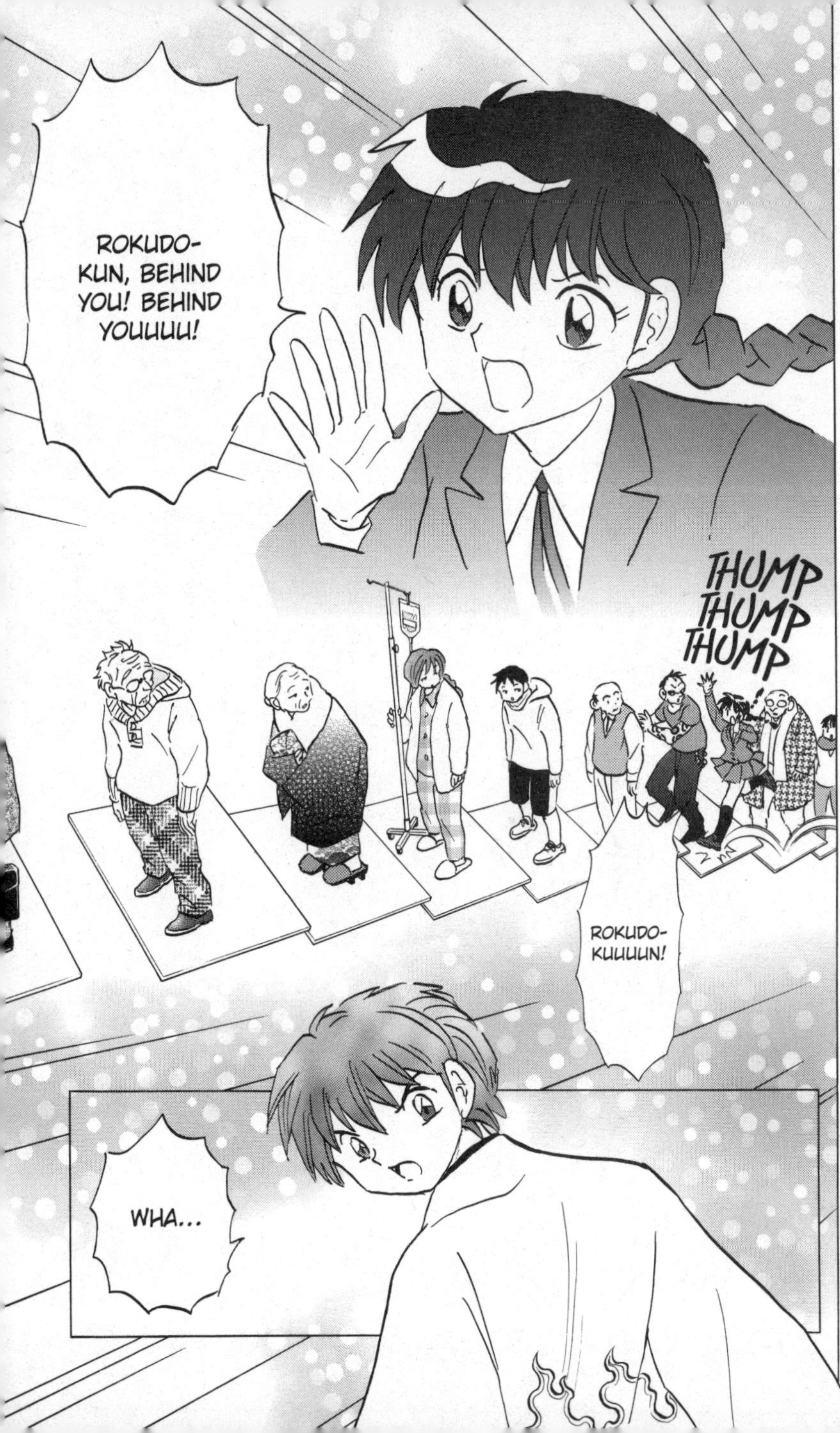
ROKUDO-KUN, BEHIND YOU! BEHIND YOUUUU!
THUMP THUMP THUMP
ROKUDO-KUUUUN!
WHA...

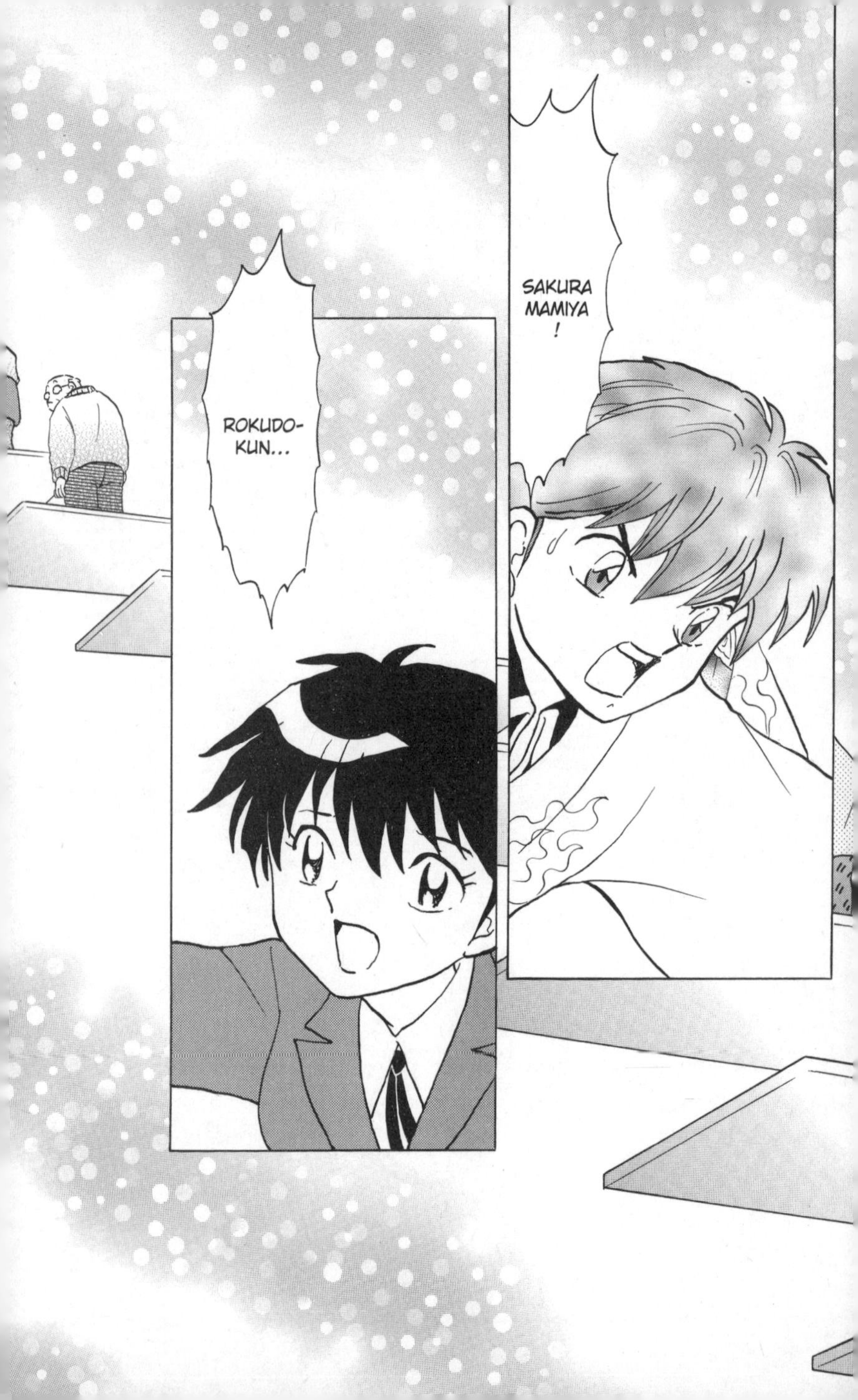
SAKURA MAMIYA!
ROKUDO-KUN...

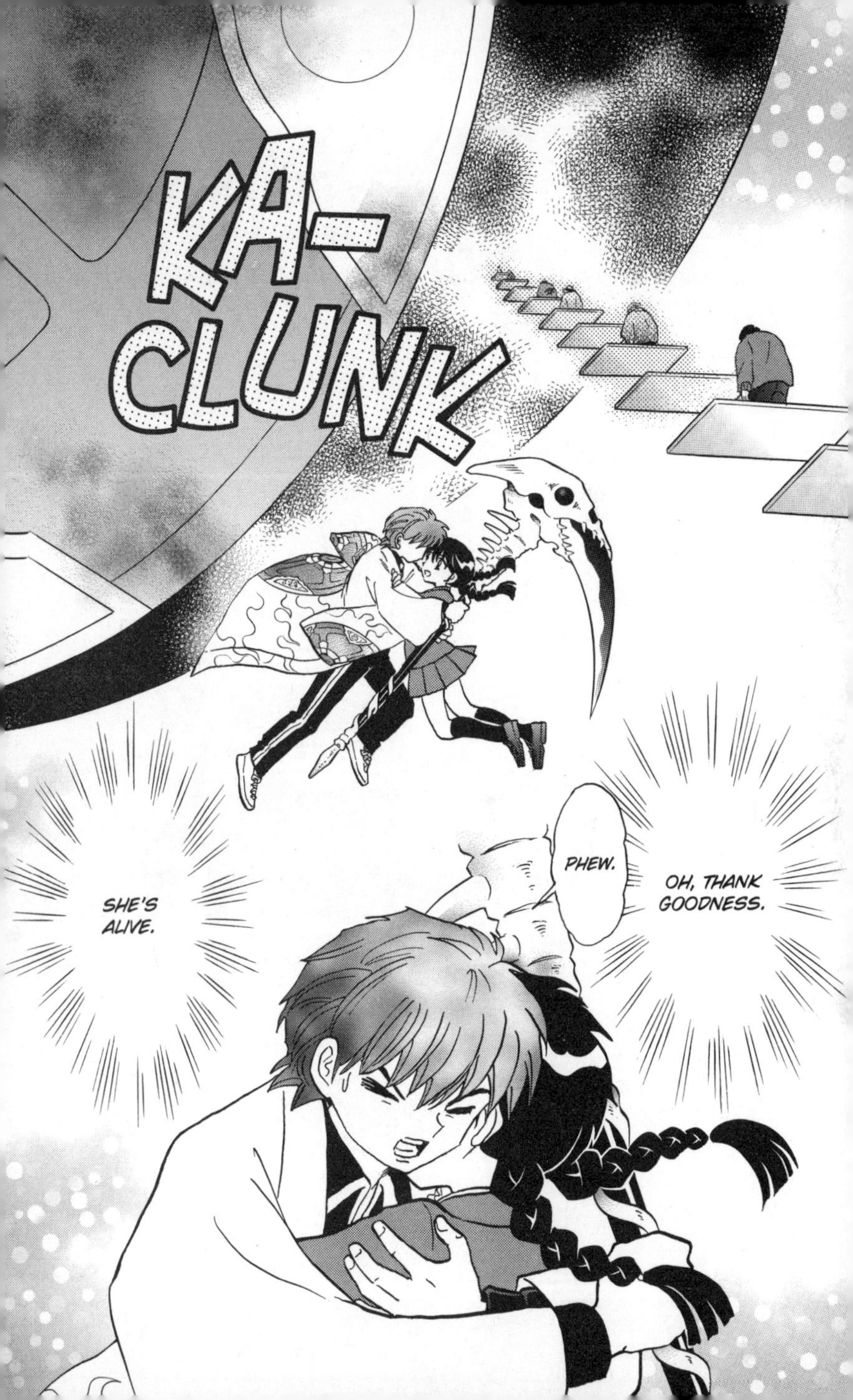
KA-CLUNK
OH, THANK GOODNESS.
PHEW.
SHE'S ALIVE.

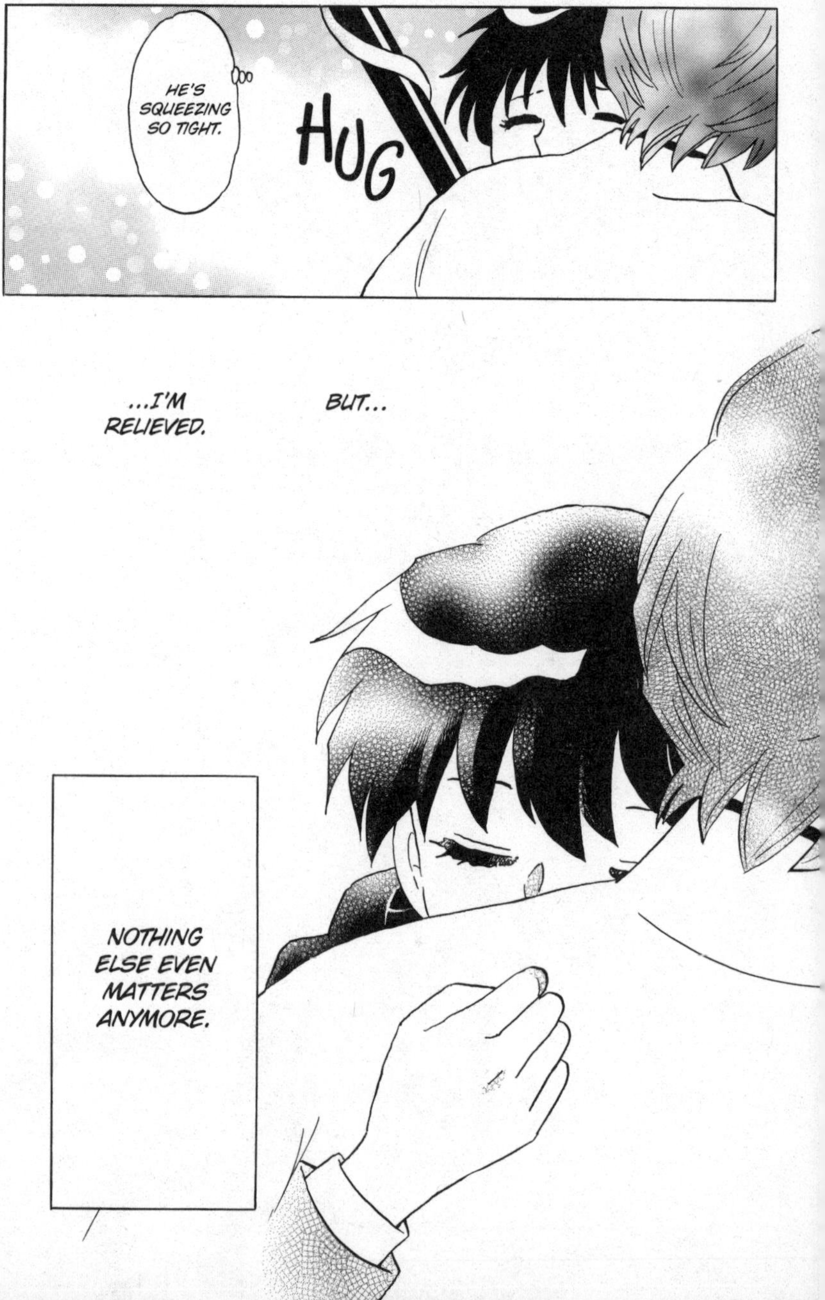
HUG
HE'S SQUEEZING SO TIGHT.
BUT...
...I'M RELIEVED.
NOTHING ELSE EVEN MATTERS ANYMORE.

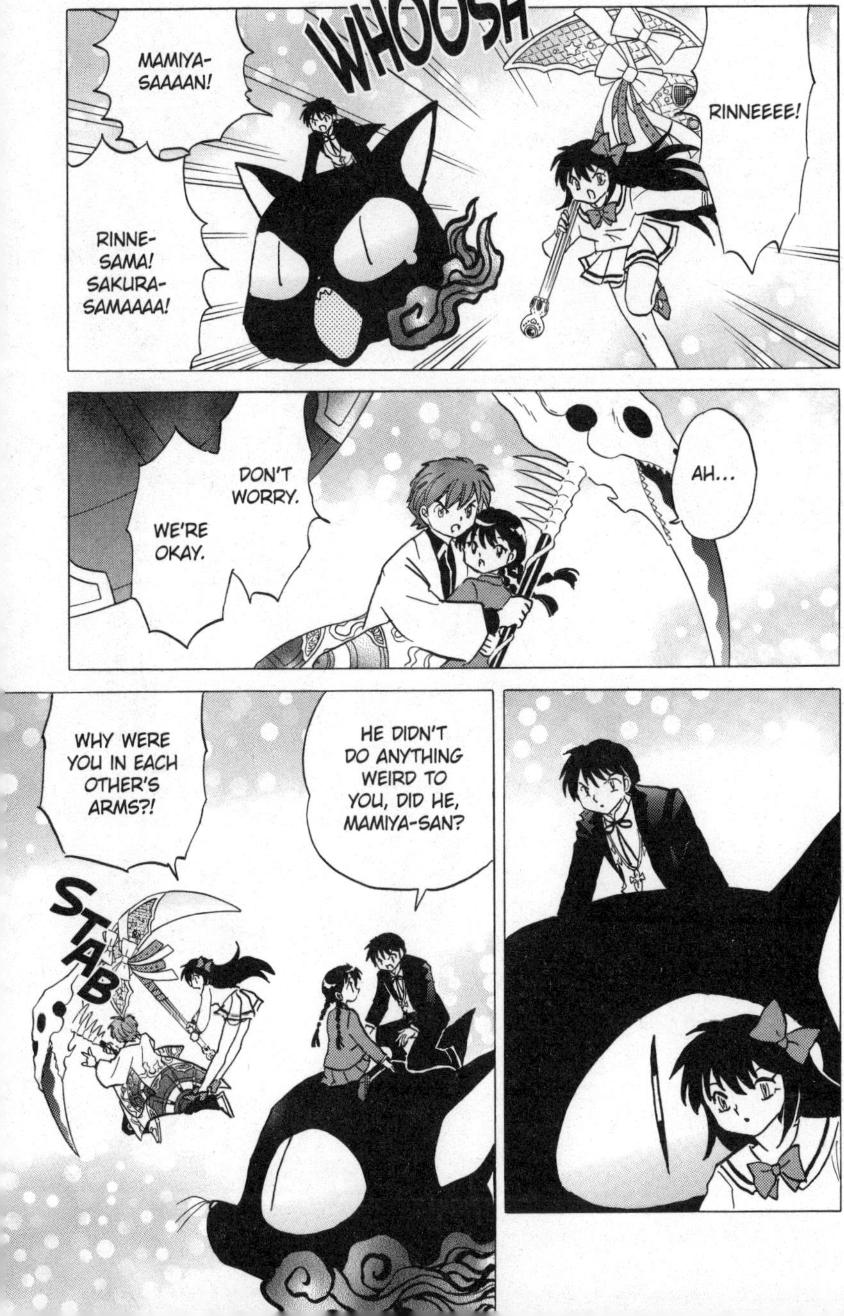
WHOOSH
RINNEEEE!
MAMIYA-SAAAAN!
RINNE-SAMA! SAKURA-SAMAAAAA!
AH...
DON'T WORRY.
WE'RE OKAY.
HE DIDN'T DO ANYTHING WEIRD TO YOU, DID HE, MAMIYA-SAN?
WHY WERE YOU IN EACH OTHER'S ARMS?!
STAB

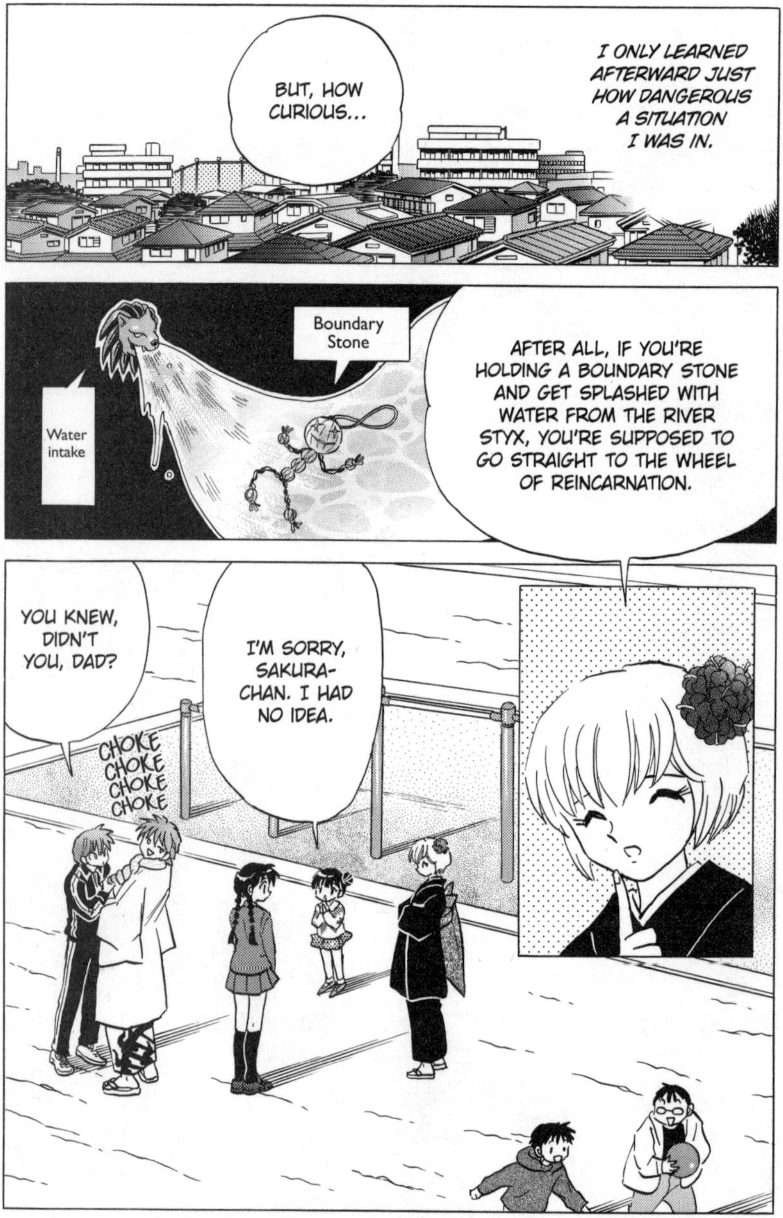
I ONLY LEARNED AFTERWARD JUST HOW DANGEROUS A SITUATION I WAS IN.
BUT, HOW CURIOUS...
AFTER ALL, IF YOU'RE HOLDING A BOUNDARY STONE AND GET SPLASHED WITH WATER FROM THE RIVER STYX, YOU'RE SUPPOSED TO GO STRAIGHT TO THE WHEEL OF REINCARNATION.
Boundary Stone
Water intake
I'M SORRY, SAKURA-CHAN. I HAD NO IDEA.
YOU KNEW, DIDN'T YOU, DAD?
CHOKE CHOKE CHOKE CHOKE

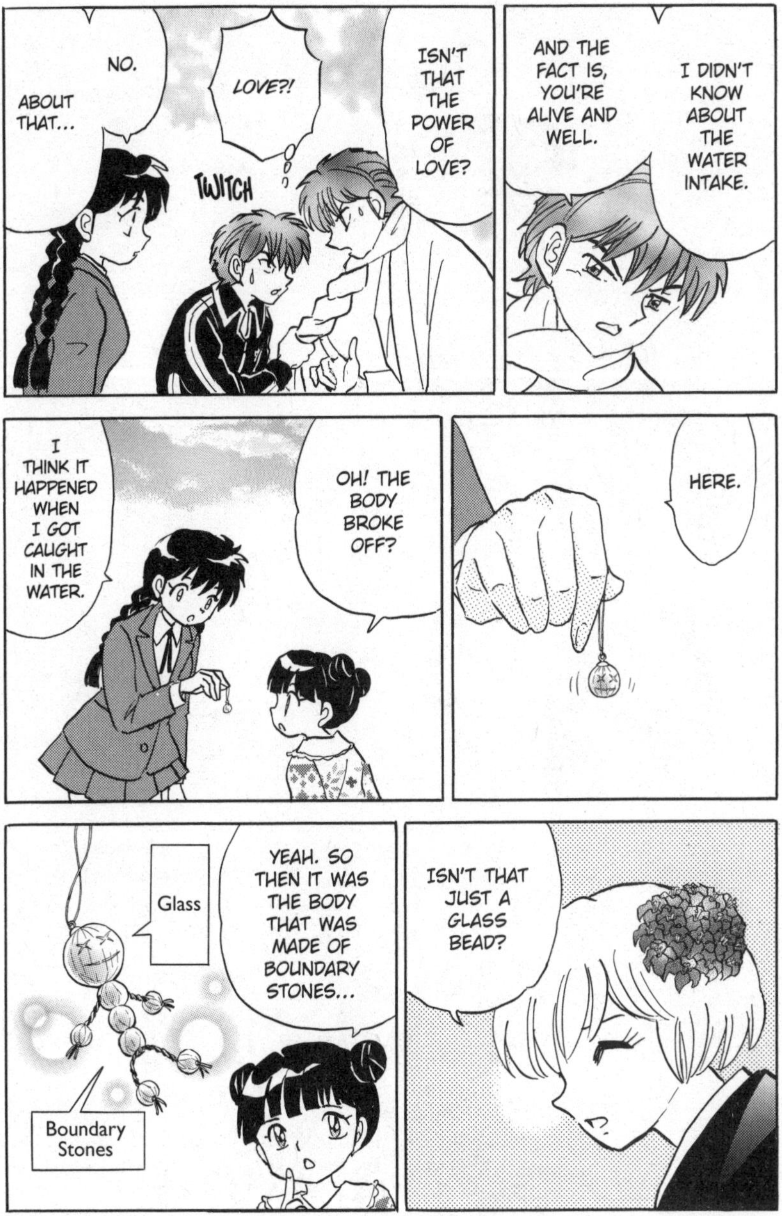
I DIDN'T KNOW ABOUT THE WATER INTAKE.
AND THE FACT IS, YOU'RE ALIVE AND WELL.
ISN'T THAT THE POWER OF LOVE?
LOVE?!
NO.
ABOUT THAT...
TWITCH
HERE.
OH! THE BODY BROKE OFF?
I THINK IT HAPPENED WHEN I GOT CAUGHT IN THE WATER.
ISN'T THAT JUST A GLASS BEAD?
YEAH. SO THEN IT WAS THE BODY THAT WAS MADE OF BOUNDARY STONES...
Glass
Boundary Stones

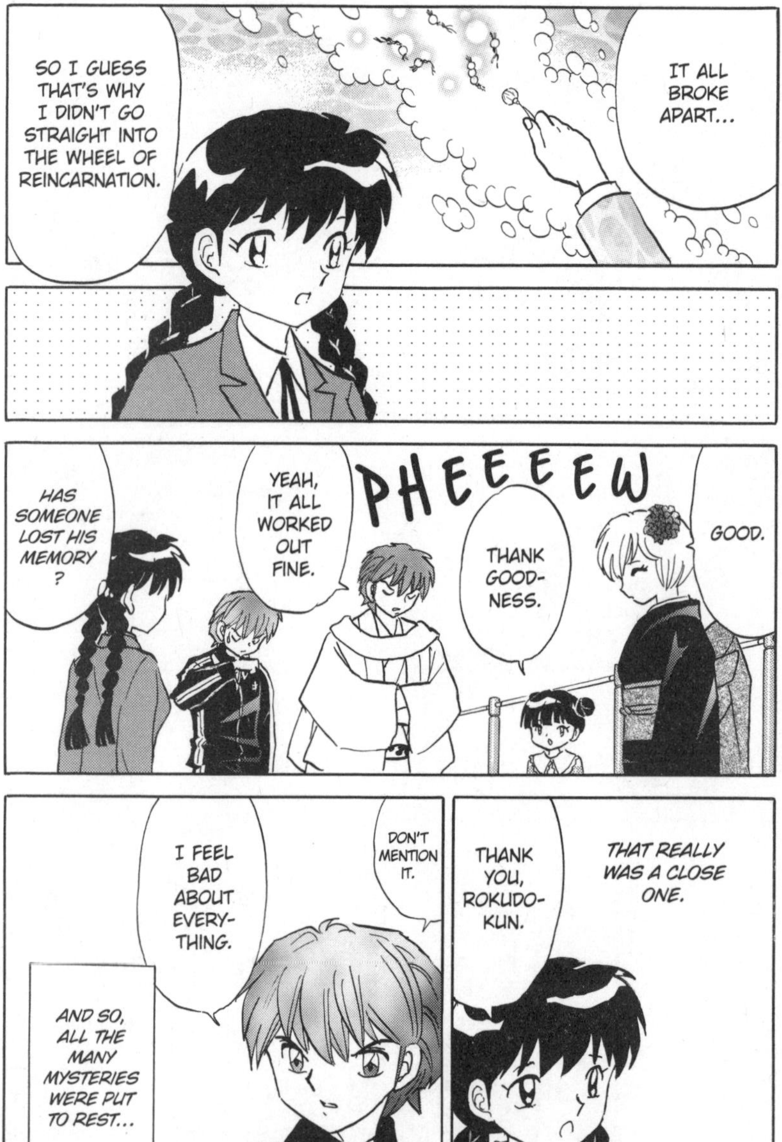
IT ALL BROKE APART...
SO I GUESS THAT'S WHY I DIDN'T GO STRAIGHT INTO THE WHEEL OF REINCARNATION.
GOOD.
THANK GOOD-NESS.
PHEEEEW
YEAH, IT ALL WORKED OUT FINE.
HAS SOMEONE LOST HIS MEMORY?
THAT REALLY WAS A CLOSE ONE.
THANK YOU, ROKUDO-KUN.
DON'T MENTION IT.
I FEEL BAD ABOUT EVERY-THING.
AND SO, ALL THE MANY MYSTERIES WERE PUT TO REST...

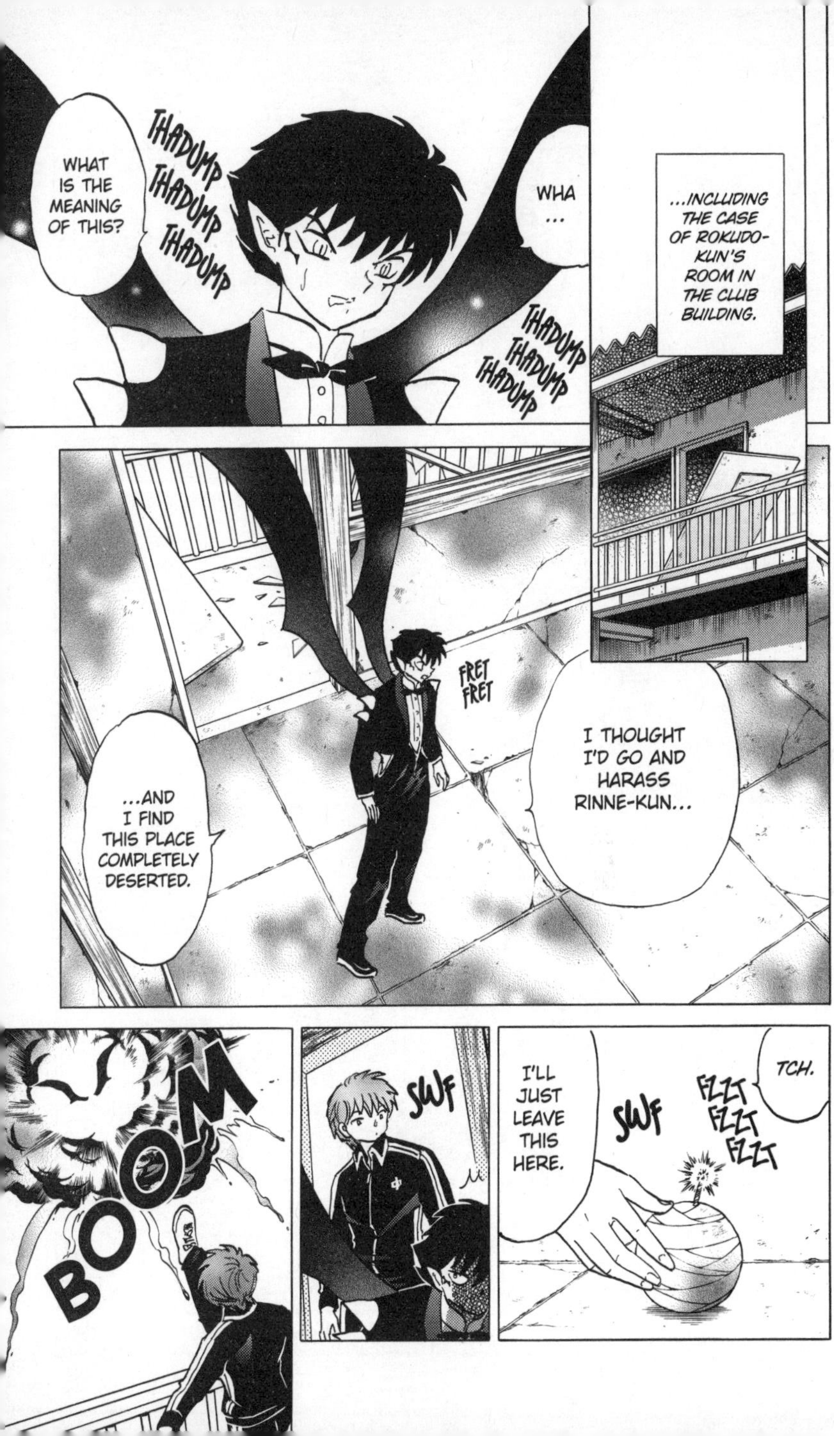
...INCLUDING THE CASE OF ROKUDO-KUN'S ROOM IN THE CLUB BUILDING.
WHA ...
THADUMP THADUMP THADUMP
THADUMP THADUMP THADUMP
WHAT IS THE MEANING OF THIS?
I THOUGHT I'D GO AND HARASS RINNE-KUN...
FRET FRET
...AND I FIND THIS PLACE COMPLETELY DESERTED.
TCH.
FZZT FZZT FZZT
SWF
I'LL JUST LEAVE THIS HERE.
SWF
BOOM

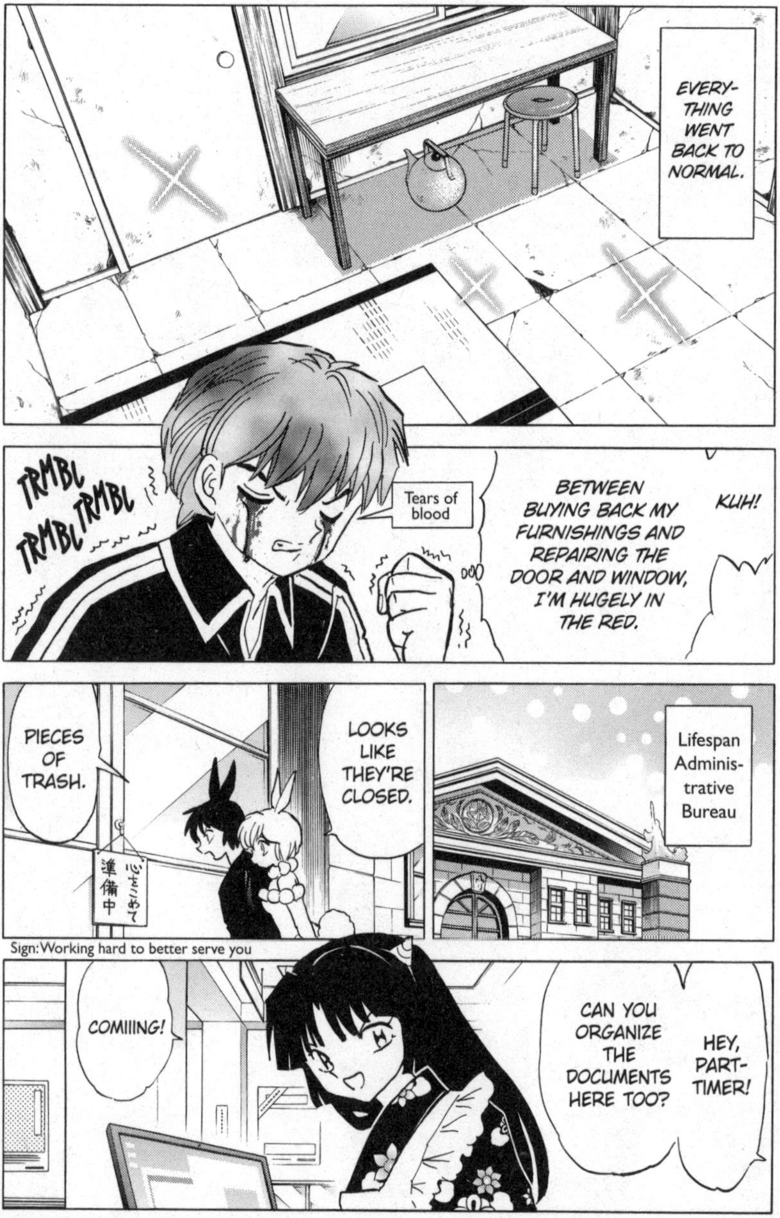
EVERY-THING WENT BACK TO NORMAL.
KUH!
BETWEEN BUYING BACK MY FURNISHINGS AND REPAIRING THE DOOR AND WINDOW, I'M HUGELY IN THE RED.
Tears of blood
TRMBL TRMBL TRMBL
Lifespan Administrative Bureau
LOOKS LIKE THEY'RE CLOSED.
PIECES OF TRASH.
心をこめて 準備中
Sign: Working hard to better serve you
HEY, PART-TIMER!
CAN YOU ORGANIZE THE DOCUMENTS HERE TOO?
COMIIING!

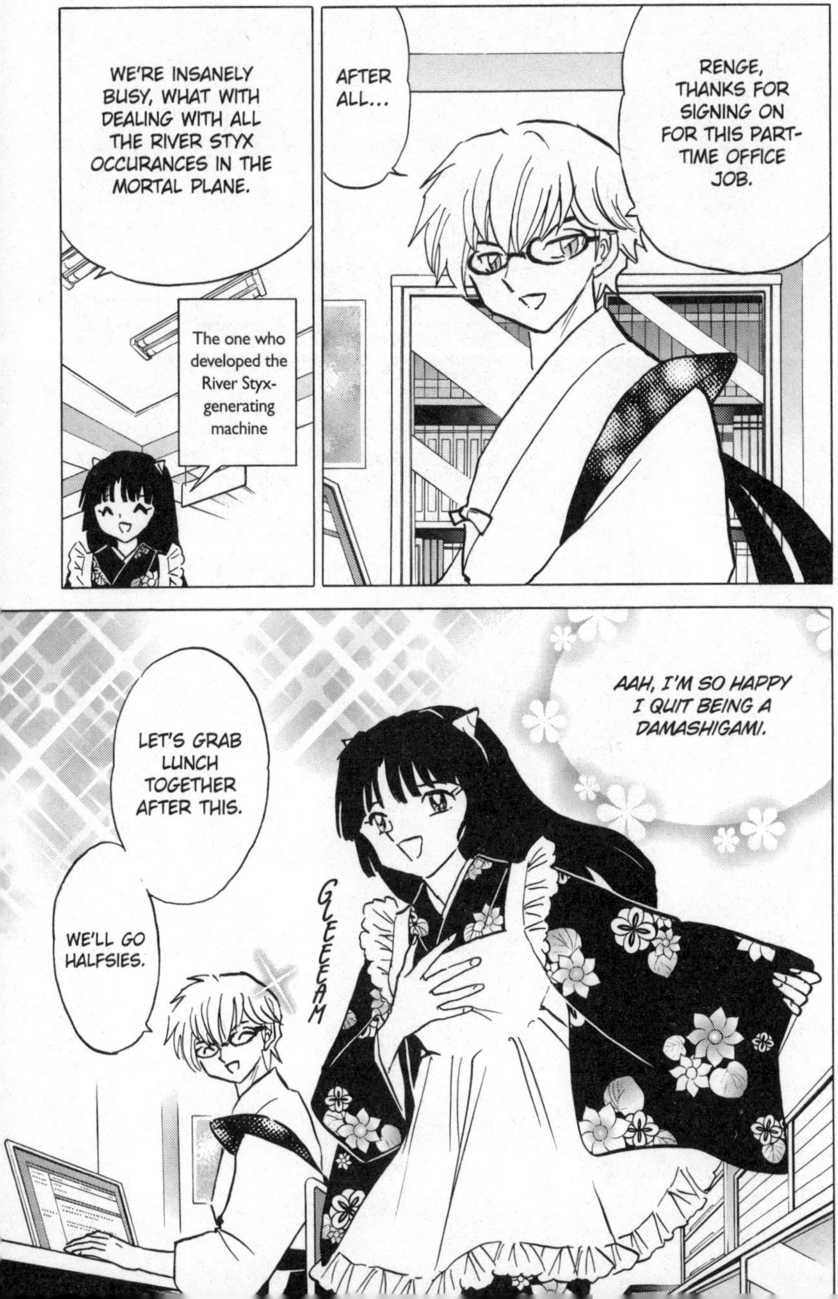
RENGE, THANKS FOR SIGNING ON FOR THIS PART-TIME OFFICE JOB.
AFTER ALL...
WE'RE INSANELY BUSY, WHAT WITH DEALING WITH ALL THE RIVER STYX OCCURANCES IN THE MORTAL PLANE.
The one who developed the River Styx-generating machine
AAH, I'M SO HAPPY I QUIT BEING A DAMASHIGAMI.
LET'S GRAB LUNCH TOGETHER AFTER THIS.
GLEEEAM
WE'LL GO HALFSIES.

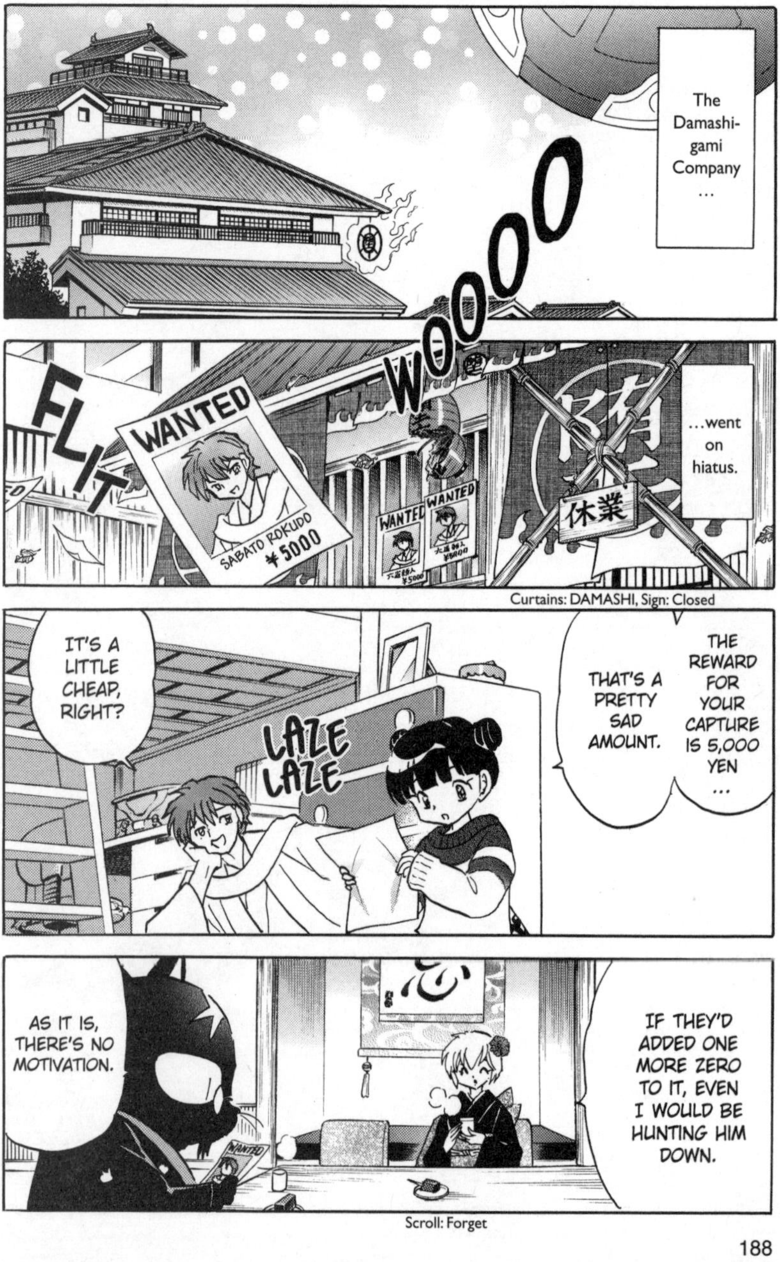
The Damashi-gami Company …
WOOOOO
…went on hiatus.
休業
WANTED
SABATO ROKUDO ¥5000
FLIT
THE REWARD FOR YOUR CAPTURE IS 5,000 YEN …
THAT'S A PRETTY SAD AMOUNT.
LAZE LAZE
IT'S A LITTLE CHEAP, RIGHT?
IF THEY'D ADDED ONE MORE ZERO TO IT, EVEN I WOULD BE HUNTING HIM DOWN.
AS IT IS, THERE'S NO MOTIVATION.
Curtains: DAMASHI, Sign: Closed

Scroll: Forget

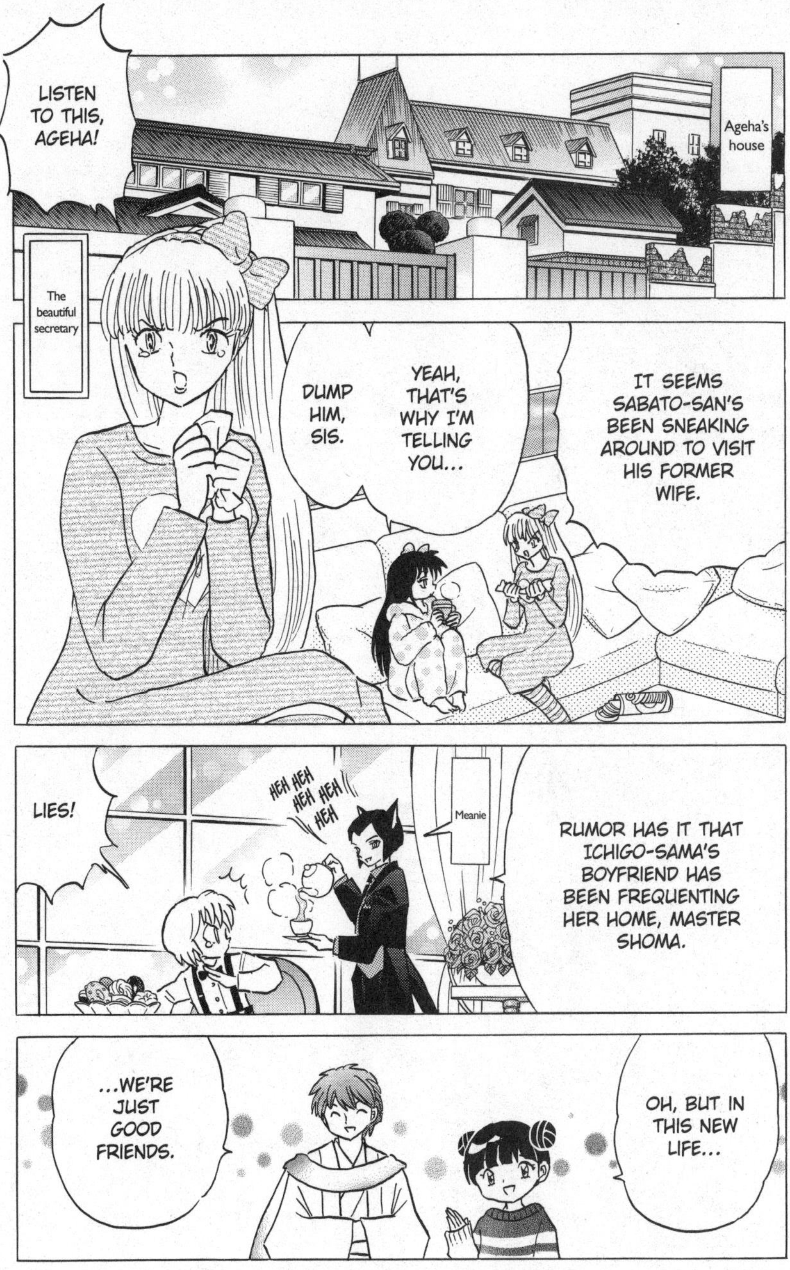
Ageha's house
LISTEN TO THIS, AGEHA!
IT SEEMS SABATO-SAN'S BEEN SNEAKING AROUND TO VISIT HIS FORMER WIFE.
YEAH, THAT'S WHY I'M TELLING YOU...
DUMP HIM, SIS.
The beautiful secretary
RUMOR HAS IT THAT ICHIGO-SAMA'S BOYFRIEND HAS BEEN FREQUENTING HER HOME, MASTER SHOMA.
Meanie
HEH HEH HEH HEH HEH
LIES!
OH, BUT IN THIS NEW LIFE...
...WE'RE JUST GOOD FRIENDS.

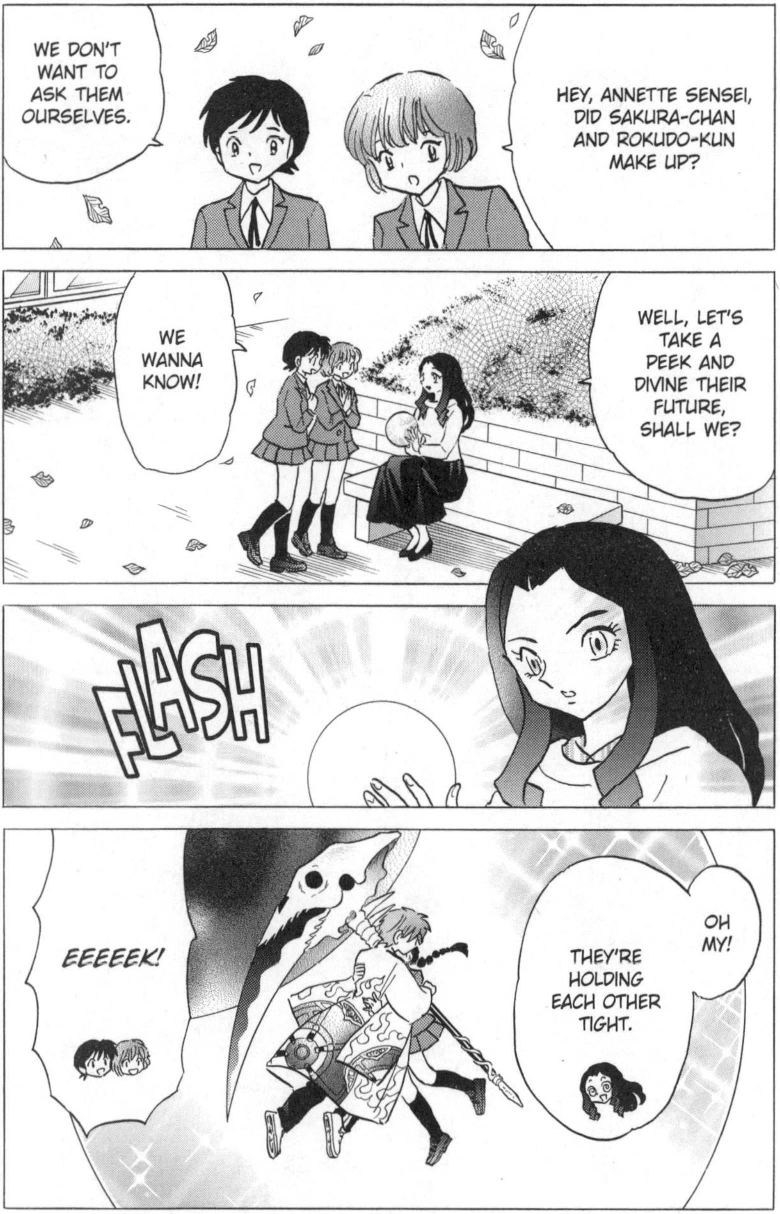
HEY, ANNETTE SENSEI, DID SAKURA-CHAN AND ROKUDO-KUN MAKE UP?
WE DON'T WANT TO ASK THEM OURSELVES.
WELL, LET'S TAKE A PEEK AND DIVINE THEIR FUTURE, SHALL WE?
WE WANNA KNOW!
FLASH
OH MY!
THEY'RE HOLDING EACH OTHER TIGHT.
EEEEEK!

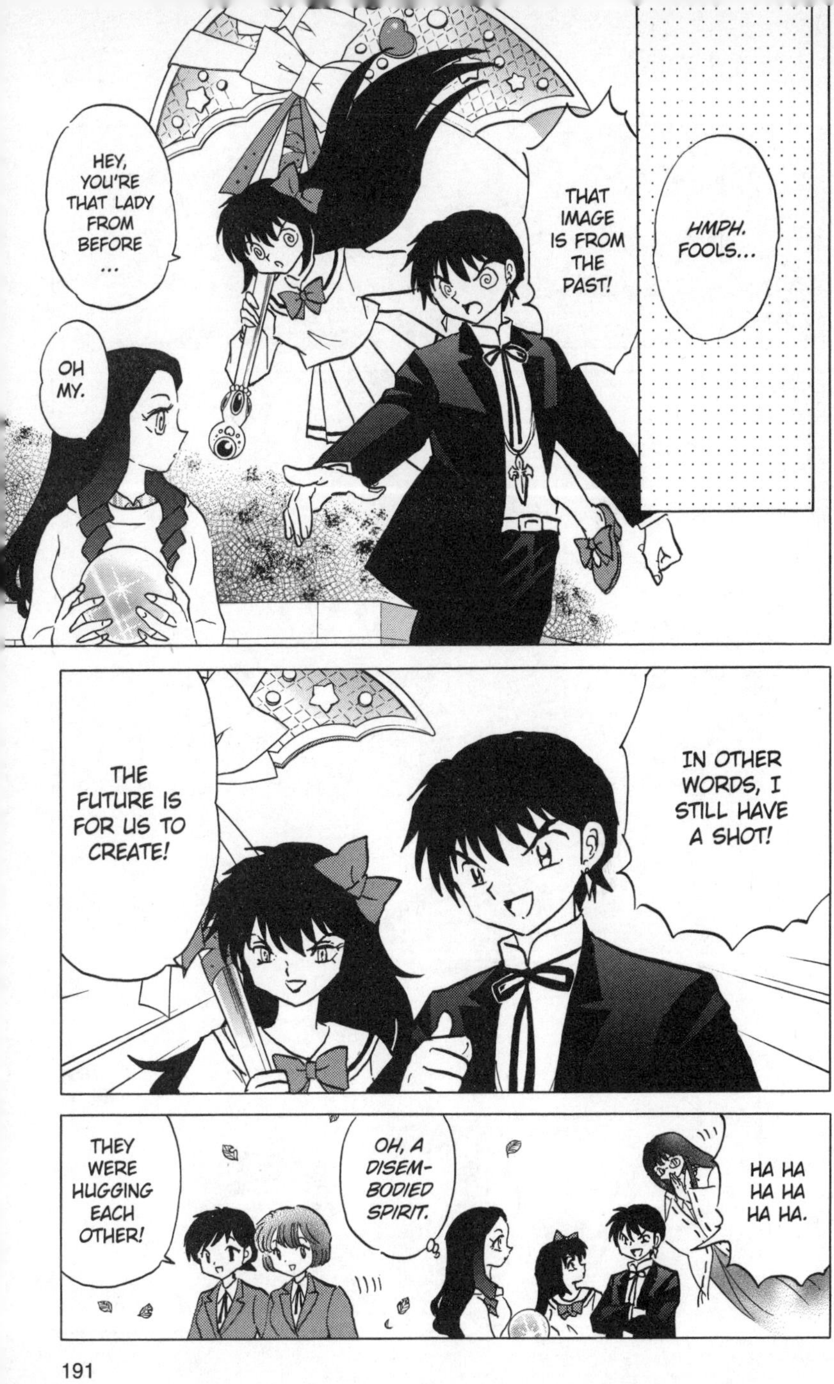
HMPH. FOOLS...
THAT IMAGE IS FROM THE PAST!
HEY, YOU'RE THAT LADY FROM BEFORE...
OH MY.
IN OTHER WORDS, I STILL HAVE A SHOT!
THE FUTURE IS FOR US TO CREATE!
HA HA HA HA HA HA.
OH, A DISEM-BODIED SPIRIT.
THEY WERE HUGGING EACH OTHER!

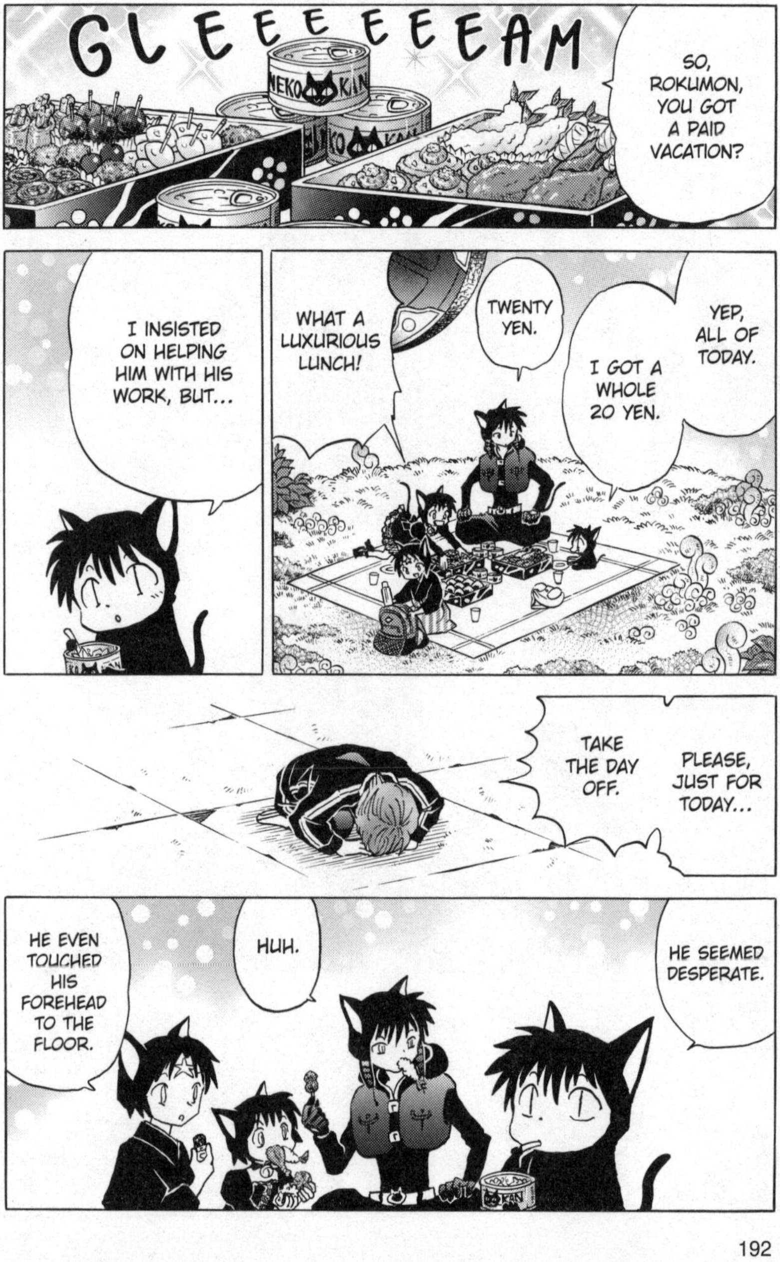
SO, ROKUMON, YOU GOT A PAID VACATION?
GLEEEEEEAM
NEKO KAN
YEP, ALL OF TODAY.
I GOT A WHOLE 20 YEN.
TWENTY YEN.
WHAT A LUXURIOUS LUNCH!
I INSISTED ON HELPING HIM WITH HIS WORK, BUT...
PLEASE, JUST FOR TODAY...
TAKE THE DAY OFF.
HE SEEMED DESPERATE.
HUH.
HE EVEN TOUCHED HIS FOREHEAD TO THE FLOOR.

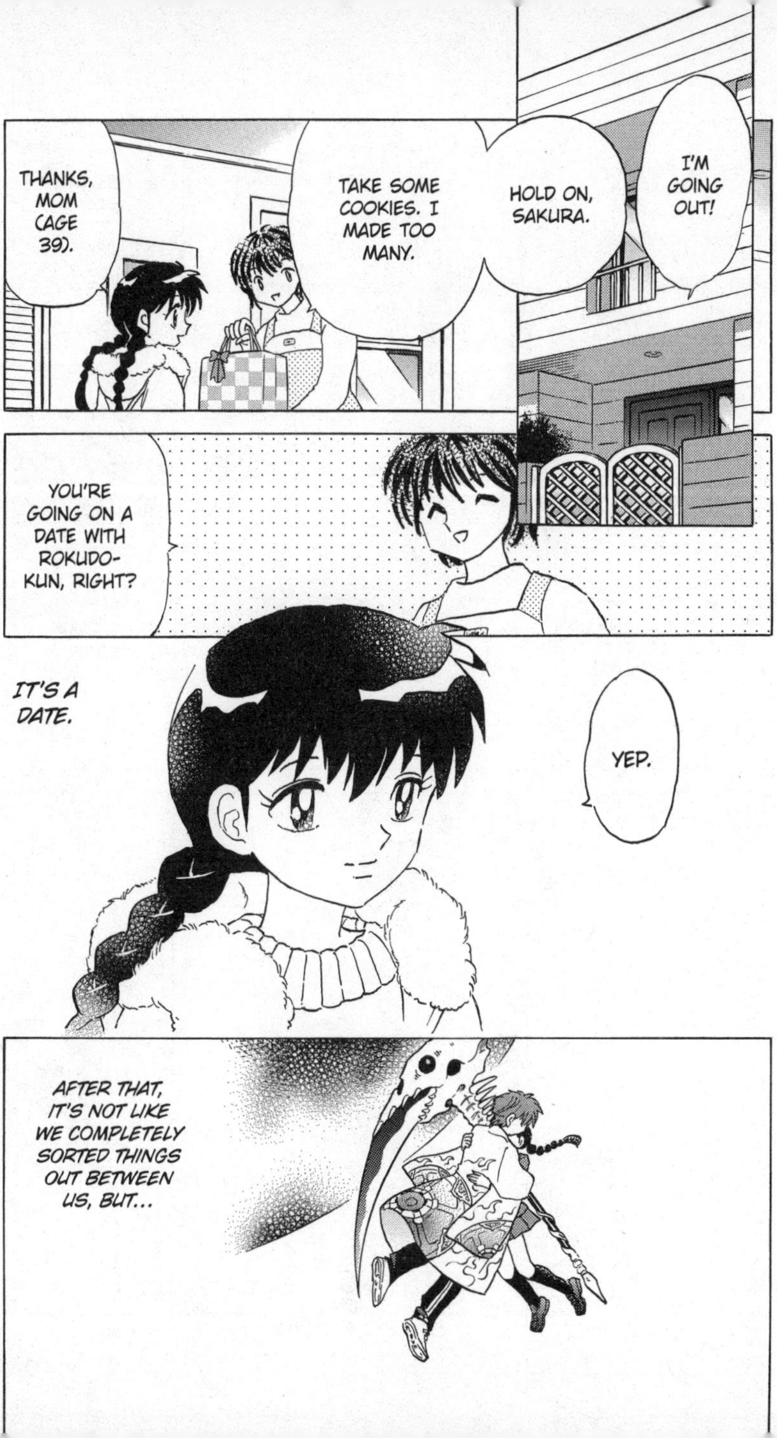
I'M GOING OUT!
HOLD ON, SAKURA.
TAKE SOME COOKIES. I MADE TOO MANY.
THANKS, MOM (AGE 39).
YOU'RE GOING ON A DATE WITH ROKUDO-KUN, RIGHT?
YEP.
IT'S A DATE.
AFTER THAT, IT'S NOT LIKE WE COMPLETELY SORTED THINGS OUT BETWEEN US, BUT...

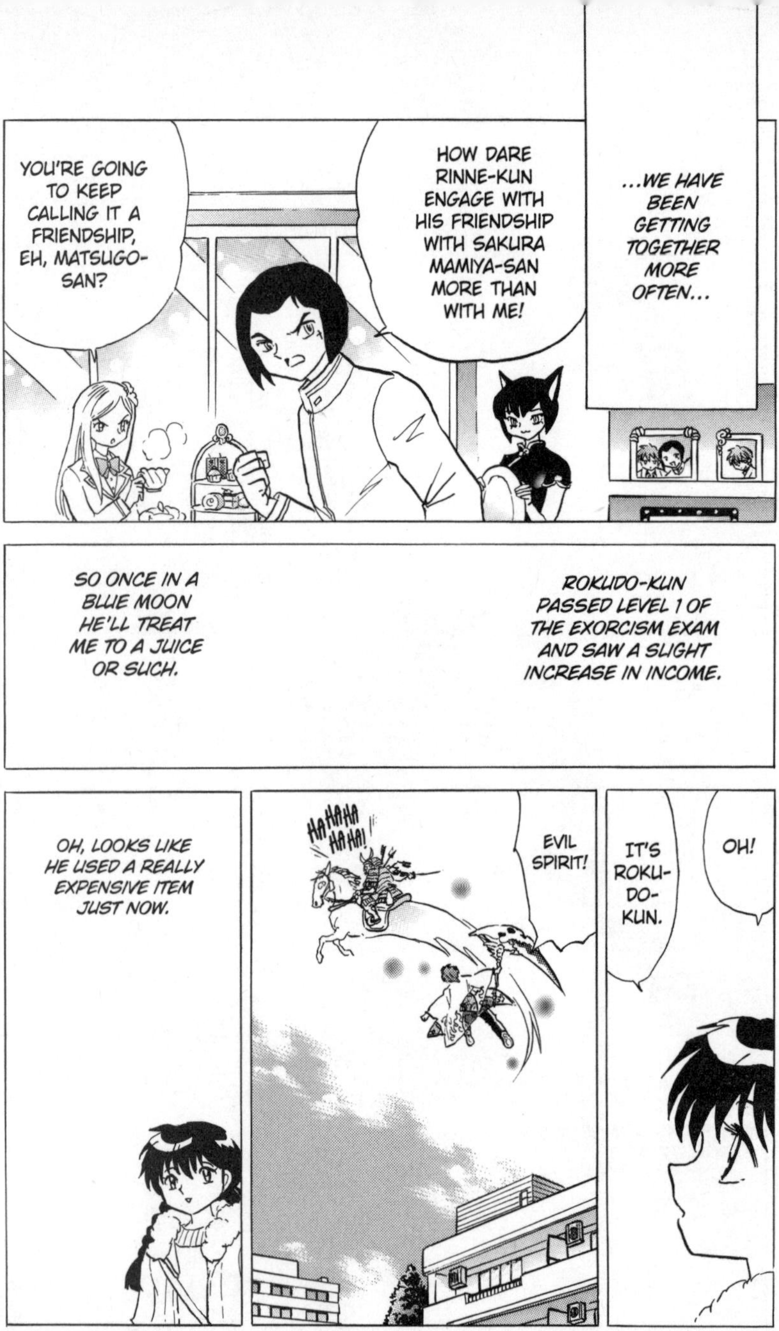
...WE HAVE BEEN GETTING TOGETHER MORE OFTEN...
HOW DARE RINNE-KUN ENGAGE WITH HIS FRIENDSHIP WITH SAKURA MAMIYA-SAN MORE THAN WITH ME!
YOU'RE GOING TO KEEP CALLING IT A FRIENDSHIP, EH, MATSUGO-SAN?
ROKUDO-KUN PASSED LEVEL 1 OF THE EXORCISM EXAM AND SAW A SLIGHT INCREASE IN INCOME.
SO ONCE IN A BLUE MOON HE'LL TREAT ME TO A JUICE OR SUCH.
OH!
IT'S ROKU-DO-KUN.
EVIL SPIRIT!
HAHAHA HAHA!
OH, LOOKS LIKE HE USED A REALLY EXPENSIVE ITEM JUST NOW.

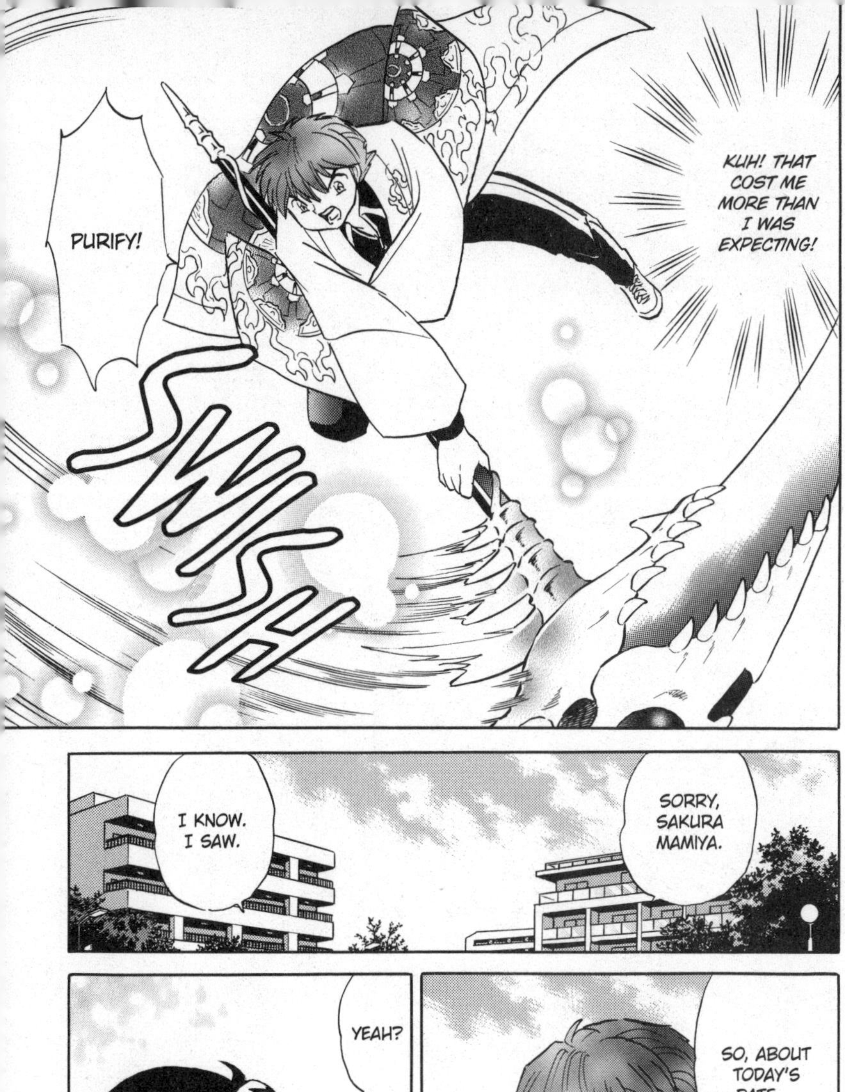
KUH! THAT COST ME MORE THAN I WAS EXPECTING!
PURIFY!
SWISH
SORRY, SAKURA MAMIYA.
I KNOW. I SAW.
SO, ABOUT TODAY'S DATE...
YEAH?

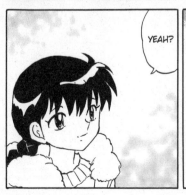

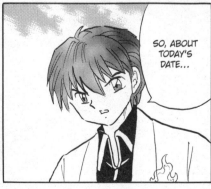

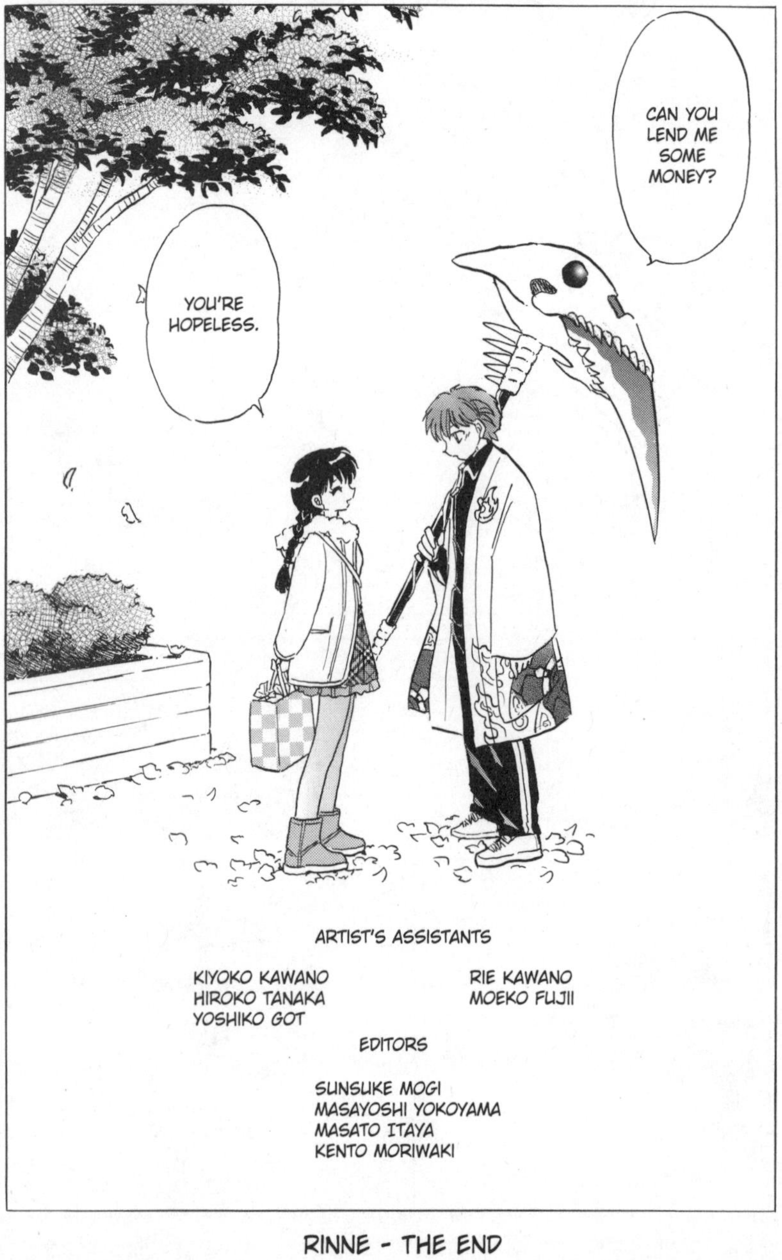
CAN YOU LEND ME SOME MONEY?
YOU'RE HOPELESS.

ARTIST'S ASSISTANTS

KIYOKO KAWANO
HIROKO TANAKA
YOSHIKO GOT
RIE KAWANO
MOEKO FUJII

EDITORS

SUNSUKE MOGI
MASAYOSHI YOKOYAMA
MASATO ITAYA
KENTO MORIWAKI

RINNE - THE END

Rumiko Takahashi

The spotlight on Rumiko Takahashi's career began in 1978 when she won an honorable mention in Shogakukan's prestigious New Comic Artist Contest for *Those Selfish Aliens*. Later that same year, her boy-meets-alien comedy series, *Urusei Yatsura*, was serialized in *Weekly Shonen Sunday*. This phenomenally successful manga series was adapted into anime format and spawned a TV series and half a dozen theatrical-release movies, all incredibly popular in their own right. Takahashi followed up the success of her debut series with one blockbuster hit after another—*Maison Ikkoku* ran from 1980 to 1987, *Ranma ½* from 1987 to 1996, and *Inuyasha* from 1996 to 2008. Other notable works include *Mermaid Saga*, *Rumic Theater*, and *One-Pound Gospel*.

Takahashi was inducted into the Will Eisner Comic Awards Hall of Fame in 2018. She won the prestigious Shogakukan Manga Award twice in her career, once for *Urusei Yatsura* in 1981 and the second time for *Inuyasha* in 2002. A majority of the Takahashi canon has been adapted into other media such as anime, live-action TV series, and film. Takahashi's manga, as well as the other formats her work has been adapted into, have continued to delight generations of fans around the world. Distinguished by her wonderfully endearing characters, Takahashi's work adeptly incorporates a wide variety of elements such as comedy, romance, fantasy, and martial arts. While her series are difficult to pin down into one simple genre, the signature style she has created has come to be known as the "Rumic World." Rumiko Takahashi is an artist who truly represents the very best from the world of manga.

RIN-NE
VOLUME 40
Shonen Sunday Edition

STORY AND ART BY
RUMIKO TAKAHASHI

KYOKAI NO RINNE Vol. 40
by Rumiko TAKAHASHI

Original Japanese edition published by SHOGAKUKAN.
English translation rights in the United States of America, Canada, the United Kingdom, Ireland, Australia and New Zealand arranged with SHOGAKUKAN.

Translation/Christine Dashiell
Touch-up Art & Lettering/Evan Waldinger
Design/Yukiko Whitley
Editor/Megan Bates

Printed in the U.S.A.

Published by VIZ Media, LLC
P.O. Box 77010
San Francisco, CA 94107

10 9 8 7 6 5 4 3 2 1
First printing, July 2021

PARENTAL ADVISORY
RIN-NE is rated T+ for Older Teen and is recommended for ages 16 and up. This volume contains adult language and supernatural themes.

ratings.viz.com RATED T+ OLDER TEEN

VIZ MEDIA
viz.com

SHONEN SUNDAY
shonensunday.com

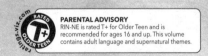

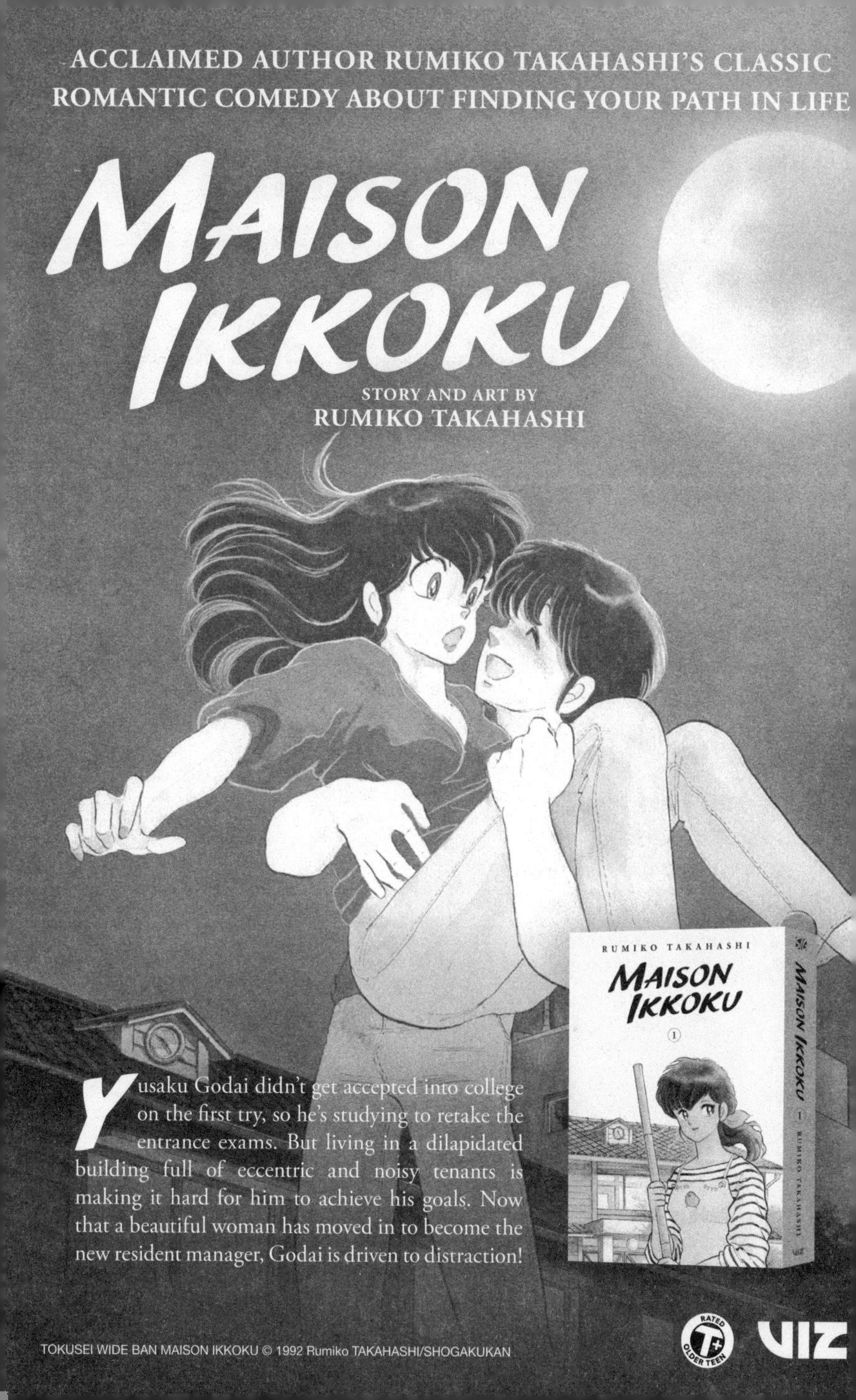
ACCLAIMED AUTHOR RUMIKO TAKAHASHI'S CLASSIC
ROMANTIC COMEDY ABOUT FINDING YOUR PATH IN LIFE
MAISON IKKOKU
STORY AND ART BY
RUMIKO TAKAHASHI
RUMIKO TAKAHASHI
MAISON IKKOKU
1
Yusaku Godai didn't get accepted into college on the first try, so he's studying to retake the entrance exams. But living in a dilapidated building full of eccentric and noisy tenants is making it hard for him to achieve his goals. Now that a beautiful woman has moved in to become the new resident manager, Godai is driven to distraction!
RATED T+ OLDER TEEN
VIZ
TOKUSEI WIDE BAN MAISON IKKOKU © 1992 Rumiko TAKAHASHI/SHOGAKUKAN

Hey! You're Reading in the Wrong Direction!

This is the end of this graphic novel!

To properly enjoy this VIZ graphic novel, please turn it around and begin reading from right to left. Unlike English, Japanese is read right to left, so Japanese comics are read in reverse order from the way English comics are typically read.

This book has been printed in the original Japanese format in order to preserve the orientation of the original artwork. Have fun with it!

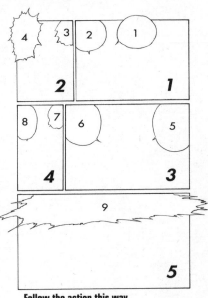

Follow the action this way